AGONY OF PLANTATION WORKERS IN NORTH-EAST INDIA

AGONY OF PLANTATION WORKERS IN NORTH-EAST INDIA

Dr. K.R. Sharma,
Mr. T.C. Das

KALPAZ PUBLICATIONS
DELHI-110052

Agony of Plantation Workers in North-East India

Rs. 750

ISBN: 81-7835-571-X

Published in 2008 in India by
Kalpaz Publications
C-30, Satyawati Nagar,
Delhi-110052
E-mail: kalpaz@hotmail.com
Phone : 9212729499

Lasser Type Setting by: Quick Media, Delhi
Printed at : Vishal Kaushik Printers, Delhi

Dedicated

To

Central Board for Workers Education,

Ministry of Labour and Employment,

Government of India,

Nagpur, India

CONTENTS

LIST OF TABLES

SECTION I : ARUNACHAL PRADESH

SECTION II : SIKKIM

SECTION III : DARJEELING

PREFACE

Agony of Plantation Workers in North East India is a piece of research work conducted to penetrate into the socio-economic dynamics of immigrant labour force to the soil of Arunachal Pradesh and local Nepalis of Sikkim and Darjeeling Himalayas of North East India. The plantation workers have been deployed at the plantations due to the declared objectives of the Government of Arunachal Pradesh for the industrialisation of the state after 1987. The industrialisation of the state calls for the import of manual workers to the plantations simply on the ground that the local tribes of the state did not accept the plantation jobs. The study explored the fact that though the plantation workers are employed as an industrial labour force, the agonies that they have to face with is really unspeakable and unheard of. Being immigrants from the Nepal Himalayas and Assam plains, their destiny is uncertain which make them utterly agonised while leading their socio-economic life at the plantation industry of the state. Agonising is rather the way of life of the workers as they any time may be ousted by the tribal planters/owners and the Government of Arunachal Pradesh because they have been allowed to stay at the plantations temporarily under the Inner Line Permits of Government of India. In fact, they are unorganised workers without having any trade union organisation and therefore they are readily succumbed to any threat and coercion. Being as good as agrarian folk, the plantation workers are not regulated by any government legislation considering Arunachal Pradesh as a tribal state of North East India. The tribal planters are all the local tribal elites who are associated with politics and administration of the state. This has resulted into the formation of tea industry with enclave societies at the Maynmar (Burma) and Chinese borders of the state of Arunachal Pradesh. However, according to the government directives, the enclaves have been formed for the safety and sovereignty of the eastern frontiers of the country. This has enforced the labours to be in close touch or contact with their places of origin.

Even if they are extremely exploited at the plantation industry, they are highly enchanted with the planation system that has provided them with ample opportunity for pursuing agrarian jobs and animal husbandry culture which they have borrowed from their places of origin. Their commitments, loyalty, perservance and semi-tribal (Mongoloid) culture have positively entertained by the tribes of Arunachal Pradesh in general and universe of the study (Anula Shagun T.E.) in particular. The culture of raising the terraces in stiff Himalayas has enabled the Nepalis to be warmly accommodated by the people of North East India including the state of Arunachal Pradesh, Sikkim and West Bengal. This is found to be the actual reason why the tribals have given their village lands on share cropping to the Nepalis. The Nepalis being share croppers of the tribals have been able to stick to their traditional agrarian economy including the animal husbandry. Agriculture and animal husbandry along with settled life have been considered by themselves as the pull factors for their immigration to the planation industry and agrarian belts of the state in particular and North East India in general. Hundreds of miles together in remote villages of various states of North East India are flooded with **Gai Goths** (cow shades) of the Nepalis. The **Gai Goth** which is the symbol of Gurkha identity and agrarian fields (Pather) provide handsome revenue to the state governments of North East India. This might be the apparent reason for encouraging Nepalis immigration though some Nepalis are very often uprooted or threaten to be uprooted by the terrorist outfits of the eight sister states of North East India.

In the study, issue like immigration and settlement history of various ethnic communities, social transformation, occupational mobility, cultural integration, inter-ethnic relationships, health dimension, religious conversion into Buddhism and Christainity, ethnicity and resource allocation etc. have been elaborately discussed with particular reference to the Anula Shagun T.E. of the state of Arunachal Pradesh, Sikkim (Temi T.E.) and Darjeeling tea plantations.

Working in the research project, we were completely encouraged by the authorities of Central Board for Workers Education both at the Regional Directorate headed by Shri S.P. Singh (Regional Director), Tinsukia (Assam) and the Directorate of the CBWE headed by Shri V. Parmeswaran, (Director), Nagpur, India for which we are extrememly thankful to them. We are thankful to the workers of the Anula Shagun T.E. for cooperating us while we were conducting field survey at the plantation during 2002 to 2003. The work would not have been completed unless we received the complete cooperation of Mr. Chowkhamoon Gohain, the owner cum Managing Director of the Guna Tea Industries (P) Ltd. of Gunanagar (Chowkham) in Namsai sub-division of Lohit district of Arunachal Pradesh manage of Temi T.E. (Sikkim) and other managers of Darjeeling tea industry. So, we extend our heartful gratitude to them. We are also thankful to our wives, children and parents for bearing pains caused to them, their tender love and affection while we were effectively working in the project. Our special thank goes to Shri A.K. Chakraborty, Education Officer (SG) of the Central Board for Workers Education, Siliguri for providing us with additional information and suggestions. Shri K.K. Sharma, Regional Director of CBWE, Siliguri has also been acknowledged for his academic inspirations.

Finally, we are thankful to Kalpaz Publications, Delhi for taking keen interest to publish the book.

Dated : 31.7.07 **Dr. K.R. Sharma**

Siliguri **&**

West Bengal **Shri T.C. Das**

SECTION–I

ARUNACHAL PRADESH

1

INTRODUCTION

The emergence of tea industry in the state of Arunachal Pradesh of North East India is a saga of Arunachal Government process of industrialization in the late eighties of 19 th century. For the first time in 1977, the Arunachal Pradesh Forest Development Corporation Ltd. was established by the Government of Arunachal Pradesh to streamline the process of industrialization so as to regularize and then systematize the then wood cutting process of forests or to continue the then wood based industries of the state more and more scientifically (Bose: 1997). Exploring the plantation potentials into the territory (North Eastern Frontier Agency), the Arunachal Pradesh Forest Development Corporation Ltd. (Ibid) could successfully open tea plantations one at Kanubari and another at Medo in Tirap and Lohit districts respectively in 1991 of the state. Similarly, during the period, two private tea estates also emerged, viz, M/S Siyang Tea and Industries (P) Ltd. and M/S Namsoom Tea Company Ltd. in East Siyang and Lohit districts respectively of Arunachal Pradesh. It is however observed that the climatic conditions, altitude and topography of the eastern districts of the state mainly East Siyang, Lower Dibang Valley, Lohit, Tirap and Changlang are very congenial for the introduction and development of tea industry. The introduction of tea industry in those districts of the state was strongly endorsed by various expert committees (Das: 1995) appointed earlier during the late seventies of 19 the century for the purpose. But due to the non-compliance to the recommendations of the expert committees on tea by the Government of Arunachal Pradesh, tea industry could not be introduced successfully before 1991 in the state. This may be the obvious reason why tea plantations under the Arunachal Pradesh Forest Development Corporation Ltd. are presently running at tremendous loss. Although the private tea plantations of the state are flourishing day by day, there are number of inherent constraints hindering the expansion of tea industry in the state. The main constraint is the land reform policy of the state government which does not allow outside corporate houses on tea to make an easy access into this aspect of industrialization process. It is because of the fact that most of the land in Arunachal Pradesh is community based land and such land can not be leased out to any outside agency for tea cultivation. This may be one of the reasons why banks are also not much interested to remit loans to such community owned land owners of the state for want of mortgages.This has been further supplemented by the Arunachal Pradesh Land Settlement and Records Act (Act No. 10 of 2000 A.D.) which interalia statutorily recognized community (tribal) property. The act also sufficiently provides that several aspects of land administration would be guided by the local (tribal) customs.

Over the last three decades, it has been thoroughly experienced by the Government of Arunachal Pradesh that the community based land owners of the state can not be forced to lease out their land for tea cultivation. Secondly, there is an acute problem of labour shortage in the state tea plantations due to the restriction imposed on the import of outside labourers as per the Inner Line Permit Policy of Government of India (Ibid) for Arunachal Pradesh. The local tribal people do not at all prefer to work as tea plantation labourers (unskilled/manual jobs) for they are the owners of cultivable or rich (fertile) wet land (Ibid) known as Pather and other natural resources of the region. Due to those factors, many pioneering projects being designed by the Government on tea plantation industry had been wind up in the state during 2001 to 2002 A.D.

According to a report (1996) of the Consultative Committee of Plantation Associations (CCPA), Calcutta, there were seventeen tea estates in Arunachal Pradesh in 1996 having 11,005 hectares of land under tea. About 325 thousand kilograms of made tea had been produced by those seventeen tea estates in the state. The average daily employment of labourers as per their Muster Roll was 1,329 and another 450 labourers were employed on casual basis during the peak plucking season. It has been mentioned in the report of CCPA (1996) that although a small tea estate of only 20 hectares was established in 1981, its real expansion could take place in the state only after 1987. There were sufficient amount of land available for tea cultivation in the state of Arunachal Pradesh from the Jhum areas of about 70,000 hectares as per the report of North Eastern Development Council. The CCPA (1996) has also categorically projected that by the year 2006 A.D., there will be 6,325 hectares of new land under tea with 9,225 kilograms of made tea having 1,459 kilograms yield per hectare. The Tea Board of India too has projected that there will be another 13,932 kilograms of made tea with 8,224 hectares of new land under tea bushes having 1,694 yield per hectare by the year 2006 A.D. in Arunachal Pradesh.

After 1995, a large number of local tribal entrepreneurs entered into the agro-based industry as an alternative to the then closing Plywood industry due to the prohibition for deforestation duly imposed by the Government of

Arunachal Pradesh. But unlike other manufacturing or processing units, the plantation sector requires a large number of stable labour force within the territory. In view of her sparse population (Ibid) of tribal origins and their utter reluctance to join the private sector industries during the late nineties of 19th century, the Arunachal Government started widely to accommodate a huge labour force from outside required for the development (Ibid) of tea plantations in the region. Because of this step being undertaken by the Government of Arunachal Pradesh, number of tea estate has been calculated to be more than twenty today with more than three thousand regular workers and another one thousand casuals are employed in peak plucking seasons in the tea plantations of Arunachal Pradesh. Today, there are approximately 6500 hectares of land under tea cultivation in the state. Almost 42,000 workers were working in medium and small scale industries (Bose : 1997) of the state.

The North Eastern Enclaves

As stated above in the study, tea plantations of the state of Arunachal Pradesh are located at her eastern most districts. Over the centuries, it has been proved that the eastern most districts of the state appear to have been the safety enclavės for the Government. The tea plantation industry is located either at the Myanmar (Burma) border or near the Chinese (Mc Mohan Line) mainland. The introduction of tea industry has a historical relevance (Ibid). Except two tea estates under the Arunachal Pradesh Forest Development Corporation Ltd., all the eighteen tea estates located at the eastern most districts of the state are under the ownership of local tribal elites to support the tribal based development policy of the state (Das : 1995). For example, Mr. Chowkhmoon Gohain, Ex.-Member of Parliament from Khampti tribe of Lohit district, Mrs. Yapang of East Siyang, Mr. W. Raj Kumar, Ex-Speaker of Legislative Assembly from Lower Dibang Valley district, Mr. Aken Lege of Roing (Lower Dibang Valley district) etc. have owned tea plantations in the eastern enclaves of the state of North East India. Thus, elites associated with politics and administration have entered accurately into tea plantation industry of the state (Mishra : 1994). Except two tea estates, one each in Lower Dibang Valley and another in East Siyang districts, all the eighteen tea plantations of the state are located at Lohit, Tirap and Changlang districts. There are certain pertinent historical antecedents as mentioned above for such enclave formation. These locations are either at the foothills of the eastern most Arunachal Pradesh or Maynmar (Burma) border being fully encircled by the dense forests. Till 1995, all tea leaves so plucked in the Arunachal plantations had to be sent to Assam plantations for manufacturing etc. But due to the increasing sense of regionalism and communal terrorism in the Assam plantations, separate factories had to be established after 1995 in the Arunachal tea plantations only. In that venture, they got sufficient loans from

Tea Board of India with handsome subsidy being given to the tribal tea plantation owners of the state of Arunachal Pradesh. Take for instance, in 1996, the Tea Board of India provided Rs. 292.9 lakhs as loans and Rs. 160.10 as subsidy (CCPA : 1996) to the tribal tea plantation owners of Arunachal Pradesh.

The development process of the Arunachal Government helped the tribal tea garden owners of the state to make their respective areas as complete enclaves as the Britishers used to convert their plantations into Plantocracy (Devi : 1989) or the Planters' Raj (Guha : 1977) or the Sahib-Coolies Raj (Sharma : 2003) in Assam and West Bengal. The onslaught of Liberalisation, Privatisation and Globalization policy for Indian industries in general (Ratnam : 2001) and the tea plantation industry in particular (Bhowmik : 1995) after 1991 has further encouraged the tribal tea planters to convert their plantations into their complete sovereignty (Raj). For example, Mr. Chowkhamoon Gohain, the owner of the Guna Tea Industries (P) Ltd. has named the area as Gunanagar after the name of his late son 'Guna'. Secondly, such enclave formation process appears to have been officially approved by the Government of Arunachal Pradesh due to two primordial reasons, viz., to restore safety and sovereignty of the eastern most frontier of the state of Arunachal Pradesh and to earn good revenue for the government exchequer as the cost of production is very low of Rs. 20/- only per kilogam of made tea while the Arunachal tea fetches Rs. 80/- per kilogram of made tea in the national and international markets due to young tea bushes of hardly twenty years old. Except the wages of Rs. 35/- per worker per day, no other welfare benefit is given to the workers. This is very much possible for the tribal planters/owners because the workers are either the Nepalis from the Nepal Himalayas or Adivasis from the Assam plains tea gardens. The Adivasis immigrated to the Arunanchal plantations as they had been covertly involved in anti-social activities or terrorism of course, under the banner of United Liberation Front of Assam (ULFA) in the Assam tea plantations. Though these Adivasis are simply called 'Tea Tribes' in Assam and 'Scheduled Tribes' in West Bengal tea plantations, they are simply treated as 'Non-Tribals' in Arunachal Pradesh along with the Nepali workers in the plantation industry. Thus, tribal-non-tribal polarization of the society has been sensed quite sufficiently in the state tea plantations. The enclaves have been persisting safely as the local tribal planters have received solid supports from their own tribes on the one hand and the state political elites of the government on the other. Eventuality of this kind has been further enunciated by the fact that the non-tribal tea plantation workers have weak social foundation as they are the recent immigrants from the Nepal Himalayas, Assam plains and other parts of the country.

They are brought there with temporary Inner Line Permits, the period of which has in most cases already lapsed. Most of them do not go for the renewal of their Inner Line Permits anticipating legal complicacies (Das : 1995). This fact is well known to all the tribal planters and local tribal population as well. As a result of this, their staying in the plantations is inherently considered to be totally illegal. Due to this reason, the non-tribal tea plantation workers do not have courage enough to raise their voice against the exploitation of the tribal planters/owners. Because of this weakness, they are readily succumbed to any threat or coercion (Ibid). This is the actual reason why the tribal people do not just want to join the tea plantation jobs especially in the unskilled category. Therefore, it is presumed that such enclaves would not have been formed provided the tribal people of the region would have joined the plantation jobs. It is also conjectured that among the Nepali workers, there is no upper caste Hindu such as Bhramin (Bahun) or priestly double born caste in the plantations (e.g., The Anula Shagun T.E.) as an integral part of the unskilled work force. In the Nepali society, most Brahmins are found to be very talented both in Nepal and the Eastern Himalayas (Sharma : 2000). It is not that the skilled industrial workers immigrated to the Arunachal tea plantations because of low wages, the story supplements that the unskilled non-tribal reserve army of workmen have been immigrated to the Arunachal tea plantations in search of their livelihood.

The unskilled labour force are mostly illiterates or semi-literates and thus they do not at all know the terms and conditions of works or services. This has further enabled the planters/owners to convert the Arunachal frontiers into the strong enclaves.

Problems of the Study

This is a Sociological study of Nepali tea plantation workers in Arunachal Pradesh of North East India. For the sake of analytical convenience, the Anula Shagun T.E. of Lohit district of Arunachal Pradesh has been methodologically selected for the study. There are 150 households of Nepali community consisting of 300 workers. Besides, there are another 100 Adivasi workers in the plantation. Therefore, the study of Nepali tea plantation workers in Arunachal Pradesh invites an interesting empirical proposition. They are working under a tribal planter/owner from the Khampti tribe who was once a Member of Parliament from Namsai sub-division of Lohit district of Arunachal Pradesh. So far, hardly any study has been conducted on tea plantation workers of Arunachal Pradesh. The tribal planter as the owner of the Anula Shagun T.E. along with other two tea estates in Tirap and Changlang districts belongs to the elite group of the state. He hardly allows any outsider to penetrate into his gardens. The immigration of Nepali workers to the Anula Shagun T.E. has portrayed the fact that industrialisation process has evolved in the eastern most frontiers of the state. The Anula Shagun T.E. is the garden of a Khampti family. The pull factors for Nepalis immigration as tea plantation workers in the tea estates of Arunachal Pradesh are delineated below.

Firstly, the Nepalis can have their permanent settlement in the plantation environment which is perfectly an agro-based industry. Unlike other industries, tea industry possesses both the agrarian and industrial characters (Xaxa : 1997) in the real sense of the term.

Secondly, the agrarian environment of tea plantation has enabled the agrarian Nepalis of Nepal Himalayas having landless occupational background, of the past to adapt the industrialisation process of Arunachal Pradesh very easily (Sharma : 2005).

Thirdly, the Nepalis, by tradition, not only cultivate the land for crops but they are also the staunch practioners of animal husbandry. The plantation industry provides them with ample opportunity for animal husbandry as well as agriculture.

Fourthly, inspite of having tribal-non-tribal differences in the state of Arunachal Pradesh, the Nepalis, due to their perseverance, could help to pay good revenue to the Government of Arunachal Pradesh because the Jhum (shifting) cultivation of the tribes as the major constraint for development process of the state, could not at all provide such revenue to the government. Unlike the Jhum cultivation of tribes having short term sustaining capacity of land productivity (Sahu : 1986) and susceptible to higher rate of soil erosion and landslides in the hill areas of Arunachal Pradesh, the settled cultivation sustains the land productivity for ever due to the presence of peripheral forest resources (Borthakur : 1981; Rai : 1994). The Nepalis have deep affection and love for both the forest resources and settled cultivation in the Himalayas (Sharma : 2003) including the state of Arunachal Pradesh of North East India.

Fifthly, basically Nepalis have close resemblance in respect of their physical appearance (Parmer : 1990) and way of living with rest of the Himalayan or sub-Himalayan Arunachal tribes. For instance, the Khamptis of Namsai sub-division of the state of Arunachal Pradesh have identical physical appearance as of the Nepalis. This may be one of the reasons why most of the Khampti agrarian elites of Chowkham block, where the Anula Shagun T.E. is located at, have given their land on share cropping to the Nepalis (Dubey : 1978) only. This has generated a prior stimulus for complete comprehension and integration of the Nepalis with the tribal way of life in the region under study.

Inspite of above mentioned areas of comprehension and integration of the Nepalis with the local tribes of the region, the Nepalis have retained their distinct ethnic identity (Subba : 1990) in their day today life in respect of language, marriage and culture by internalizing some of the cultural traits of dominant tribes of the region. Historically, the Nepalis as Jawans (soldiers) of the British Assam Rifles (Subba : 2003) were deployed in Arunachal Pradesh in 1873. Henceforth, they started to settle down there having similar Himalayan habitat and people as of their places of origin. That was most apparent for them as traditionally they were mainly tribes on sub-tribes of the Nepal Himalayas (Sharma : 2000). The most glaring instance of their cultural integration is in respect of language as duly encouraged by the Government of Arunachal Pradesh (Das : 1995). The popular local Assamese language of the region under reference has been totally internalized in day today life by the Nepalis. Besides the Assamese language, tribal dialects are also fluently spoken by the Nepalis in Arunachal Pradesh in general and the garden universe in particular. This is the reason why the Khampti tribes prefer Nepalis than Hindustanis in the plantation. It is proved over the centuries that their ingenuity to work and agrarian versatality have been positively ascertained to the Government of Arunachal Pradesh and people thereof though the Nepalis have been accustomed to bear the curse of being called immigrants in North East India. Sincere endeavours of the Nepalis have been profusely applauded by the tribes of North East India including the state of Arunachal Pradesh. The Government efforts to convert Jhum (shifting) cultivation into settled ones have been supported by the culture of terrace cultivation which the Nepalis used to be habitually done since time immemorial in the Himalayas. Therefore, the Nepalis proved themselves to be the agrarian experts possessing the expertise for wet rice cultivation (Sharma : 2000) in Arunachal Pradesh also. Even the rough terraces for tea cultivation appear to have been raised following the Nepali instances of agrarian terraces raised in the Himalayan or sub-Himalayan regions of Arunachal Pradesh. The perseverance to duty on agrarian/other assignemts has characterised the Nepalis as "Khati Khanee Machees/Jati" in India meaning thereby the community which survives by hard work and hard work alone (Ibid). The same thing happened in case of the Anula Shagun T.E. also where Mr. Chowkhamoon Gohain, the Khampti owner of the plantation had no other alternative except to accommodate the Nepalis as tea plantation workers in the plantation for his tribesmen did not accept the plantation jobs for two simple most reasons, *viz.*, most Khamptis were the owners of wet rice field (Pather) and Jhum lands at that time at Chowkham and secondly, the Khamptis are basically commercial minded tribes among other tribes (Das : 1995) of Arunachal Pradesh. Apparently, the Khamptis always endeavour to involve themselves with some sorts of trade and business in the region (Bose : 1997) rather than engaging themselves in the agrarian pursuits completely. It is found that the Khamptis prioritize business first and then agriculture in Chowkham (Mishra : 1994).

From the above discussion, it is transparent that although the Nepalis have integrated fully into the garden environment, quite often they feel unsafe of their living at the plantation due to the increasing communal terrorism in North Eastern region of the country. This has strongly enforced them to be in close touch or contact with Nepal Himalayas or other places of their origin because the Khampti as well as other dominant tribes of the region may one day ask the Nepalis to vacate the land of tribals for ever in Arunachal Pradesh in general and the garden universe in particular.

Heterogeneity, low wages, coercion and isolation were the characteristic features of the plantation system (Bhowmik : 1981). Historically, such heterogeneity was completely sustained by the isolated enclaves all over the plantation world. The same characteristic features are also found today in the Anula Shagun T.E. Though there are Adivasi workers in the plantation, the Nepali workers have been kept in separate labour line known as the Nepali labour Dhura. This has generated a kind of interesting, Sociological proposition for studying the socio-economic agonies of the plantaton workers.

Most scholars, while defining the plantation system, normally overlook the socio-economic agonies of the workers. They have either elucidated the production relations or described the production unit itself (Sharma : 1994).

The International Labour Organisation (ILO) notes the term "plantation" at first as groups of settlers or the political units formed by it under the British colonialism especially in North America and West Indies (ILO : 1950). Prof. Hla Myint (1973) has distinguished the plantation from peasant agriculture by its large scale enterprise which normally requires more labour per unit of land, producing relatively large number of unskilled labourers whose activities are closely supervised and the primary skill of the labours is to follow orders. The emergence of tea industry was of alien origin (Greaves : 1957). Further, migration and coercion are other characteristic features of the plantation system (Jones : 1968). Therefore, defining plantation and conceptualising relationship as a whole, mere elucidation of the economic characters or economic benefits for the owners of the industry is not at all adequate. The social relations and thereby the emerging agonies at the inter-personal and inter-community levels are also to be taken into due consideration (Sharma : 2003) with thorough caution (Sharma : 1997).

The Nepali tea plantation workers of the Anula Shagun T.E. have no high Hindu caste background. Except the Chhetris, they belong to Matwali group of the Nepali society of Nepal Himalayas and Assam plains. Historically, the Nepali Matwalis were toiling mass of the Nepal Himalayas (Pradhan : 1991). They had high proneness towards the Matwalisation (Tribalisation) process both in Nepal and the Eastern Himalayas (Sharma : 1997). Whether such proneness towards the Tribalisation (Matwalisation) process has helped them to adapt the local tribal (Khampti) environment of the Anula Shagun T.E.? This is another aspect of the study. The interactions between the Hinayani Buddhist Khampti tribes and Hindu Nepali castes in regard to their day today economic activities have shaped to the tune of industrial environment in a loose form of the term having specific organisational hierarchy with prescribed goals of the plantation industry. The management and office staffs are completely Khamptis by ethnicity. It has been observed that except the wages and house building materials for constructing labour huts, no other industrial facility is given to the workers. This may be the clear reason why the Nepali workers always remain busy after their garden duty with non-plantation jobs and animal husbandry. This has been amply coordinated by the fact that the Nepalis are very popular for cattle farmings not only in Assam but also in Arunachal Pradesh. The city/town dwellers of Assam like Guwahati, Tezpur, Lakhimpur, Tinsukia, Jorehat, Dibrugarh etc. and Tezu, Itanagar, Bomdila, Namsai etc. of Arunachal Pradesh purchase cow milk from the Nepalis. Quite a good number of Nepalis have huge **Gai Goths** (cow sheds) in the state of Assam, Arunachal Pradesh, Nagaland, Manipur, Meghalaya and Mizoram of North East India. They are called Gwalas or cow milk suppliers. The Kheti (cultivation) and Gai Goths (cow sheds) are part and parcel of agrarian economy of the Hindu (Gurkhas – protectors of Gau Dharma) Nepalis in North East India. In the Eastern Himalayas, they are treated as the founders of white revolution (Sharma : 2000; Balaraman : 1994). It is observed that off 150 Nepali households of the Anula Shagun T.E., altogether 148 households have animal husbandry along with agriculture in the neighbouring Khampti villages of Chowkham. In fact, the Nepalis immigrated to North East India and Burma mainly for cattle farmings and agriculture.

Although the Anula Shagun T.E. is an agro-based industry which was established after the abandonment of Namsoom Saw and Veneer Mills OP) Ltd., the workers feel that they do not by and large bother about their future as they have deep confidence on Mr. Chowkhamoon Gohain as god father of the area. He will definitely save them in hard days as he did the same at the time of closure of Namsoom Saw and Veneer Mills (P) Ltd. at Gunanagar (Chowkham) in 1987.

In this way, they are unorganised sector workers as no labour legislation of Government of India has been implemented in the plantation so far of its fifteen years of establishment. The workers have not earned any consciousness for the formation of trade union in the plantation. It means that whatever the owner of the garden provides them, they have to accept it forcefully. This shows that the workers are in the colonial system of production relations. A kind of industrial autocracy has taken place between the workers and management hailing from the family of Chowkhamoon Gohain.

In this way, the garden workers of the Anula Shagun T.E. have hardly come across the concept of trade union movement and working class solidarity. The industrial relation between the workers and management is the relation of Master-Servant in nature (Bhowmik : 1996). The workers being immigrants have been made scared of ousting from the garden by the management system inspite of their staying at the plantation for more than fifteen years or more of its existence. This is one of the main reasons why they always remain silent of their exploitation by the management system which is autocratic in form as the Managing Director, Directors and Managers of the plantation belong to the same Khampti family. Even most of the supervisory (Mauri) and office staffs of the plantation hail from the Khampti tribes of the region. In this way, management of the plantation is ethnically well organised. Another reason for complete sustenance of such technique of taming coolies in colonial fashion is due to the fact that the state government is represented by a Khampti man as a Member of Legislative Assembly of Arunachal Pradesh from Namsai constituency.

Therefore, it is transparent from the above discussion that the tribal ownership of tea industry being absolutely patronized by the Government of Arunachal Pradesh is as good as a British colonial enclave in the state to encourage as well as flourish the community based industrial development (Das : 1995) process and locals participation in the process. All the contracts regarding supply of necessary articles and goods for the garden are given to the local Khampti youngsters. Thus, coercion of workers as exercised by the management (Bhowmik : 1996) is widely supported by Khampti population of the region. Historically, the Khamptis immigrated to Sadiya of Assam from Upper Burma and later on from Sadiya to Chowkham area of Arunachal Pradesh (Gogoi : 1971). Thus, Chowkham is the den of Khamptis due to the existing dense forests and fertile arable land ever since the British days (Bose : 1997). The Khampti elites feel it very comfortable to lease out their agrarian land on share cropping mainly to the Nepalis of Nepal Himalayas and Assam plains of North East India. Doing this, the tribal elites are profitably utilizing their land resources on the one hand and victory in elections on the other.

Operationalisation of the Concept of Study

There is hardly any study ever conducted on tea plantation workers of the state of Arunachal Pradesh. Except a few stray reports that are available at the archieves of the Directorate of Industries, Government of Arunachal Pradesh, there is no other report on tea industry of the state. Hence, the Anula Shagun T.E. is also not an exception in this regard. The reports of the Directorate of Industries, Government of Arunachal Pradesh reveal some ideas about their production figure, target, marketing situation etc. Not a single report of the Directorate of Industries, Government of Arunachal Pradesh has stated anything about the socio-economic agonies of work force of tea estates of the state. The reports available with Tea Board of India also reveal some information about the quantum of subsidy sanctioned to the tribal tea garden owners along with the actual loans provided for extension and expansion of tea industry in the state. This may be the accurate reason why Mr. Gohain of the Anula Shagun T.E. had only 30 hectares of land under tea in the year 2000 A.D. but during our survey period (2002 to 2003), the area had been very fastly expanding to the tune of 219 hectares under tea bushes with three lakh and fifty thousand kilograms of made tea per year. Being the sole landowner of most of the villages of Gunanagar (Chowkham), it is explored that he is going to expand the land under tea bushes to the tune of 700 hectares by the end of 2006 A.D. While tea plantations under the Arunachal Pradesh Forest Development Corporation Ltd. (two in number) are in very deplorable condition due to non-availability of land for expansion as the neighbouring tribal villages and forest land of the state government can not be brought under tea cultivation. Moreover, the cost of production is very high of Rs. 70/- per kilogram of made tea in the corporation gardens while it is as stated above, even less than Rs. 20/- per kilogram of made tea in the private sector gardens because the workers are devoid of any industrial incentive except the wages and house building materials. Above all, the age of tea bushes is very young of hardly fifteen years old and labour productivity is very high of 850 kilograms of made tea per worker per year.

The theoretical approach adopted in the study is Social Anthropological ones as the society of the Anula Shagun T.E. is neither purely a Hindu caste oriented nor perfectly a tribal in nature. In fact, it is a Hindu-Buddhist integrated zone of the Arunachal Pradesh. Historically, the area was directly under the influence of Assamese kings ever since the days of Ahom rule (Dutta Choudhary : 1978; Bose : 1997). The Assamese society is predominantly a Hindu one. Three major communities of the Anula Shagun T.E., viz, Khampti, Nepali and Adivasi have common habitation with separate labour lines for the workers and independent land holding for the Khamptis. A kind of social stratification has been emerged between the tribals and non-tribals. Former claimed themselves as the "Sons of the Soil" of Arunachal Pradesh while later are considered as the "Immigrants" or unskilled plantation coolies from outside the Arunachal Pradesh.

Under the situation as stated above in the study, it is agreed by all the Nepali castes that the industrialization process of the Anula Shagun T.E. is an extra stimulus for their living. For them, agriculture minus industry is not a misnomer while industry minus agriculture is completely a myth (Sharma : 2003) for their living at the plantation. This is the inherent reason why they have been closely associated with the industry inspite of their complete exploitation by the management system of the plantation.

The present study focuses not only on socio-economic agonies of tea plantation workers but also on their health dimension, nature of Hindu-Buddhist relationships, changing social structure of Nepali society, family, marriage, education, religious structure, caste-tribe fusion and fission processes in the poly-cultural universe etc. in various chapters of the study. In regard to economic life of the workers, their occupational structure, migration pattern, place of birth, land holding pattern, animal husbandry, income, borrowing etc. have been analyzed thoroughly. The migration history of Khamptis has also been incorporated in the study.

Methodology of the Study

For the first time, we visited the Anula Shagun T.E. in June, 2002 to introduce ourselves with the workers, management and other important personnel of the plantation. Being the scholars from North East India, we were out and out accepted by the plantation workers of the Anula Shagun T.E. At first, Mr. Chowkhamoon Gohain, the Managing Director of Guna Tea Industries (P) Ltd. was found to be little indifferent to us when we advertently explained the cardinal objectives of our research project. But later on during our survey period (2002 to 2003), he was convinced with the research project to such an extent that he not only supported us morally but also provided us the literature that was available with him about the emergence and growth of tea industry in the state of Arunachal Pradesh. Besides this, the Government Gaon Burah of Gunanagar Gaon Panchayat, few old Khampti village chiefs and other influential people were also interviewed on the history of the plantation and recruitment of workers in the plantation in particular and the state of Arunachal Pradesh in general.

The Anula Shagun T.E. represents the emergence of tea industry in the state of Arunachal Pradesh as a whole on the logic that it is located at the eastern most enchanted district of not only the state of Arunachal Pradesh but also of the country adjoining Myanmar (Burma). Secondly, the plantation has accommodated 300 Nepali and 100 Adivasi workers. No other tea plantation of the state has employed such a large number of Nepalis as manual labourers. All 150 households of the Nepali community with 300 workers were covered under the study. The present study does not exclusively rely on the theoretical sophistications but based on the empirical data collected from the Anula Shagun T.E. of Arunachal Pradesh during 2002 to 2003 A.D.

Methods of Data Collection

Considering the problem of the study, following sample questionnaire had been prepared. The first section deals with the household census.

1. Name of the Respondent
2. Relation with the head of the family
3. Age structure of the family members
4. Sex structure of the family members
5. Birth place of family members
6. Educational standards of the family members of the workers
7. Religious structure of the families of the workers
8. Occupational structure of the family members of the workers
9. Landholding pattern of the workers
10. Cattle stock Population of the workers
11. Modern equipments of the workers
12. Wage structure of the workers
13. Number of working population in the families of the workers
14. Name of the festivals/rituals observed in the families of the workers
15. Name of festivals/rituals attended in others' households
16. Name of languages/dialects known to the workers.

The above structured questionnaire were administered in the pilot study in order to frame the following semi-structured questionnaire for conducting the survey in the Anula Shagun T.E. on the socio-economic agonies as well as the cultural integration of the workers.

1. Why you immigrated to the Anula Shagun T.E.?
2. Who brought you to the Anula Shagun T.E.?
3. Where did you work before joining the Anula Shagun T.E.?
4. What did you do in your place(s) of origin?
5. How much you get at the plantation as wages?
6. What are the other job incentives you get from the plantation? (Details).
7. How many hours you have to work in a day at the plantation?
8. What are the main duties you have to do during twelve months in a year?
9. How your management recruit the workers at the plantation?
10. What type of industrial relation is there in your plantation between the workers and management?
11. Is there any social organization in the plantation?

12. Which community is most dominant in the plantation?
13. Whether Gaon Panchayat has any role to play in the affairs of the plantation?
14. What are the relationships between the Nepalis and Khampti tribes in the plantation?
15. What kind of marriages have taken place in your family?
16. Number of marriages within the same caste/community.
17. Number of marriages with other castes/communities.
18. Do you accept Puccka foods from other communities?
19. Do you accept Kuccha foods from other communities?
20. Do your management personnel attend the marriage and death rituals in your house if they are called for?
21. Do you sacrifice animals' blood while observing your household rituals/festivals?
22. What are the common festivals of your plantation?
23. Do you invite other communities in such festivals/rituals in your household?
24. What are the major food items you use in celebrating the festivals/ rituals?
25. Do you offer wine and meat to a Brahmin?
26. Do you accept inter-community marriages?
27. Do you think that there is inter-ethnic conflicts between the tribals and non-tribals in the plantation?
28. Do you celebrate the communal festivals? If yes, why? And if no, why?
29. Where do you go first if any member of your family falls sick? To a Jhankri (Shahman) or to a Doctor? If to a Doctor, why? And if to a Jhankri, why?
30. Does a community helps others in case of emergency? If yes, how? And if no, why?
31. Do you think that there should be trade union or workers organization in the plantation?
32. Is there any Bhatti (liquor furnace) at the plantation?
33. Do the tribal neighbours invite you in their festivals? If yes, how? If no, why?
34. Do you cast votes? If yes, since when? If no, why?

35. Whether you share crops with the tribal owner? If yes, how much in a year?
36. Do you pay tax? If yes, whom-the land owner or the Government?
37. Do you have to pay anything for keeping cattle stocks at home? If yes, to whom?
38. Whether you visit your places of origin in a year/two? If no, why?
39. Whether any communal riot has taken place in the plantation between the tribals and non-tribals?
40. Whether you have to face threats from the terrorist organizations?
41. How the government officers of Arunachal Pradesh treat you?
42. Whether you can avail forest resources as enjoyed by the tribals in the region?
43. Do you left the plantation if your management ask you to leave? If yes, why? If no, why?
44. What are the division of roles among your family members?
45. How many new babies were born in your household during the last ten years?
46. How many members died in your family during the last ten years?
47. Do you heard anything about family planning? If yes, has any member of your family undergone vasectomy or tubectomy operation?
48. Do you believe on 'Small Family Norm' If yes, why? And if no, why?
49. Whether the local Khampti tribes (Buddhists) try to convert the Nepalis or other communities into the Buddhist religion?

2

THE ANULA SHAGUN T.E.: BACKGROUND AND SCOPE

The Anula Shagun T.E. is located at Chowkham block of Namsai sub-division of Lohit district of Arunachal Pradesh. It is near the Indo-Maynmar border. The actual area where the plantation is located at is locally known as Gunanagar. There is a small town in Gunanagar. Gunanagar is named after the name of late son 'Guna' of Mr. Chowkhamoon Gohain, the Khampti owner of the Anula Shagun T.E. In fact, the real name of tea industry is known as 'Guna Tea Industries (P) Ltd'.

The Anula Shagun T.E. is named after the name of granddaughter of Mr. Chowkhamoon Gohain who was a Member of Parliament from Arunachal Pradesh at the time of Pandit Jawaharlal Nehru, the first Prime Minister of independent India. The Arunachal Pradesh was then known as North East Frontier Agency (NEFA) under the administration of Government of Assam (Bose : 1997) at Shillong. The Anula Shagun T.E. was established in 1987. Prior to 1987, there was an wood based industry of Mr. Gohain in Gunanagar where about five hundred workers of Assam origin used to work as wage labourers. It was known as Namsoom Saw and Veneer Mills (P) Ltd., Gunanagar (Chowkham) of Arunachal Pradesh.

Following the example of Mr. Gohain, another saw mill was established by a Marwari from Tinsukia (Assam) in Gunanagar of Chowkham. It is still there in Gunangar. Before 1987, Mr. Gohain had a tea estate known as Lallong T.E. at Bordumsa (Changlang district) where tea leaves of the Anula Shagun T.E. used to be sent for manufacturing etc. This along with the cost effectiveness (Asopa : 2004) of production, a separate factory was established at the Anula Shagun T.E. itself in 1999 A.D. Under the prohibition of Government of Arunachal Pradesh for deforestation, the Namsoom Saw and Veneer Mills (P) Ltd. was to be completely abandoned by 1987 in Gunanagar. To begin with an experimental basis, there were only thirty hectares of land under tea in the Anula Shagun T.E. till 1996 (CCPA : 1996). With the increasing popularity of Arunachal tea in national and international markets, area under tea had to be expanded very fastly ever since 1995 and today, there are 219 hectares of land under tea in the Anula Shagun T.E. On the east of the Anula Shagun T.E., there is Na-Dehing river, on the west, there is Chowkham town, in the north, there is a Chakma village and in the south, there are 52 National Highway, Satkilu village and Gunanagar town.

The Lallong T.E. of Mr. Chowkhamoon Gohain had to be abandoned in 1998 due to Naga terrorism in Changlang and Tirap districts of Arunachal Pradesh.

Labour Recruitment : An Inherent Constraint

One of the major objectives behind the introduction of tea industry at Gunanagar was to industrialise the local Khampti tribes so that the then Jhum (shifting) cultivation of the Khamptis and other tribes could be discontinued under the industrial policy of Government of Arunachal Pradesh (Das : 1995). Being one of prominent elites of the area, Mr. Chowkhamoon Gohain introduced the plantation industry. Unlike other sophisticated industries involving high level of technology (Bhowmik : 1981), the tea plantation is an agro-based industry, which is also a society of permanent nature (Bhowmik : 1996) employing a large number of manual resident labourers (Das : 1995). Opening the Anula Shagun T.E., Mr. Gohain thought that he would easily procure his Khampti neighbours as labour force in the Anula Shagun T.E. But as Eric Wolf (1959) stated that the introduction of an industry would destroyed their cultural heritage or culture, the Khamptis also felt that their culture of Jhum (shifting) cultivation that designated their cultural heritage was going to extinct. That could so deeply antagonised the local Khampti inhabitants that they neither joined the tea plantation jobs nor did they cast their valuable votes in favour of Mr. Chowkhamoon Gohain for his candidature to the Indian Parliament. In this way, not a single Khampti including previous slaves of the Khampti (Bose : 1997) community joined the plantation manual or unskilled jobs. The problem was immediately placed before the state Legislative Assembly session of Arunachal Pradesh which decided to allow outside labourers for the tribal planters/owners by issuing the workers with temporary Inner Line Permits (Ibid). However, it was stated in the resolution taken in the Legislative Assembly session of the state that the tribal planters/owners of the plantations had to shouldier the responsibility of renewal of Inner Line Permits for the workers before the expiry of renewal dates. But the tribal planters/owners did not venture to renew the Inner Line Permits for the workers. Instead, they enrolled the name of the workers in the voter list which benefited the planters/owners in two ways, viz, procurement of cheap labour force and victory in elections. Later might be the apparent reason why Mr. Kung Inju (Rajen), the son of Mr. Gohain of the Anula Shagun T.E. won elections for two consecutive periods (1987 to 1992 and 1992 to 1997) as a

Member of Indian Parliament from Arunachal Pradesh. Even the daughter-in-law of Mr. Gohain won election in 1998 as a Member of Legislative Assembly of the state of Arunachal Pradesh.

After 1999, the policy of industrialisation of Union Government through her integration rather than assimilation (Das : 1995) process as introduced by the British administration in Arunachal Pradesh, helped the tribal planters/owners to import as many labourers as possible because the credibility of Inner Line Permits became less effective (Ibid) in the state except in some places of national improtance.

Following the integration process of Government of India, Mr. P.K. Thungon, the then Chief Minister of Arunachal Pradesh stated that the "Policy of the Government has been to encourage evolution into the modern world of the traditional structure of every society of Arunachal Pradesh. Where aspects of the traditional structure are inconsistent with modern needs or national policy, the aim is to reform them within and avoid any sudden or drastic abolition without adequate replacement (of emotional aptitudes relating to the tribal culture : Government of Arunachal Pradesh : Itanagar : 1997)". That gave rise to the end of slavery system in the state (Bose : 1997).

Considering the above contention and to appease the local Khampti educated unemployed youths, the owner of the Anula Shagun T.E. appointed a few Khamptis as supervisory staffs in 1998 at the plantation.

However, to meet the labour problems of the plantation, Mr. Gohain, the Khampti owner of the Anula Shagun T.E. asked a Mangar, Rai and Chhetri workers of the Nepali community who were working under him since the introduction of Namsoom Saw and Veneer Mills (P) Ltd., to bring required number of Nepali workers at the plantation and therefore, he appointed them as labour recruiters to entice respective caste members from the Assam plains and Nepal Himalayas or elsewhere the country for which the labour recruiters were promised to be provided with some rewards (Baksis) by the planter/owner in the form of cash or kind during the Dashara (Dasai) festival.

Accordingly, the Rai labour recruiter went to Upper Assam and enticed as well as recruited ten workers from Lakhimpur district. Similarly, the Mangar labour recruiter enticed and recruited 70 labourers from Nepal Himalayas. In the same way, the Chhetri labour recuiter enticed and recruited five workers from Upper Assam and 45 labourers from Nepal Himalayas. The workers were to be enticed due to the ban for labour recruitment then in Nepal. Other Nepali castes joined the plantation following the Chhetri, Mangar and Rai workers who were their relatives and neighbours in Nepal Himalayas or Upper Assam. Interestingly, it is also observed that most of the Nepali immigrants as workers belong to western Nepal Himalayas. The Nepalis immigrated to the plantation from Assam plains were ousted selectively by the United Liberation Front of Assam (ULFA) mainly from Sibsagar, Lakhimpur, Tezpur, Dibrugarh and

Tinsukia districts. All the Adivasi workers of the Anula Shagun T.E. immigrated before 1990 due to their involvement, of course forcefully by ULFA, in anti-social activities or terrorism in the Assam plains gardens. They reported that now they are free from any terrorist threat. This is sufficiently supported by the fact that Arunachal Pradesh is basically free from terrorism both within and outside the state. Secondly, local Khamptis are the ardent believers of "Ahimsa Paramo Dharma" or non-violence as the greatest religion in Buddhist philosophy of life. All the Khamptis are the followers of Hinayana sect of Buddhist religion (Bose : 1997).

The above discussion makes it very clear that inspite of complete exploitation by the management system, the workers of the Anula Shagun T.E. are silent as they feel that Mr. Chowkhamoon Gohain (owner) is their god father. In this way, Mr. Gohain appears to be the don of the plantation. One Mr. Nagen Baruah (senior-most man of the plantation as vehicle driver) informed us that he has told Mr. Gohain that he will work at the plantation till Mr. Gohain is alive. Mr. Barauh as vehicle driver has been working under Mr. Gohain ever since 1967 when the Namsoom Saw and Veneer Mills (P) Ltd. was established at the Namsoom Gaon (present Gunanagar).

After enticing and recruiting the workers from Upper Assam and Nepal Himalayas, all three hundred Nepali workers with 150 households were kept at the Nepali Labour Dhura or Nepali Labour line near the present factory premises of the plantation. But it is observed that all the Adivasi households are located in proper plantation area which is actually four kilometres away from the factory premises. The idea behind keeping the Nepali and Adivasi workers in two separate labour lines of the plantation is to discourage them to interact freely and share their sorrows and melanchony openly. Secondly, the plantation has two divisions, *viz,* Anula and Guna. All the Adivasi workers work at the Anula division while all the Nepali workers work at the Guna division. Thirdly, the Nepalis are better educated and hence they are leading better quality of life than the Adivasis. Fourthly, Mr. Gohain has some Nepali Mits and therefore he often visits the Nepali households while he hardly visits the Adivasi households.

Fifthly, the Nepalis supply vegitables, milk, crops and other edible goods to the tribal planter. This is due to the reason as mentioned above in the study that in Nepali society agriculture and animal husbandry go hand in hand while the Adivasis do not have much wet rice land and animal husbandry in the plantation or outside. The Nepalis are fond of floriculture. Altogether, it is observed that four Newar households of the Nepali community of Satkilu village have established flower beds for business purpose.

Finally, the Nepalis are stubborn, sincere to their work and martial by character (Northey and Morris:1976). These might be the obvious reasons why Mr. Gohain has constructed his bunglow near Nepali Dhura of the plantation.The following example shall show as to how the Nepalis belong to a martial race of the Himalayas. This is apparently related to an incident which took palce in the plantation in 1969 when the Bengladeshi Chakmas attacked the Khamptis in Chowkham region. In the incident, Mr. Gohain was brutally injured. A Limbu (Nepali) body guard saved him and the body guard was butchered on the spot by the Chakma agitators. The Bengladeshi Chakmas and Assamese Deoris were creating ethnic problems (Das:1995) then in the Lohit district of Arunachal Pradesh. However, the problem was sorted out amicably by rehabilitating the Chakmas and Deoris under the rehabilitation scheme of Government of India on the other side of river Na-Dahing of Chowkhm. The incident of Chakma attack to Mr. Gohain was officially reported to the provincial Legislative Council of Arunachal Pradesh and Indian Parliament. This may be the distinct reason why Mr. Gohain has still kept a Nepali Driver, Cook and body guard at his bunglow even today. It is learnt from the senior workers of the plantation that the Chakmas as well as Deoris revolted against the Khamptis because the Chakmas and Deoris were tried to make slaves of the Khamptis in Chowkham region of Arunachal Pradesh.

Replying to our query of the Khampti reactions about the import of Nepali plantation workers into his gardens. Mr. Gohain said that he is the only pioneer of industrialisation process in Chowkham region. Therefore, he does not allow for complete domination of Khampti (tribal) culture in his industrial pursuits (Kumar : 2001). He fells that an industrialist should always think about the spill over impacts of industrialisation in the society. Because of the opening of tea industry in the eastern most enchanted frontiers of Arunachal Pradesh, towns like Gunanagar, Chowham, Khonsa, Changlang. Wakro, Medo, Roing, Miao, etc., of the eastern districts of the state have emerged where sizeable population have got good earning sources through trade and commerce. Again, the industrialisation through tea industry has helped to have a balanced ecology of the region as the local forests have been saved from rampant deforestation. Simultaneously, the planters have nicely maintianed shade trees in their gardens. In this way, tea industry is found to be most suited to the Arunachal ecology by maintaining environmental balance of the state. It is also found that the Nepalis have immense love and affection for forests in order to possess good number of animal husbandry at their disposal. It requires sufficient cattle fodders to be collected from the forests. Thus, they collect cattle fodders safely from the branches fo trees (Sharma: 2005) without destroying trees of the forests as such. This has been found to be most scientific reason to the Government of Arunachal Pradesh to encourage Nepalis to settle down in agrarian belts and tea plantations of the state. Similar picture is also found in other states like Assam, Mizoram, Nagaland, Manipur and West Bengal particularly in the hill areas of Darjeeling, Kalimpong and Kurseong sub-division of Darjeeling district (O' Malley: 1985; Sen: 1989) and the state of Sikkim (Sharma: 2003). It is also explored from the study that the Nepalis, by nature, are loyalists. Over the pages of Indian history, it is written with profound appreciations that they were absolutely loyal to the Pandavas. They worked and have had shade their blood and sweats for the Britishers and then the independent Indian Government by serving themselves in Gukha Regiment of Indian army (Singh and Singh:1987) . They are very much loyal to their masters. Take for instance of Mr. Dil Bahadur Limbu (Nepali), cook of Mr. Gohain of the Anula Shagun T.E. who informed us that he will left the plantation for Nepal or Assam aftermath of Mr. Gohain's death. It shows that the offsprings of Mr. Gohain as planters are by heart and soul not acceptable to the cook. The same thing is also found among aged workers of the plantation.

Still another reason for deployment of Nepali workers at the plantation was that the local Khampti tribes including their earlier slaves (Bose : 1997) tested the salt of industrialisation process of the state government in such a way that they have started earning sufficient wealth from the forest-based industries of Chowkham. All the petty business/contracts of the forests and plantations are being given to the Khamptis only. The ninety nine percent of supervisory (Mauri) and office staffs of the plantation are Khamptis. As overtly reported by the Government Gaon Burah (village headman) of Gunanagar, there are about ten thousand Khamptis today in Chowkham block of Lohit district of Arunachal Pradesh. Their strength as non-workers is harldy one hundreed in the Anula Shagun T.E. Rest of them are staying outside the plantation in Gunanagar, Chowkham, Wakro and Medo areas as the owners of fertile wet rice land (Pather) and forest resources.

Evolution of Work Force in Arunachal Pradesh Tea Plantations

The emergence of tea plantation workers in the state of Arunachal Pradesh is the creation of state sponsored tribal process of industrial development. Loosening the efficacy of Inner Line Permit policy of Government of India, tea plantation workers were imported to Arunachal Pradesh after 1995. This is evident from the table 2.1 of the study.

Table 2.1

Evolution of Work Force in Arunachal Tea Plantations

Year	*Workers*				*Total*
	Male	*Percentage*	*Female*	*Precetage*	
1995- 1998	400	30.1	929	69.9	1329
1998-2001	500	31.6	1080	68.4	1580
2001-2003	726	24.2	2274	75.8	3000

Another 1000 casuals are estimated to have been employed in tea plantations in peak plucking season.

Source: Directorate of Industries: Government of Arunachal Pradesh: Itanagar: 2003.

The table No.1 of the study indicates that throughout the origin and growth of tea plantation industry in the state of Arunachal Pradesh, the percentage of female workers went on increasing from 69.9% in 1995 to 1998 to 75.8% in 2003 while the percentage of male workers has been decreased from 30.1% in 1995 to 1998 to 24.2% in 2003. Reasons for employing more female workers have been described in the later pages of the study.

Structure of Work Force

To comprehend the tea plantation as an agro-based industry, a peep at the structure of labour force is indespensible. In the following section, an attempt has been made to study the structure of labour force in the Anula Shagun T.E. of Arunachal Pradesh.

Table 2.2

Structure of Work Force in the Anula Shagun T.E.

Sl.No.	*Caste/ Community*	*Hosehold*	*%*	*Male*	*%*	*Female*	*%*	*Total*
1.	Nepali = Chhetri	30	15.0	20	12.9	40	16.3	60
2.	Nepali = Mangar	50	25.0	40	25.9	60	24.5	100
3.	Nepali = Gurung	10	5.0	9	5.8	11	4.5	20
4.	Nepali = Kami	12	6.0	15	9.7	9	3.7	24
5.	Nepali = Tamang	6	3.0	6	3.9	6	2.4	12
6.	Nepali = Rai	30	15.0	19	12.3	41	16.7	60
7.	Nepali = Limbu	10	5.0	4	2.6	16	6.5	20
8.	Nepali = Newar	1	0.5	1	0.6	1	0.4	2
9.	Nepali = Thami	1	0.5	1	0.6	1	0.4	2
10.	Adivasis	50	25.0	40	25.8	60	24.5	100
	Total	200	100.0	155	38.7	245	61.3	400

Source: Field Work: 2003.

On the whole, the table 2.2 of the study indicates that the percentage of female tea plantation workers (61.3%) is almost double to the male counterpart (38.7%) in the Anula Shagun T.E. It is also observed from the table that the planter/owner prefers female workers due to manifold reasons. Firstly, historically, the British planters established the fact that fingertips of the female workers as pluckers are much more sensitive (Sharma: 2003) than the male counterpart. Secondly, the females are simple minded and sincere enough to their works (Bhadra: 1992) than males. Thirdly, the females tender similar care and affection to tea bushes and leaves as they do in case of their own children (Sharma: 2000). Caste-wise, Mangar and Adivasi workers (25.0% each) have highest percentage among other male tea plantation workers in the plantation.

Next to Mangar and Adivasi workers, 12.9 % of male workers belong to Chhetri caste. Similarely, 12.3% of male plantation workers belong to Rai caste. Among the plantation workers, 24.5% of female workers belonging to Adivasi community is very significant. Another 16.7% and 16.3% of female plantation workers belong to Rai and Chhetri castes respectively. The percentage of rest of caste/community workers is more or less same. Interestingly, it is also observed from the table that all these castes of Nepali and Adivasi communities were historically toiling mass in their places of origin (Sharma: 1997: Bhowmik: 1981). This may be simple most reason why they have settled here with permanent garden jobs and they are living with calm and quiet industrial enviroment. On the contrary, neighbouring tea plantations of Assam have been fully shattered by terrorism obviously under the agency of United Liberation Front of Assam (ULFA) with lack of tranquility and freedom of living.

Age Structure of the Workers

In order to ascertain the working potentiality or productivity of the workers, an understanding regarding their age structure is indespensible in order to draw a concrete empirical generalization. This will be clear if we see the table 2.3 of the study.

The table 2.3 of the study portrays the fact that 56.0% of the workers belong to the age group of 18 to 28 years; 21.2% of them belong to the group of 29 to 39 years; 9.7% of them belong to 40 to 50 years; 6.7% of them belong to the age group of 51 to 60 years and 6.2% of them belong to 60 years plus who have been working in the plantation with their long experience in the industrial job. They are working in the plantation because of their close association with Mr. Gohain ever since 1967. They stated that they will work as long as they can. It show that there is no age bar for the tea garden jobs as we found in the agrarian belts of Arunachal Pradesh. This is due to the fact that no labour legislation of Government of India is being implemented so far to regulate the terms and conditions of works or services for the plantation workers because they do not have any organisation or trade union of their own to fight for their just rights and responsibilities. The trade union movement taken place in other tea plantations of far and wide corners of the country has not yet been penetrated (Sharma: 1991) into the Arunachal tea plantations of North East India in general and the Anula Shagun T.E. in particular. In fact, there is no appropriate mechanism of the Government of Arunachal Pradesh to regulate various central labour legislations.This is overtly possible in the state tea plantations for no outside trade union leader is allowed to enter (Mamkottam: 1994) into the plantations and impart trade union education (Bhowmik: 1995) to the workers. Thus, the birth of working class consiousness in the state tea plantations is a distant dream (Sharma:2000) for the workers.

Table 2.3

Age Structure of the Workers

Sl. No.	*Caste/ Community*	*18 to 28 Yrs.*	*%*	*29 to 39 Yrs.*	*%*	*40 to 50 Yrs.*	*%*	*51 to 60 Yrs.*	*%*	*60 Yrs. Plus*	*%*
1.	Nepali = Chhetri = 60	40	17.8	10	11.8	9	23.1	1	3.7	–	–
2.	Nepali = Mangar = 100	65	29.1	20	23.5	2	5.1	10	37.1	3	12.0
3.	Nepali = Gurung = 20	8	3.6	4.7	1.7	2	5.1	3	11.1	3	12.0
4.	Nepali = Kami = 24	10	4.5	6	7.1	5	12.8	2	7.4	1	4.0
5.	Nepali = Tamang = 12	2	0.9	1	1.2	7	17.9	1	3.7	1	4.0
6.	Nepali = Rai = 60	31	13.8	10	11.8	8	20.5	3	11.1	8	32.0
7.	Nepali = Limbu = 20	8	3.6	3	3.5	2	5.1	3	11.1	4	32.0
8.	Nepali = Newar = 2	–	–	–	–	1	2.6	1	3.7	–	–
9.	Nepali = Thami = 2	–	–	1	1.2	–	–	1	3.7	–	–
10.	Adivasis = 100	60	28.8	30	35.3	3	7.7	2	7.4	5	20.0
	Total = 400	224	56.0	85	21.2	39	9.7	27	6.7	25	6.2

Source: Field Work : 2003.

Labour Migration in Arunachal Pradesh

Das (1995) observed "The emergence of non-agricultural labour force in the state of Arunachal Pradesh economy is concomitant outcome of externally thrusted process of development in the post independent period. The process of development not only needed the flow of fund from the centre but also manpower from outside". Further, he observed that not only skilled man-power had been recruited in different services but a large number of unskilled workers had also been brought. This is due to non-participation of tribal people in the affairs of the plantation frontiers of Arunachal pradesh. Thus, the process of transition of tribal labour force from the agriculture and Jhum belts (Mishra: 1994) to the industrial sector with particular reference to the plantation frontiers is not at all significant in the state. The observation made by Das (1995) that money wages in different private sector industries in Arunachal Pradesh are by and large same to that of the plain workers of Assam and

West Bengal is found to be obviously contradictory in case of tea plantations of Arunachal Pradesh where a worker is simply paid Rs.35/- per day. In most of the cases, the plantation workers were unemployed or disguishedly employed at their places of origin. They moved to Arunachal Pradesh to join the plantations and agricultural belts as unskilled labour force. As a result, it is not that the skilled labour force immigrated because of wage differentials rather the fact is that the unskilled labour force immigrated to the plantation frontiers (enclaves) of Arunachal Pradesh in search of their livelihood.

In regard to health dimension of the workers, it is entirely left to the discretion of employers/planters whether to provide the medical incentives or not to the workers. It is observed that in case of minor injuries during the working hours, the workers are generally provided with little amount of money for their medical treatment. Sometimes, they are sent to their homes for the same and generally reinstated later on when they come back. Thus, for all practical purposes, the job security of the workers is under the mercy of planters/owners. All the planters/owners do not follow the legal formalities in the light of the provisions of Plantation Labour Act, 1951 while recruiting and employing the workers. The length of service life of the workers continues till it is mutually beneficial to both the management and workers.

Again, in regard to the facility like sanitation, housing etc., the immigration of workers to the plantation frontiers does not make much difference from that of their places of origin. Here, the river water is also used for all purposes at homes and jungles are the source of fuel (Ibid) and cattle fodders to the workers.

The immigrant workers of other tea plantations of Arunachal Pradesh have been agonised with the same platitude as described above regarding their health and sanitation. The workers themselves have to maintain their homes and procure fuel from nearby forests for cooking their food at homes.

Place of Birth of the Workers

The foregone discussion has categorically depicted the fact that all plantation workers of Arunachal Pradesh are immigrants from the Nepal Himalayas, Assam plains and other parts of the country. Let us see the place of birth of workers with particular reference to the Anula Shagun T.E.

The table 2.4 of the study transpired the fact that 74.7% of Nepali workers of the Anula Shagun T.E. immigrated from the Nepal Himalayas. Another 11.3% of them immigrated from the Assam plains particularly Lakhimpur, Tezpur, Tinsukia, Dibrugarh and Sibsagar districts due to communal riots there as led by the United Liberation Front of Assam (ULFA). Only 14.0% of workers were born at the plantation. The parents of these workers (14.0%) were employed at the Namsoom Saw and Veneer Mills (P) Ltd. of Mr. Chowkhamoon Gohain ever since 1967 at Gunanagar. Among the Nepali castes, 31.2% of

Mangar, 20.1% of Chhetri and 18.7% of Rai workers immigrated to the plantation after 1995 from Nepal Himalayas due to the Maoist movement in Nepal. Similarly, other castes like Gurung, Kami, Tamang, Limbu, Newar and Thami immigrated to the plantation due to poverty (Regmi: 1971) and terrorism being whimsically launched by the Maoists in Nepal. The workers said that now they are at least at peace here though they have been looked down upon by the Khampti tribes of the region. It is also observed in the table 4 that 47.6% of Mangars, 23.8% of Chhetris and 19.1% of Rais were born in the plantation. Not a single Brahman as plantation worker is found in the plantation. In the same ways, 29.4% of Rai and 14.7% of Chhetri workers immigrated from the Assam plains and other parts of the country. Another reason for labour migration to the plantations and agrarian belts of Arunachal Pradesh as a whole is due to the fact that the state has full of forest resources for the agrarian Nepalis (Sharma: 2000) of Nepal Himalayas and Assam plains.

Table 2.4

Place of Birth of the Workers

Sl.No.	*Caste*	*Born in the Garden*	*%*	*Born in Assam/ Country*	*%*	*Bron in Nepal*	*%*
1.	Chhetri=60	10	23.8	5	14.7	45	20.1
2.	Mangar = 100	20	47.6	10	29.4	70	31.2
3.	Gurung = 20	–	--	2	5.9	18	8.1
4.	Kami= 24	2	4.8	3	8.8	19	8.5
5.	Tamang= 12	1	2.4	2	5.9	9	4.1
6.	Rai= 60	8	19.1	10	29.4	42	18.7
7.	I imbu= 20	1	2.4	2	5.9	17	7.6
8.	Newar= 2	–	–	–	–	2	0.9
9.	Thami= 2	–	–	–	–	2	0.9
	Total= 300	42	14.0	34	11.3	224	74.7

Source: Field Work: 2003.

Workers Connection with their Places of Origin

Exploring the recurrence of workers' contacts with their places of origin, the following picture has evolved in the Anula Shagun T.E. of Arunachal Pradesh.

Analyzing the table No.5 of the study, it is observed that 54.5% of workers do not at all visit their places of origin in Nepal Himalayas and Assam plains. The workers who visit once in five years (4.0%), once in four years (3.2%) and once in three years (8.7%) may be treated as the people (workers) who

Table 2.5

Workers Contact with their Places of Origin

Sl. No.	*Caste/Community*	*Inl Yr.*	*%*	*3In2. Yr.*	*%*	*In3. Yr.*	*%*	*In4. Yr.*	*%*	*In5. Yr.*	*%*	*No Cont.*	*%*
1.	Nepali = Chhetri = 60	35	48.6	15	32.6	3	8.6	1	7.7	1	6.2	5	2.3
2.	Nepali = Gurung = 20	2	2.8	1	2.2	2	5.7	1	7.7	1	6.2	13	6.0
3.	Nepali = Mangar = 100	10	13.9	15	32.6	20	57.1	3	23.1	4	25.0	48	22.1
4.	Nepali = Kami = 24	3	4.2	7	15.2	2	5.7	1	2	12.5	9	9	4.1
5.	Nepali =Tamang = 12	1	1.4	1	2.2	2	5.7	1	7.7	1	6.2	6	2.8
6.	Nepali = Rai = 60	10	13.9	3	6.5	3	8.6	2	15.4	1	6.2	41	18.8
7.	Nepali = Limbu = 20	1	1.4	2	4.3	1	2.9	3	23.1	2	12.5	11	5.1
8.	Nepali = Nwar = 2	–	–	–	–	–	–	–	1	1	6.2	01	0.5
9.	Nepali = Thami = 2	–	–	-	–	–	–	–	–	1	6.2	01	0.5
10.	Adivasis = 100	10	13.9	2	4.3	2	5.7	1	7.7	2	12.5	83	38.1
	Total = 400	72	–	46	–	35	–	13	–	16	–	218	–

Source: Field Work: 2003.

do not have much contact with Nepal or Assam. Moreover, 29.5% of the workers who pay their casual visits to their places of origin every year can roughly be comprehended as the first generational immigrants to the plantation. But it is obviously wrong to brand 57.7% of workers of Nepali origin as immigrants. It is rather a curse or myth in the real sense of the term to call them as immigrants. They do not even know the actual places from where their grandparents hailed to Arunachal Pradesh in particular and North East India in general. Their commitments with ample contributions to the state economy (Sarkar and Lama: 1986) is being absolutely counted upon and given due importance by the Government of Arunachal Pradesh and the tribes. So, in view of participative economic development approach or policy (Das: 1995) of the Government of Arunachal Pradesh, Nepalis appeared to have been totally merged (Ratnam:2001) as part and parcel of Arunachal state population. To Mr. Chokhamoon Gohain, the Nepalis are first and foremost his loyal resident workers and then bonafide citizens of the state of Arunachal Pradesh. To him, no more, the Nepali tea plantation workers of the state can be rationally branded as immigrants to the soil of Arunachal Pradesh of North East India.

Education of the Workers

The question of educational standard is very vague (Chakraborty: 1997) among the Nepali tea plantation workers as they belong to unskilled category at the Anula Shagun T.E. However, in the following section, we shall be able to roughly comprehend the educational standards of the workers.

Table 2.6

Educational Standards of the Workers in Anula Shagun T.E.

Sl No.	*Caste*	*Illiterate*	*%*	*I to IV*	*%*	*V to X*	*%*	*XII to XII*	*%*
1.	Chhetri = 60	40	21.5	10	12.2	8	34.8	2	22.2
2.	Mangar = 100	65	34.9	30	36.6	4	17.4	1	11.1
3.	Gurung = 20	18	9.7	2	2.4	–	–	–	–
4.	Kami = 24	15	8.1	7	8.5	1	4.3	1	11.1
5.	Tamang = 12	8	4.3	3	3.7	1	4.3	–	–
6.	Rai = 60	29	15.6	20	24.4	7	30.4	4	44.4
7.	Limbu = 20	11	5.9	7	8.5	1	4.3	1	11.1
8.	Newar = 2	–	–	2	2.4	–	–	–	–
9.	Thami = 2	–	–	1	1.2	1	4.3	–	–
	Total = 300	186	62.0	82	27.3	23	7.7	9	3.0

Source: Field Work: 2003.

The table 2.6 of the study shows that 62% of the workers are illiterates. Interestingly, the table also show that 7.7% of them have V to X standard of education and 3.0% of them have higher secondary level of education. Altogether, 38.0% of tea plantation workers of the Anula Shagun T.E. are literates. The reason to have high level of education among the Nepali tea plantation workers in the Anula Shagun T.E. is due to the reason that there are three primary and one higher secondary schools in Gunanagar and Chowkham areas. Secondly, unlike in the past till 1987, the medium of instruction in schools and colleges of Arunachal pradesh is in Hindi and English languages (Bose : 1997). Prior to 1987, the medium of instruction in the state schools and colleges was in Assamese language only. The Nepali lingua franca is based on Devnagari script and Hindi language is also written in Devnagari script. Thirdly, the Nepalis prefer Hindi language and pick up the same very fastly through conversation and other communication media like television, radio, newspapers, magazines etc. Also they prefer to send their children to Hindi and English medium schools and colleges. Possessing the cosmopolitan characters (Northey and Morris: 1976; Chaube: 1985), everywhere Nepalis adapt the local languages, dialects and cultures within a very short apan of time. The Government of Arunachal Pradesh encourages to teach the students in Hindi and English languages at the state schools and colleges. In the process, the Nepalis have come up in much better way than the local tribes and hence they wirte Hindi and English quite perfectly. Moreover, they speak Hindi and English languages fluently. Because of this quality possessed by the Nepalis, many topmost government and semi-government bureaucrats of Arunachal Pradesh hail from the Nepali community. But interestingly, insptie of possessing such a quality, most of the Nepalis are not given even the supervisory and clerical posts in the state tea plantations.

Demography

Altogether, the Anula Shagun T.E. consists of one thousand population. They are directly or indirectly dependent upon the tea plantation economy. Considering the existing demography of the plantation, an attempt has been made in the following sections to study the nature of mortality and fertility rates of the plantation workers.

The table 2.7 of the study transpired the fact that fertility rate of Rai caste is very high (18.1%) followed by the fertility rate of Tamang (17.5%) and Mangar (15.1%) castes at the plantation. The table also indicates that fertility rate among rest of the other castes is more or less same. The fertility rate of Rai caste is very high as most densely populated caste is from the Rai group of the Nepali community not only in North East India but also

Darjeeling-Sikkim Himalayas (Sharma: 2003). In fact, the Rais have highest immigration trend from the Eastern Nepal known as Panthar. Traditionally, Panthar was the native place of Rai caste (Pradhan: 1991) of the Nepali community.

Table 2.7

Fertility and Mortality Rates of the Workers Households*

Sl.No.	*Caste/Community*	*Fertility*	*Percentage*	*Mortality*	*Percentage*
1.	Napali = Chhetri	18	10.8	4	3.6
2.	Napali = Mangar	25	15.1	13	11.6
3.	Napali = Gurung	14	8.4	19	17.0
4.	Napali = Kami	10	6.1	7	6.2
5.	Napali = Tamang	29	17.5	19	17.0
6.	Napali = Rai	30	18.1	13	13.6
7.	Napali = Limbu	15	9.0	7	6.2
8.	Napali = Newar	2	1.2	1	0.9
9.	Napali = Thami	3	1.8	–	–
10.	Adivasis	20	12.0	29	25.9

*The data were collected for the period of last ten years.

Source: Field Work: 2003.

Looking at the mortality rate of various castes, it is observed from the table 2.7 that castes like Gurung (17.0%). Adivasis (25.9%) and Mangar (11.6%) have higher mortality rate. Rest of the castes like Chhetri (3.6%), Kami (6.2%) and Limbu (6.2%) have by and large similar mortality trend in the plantation. The Newar has lowest percentage (0.9%) of mortality rate.The Adivasis have highest mortality rate because of the fact that they hardly bother about their health aspect of life. This may be the reason why their quality of life is very low compared the same with the Nepali counterpart in the plantation. The Nepali castes like Gurung, Rai, Tamang and Mangar have higher mortality rate because they are habitually addicted to alcoholism in their day today life. The caste like Chhetri, Newar, Kami and Limbu appear to be more and more conscious by not indulging themselves in alcoholism both in the plantation and outside. The occurance of tuberculosis is very high among the Adivasis as well as Rai, Tamang, Gurung and Mangar castes of the Nepali community in the plantation. This has been nicely supplemented by a report of local government hospital of Chowkham (Gunanagar) in Namsai sub-division of Arunachal Pradesh. The health services rendered by the Department of Health of Government of Arunachal Pradesh (Bose: 1997) have not yet received by the workers of the Anula Shagun T.E. of Gunanagar (Chowkham).

3

ECONOMIC LIFE OF THE WORKERS

In the present chapter, we shall discuss about the economic life of the plantation workers belonging to Nepali community of the Anula Shagun T.E. How the heterogeneous working population of the plantation has been categorised as the homogeneous work force as they are all the sellers of their physical labour (Bhowmik: 1995)? Discussing the economic life, we shall look into the caste and landholding, caste and cattlestock population, caste and working population and caste and years of service of the workers in the Anula Shagun T.E. We shall also see the nature of secondary occupations and traditional occupations of the Nepali castes and how the traditional occupational structure of the Nepalis has been transformed after their immigration from the agrarian Nepal Himalayas and Assam plains to the industrial environment of plantation economy of the Anula Shagun T.E. of Arunachal Pradesh of North East India?

Organisational Structure of the Anula Shagun T.E.

Unlike other tea plantations of Assam and West Bengal or any other tea plantation of North East India, the organisational structure of Arunachal tea plantations in general and the Anula Shagun T.E. in particular is very simple. It is because of the fact that as mentioned in the previous chapters of the study that tribal family members occupy the top management hierarchy. Take for instance of the Anula Shagun T.E. where Mr. Chowkhamoon Gohain, the owner of Guna Tea Industries (P) Ltd. is the Managing Director. Below him, his son is the Director Incharge of the plantation. Below the Director Incharge, daughter-in-law of Mr. Gohain is the Director of the plantation. No Manager or Assistant Manager has been appointed for the plantation. Below the Director, ten Khampti and two Nepalis have been appointed as supervisory staffs (Mauris) in the plantation. Locally, the supervisory staffs are called Mauris and factory workers numbering about twenty have been employed from the Nepali community. Four Vehicle drivers one each from the Assamese, Nepali, Khampti and Bengali communities have been employed at the plantation. Tea plantation workers are at the bottom of organisational hierarchy. By "plantation workers" here we mean both the daily rated plantation and monthly rated factory workers. They work on "No Work No

Pay" basis (Ramaswamy: 1995). Although a Muster Roll is maintained at the plantation, they are treated as daily rated 'regular' working force of the agro-based industry. In this way, they are as good as casual workers. It may be due to the liberalization policy of Government of India as casualisation and liberalization are two sides of the same coin (Bhowmik: 1995).

Interestingly, it is well observed that fifty percent of workers in Muster Roll go on changing every week among the Adivasi workers. Thus, keeping a stable labour force in the plantation mainly at the Anula division is very big problem for the management (Choudhury: 2000). The Adivasis as reported by the Mauris, do not attend the work regularly and thus very frequently they remain absent at their duty places. Again, some Adivasi workers are not found reporting to the Mauris may be due to the absence of welfare incentives for the workers like Provident Fund, Gratuity, Bonus etc. coupled with other industrial facilities as enshrined in various labour legislations of Government of India. However, such problem is not noticed with the Nepali tea plantation workers of the Anula Shagun T.E. This will be more clear if we see the table No. 3.1 of the study.

It is observed from the table No. 3.1 of the study that 31.3% of the workers are working at the plantation for more than ten years. Again, another 34.7% of them are working for more than five years but less than ten years.Similarly, 34.0% of the workers are working at the plantation for less than five years. It is also found that 31.3% of the workers are associated with the plantation ever since its inception (1987) while 68.7% of them were recruited in phase manner with the extension of the plantation from 30 hectares in 1987 to 219 hectares under tea bushes till 2003 A.D. Interestingly, in the beginning, more and more importance was given to the recruitmnent of Adivasi workers from the neighbouring state of Assam but later on more and more Nepalis had to be recruited from the Assam plains and Nepal Himalayas because the Adivasis did not ordain required commitments to the plantation industry. This might be the apparent reason for employing 300 Nepali workers while only 100 Adivasi workers have been employed today at the plantation.

Therefore, it is very clear from the above discussion that the Nepalis have shown deep patronage to the industrial autocracy of a Khampti family of the Anula Shagun T.E. Interacting with Mr. Gohain, it is learnt that he has kept a Nepali (Rai) Chowkidar with full confidence at his bunglow Mr. Gohain even takes the Chowkidar to Tezu and Tinsukia towns while transacting his bank accounts for weekly wage payment of the workers. Thus, the Nepalis have exhaustively proved their loyalty, perseverance and commitment to the cause of tribal process of industrialisation of Government of Arunachal Pradesh. Adherence to such commitment for the landlord or planter as Thulo Manchee (big sort) is the prominent hereditary quality of the Nepalis which they have mainly borrowed from their places of origin. In the traditional Nepali society, each caste was to be fully commited to its masters with respective caste occupation. This will be evident if we see the table 3.2 of the Study.

Table 3.1

Years of Service of the Workers at the Anula Shagun T.E.

Sl.No	*Caste/Comunity*	*1 to 5Yrs.*	*%*	*6 to 10 Yrs.*	*%*	*10 Yrs. plus*	*Percentage*
1.	Nepali = Chhetri = 60	40	29.4	15	10.8	5	4.0
2.	Nepali = Mangar = 100	30	22.1	40	28.8	30	24.0
3.	Nepali = Gurung = 20	5	3.7	3	2.2	12	9.6
4.	Nepali = Kami = 24	4	2.9	15	10.8	5	4.0
5.	Nepali = Tamang = 12	1	0.7	2	1.4	9	7.2
6.	Nepali = Rai= 60	20	14.7	10	7.2	30	24.0
7.	Nepali = Limbu = 20	5	3.7	3	2.2	12	9.6
8.	Nepali = Newar = 2	1	0.7	–	–	1	0.8
9.	Nepali = Thami = 2	–	–	1	0.7	1	0.8
10.	Nepali = Adivasis = 100	30	22.1	50	36.0	20	16.0
	Total = 400	136	34.0	139	34.7	125	31.2

Source: Field Work: 2003.

Table 3.2

Traditional Occupations of the Nepali castes

Sl. No.	*Caste*	*Traditional Occupation*
1.	Chhetri	Warriors
2.	Mangar/Rai/Limbu	Agriculturists
3.	Gurung	Shepherds
4.	Tamang	Horse Traders/Cavalry
5.	Newar	Goldsmiths/
6.	Thami	Carriers/Bodyguards
7.	Kami	Ironsmiths.

Source: Field Work: 2003.

The table No. 3.2 of the study makes it very clear that traditionally all the Nepali castes of the plantation belonged to toiling class of Nepal (Pradhan:1991) and the Eastern Himalayas (Sharma: 1997). However, the Nepali occupational structure undergone a drastic change in Nepal also after 1926 (Haimendorf: 1966) with the abolition of slavery system. Thereafter, the occupational structure of the Nepali castes became primarily agrarian in nature. The formation of new agrarian social structure in Nepal Himalayas made those castes 'landless' toiling mass for they were thereafter exposed to new type of agrarian hierarchy into Pattadar (landowner) and Pakhurey (share cropper) groups (Regmi:1971). It is explored from the study that the workers who have been immigrated from the agrarian Nepal Himalayas belonged to Pakhurey group doing various agrarian manual jobs. The drastic change that is being taken place at the plantation is that they are all the owners of kitchen Ganders that have been provided by the plantation management and wet rice land (Pather) provided by the Khamptis in Satkilu village of Chowkham. Occupationally, they have dual characteristics (Xaxa: 1997), viz, agrarian and industrial. No more, they are purely Pakhureys by land ownership pattern. The nature of dual characteristics of Nepali castes can be understood very distinctly if we see the table 3.3 of the study.

The table 3.3 of the study indicates that 76.0% of families of the plantation workers are engaged in different kinds of job either agriculture, petty business or government services. These are secondary occupations of the workers. Rest of family members of the workers numbering 170 are either the students, small kids, retired or aged persons. It is further obseved that these retired or aged persons also look after the small kinds at homes and cattlestocks in jungle and field. Therefore, occupationally, they are to be treated as good as working population of families of the workers. Again,it is very much transparent from the table No. 10 that 56.7% of families of the workers have double working persons. Still another 14.3% of the workers' families have triple working persons. Above all, 3.1% of their families have four working persons and 1.8% of their families have five working persons.

The above discussion has portrayed an interesting fact that hardly any family member of the workers except small kids stays idle without work in the plantation. To the wokers, human life is part and parcel of work and without work they can not just survive. Hour - wise, they work for 12 to 13 hours a day of which 8 hours have been devoted to the garden duty and five hours either in agrarian or other agrarian related jobs. Each family devotes at least two to three hours everyday for rearing and dearing the cattlestock population. This will be more clear if we see the possession of cattlestock population by the workers.

The table 3.4 of the study indicates that comparatively Chhetris have highest number of milched cow population considering their numerical strength in the plantation. Next to Chhetris, Mangars have domesticated much milched cows at their households. It is because of the fact that historically only the Chhetri, Mangar and Gurung castes of the Nepali Community were considered to be purely Gurkhas - the protectors of Gau (cow) Dharma (religion) and hence they were to be overtly considered as pure Hindus (Sharma : 1997) in Nepal Himalayas (Pradhan: 1991: Haimendorf: 1966). Caplan (1970) has also made similar observation in the Eastern Nepal.Interestingly, it is also observed in the table 11 of the study that the Matwalis (Rai, Limbu, Mangar, Gurung, Tamang, Kami, Newar and Thami) have large number of fowl population (40.8%) in their huseholds. They are Matwalis who are suppose to use wine and sarcrifice animals' blood/flesh while performing their rituals but the Chhetri being a Tagadhari caste has to wear sacred threads. The Chhetri is to be considered as double born Hindu caste along with the Brahmins (Bahuns) of the Nepali society (Sharma:2000). This will be elaborately discussed in next chapter of the study. The Mangars and Gurungs being highly Hinduised castes (Srivastava:1966) in the past in Nepal Himalayas have the habit of keeping large number of milched cow population at their homes. This is also very evident from the table 3.4. Another interesting point to note here from the table is that not a single Matwali household has kept or domesticated pigs. Keeping or rearing piggery is strictly prohibited by the plantation owner who has constructed/maintatined a Budhist Monastry (Gumpha) near the Nepali labour line (Dhura) of the

Table 3.3

Structure of Working Persons of the Workers

Sl.No.	*Caste/Community*	*Double*	*Triple*	*Four*	*Five*	*Total*
1.	Nepali = Chhetri = 102	60	3	–	–	63
2.	Nepali = Mangar = 180	100	20	–	–	120
3.	Nepali = Gurung = 32	20	2	2	1	25
4.	Nepali = Kami = 38	24	2	2	1	29
5.	Nepali = Tamang = 19	12	2	1	1	16
6.	Nepali = Rai= 120	60	30	5	3	98
7.	Nepali = Limbu= 37	20	3	1	1	25
8.	Nepali = Newar = 4	2	–	1	–	3
9.	Nepali = Thami = 4	2	–	–	1	3
10.	Adivasis = 170	100	39	10	5	154
	Total = 706	400	101	22	13	536
	Percentage –	56.7%	14.3%	3.1%	1.8%	76.0%

Source: Field Work: 2003.

plantation. Secondly, it is also prohibited by the Government of Arunachal Pradesh because in 1995, a malarial fever from the mosquitoes after their bitting the pigs contaminated the entire Lohit district of the state in an epedemic form. Again, it is seen that 2.4% of bulls have been kept at their households because the bulls are necessary animals for ploughing the land and mating with the cows. Chicken and cow milk are mainly sold for the Gunanagar and Chowhkam dwellers who do not mostly rear and dear milched cows at their households. In fact, most of the Khamptis are not accustomed to domesticate milched cow population as they were Jhumias (shifting cultivators) in their own way till the recent past. Keeping goats at homes is mainly for their household consumption. On the average, each Nepali household has kept at least five domesticated animals at its disposal. It shows that agriculture cum industrial economy of the planation have enabled the agrarian Nepalis to keep such a large number of cattlestocks at their households.

Table 3.4

Cattlestock Population of the Workers

Sl.No.	*Caste*	*Cow*	*Goat*	*Bull*	*Hens/Cocks*	*Total*
1.	Chhetri = 30	60	10	2	–	72
2.	Mangar = 50	120	30	4	30	184
3.	Gurung = 10	25	25	2	50	102
4.	Kami = 12	24	30	2	30	86
5.	Tamang = 6	13	15	2	35	65
6.	Rai = 30	30	20	4	46	100
7.	Limbu = 10	12	10	2	60	84
8.	Newar = 1	1	–	–	30	31
9.	Thami = 1	1	–	–	25	26
	Total = 150	286	140	18	306	750
	Percentage =	38.1%	18.7%	2.4%	40.8%	100.0%

Source: Field Work: 2003.

Landholding Pattern of the Workers

The landless Nepalis of Nepal Himalayas immigrated to the Anula Shagun T.E. as they were assured of settled life with agrarian field both in and outside the plantation. In general, that was the pull factor for the Nepalis immigration to North East India including the state of Arunachal Pradesh.

Every worker has been provided with the kitchen garden at the plantation. Historically, to attract the poverty ridden tribals to join as manual workers in the plantations, the British planters used to provide kitchen gardens to the workers due to the isolated locations or enclaves of the plantations where the workers could not have frequent access to market except once in a weekly Hat (small bajar taken place in open space of the plantations) to purchase vegitabels etc. After joining the plantation job, they got ample opportunity to clear up the dense forests around the plantations and raised terraces for settled cultivation.The work relating to forest clearance had been accomplished by the Nepalis following the state policy for terminating Jhum (shifting) cultivation in the area under reference. The same thing is also found today in all the Nepali dominated villages of the state of Arunachal Pradesh. It is also found that unlike other state governments of India, the Government of Arunachal Preadesh wants that the tribals of the state should clear up the forests and have their settled cultivation for ever particularly in hill regions of Tirap, Changlang and Lohit districts adjoining the Maynmar (Burma) and China.

Table 3.5

Land Holding Pattern of the Workers

Sl.No.	*Caste*	*Kitchen Garden (in Khatta)*	*Percentage*	*Wet Rice land (Pather) in Bigha***	*Percentage*
1.	Chhetri =30	150	21.4%	60	21.0%
2.	Mangar = 50	250	35.7%	100	35.0%
3.	Gurung = 10	30	4.3%	20	7.0%
4.	Kami = 12	36	5.1%	24	8.4%
5.	Tamang = 6	18	2.6%	20	7.0%
6.	Rai = 30	180	25.7%	40	14.0%
7.	Limbu= 10	30	4.3%	10	3.5%
8.	Newar = 1	3	0.4%	5	1.7%
9.	Thami = 1	3	0.4%	7	2.4%
	Total = 150	700	99.9%	286	100.0%

* One Khatta = 720 Sq. feets,

** One Bigha = two acres.

Source: Field Work: 2003.

The table 3.5 of the study shows that 286 Bighas of land are wet rice fields (Pather) which are cultivated by the Nepali workers of the plantation at Satkilu village. It transpired the fact that every Nepali caste of the plantation has been cultivating the land for paddy, maize, wheat and vegitables. The field provides cattle fodders also such as straw and grass of variety to the agrarian Nepalis. Only paddy has to be distributed equally with the landowners (Khamptis) as the land holding right lies with the Khamptis only. But operationally, the Nepalis are the real owners of wet rice fields (Pather) known as Panikheti in the Nepali society, because the Khampti tribal owners of the land hardly visit the wet rice fields and therefore they do not virtually encroach upon the management right of the land being solely given to the Nepalis. In the plantation, 35.7% of the kitchen land is owned by the Mangars. Another 25.7% of the kitchen garden is owned by the Rai caste. Similarly, 21.4% of the kichen garden is owned by the Chhetris. Logic behind holding more kitchen gardens by the Mangar, Rai and Chhetri than other castes is closely associated with their immigration and settlement histroy in the plantation. These three castes of the Nepali community were earlier immigrants while other castes were recent immigrants at the plantation of the state of Arunachal Pradesh. Similarly, in regard to holding wet rice land or paddy field on share cropping, these three castes have higher quantum of land at Satkilu village of Chowkham. The percentage of agrarian wet rice land holding on share cropping is lesser among other castes of the plantation because they are the recent immigrants. The earlier immigrants called themselves as "Raithanees" and the later immigrants are called by the Raithanees as "Sukumbasis". The Sukumbasis being not fully acquainted with the local Khampti land owners, have lesser amount of land on share cropping in the area under reference. On the whole, it is observed that the Mangars are much better off than other castes in so far as the question of holding wet rice land on share cropping is concerned.

Style of Life of the Workers

To operationalise the issue "Style of Life" of the workers, holding valuable articles is taken as the main parameter in the study. This is evident from the table 3.6 of the study.

The table 3.6 of the study indicates that the Mangar, Rai and Chhetri castes appeared to have been leading better quality of life than other castes in the plantation. Holding modern equipments and mechanical goods is more with Rai, Mangar and Limbu castes than other castes.This is evident from the ownership of scooters by Limbu, Rai and Mangar castes. The Gurungs have also good number of scooters of their own. Rest of the castes have lesser number of such modern equipments. Interestingly, not a single worker's family has four wheeler vehicle. It is because of the fact that the location of plantation is as such that they can not just go to Tinsukia or Tezu (district headquarter of the Lohit district) towns regularly for shopping or other works. Whenever they go to Tezu which is 30 kilometres away from the plantation, they go by bus only. They openly expressed the fact that it is very difficult to keep four wheeler vehicles at their homes as there is no servicing centre nearby the plantation to repair the vehicles in case any defect is noticed with the vehicles. Moreover, they do not want to purchase the vehicles because of their low level of living at the plantation. In fact, keeping such vehicles and expensive articles at homes carry higher social status that reflects hierarchy, utility and attractiveness (Bose: 1997). Acquiring such social status is absolutely absent among the plantation workers. Above all, they stated that they do not want by heart and soul to spend money so that they can invest their money in Terai belts of Nepal (adjoining the Indian border) considering their uncertain future in the region.

Table 3.6

Possession of Valuable Articles by the Workers

Sl. No.	*Caste*	*Television*	*Radio*	*Sofa Seats*	*Watch*	*Clock*	*Bycycle*	*Scooter*
1.	Chhetri = 30	20	8	2	19	25	20	2
2.	Mangar = 50	45	4	45	40	50	35	12
3.	Gurung = 10	8	1	8	18	10	17	8
4.	Kami = 12	10	1	7	8	13	21	4
5.	Tamang = 6	5	2	4	9	7	2	3
6.	Rai = 30	25	10	28	52	32	21	19
7.	Limbu = 10	9	5	7	17	12	9	10
8.	Newar = 1	1	1	1	2	2	1	1
9.	Thami = 1	1	1	2	2	2	1	1
	Total = 150	124	33	104	167	153	127	60

Source: Field Work: 2003.

Working Hours for the Workers

With the garden siren at 7 A.M., the workers have to report to the Mauris (supervisors) for work. The work starts sharp at 7 A.M. and continues till 11 A.M. At 11 A.M., they go home for their lunch and come back to the work places sharp at 12 Noon. From 12 Noon to 4 P.M., work continues for the workers. The workers have to work for six days in a week. The sunday is a holiday without wages. Each worker has to pluck 32 kilogram of green tea leaves per day. It is known as Thicka. If the workers pluck extra green tea leaves than rupee one is given to the workers per kilogram of plucked green tea leaves. During the pruning season, each worker has to prun ten Tangs (tea bushes) per day. Unlike other tea plantations of Assam and West Bengal, here the workers have to work for the whole day (eight hours) in the pruning season also.

Benefits to the Workers

Except four day puja holidays, 15 th August (Independence Day) and 26 th January (Republic Day), no other holiday or leave is being given to the workers in the plantation. There is no system of providing Annual Leave to the workers as per the provisions of Plantation Labour Act, 1951. The house building materials are provided to the workers by the management, while the constructing cost of labour huts is to be entirely incurred by the workers themselves from their own purse.

There is neither the system of Employees Provident Fund deduction from the wage payment bill of the workers nor the contribution of management towards the Provident Fund for the workers. Each labour line has been provided a tube well for drinking water. The workers have to collect fuel from the local reserve forests of the Government of Arunachal Pradesh.No children education incentive has been given to the workers. The creche facility has also not been provided to the workers' children below six years of age as per the provision of Plantation Labour Act, 1951 of Government of India. There is electricity supply to the labour lines but the electricity bills have to be paid by the workers themselves. In the name of recreational facility, there is a labour recreation club at Guna division of the plantation without any recreational item. The workers are also not provided Bonus and Gratuity. In regard to the medical facility for the workers, the garden management do not at all pay anything except one or two days leave without deducting wages of the workers. All the medical expenses are to be met by the workers themselves from their own purse. A cooperative ration shop has been opened at the plantation where the workers can procure necessary edible goods costing to the tune of actual wages received from the plantation. A ration Khata (copy) has been provided to the workers to draw the edible goods from the cooperative ration shop.

As there is no Badli (substitute) system of labour recruitment as we found in Assam and West Bengal tea plantations, the workers are recruited as good as casuals (Bhowmik: 1995) and employed on "No Work No Pay" basis. Under the Badli system, the dependent members of the workers are given garden jobs when the workers retire on superannuation. This may be the transparent reason why the plantation workers normally remain absent on duty. Mostly, with the commencement of agrarian sowing and harvesting seasons every year, they remain absent on their duty at the plantations. The workers prefer jobs at the agrarian sector because they can earn more money. For instance, if a worker holds a pair of bulls and if he tills the land of others for six months in a year than he can easily earn the whole year's bread and butter for his family. This may be the justification why most of the Adivasi workers of the plantation do not like to attend the garden jobs regularly. They stated that there is no prospect for their promotion to the supervisory category. So, a worker joins as a worker and retires as a worker (Sharma: 1994) only.

Therefore, industrialisation of the Indian workers as brought about by the Liberalization, Privatisation and Globalization policy (Bhowmik: 1996: Sharma: 2005) of Government of India has also left ample impacts on the plantation (Asopa: 2004) frontiers of Arunachal Pradesh. To cut down the incentives of workers so as to make prospered the industrialisation process of the state is observed to be the easy means for managing the tea industry of the state. The Government intervention in the industrial relation issue is very very negligible especially in regard to the welfare schemes for the workers as the political leaders, government bureaucrats and plantation owners of the state as mentioned above in the study belong to the middle class elites (Mishra: 1994) of the tribal society. In fact, the state sponsored industrialisation process of Arunachal Pradesh is mainly meant for the local tribes of the tribal state of North East India.

The above cited illustrations help us to generalize that the so-called industrialisation process of Arunachal Pradesh has hardly evolved an ideal industrial society in truest sense of the term. Rather, to safeguard the protectionist approach of the Government of Arunachal Pradesh by patronizing the tribal way of industrialisation process, the plantation frontiers have become protective enclaves for the country in the absolute sense of the term. Therefore, tea industry appears to have been the extension of agrarian economy of the state of Arunachal Pradesh.

Housing Conditions of the Workers

All the Nepali households of the Anula Shagun T.E. are of Puccka type with corrugated galvanised Iron Sheet roofs and wodden walls. It is collated from the responses of the workers that the houses which were provided to them are all of Puccka type. The Puccka houses were constructed during the late sixties of 19th century when the Namsoom Saw and Veneer Mills (P) Ltd. was established at Gunanagar in 1967. But, now the workers have to maintain and repair the same as the management of the plantation do not at all provide housing maintenance expenses and repair cost.

Interestingly, it is also observed that the houses constructed after the introduction of Guna Tea Industries (P) Ltd. in 1987 are all of the kuccha type with thatched roofs and bamboo framed mud walls. It is learnt from the workers of the plantation that Mr. Gohain had constructed the Puccka houses in 1967 when the Chowkham was full of forest resources that enabled him to construct wooden quarters for the Nepali workers with Corrugated Galvanised Iron Sheet roofs at very low cost. The situation underwent a sea change after 1987 when the Government of Arunachal Pradesh selectively banned for deforestation in the state. This is the main reason why the Adivasi households of about fifty in number are of Kuccha type today because now the approximate cost for constructing a single Puccka house is Rs. 60,000 or more and because of this reason, they do not dare to approach the management for the same due to the obvious reason as mentioned above in the study. If they do so, then they are threaten to be ousted from the plantation without possessing the current Inner Line Permits. So, the workers feel it much better to keep themselves mum rather than inviting troubles for their peaceful living at the plantation. Hence, the issue of new house construction does solely depend on the mercy of the planters. The size of Kuccha houses are of 40' by 30' while the size of Puccka houses are of 80′ by 100′. It is because of the fact that the Puccka households are there due to the reason that in 1967, there was sufficient land available for the planter to construct such Puccka houses at Gunanagar area of Chowkham. It is also observed that the size of Puccka trouses is quite sufficient to accommodate the entire family members of workers, as the population structure of the plantation workers is not so high. Almost 30.0 % of the plantation land is still vacant. Even the whole Chowkham region does not have more than ten thousand households. About two thousand Khampti tribal population (Mishra:1994) have occupied the villages on both sides of 52 National Highway that destines the Hindu pilgrims to their famous religious place known as Parsuram Kund which is located at the Lohit river of Arunachal Pradesh.

Caste and Income of the Workers

It is transparent from the table 3.7 of the study that the annual income of the plantation workers is quite high. The gross income of the workers has been calculated from all their earning sources like agriculture, plantation (wages), animal husbandry and government services.

Table 3.7

Caste/Community and Income Structure of the Workers

Sl. No.	*Caste (Household)*	*Monthly Income (In Rs.)**	*Annual Income (In Rs.)***
1.	Nepali = Chhetri = 30	63.000	7, 56.000
2.	Nepali = Mangar = 50	1,26.000	15,12.000
3.	Nepali = Gurung = 10	30,450	3,65.000
4.	Nepali = Kami = 12	30,450	3,65.000
5.	Nepali = Tamang = 6	16,800	2,65.000
6.	Nepali = Rai = 30	10,2,900	12,34,800
7.	Nepali = limbu = 10	26,250	3,15,000
8.	Nepali = Newar = 1	3,150	37,800
9.	Nepali = Thami = 1	3,150	37,800
10.	Adivasis = 50	1,61,700	19,4,000
	Total = 200	56,3,850	50,19,800

*+** = Gross Income from all earning sources.

Source: Field Work: 2003.

Among the Nepali castes, Rai, Tamang, Kami and Mangar are much better off than other castes in so far as their income structure is concerned. They are economically much proficient than others because they have owned good amount of agricultural land on share cropping from the Khamptis. Moreover, they were earlier immigrants to the plantation. Although the Adivasi workers of the plantation earn at par with the Nepali counterpart, their level of living is comparatively much lower than that of the Nepali counterpart. The Adivasis had since time immemorial little inclination towards decent living (Bhowmik: 1981) with the income they used to earn from various sources of their economy.

Interestingly, all the workers stated that 40.0% of their income is spent in maintianing their homes. Again, a substantial amount of money of the workers has been spent for the medical treatment of their family members every year in Tezu, Tinsukia, Dibrugarh or Guwahati hospitals and nursing homes.

Caste and Borrowings

It is comprehended from the discussion with the plantation workers that hardly they borrow from others except on emergency. An analysis has been made in the following section to understand the nature of borrowing. This will help us to know the nature of borrowing as to which caste or community borrows from which other castes or communities of the plantation and its neighbourhood.

Table 3.8

Caste/Community and Borrowing of the Workers

Sl.No.	*Caste*	*Caste/Community*
1.	Nepalis	Nepalis/Khamptis/Marwaris/Biharis
2.	Adivasis	Adivasis/Khamptis /Nepalis/Marwaris/Biharis

Source: Field work: 2003.

Very interestingly, it is observed from the table 3.9 of the study that normally at emergency, the Nepalis borrow from their own community. If they do not get loans from their own community, they go to the Khamptis who are their masters in the plantation and Chowkham which is their neighbourhood and if they do not get loans from the Khamptis, then they go to Marwaris and Biharis. The picture is also found same among the Adivasis but the Adivasis go for loans to the Marwaris and Biharis if they do not get loans from their own community, Khamptis and Nepalis.It indicates the fact that Marwaris and Biharis are not much preferred for loans by the workers due to high interest rate charged (18.0%) per thousand per month.

It shows that on the whole, the Marwaris and Biharis have good source of income from the interests charged for loans from the workers. However, the nature of borrowing indicates the area of cultural integration among the communities of the plantation. However, the workers are fully convinced that Adivasis, Nepalis and Khamptis are their actual permanent neighbours while the Biharis, Marwaris and other Indians are temporarily settled here in Gunanagar (Chowkham) for trade and commerce. The moment their business dwindle they will left the place for elsewhere for ever. Borrowing is therefore found to be a strong thread or bond for cultural integration among the Nepalis, Adivasis, Khamptis and other communities in Gunanagar of Chowkham in particular and Arunachal Pradesh in general.

Plantation Workers and Trade Union Movement

The study reveals that there is no trace of trade union movement in tea industry of Arunachal Pradesh. Whatever the trade unions are there in the state, they are mainly centered around Itanagar printers, constraction, Public Works Department and two wood based industries (Das: 1995) of the state. Tea plantation workers of the state are mainly the in migrants under the short term Inner Line Permits of the government. They fear to talk about the union or unionization (Bhowmik: 1995) of the workers. Even there is not a single recognised social welfare organisation in tea plantations of the state which could fight for the welfare of the plantation workers. Whatever the social problem emerges at the plantation, it is to be solved by the Government Gaon Burah of the area. The Government Gaon Burah (village headman) of every village has been paid an honoririum of Rs. 1000/- per month by the Government of Arunachal Pradesh. He looks after the general problems of the society.

In the Anula Shagun T.E., there is a Khampti Government Gaon Burah who tries to solve the social problems of the workers. But very interestingly, it is noted that a rift has taken place between the Government Gaon Burah and the owner of the plantation.It is explored from the study that the Government Gaon Burah belongs to another clan of the Khampti tribal society while the planter belongs to the Namsoom clan which was historically considered as the most superior clan than other clans of the tribal society. Traditionally, the Namsoom clan of the Khampti tribal society was the ruling clan (Gogoi: 1971; Mishra: 1994). Secondly, the Government Gaon Burah wants to make the workers conscious about their rights and responsibilities at the plantation industry. This is against the interest of the plantation owner who by heart and soul wants to keep the workers in utter darkness. Even the government schemes which are not liked by him can hardly be implemented at the plantation. In other words, if he does not like any scheme of the government, he straightway rejects the same. Nobody except his pet persons can penetrate into his gardens. Thus, the plantation industry is his personal colony and the society thereof is enclave society of the state of Arunchal Pradesh.

In this way, from the point of view of the Government legislations, tea plantation workers of Anula Shagun T.E. in particular and Arunachal Pradesh in general can be called as unorganised sector workers. The workers are unorganised as the owner of the plantation has fully owned the industry but he has nothing to own the labour force of the industry both in their industrial and social life (Mamkottam: 1994). Thus, there is every doubt as to whether any trade union movement as we found in neighbouring Assam tea plantations can have an easy access (Seth: 1994) into the Anula Shagun T.E. in future. The same platitude is also found in case of other tea plantations (Sampath: 1994:Dubey:1994) of the state of Arunachal Pradesh in so far as the unionisation of (Sinha:1994) the workers is concerned.

Labour Commitments to Tea Industry

Inspite of complete exploitation of workers at the Anula Shagun T.E., the workers are found to be fully committed to the industry as no work remains pending right from the plucking of green tea leaves to the packaging of made tea. Even they work for eight hours in the pruning season also while in Assam and West Bengal tea plantations, the workers have to work for only four hours in a day during the season. This really supplements the hypothesis that Nepalis are hard working people. Had there been any other dominant working community like Khamptis, Chakmas, Deoris or Hill Miris of the region then the Anula Shagun T.E. had to be abandoned long back for ever. This may be the reason why Mr. Gohain has also started another tea plantation at Medo area by recruiting the Nepalis as manual workers from his Bordumsa (Changlang district) and the Anula Shagun (Lohit district) tea estates. The commitment of the Nepali tea plantation workers along with the young tea bushes of hardly fifteen years old and low cost of production of only Rs. 20/- per kilogram of made tea (Asopa: 2004) has given encouraging direction to the tribal tea garden owner of the Anula Shagun T.E. In general, the higher rate of Tea Board's subsidy schemes for introducing new factories and field (CCPA:1996) has given further stimulus to all the tribal planters of the state. Tea garden owners of the state are paying very handsome revenue to the Government of Arunachal Pradesh by fetching selling price of Rs. 70/ - on the average per kilogram of made tea in the market. Here, an instance has been cited regarding the prices that Arunachal tea gardens got in 1999-2000 in the market that portrays the fact that tea industry of Arunachal Pradesh has a promising or bright future.

The table 3.10 of the study shows that on the average, Arunachal tea of C.T.C. variety got Rs. 70.84 in 1999-2000 per kilogram of made tea. The price level of Arunachal tea is higher than any other tea of Assam and west Bengal plantations in so far as the C.T.C. variety is concerned. The apparent reason besides cheap labour for getting such higher level of prices in the market is due to its better quality of tea leaves being plucked from the young tea bushes. It indicates the ground reality that tea plantation industry is quite lucrative to the state economy of Arunachal Pradesh.

Table 3.10

Tea Prices for Arunachal Pradesh (1999-2000)

Garden	*C.T.C. Leaf Qty. in thousand kg.*	*Average Price (per kg.)*	*Orthodox Tea Leaf (Qty. in kg.)*	*Price per kg.*	*DUST*	
					Qty. in kg.	*Price*
Ganesh Tea	2039.1	45.77	–	–	–	–
Tayang Shreenanda	28982.4	74.88	–	–	17980.21	61.20
Tayang	830.0	32.16	–	–	–	–
Total	31841.5	67.02	–	–	17980.21	61.20
Excise Zone II Total	4938051.6	67.02	1448696.0	78.65	1183904.0	53.42
Grand Total	13651351.6	70.84	4978633.4	69.85	6518000.4	58.91

Source: Assam Tea Review: May, 3-5-2000.

4

SOCIAL LIVING OF THE WORKERS

In this chapter, we shall elaborately discuss about the social life of the workers. Discussing the social life of the workers, changing social structure of the Nepali castes, caste and family, caste and marriage and caste and commensal relations shall be highlighted. Further, special stress will be given on the relationship between the Nepali and Adivasi as well as Nepali and Khampti communities of the plantation. Highlighting the changing social relationship, we shall also see as to how the traditional Nepali social structure based on hierarchical divisions has been transformed in the plantation industrial environment of the Anula Shagun T.E. of Arunachal Pradesh?

The Anula Shagun T.E. : Land of Immigrants

Historically, the dominant Khampti of the region under reference had immigrated from the Bor Khampti country of Maynmar (Burma) at the source of river Irrawady in early 18th century (Gogoi: 1971). First, they settled down at Tengapani areas of Tirap district of Arunachal Pradesh where they were very badly defeated and ousted by the Singhpo tribe (Ibid). After being badly defeated and ousted by the Singphoes from Tengapani, the Khamptis moved towards Sadiya of Assam (Das:1995) and settled down there by defeating the local Assamese people. Prof. M.L. Bose, the historian (1997) has very lucidly described about the origin and settlement history of the Khampti tribes in Arunachal Pradesh. He observed "The British came into contact with the Khampti tribe when they came to Assam during the Anglo–Burmese War of 1824 to 1826. The Khamptis were immigrants from the land called Bor Khampti between the eastern extremity of Assam and river Irrawady". At first, they had settled around Tengapani in the Tirap district of Arunachal Pradesh. In 1799 to 1800, the Barasiriagis (the dominant Assamese people) revolted at Sadiya, the Khamptis along with other tribes joined Assamese people) revolted at Sadiya, the Khamptis along with other tribes joined the Asamese Governor of Sadiya (Bhuyan: 1947). The Thungkhangia Burangi records that they occupied Sadiya in 1797 and title and dignity of Assam Governor were assumed by the Khampti tribal chief

(Ibid). The Ahom kings had no formal relations with the Khamptis nor had the Posa (tax) of any kind had levied to them by the Ahom kings. The Khampti chief ruled like an independent prince.

Further, Prof. Bose observed He had succeeded in keeping his Sadiya free from the Anglo-Assamese turmoil when Scot, the British Agent to the Governor-General came to Upper Assam in 1824, the Khamptis of Chowkham had rendered him good service. Therefore, Scot recognised the Khampti chief "Chousalan Sadiya Khawa Gohain" as their cheif and permitted him to collect taxes from the Assamese people within his jurisdiction. The Khampti chief himself and other Khamptis did not pay any tax and instead undertook to maintain a contingent of 200 men to be armed by the British as per the terms of an agreement entered to obey orders of the British Government sent through the Political Officer of Upper Assam to whom they were to bring all serious crimes for trial.

The relation between the Khamptis and British remained friendly and peaceful till 1839 though rumours of the Khampti intrigues were reported occasionally. As late as 1838, Captain White, the Political Agent of Sadiya wrote that they were faithful to their engagements and gave no cause for anxiety though a report of the year shows that the Khamptis had become disgusted over Sadiya which they considered to be their own territory. In 1835, a fresh batch of immigrants from Bor Khampti land entered Assam and sought permission to settle under the British Government. They asked for the remission of taxes for ten years and fire arms. The British were anxious to settle them as barriers between Assam and Burma because still they were haunted by a dread of fresh Burmese invasion. Therefore, the Khamptis were allowed to settle without paying taxes for three years but no fire arms were supplied to them.

In 1838, a dispute arose between the Khampti chief of Sadiya and Bor Senapati of Muttuck, the Moamaria chief of Upper Assam in regard to the tract of land on south bank of Brahmaputra. The Political Agent (officer) asked both the parties to appear before him. The Khampti chief took possession of the land in defiance of the order whereupon the Political Agent in vindication of his authority attacked the land in dispute. He ordered first the suspension and then removal of the Khampti chief from the post of Khawa Gohain. The Khawa Gohain was thereafter removed to a distant station down the river out of reach of easy intrigue and his post was abolished. His territory was brought under the administration of the British officer at Sadiya who collected taxes from the Assamese people and administered justice to them. But the Khamptis and Singhpoes of this territory were left under their own chiefs, no tax was levied upon them.

Apparently, the Khamptis seemed contend and during the Singhpoes rising of 1838, they along with Khamptis of Chowkham rendered good service to the British. The ex-Khawa Gohain was allowed to return to Sadiya in his private capacity in recognition of the Khampti service. But this hatred to the British and fear of being brought under the regular jurisdiction of the British administration resulted premediated outbreak on 19th January in 1839, when about 500 Khamptis in arms attacked the British post at Sadiya, butchered Col. White and his men and burnt the lines in the ground. The Khamptis on the south bank of the Brahmaputra (Chowkham) also revolted but they were put down by the British troops. The successful Khamptis on north bank of the Brahmaputra, however retreated with their adherents and took refuge among the Dibang Mishmis. Compelled by distress in their jungle refuge, one chief, Conking Gohain, surrendered and then led a British force to compel others to follow him. In 1839 to 1840, more expeditions were sent to disperse the Khamptis from the hills and finally in 1843, all the Khamptis surrendered to the British under agreement of good behaviour.

After that the Khamptis were divided into four groups, as suggested by the Captain Vetch who suppressed the Khampti rebellion. With a view to weakening them they were dispersed by the British in four divisions. One group was settled at Choonpura above Sadiya under the Captian Gohain, cousin of late Khawa Gohain. Another division which was formerly near Tengapani was settled near Saikhawa to the south of river Brahmaputra. The third party under Chowtang Gohain was settled at Dhemaji and fourth sent to Bhodia, west of Lakhimpur under the son of late Khawa Gohain. Since then, they could not be united and as a result, they failed to acquire any political importance.They involved in agricultural pursuits. Those who settled in Choonpura and below Saikhawa (Chowkham) did not pay any tax or revenue to the British Government, the rest in Bhodia and Dhemaji paid regular taxes to the Government.

The British relation with the Khamptis did not face any strain thereafter. Rather, henceforth, the Khamptis and their chiefs always acted as regular guides to the British officers in their tours to Mishmi and Singhpo hills. Needam, Williamson and Dunda took Khampti Gohains in their tours. The Khampti chief of Chowkham was granted a pension and a gun in recognition of British favour to him. As late as 1916, he claimed restitution of his independence and titile. Though the request was turned down, his pension was increased to Rs. 50/- from Rs. 30/- and his people were exempted from taxation when poll taxes began to be levied in the central and eastern districts of North East Frontier in which some Khamptis were included after 1914". Today, the other Khamptis as dispersed by the British appeared to have been completely assimilated with other tribes of the places of their settlement. This may be the reason why today the Khamptis are found to be concentrated in Chowkham area of Lohit district of Arunachal Pradesh.

After their settlement in Chowkham in 1785 (Mishra: 1994), the Khamptis started settled cultivation along with business on the Khampti tribal arts and crafts. Their "Lungi" making profession has become very prominent in the state along with the continuation of village dormitory system which they inherted from their tradition. According to the Khampti custom, village chief used to allot the common land to the individual villagers. With the abandonment of any land by the individuals, it automatically reverted to the village common land (Das:1995).

The institution of chieftainship among the Khamptis had been instrumental in dividing their societies into two classes, viz., the patricians and plebians. In the Hinayani Budhist society, chiefs occupied the highest position and they were folllowed by priests. Below them, there was a class of free men. At the bottom, there were slaves. The chiefs and priests-patricians being the leisured class were largely dependent on the labour of the commoners-the plebians and slaves (Mishra: 1994).

Such a system was supported by the British colonialists so as to keep the tribal Arunachal Pradesh isolated under their policy of "Excluded Areas" and "Partially Excluded Areas". The situation changed after 1947 when the Government of India started to follow the policy of integration in Arunachal Pradesh as elsewhere the country so as to keep the tribal identity intact. Doing this, the development process through industrialisation started in Arunachal Pradesh and Chowkham also. With the formation of a full fledged state in 1987, Arunachal Government officially abolished the slavery system (Bose:1997). That gave a new social structure in Arunachal Pradesh, viz, landowners and landless categories in rural areas of the state. Along with the introduction of Panchayat Raj system in village Arunachal ever since 1967 (Ibid), the whole social structure started changing very fastly. All the slaves became free citizens of the state. The impact of changes also equally affected the industrially developed Lohit district of the state, viz, village chief/ Gaon Burah, middle class elites and low class Khamptis. Interestingly, village chiefs and Gaon Burahs have formal powers being delegated by the Government of Arunachal Pradesh while the real power lies with the hands of middle class Khampti elites (Mishra: 1983) in the villages of Chowham (Gogoi: 1971) while the lower class Khamptis are purely agrarian people today. The agrarian pursuits is much more lucrative to the lower class Khamptis and other tribes than working in tea plantation industry of the region. That had really called for the import of plantation labours from the Assam plains and Nepal Himalayas in the eastern most districts of Arunachal Pradesh. The discussion makes it very distinct that the Khamptis along with Singhpo and Nocte tribes were mainly the early immigrants to the most enchanted districts of the state of Arunachal Pradesh from Maynmar (Burma). The question of survival made the Khamptis more proactive in business and agriculture in their own way from the beginning in Chowkham (Mishra: 1994) block of Namsai sub-division of Arunachal Pradesh.

It is observed that the power and authority of Gaon Burah is secondary in the present Khampti society of Chowkham as the newly emerging middle class educated elites (Ibid) among the Khamptis are now moulding the society, polity and economy (Das: 1995) of the region. Almost all the land of Satkilu village near the Anula Shagun T.E. is owned by the Khamptis. The Gohain family of the Anula Shagun T.E. has owned three tea estates one each in Chowkham and Medo of Lohit district and Bordumsa of Changlang district of Arunachal Pradesh.

Traditional Social Structure of the Nepalis

The study of existing social structure of a community calls for thorough pondering over its traditional social framework. In the traditional Nepali society, the whole population was divided into three groups, viz, Tagadhari, Matwali and Untouchable in Nepal (Haimendorf: 1966) and even in Darjeeling-Sikkim Himalayas (Sharma: 2000) of the Indian sub-continent. The caste falling in each category had specific occupation. Thus, prior to their immigration to the Anula Shagun T.E., the Nepali castes had their specific occupations. The society was typically an agrarian in nature. This will be more clear if we see the table 4.1 of the study.

Table 4.1

Traditional Nepali Caste System

Sl.No.	*Varna*	*Caste*
1.	Brahmin	Upadhaya, Kumai, Jaisi, Deb Bhaju (Newar)
2.	Kshatriya	Thakuri, Chhetri, Khatri
	Double Order*	Gurung and Mangar
3.	Vaisya	Newar High Castes
4.	Shudra	Rai, Iimbu,low caste Newars, Sherpa, Sunuwar, Murmi, Thami, Tamang etc.
5.	Untouchables	Kami, Damai, Sarki, Jyapu, Pore (Newars) Etc.

* Converted into Hindu religion from Budhism and other forms of Animism of the Nepal Himalayas.

Source: Nepali; 1965; Sharma: 2003.

The table 4.1 of the study shows that the Nepali caste system emerged after 1769 (Unification of Nepal by Prithivinarayan Shah) in Nepal underwent a sea change afterwards. The five fold classification of the Nepali society underwent a drastic change. Prof. Haimendorf (1966) has classified the Nepali society into three fold groups, viz, Tagadhari, Matwali and Untouchable. Caplan (1970) has also classified the Nepali society into three groups, viz., Tagadhari, Matwali and Untouchable considering the overt changes that had taken place in Nepal after 1926–the year of the abolition of slavery system by the Nepalese Government.

The traditional caste system was associated with the specific occupation of each and every caste.This is evident from the table 4.2 of the study.

It is very much transparent from the table 4.2 of the study that most of the Nepali castes were by and large toiling mass of Nepal and the Eastern Himalayas. They were mainly concentrated in the agrarian belts of Nepal, Darjeeling, Sikkim as well as Bhutan Himalayas (Sharma: 2003).

Table 4.2

Occupational Structure in the Traditional Nepali Society

Sl. No.	*Caste*	*Traditional Occupation*
1.	Bahun	Priests
2.	Chhetri	Warriors
3.	Thakuri	Aristocrats
4.	Newar	Businessmen
5.	Rai/Iimbu/Yakha/ Mangar	Agriculturists
6.	Thami/Sunuwar/Gurung	Shepherds
7.	Tamang	Horse Traders/Cavalry
8.	Bhujel	Beaten rice makers
9.	Jogi	Ascetics
10.	Yolmu	Paper Makers
11.	Sherpa	Porters
12.	Lepcha	Shifting (Jhum) cultivators in Eastern Nepal/Sikkim
13.	Bhutia	Landlords (Kajis) in Eastern Nepal, Darjeeling-Sikkim Himalayas.
14.	Kami	Ironsmiths
15.	Damai	Tailors/Musicians
16.	Sarki	Cobblers.

Source: Sharma: 2005.

The Nepali castes like Bahun, Chhetri and Thakuri belonged to Tagadhari group. The Tagadharis meant those castes who used to wear sacred threads and they were to be purely vegitarians by food habit. The caste like Mangar and Gurung were partially Hindus and again partially Budhists because they were used to practice Budhist rituals along with Hindu cultural (Matwali) ceremonies. The Mangar , Gurung along with Rai, Limbu, Yakha, Newar, Sunuwar, Tamang, Bhujel, Yolmu, Sherpa, Lepcha, Bhutia etc. were broadly considered as Matwalis who were suppose to use wine and meat compulsorily as ritual items. The castes like Kami, Damai, Sarki, Cheme, pore etc. were cpnsidered as untouchables in the traditional Nepali society. But those untouchable castes remained vibrant in Nepal till 1926 only after which the concept of untouchability underwent considerable changes. However, the Tagadhari group has been categorised in the present study into two sub-groups, viz, Jharra (pure) and Thimaha (Non-pure). The Jharra Tagadharis have to wear sacred threads of nine strings while the Thimaha Tagadharis have to wear sacred threads of six strings only. The Thimaha Tagadharis are very much akin to the Matwali way of life as they too sacrifice animals' blood while observing their rituals. Again, the Matwali category has been classified into Setho (White) and Kalo (black) groups. The castes like Rai, I imbu, Mangar, Gurung, Sunuwar, Sherpa, Newar, Tamang, Thami etc. are theoretically conceptualised here in the present study as Setho as they appear to belong to Mongoloid race of the Himalayas. The Kami, Damai and Sarki-the untouchables of the past have been categorised as Kalo (Ibid) type. They appear to possess the Aryan like characters as of Bahun, Chhetri and Thakuri castes of the Nepali society.

The traditional caste hierarchy of the Nepali society got complete transformation at the Anula Shagun T.E. of Arunachal Pradesh. This will be evident from the table 4.3 of the study.

Table 4.3

Caste Hierarchy in the Anula Shagun T.E.

Sl.No.	*Caste Status*	*Caste Hierarchy*
1.	Tagadharis (Thimaha)*	Chhetri
2.	Matwalis (Setho)	Mangar, Gurung, Rai, Limbu, Newar, Tamang, Thami
	Matwalis (Kalo)**	Kami
	Others	Assamese/Marwari/Bihari/ Bengali/Khampti/Adivasi

* No Jharra Tagadhari (Bahun) is here in the plantation.

** Damai and Sarki castes of the Nepali society are not there in the plantation.

Source: Field Work: 2003.

It is very distinct from the table No. 19 of the study that there is no Jharra (Pure) Tagadhari (Bahun) caste in the plantation. Thus, only Thimaha Tagadharis are there as the plantation workers. Again, the Matwalis have been operationalised into Setho and Kalo types. The Kalo Matwalis are part and parcel of Matwali group as a whole as ritually they are very much akin to the Setho Matwalis. Below Matwalis, Assamese, Marwari, Bihari, Bengali and Khampti are there who have been conceptually occupied the position in the hierarchy on the ground that socio-economically as well as culturally they are more sophisticated than Adivasi tribes of the region. Culturally, the Adivasis are conceptualised as untouchables by the plantation society because they are butchers and take beef, Interestingly, there is no Damai and Sarki castes of the Nepali society in the plantation. The Sarkis used to kill cattles mainly the cow and bull and make shoes from the fleshes of the cattles in the past in Nepal and Eastern Himalayas. The Damais were tailors and musicians by occupation. Moreover, the untouchables used to take beef along with Rai, Limbu, Gurung, Mangar, Tamang, Thami and Bhujel castes in Nepal (Pradhan:1991) Himalayas. That was the immediate cause for their outmigration to Munglan (India) as beef eating was strongly prohibited by the then Nepalese Government. This may be the reason why only 10.0% of the them belong to the Tagadhari group today (Subba: 2003) in N.E. India. No Nepali caste kills cattles especially cows and bulls at the plantation. But the Adivasis are found to have been slaughtering the cattles and taking beef. This might be the scientific justification to put the Adivasis at the lowest stratum of the plantation system of the Anula Shagun T.E.

However, living in the industrial environment of tea plantation, a new type of social stratification has been emerged at the plantation considering the prevailing situation in Gunanagar and other areas of Arunachal Pradesh. This is clear from the table 4.4 of the study.

It is observed from the table 4.4 of the study that there is an absolute polarization of the plantation society into tribal and non-tribal groups. Such a polarization of the plantation society is the concomitant impact of Arunachal society as a whole which has very clearly classified the state population into tribal and non-tribal groups. However, the table also indicates that the tribal Khamptis have occupied the higher positions in social structure of the plantation. They are at the higher echelons of the society while the non-tribals occupy the lower positions as they are all the immigrants and the Khamptis consider the immigrants as developed or forward ouside communties of the country or abroad. Moreover, occuptionally, they belong to toiling class of the plantation system. In fact, the immigrants are looked down upon by the local Khampti tribes who think that the immigrants being forwad people want to exploit the innocent or backward tribes of the plantation in particular and Arunachal Pradesh in general. Such a polarization of the plantation society has enabled the tea garden management to divide the society into various groups and exploit the workers as far as possible for the sake of so-called industrial development of Chowkhm.

Table 4.4

Social Stratification in the Anula Shagun T.E.

Sl.No.	*Social Status*	*Caste/Tribe*
1.	Tribals (Sons of the Soil)	Khamptis (Backward)
2.	Non-Tribals (Immigrants)	Nepalis/Assamese/Marwaris/ Biharis/Bengalis/Adivasis etc. (Developed).

Source: Field Work: 2003.

Family

Traditionally, the Nepalese peasants and landless agricultural workers had joint families in agrarian Nepal (Sharma: 2003) Himalayas. A family used to be patriarchal in nature consisting of a man, his wife, sons, daughters, married sons, daughter-in-laws, grandsons and granddaughters. In the present study, the term 'family' denotes a group of persons sharing the same hearth and living together in the same house whether related or not. The workers are not allowed to construct private houses in the plantation. The garden has provided labour quarters of 100' by 80' by length and breadth respectively. Considering this, the present study has planned to classify the family into Nuclear and Joint types. The Nuclear family denotes a family composed of parents and unmarried children. The Joint family denotes a family consisting of parents of a couple, unmarried brothers, sisters, father-in-law, mother-in-law, grandsons and granddaughters. The family structure of the Anula Shagun T.E. will be very distinct if we see the table 4.5 of the study.

It is observed from the table 4.5 of the study that 71.3% of family of the workers are of Nuclear type while only 28.7% of them are of Joint type. Unlike in the traditional Nepali society, the structure of family in the plantation is different in the sense that it may not always be patriarchal in nature. The percentage (100.0%) of Nuclear family is highest in case of Newar and Thami castes. But this percentage of Newar and Thami castes does not carry any significant meaning as only one each house of Newar and Thami castes is there in the plantation. The 90.0% of Rai, 80.0% of Kami, 80.0% of Gurung and Iimbu castes have Nuclear family. The percentage of Joint family is highest among the Chhetri (40.0%) and Mangar (40.0%) castes in the plantation. Next to them, Gurung (20.0%) and Limbu (20.0%) castes have

Table 4.5
Family Structure of the Workers

Sl.No.	*Caste*	*Nuclear*	*Percentage*	*Joint*	*Percentage*
1.	Chhetri =30	18	60.0	12	40.0
2.	Mangar =50	30	60.0	20	40.0
3.	Gurung =10	8	80.0	2	20.0
4.	Kami =12	10	83.3	2	16.7
5.	Tamang =6	4	66.7	2	33.3
6.	Rai =30	27	90.0	3	10.0
7.	Iimbu =10	8	80.0	2	20.0
8.	Newar =1	1	100.0	–	–
9.	Thami =1	1	100.0	–	–
	Total =150	107	71.3	43	28.7

Source: Field Work: 2003.

joint familkes. Again, the Kami (16:7%) and Rai (10.0%) castes have joint families in the plantation. The table also indicates that the Nuclearisation process of family (Sharma: 1994) got complete shape in the plantation system. Socially, the separation of newly married couples from their parental homes under the Ansa Banda (division of ancestral property among the sons) system of the traditional Nepali society is a driving force (Sharma: 2003) which has also accepted by the plantation system of the Anula Shagun T.E. The table also portrays the fact that still the joint family system is persisting in significant percentage at the plantation due to widespread agrarian economy of the region under study. It is observed that the agrarian economy requires more and more joint families to have sufficient manpower resources for successful cultivation in the land (Pather).

Changing Roles of the Family Members

The Anula Shagun T.E. is basically a patriarchal society in which the main authority lies with the male members of the families. This is based on the bare fact that they are the recent immigrants who have predominantly male dominated society in Nepal Himalayas (Bannet:1978). Thus, the decision making power of the families lies with the male members only. Of course, a bit differnence is noted among the Tamang, Thami and Gurung castes. Among these three castes, the power and authority are by and large equally shared by the male and female members.It is because of the fact that basically they were Budhists in Nepal Himalayas before their immigration to the Anula Shagun T.E. In Budhist society, the females are given more prominence than the males (Srivastava:1966). The authority structure of family is more or less same among the Rai, Limbu, Chhetri, Mangar, Kami and Newar castes as of their places of origin. However,in regard to the traditional liabilities that parents had to shouldier especially at the time of marriage ceremony of daughters by offering Daijo (a kind of Dowry) in Nepal (Sharma: 2000) Himalayas has been changed as the females are also the earning members of the families at the plantation. Unlike in the past, the elder sisters of the family (Ibid) need not to be respected. With the continuation of traditional kin based joint family (28.7%) system in the plantation, the domestic roles of family members are by and large same as in the past. The males have to do more difficult jobs than the females who normally look after the small kids, cook, food, collect fuel, cattle fodders etc. The field leveling, breaking the mud clouts, ploughing the land etc. are to be exclusively done by the male members only. Transplanting of seedlings or saplings is to be done by females only, clearing the wild shrubs among the paddy bushes and maije trees are jointly done by both the males and females.

Due to industrial environment of the plantation, female mobility is much more regular here than in the traditional Nepal Himalayas specially in relation to attending marriage ceremonies, death rituals, and shopping at Gunanagar, Chowkham, Doom Doma, Tinsukia, Tezu, Medo, Wakro and Dibrugarh towns. However, as Sharma (2003) observed that such liberty is very much restricted among the Tagadhari women. The Matwalis also do not like to see their females are freely mixing with other males specially in regard to sexual matter.

The on going movement for women empowerment duly launched by the various tribal women organisations in Arunachal Pradesh (Chakraborty:1998; Durah:1998), encouraged the women workers to emancipate themselves from the clutches of their mother-in-laws, husband's brothers, female affines and kin bonds of the family as a basic unit to sustain the traditional values of the social system (Bhadra: 1992). The Nepali women workers have earned the capacity to emancipate themselves in the industrial environment from the traditional social myths, prejudice and misconceptions (Bose: 1997). Very recently, the women workers of the plantation have formed a Mahila Samity (Chowkham) having a Khampti woman as its President and a Nepali woman as the secretary. The name of Mahila Samity is known as Gunanagar Mahila Samity (Chowkham). The woman organisation is working for the elimination of alcohol practices and awareness on HIV AIDS among the workers and neighbours in the universe of the study.

Marriage Patterns of the Workers

Marriage as a social institution appears to be very optional in the Nepali society especially while selecting the marital partners. The following table shall clearly depicts the marriage patterns of workers in the plantation.

Table 4.6

Marriage Patterns of the Workers

Sl.No.	*Caste*	*Intra-Caste*	*Percentage*	*Inter-Caste*	*Percentage*
1.	Chhetri = 42	39	92.9	3	7.1
2.	Mangar = 70	40	57.1	30	42.9
3.	Gurung = 12	5	41.7	7	58.3
4.	Kami = 14	8	57.1	6	42.9
5.	Tamang = 8	7	87.5	1	12.5
6.	Rai = 33	18	54.5	15	45.5
7.	Iimbu = 12	4	33.3	8	66.7
8.	Newar = 1	1	100.0	–	–
9.	Thami = 1	1	100.0	–	–
	Total = 193	123	63.7	70	38.3

Source: Field Work: 2003.

If we analyze the table No.22 of the study, it is found that 63.7% of their marriages have taken place within their own castes only while 38.3% of their marriages have taken place among various castes and tribes of the plantation or Chowkham region. Caste-wise, the Newars (100.0%) and Chhetris (92.9%) have married within their own castes. In regard to inter-caste marriage, the Iimbus (66.7%), Gurungs (58.3%), Kamis (42.9%) and Mangars (42.9) have married with other castes and tribes of the region. But as the workers view that marriages among the Matwalis including the local tribes are not considered as inter-caste/tribe marriages due to similar ritual practices of the Matwalis of Nepali society and local tribes. Many Tamangs, Gurungs, Rais, Iimbus and others have married Khampti women in order to make sure of their destiny at the plantation of Arunachal Pradesh for ever. It shows that the traditional concepts of Jat Bibaha (marriage within own caste), Ajat Bibaha (marriage with other lower castes) and Kujat Bibaha (marriage with untouchable castes) have still some continuities at the plantation. But in almost all the cases, marriage choice is becoming very much optional for all castes and tribes. Some castes like Newar, Kami and Chhetri appear to be more and more conscious than others about their marriage alliences as they mostly do the same within their own castes only. At the present situation in the plantation, most of the youngsters are very much anxious to opt for love marriages rather than Mangi (arrangement) Bibahas (marriages) may be due to high financial implication of marriage by arrangement. This is taking place at the plantation as the dominant Khampti tribes of the region also mostly do Chori Bibahas (marriages by elopments) as per their dormitory system of the past (Mishra:1994).

Traditionally, the Tagadhari males had to maintain a gap of four generations from their mother's side and eight generations from father's side before marrying the girls (Sharma: 2000). But since the plantation is consisting of many castes, tribes and communities hailing from various parts of the country and abroad, it is really impossible to draw the genealogy of marrying couples. The concept of endogamy or exogamy of the past is hardly found to have been affecting the marriage alliances of the workers in the plantation today. The Satto Bibaha (marriage by bride exchanges) among the Tagadharis is not found today. The polygamy is also absent in the plantation as the plantation system does not allow two wives for a male plantation workers. Again, the concept of Jat Danda (penalty for breach of endogamy) is not at all found here in the plantation as it used to take place in their places of origin (Sharma: 1997). Unlike in the past, there is no hypergamy among the Bahuns in the state of Arunachal Pradesh as a whole. Marrying the Khampti girls connotes a symbol of high dignity or social status for the Nepalis to confirm their destiny in the plantation and thereby the whole of Arunachal Pradesh specially after 1987. This fact has been nicley supplemented by the observation made by Das (1995). The marriage appers to be a strong bond or thread for restoring national integration in the development process of the state of Arunachal Pradesh. Interestingly, not a single Nepali male has married Adivasi woman in the plantation. The rationale behind marrying the Khampti woman by the males of other communities is to confirm their dsting by acquiring the citizenship certificates in the tribal state of Arunachal Pradesh at least for the children who are born from the wombs of the Khampti women. There is no system of Jat Bara Karnu (to outcaste any Tagadhari into an untouchable caste) as in the past. Such system was called as Jat Patit system in Nepal. However, some Tagadharis were to be brought back to their original caste status by doing a ceremony known as Patiya.

Very recently, the Government of Arunachal Pradesh has officially accredited such marriages if the tribal girls do willingly marry boys of other communities. After having children from the wombs of Khampti or any other tribal woman, if any male of Nepali or other communities wants to leave the Arunachal Pradesh, he can do it at his own liberty except his children who can not be taken away by him because the children who are born from the wombs of Khampti or any other tribal women are legally considered as the tribal children of the tribal state of Arunachal Pradesh. This is due to the fact that among the Khamptis or other tribes, genealogy or lineage is equally drawn from the female side also. This might be the obvious reason why most of the Khampti children speak Nepali language fluently at par with their own Tai Khampti laguage in the Anula Shagun T.E., Chowkham, Gunanagar, Medo, Wakro etc. In fact, as we asked the Khampti marriageable youths about their options for marital partners, it is found that 90.0% of the Khampti tribal boys and grils opt for the Nepalis and only 10.0% of them opt for the Khmapti or other tribes of the state for the same.To the Khamptis, Nepalis hail from the Himalayas no matter whether they are from Nepal, Arunachal Pradesh or any other parts of the Eastern Himalayas or North Eastern hill regions which they consider to be the abode of their Almighty -the Lord Budha (Bhanja: 1984).

The foregone observation shows that the Himalayan society, culture and tradition have a great bearing (Haimendorf: 1966) on the Hindu-tribal relationships in North East India including the state of Arunachal Pradesh.

The Commensal Relations

From the point of view of commensal relation, the traditional Nepali society was divided into two broad divisions, *viz,* Pani-Chal-Ne-Jats (Castes from whom water can be taken) and Pani-Na-Chal-Ne-Jats (castes from whom water can not be taken). This can be clearly understood from the table 4.7 of the study.

Table 4.7

Traditional Commensal Relation in regard to Acceptance of Water

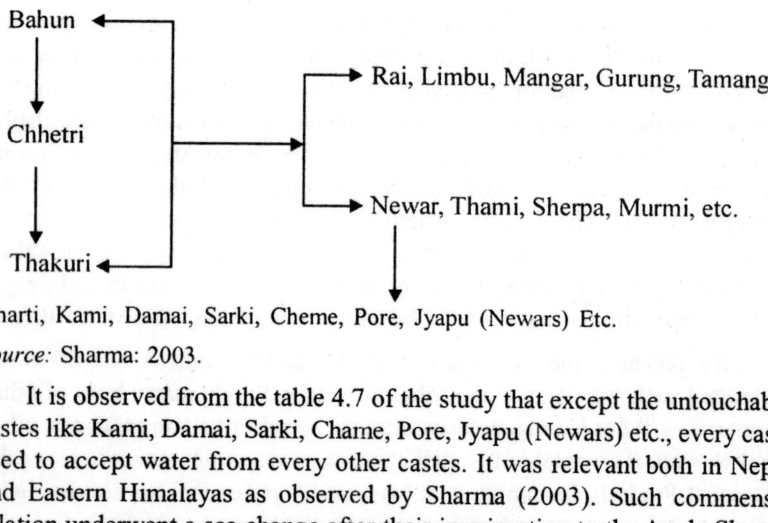

Source: Sharma: 2003.

It is observed from the table 4.7 of the study that except the untouchable castes like Kami, Damai, Sarki, Chame, Pore, Jyapu (Newars) etc., every caste used to accept water from every other castes. It was relevant both in Nepal and Eastern Himalayas as observed by Sharma (2003). Such commensal relation underwent a sea change after their immigration to the Anula Shagun T.E. of Arunachal Pradesh from their places of origin.

It is transparent from the table 4.8 of the study that the commensal relation in regard to the accepatance of water has been drastically altered at the Anula Shagun T.E. Unlike in the past, all castes and tribes take water from each other at the plantation. It is a matter of great pleasure and vanity for the plantation workers if they are being served with water, tea and snacks by the family members of the plantation owner and other Khamptis of the region.

Table 4.8

Commensal Relation of 'Water' in the Anula Shagun T.E.

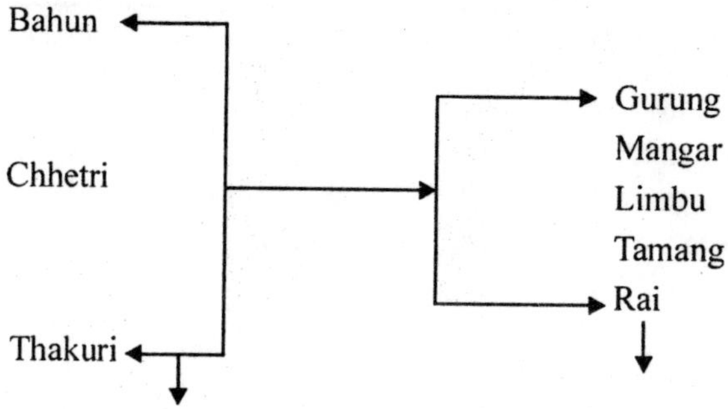

Khampti/Assamese/Bihari/Bengali/Kami/Adivasi.

Source: Field Work: 2003.

In regard to the acceptance of Kuccha food like boiled Dal (pulses) and rice, the Chhetris are found to be much conscious from other castes and tribes while in regard to the Puccka food like tea, snacks etc., all castes and tribes accept the same openly without any hesitation in their day today life. Acceptance of Kuccha as well as Puccka food is open among all the castes and tribes except at the time of observing their respective caste/tribal rituals.

Observing the Khampti Budhist Losar, Sangken and Sapwng Yawng festivals, all the Nepalis, Adivasis, Biharis, Bengalis, Assamese and other were found to have been enjoying with both Kuccha and Puccka foods openly. Similarly, the Nepali Seal Roti (cuisine) was found to be very popular among the Khamptis, Assamese, Biharis, Bengalis and other communities of the plantation as well as Gunanagar, Chowkham, Wakro, Medo and Namsai areas of Arunachal Pradesh.

Religious Practices of the Workers

From the religious point of view, all the tribes aboding the northern and western Arunachal Pradesh are Budhists while the tribes aboding the central territory of Arunachal Pradesh have their traditional tribal religion known as Animism and foot hill (eastern and southern) tribes of Lohit, Tirap and Changlang districts of Arunachal Pradesh have their original Budhist religion being brought down from their places of origin (Bose:1997). Though the religious practices of the plantation workers are related to Hindu, Budhist and Christain religions, the nature of performing the practices is predominantly tribal (Sharma:1997). The table 4.9 of the study shall clearly show the structure of religion of the workers.

Table 4.9

Religious Structure of the Workers

Sl.No.	*Caste*	*Hindu*	*Percentage*	*Budhist*	*Percentage*	*Christain*	*Percent*
1.	Chhetri = 100	29	96.7	–	–	1	3.3
2.	Mangar = 50	46	92.0	–	–	4	8.0
3.	Gurung = 10	–	–	10	100.0	–	–
4.	Kami = 12	8	66.7	–	–	4	33.3
5.	Tamang = 6	–	–	6	100.0	–	–
6.	Rai = 30	27	90.0	–	–	3	10.0
7.	Limbu = 10	8	80.0	–	–	2	20.0
8.	Newar = 1	1	100.0	–	–	–	–
9.	Thami = 1	1	100.0	–	–	–	–
	Total= 150	120	80.0	16	10.7	14	9.3

Source: Field Work: 2003.

The table 4.9 of the study indicates that the Anula Shagun T.E. is predominantly a Hindu industrial society with the Khamti tribal core culture. Interestingly, the table also transpired the fact that Tamangs and Gurungs from the Nepali society are purely Budhists by religion here at the plantation while they are mostly Hindus in the Eastern Himalayas (Sharma: 2000). This may be due to the fact that being Budhists they are very close to the Khampti tea plantation owner. A Tamang Lama (Priest) along with other Budhist Lamas from the Khampti community have been employed at the Gunanagar Budhist Monastry which was built/maintatined by the Khampti tea garden owner. Even some Mangars are on the process of reversion to their original Budhist religion. It is also observed from the table that 10.0% of Rai, 33.3% of Kami and 20.0% of Limbu castes have converted themselves into the Christainity. The conversion trend towards Budhism and christainty is found to be accrescent by leaps and bound in the plantation. This is due to the widespread influence of Budhism and Christainity among the tribals in Arunachal Pradesh. In fact, the population of North East India have mostly the Mongoloid characteristics having the admixture of Indian, Tibetan and Burmese cultural elements (Bose: 1997).

Traditionally, all the Nepali castes including Chhetri and Bahun used to practice tribal cults in Nepal Himalayas by inviting Shahmen (Jhankris) to perform their rituals. Different castes had various types of Jhankris of their own. The Animism, while observing rituals of the past has been transformed today into a mixed cultural blend of tribalism and Hinduism in the plantation.

The Khampti Budhist Sangken, Sapwng Yawng festivals, the Nepali (Hindu) Dasai, Tihar (Deepawali) and Christain Bara Din (X'Mas Day) are most common festivals of the plantation workers. The Saraswati Puja, Durga Puja, Nam Kirtan (prayers to god and goddess) at Namghar (Assamese) are equally given prominence by all the castes and tribes of the plantation.

The Assamese Bihu (thrice in a year like Bhogali, Rangali and Kangali) festival is equally given prominence by all the castes and tribes of the plantation. The observance of such festivals of the Nepalis, Assamese, Khamptis and others has not at all loaded with any religious dogmatism or conservatism. Rather these festivals are to be observed as the common festivals with the participation of all castes, tribes as well as communities. So, what is important is the total participation of all castes and tribes in the festivals that embodies a sense of cultural symbiosis (Ibid) rather than carrying the traditional religious dogmatism of the past as such in the changing industrial environment. The tea industry has also fully recognised these festivals as common festivals of the plantation society. Thus, a cross-cultural environment has been emerged at the plantation today.

Health Practices of the Workers

The health practices of the workers normally have two facets, viz, concept of diseases and measures for treatment (Sharma:1994 Sengupta:1999). The plantation workers having purely agrarian background of the past had ample knowledge of the herbal medicinal plants to cure diseases (Baruh: 2000). This along with the invitation of Jhankris (shahmen) could give them deep confidence (Macdonald: 1976) that the patients would be completely cured. By 'disease', they used to believe the misfortune that could be evaded out through the secret Mantras (prayers) of Shahmen (Barreman: 1972) at their homes (Sharma:2005). Having sufficient forests around, the workers still use the herbal medicinal plants to cure the diseases. But the use of Jhakris is decreasing in the plantation or Chowkham area. So, no more, the Jhankri system gathers much adoration from the society. Except a Kami Jhankri, there is no other Jhankri today at the plantation. The Fa-Foo or Jhar-phuk (secret prayers) of Jhankris and Chinta (Puja) or seance by the Jhankri in black nights by giving or sacrificing the blood of black cocks and home-made wine known as Rakshi to evil spirit as in the past is not at all prevalent today in the plantation. No Jogi (Ascetic) roams around the houses of the workers at black nights to evade out Bhut-Pisach (evil spirits) and bless the households of the workers with sound of horn from the human bone inviting the favourable stars for the members of the households. On the whole, health practices of the workers are their individual concern and management of the plantation industry has nothing to do about the same (Dasgupta: 1997; Bhadra:1997).

The use of Hariya made by the Adivasis and Rakshi, Jnar, etc., of fermented millets and rice made by the Nepalis are very popular among all castes and communities of the plantation. The Tongbas or Chiyang (home made beer) of Bhutia community of the Himalayas is not at all known to the workers. There is no Bhatti (liquor furnace) at the plantation. All the workers' household take drinking water from the tube wells of the labour lines (labour Dhuras) and quite often from the Jhoras (streams) and almost all the plantation workers actually go to Jhoras for their toilets and urinals. They go to Chowkham Government Hospital when their patients become serious due to tuberculosis or other diseases (Government Hospital: Chowkham: 2003). Almost 90.0% of enrolled patients of Chowkham Government Hospital are males who are mainly suffering from tuberculosis. Normally, pulses, rice, vegitables and Chapatis are common food items of the workers. Once in a week or fortnight, they prepare meat or fish at their homes.

5

THE INTER-ETHNIC RELATIONS

In this chapter, we shall try to comprehend as to how a new type of inter-ethnic relationship has evolved at the Anula Shagun T.E.? Discussing the relationship among various ethnic communities of the plantation, a stress is given on the influence of language, marriage and cultural rituals of various communities. By an "ethnic group", we understand as Federick Barth (1969) observed, a population which is largely biologically self-supporting, shares fundamental cultural values, realises in overt unity in cultural forms, makes up a field of communication and interaction, has a membership which identifies itself."

The Anula Shagun T.E. as an agro-based industry of the Arunachal Pradesh, is having poly-ethnic in nature than mono-ethnic one. Interacting with various other ethnic communities, every community tries to retain its distinct cultural identity (Dasgupta: 1997). A kind of poly-cultural symbiosis has emerged at the plantation. Here, we shall see as to how the industrial environment has established a unique form of social system keeping intact the cultural (social) separateness of various ethnic communities. In the process, some of the cultural traits of a community have been perfectly integrated in different forms and still some other traits have been apparently differentiated. The term integration and differentiation have been further explained in the study with reference to the fusion and fission processes of the plantation society. The fusion process is closely associated with socio-cultural relationship alone while fission process takes place due to inter-class relationship as being brought about by the industrialisation of the society (Bhadra:1992).

Before exploring the fusion and fission processes in the following section, let us see how the inter-ethnic relationships had taken place at the Anula Shagun T.E. (Chowkham) in the light of historical background of ethnic communities of the Arunachal Pradesh as a whole. The core- peripheral aspect of the plantation system calls for an interesting Sociological analysis of inter-ethnic relationships.

Table 5.1

Tribe Wise Distribution of Population in Arunachal Pradesh (1961)

Sl.No.	*Name of the Tribal Group*	*Population*	*Place of Origin*	*Cultural Zones (District)**
1.	Adi	1,07,880	Tibet	West Siyang/East Siyang
2.	Aka	2,195	Tibet	East Siyang
3.	Apa Tani	10,949	Tibet	Lower Subansiri
4.	Bagni	24,822	Tibet	East Kameng
5.	Bangro	1,575	Tibet	Lower Subansiri
6.	Dafla (Nishi)	35,111	Tibet	Lower Subansiri
7.	Khoa (Bagun)	659	Maynmar	Dibang Valley
8.	Khampti	2,600	Maynmar	Lohit
9.	Khamba	1,120	Tibet	West Siyang
10.	Memba	2,497	Tibet	West Siyang
11.	Miji (Dhammai)	2,144	Tibet	West Kameng
12.	Mikir	564	Tibet	East Kameng
13.	Hill Miri	5,075	Tibet	Lohit
14.	Mishmi	20,317	Tibet	Dibang Valley
15.	Monpa	21,982	Tibet	Tawang
16.	Sherdukpan	1,154	Tibet	West Siyang
17.	Nocte	19,353	Maynmar	Changlang
18.	Singhpo	983	Myanmar	Changlang
19.	Selung	1,519	Tibet	East Kameng
20.	Tangsa	10,900	Maynmar	Changlang
21.	Wancho	23,393	Maynmar	Tirap
22.	Yobin	781	Maynmar	Changlang
	Total	2,97,573	–	–

Source: Das: 1995 *Field Work:2003.

Historically, the Arunachal Pradesh as a whole, was the dens of various trading ethnic communities hailing from Assam, Maynmar (Burma), Tibet and even Bengladesh. In fact, it is already mentioned in the study that almost all the tribes of Arunachal Pradesh were immigrants from Maynmar, Tibet,

Bhutan and Bengladesh. According to 1961 Census, there were as many as 82 tribes and sub-tribes in Arunachal Pradesh. This is evident from the table 5.1 of the study.

It is very transparent from the table 5.1 of the study that tribes of Arunanchal Pradesh had either Tibet or Maynmar (Burma) background. They immigrated to Arunachal Pradesh for their livelihood from their respective places of origin. Take for instance of the Khampti tribes of Lohit district of the state. The Khamptis immigrated to Sadiya (Assam) from Maynmar and then to Chowkham of Lohit district of Arunachal Pradesh in 1785 (Mishra: 1994). It is explored from our field survey that the Khamptis tried to occupy Bordumsa of Changlang district but they were forcefully pushed to Chowkham by Singhpo tribe of the area. Today, there are at least sixty respective ecological Zones of 82 tribes and sub-tribes (Das: 1995) in Arunachal Pradesh. From the beginning, the Khamptis had been engaged themselves in business on the Khampti tribal arts and crafts along with agriculture (Bose:1997) at Chowkham. Altogether, there are 10,091,117 (Sharma: 2005) tribal population today in Arunachal Pradesh of which about ten thousand Khampti population are found in Namsai sub-division of Lohit district. It is found that from the beginning, the Khamptis had been engaged in Jhum (shifting) cultivation also in their own way.Thus, besides agriculture and business, they had also barter system on selected items that were to be procured from outside the Arunachal Pradesh. To sustain the agriculture, animal husbadry had also undertaken by the Khamptis. But they are now found almost unsuccessful in agriculture and animal husbandry. As the Chowkham is located near the Tinsukia town of Upper Assam, the Assamese society had its influence on the Khampti tribes ever since the days of Ahom kings and British administration. Due to the earthquake in Dibang Valley in 1950 (Das: 1995) and Chinese invasion to the soil the country in 1962, most of the then industries of the eastern districts of Arunachal Pradesh were to be shifted to the foothills of Lohit district after 1962. That gave rise to the influxion of Marwari entrepreneurs from Margherita, Tinsukia, Naharkatiya, Sadiya and Dibrugarh of Assam to Chowkham to open up the wood based industries. Thus, the then mono-ethnic Khampti tribal habitation of Gunanagar (Chowkham) started transforming into the poly-ethnic industrial environment (Bose: 1997). That continued till 1987. Henceforth, the earlier mono-ethnic boundary of Gunanagar (Chowham) started closing down due to the selective ban for deforestation by the Government of Arunachal Pradesh. That casued the Marwaris in good number to left Chowkham for elsewhere the country.

With the introduction of integrated industrial policy in the Arunachal Pradesh as a full fledged state, local tribal elites started tea industry in the state. In Gunanagar (Chowkham), Mr. Chowkhamoon Gohain converted his Namsoom Saw and Veneer Mills (P) Ltd. into Guna Tea Industries (P) Ltd.

in 1987. To meet the problem of labour shortage, the Nepalis of Nepal Himalayas who were denied to acquire the Inner Line Permits of the Government of India prior to 1987 (Bose: 1997) along with the Adivasis from the Assam plains were imported as tea plantation workers at the Anula Shagun T.E. Thus, the earlier poly-ethnic wood based entrepreneurial environment started slowly transforming into a labour poly-ethnic industrial habitation. The earlier ethnic boundaries (Dasgupta: 1997) had been formed with the people of Assam and Khamptis of the region while the tea plantation environment is much more complex as it is consisting of Nepali, Adivasi, Bihari, Marwari and Bengali Communitities though the plantation is purely surrounded by the Khampti villages-the core cultural niche of the region. This will be more clear if we see the table 5.2 of the study.

Table 5.2

The Poly-Ethnic Fusion Process in the Anula Shagun T.E.

A	*Assamese/Adivasi/Bengali/Bihari/Marwari*
N	Chhetris/Kamis
U	Limbus
L	Rais
A	Mangars
S	Gurungs
H	Newars
A	Thamis
G	Tamangs
U	Khamptis
N	52 National Highway
T.	Satkilu Village
E	*Source:* Field Work:2003.

The table 5.2 of the study has clearly indicated the fact that although the Khampti villages are located at the surroundings of the plantation, they form a group having ten layers of castes and communities. At the tenth layer, there are Assamese, Adivasis, Biharis, Bengalis and Marwaris in so far as the dynamics of inter-ethnic relationships are concerned. Each layer maintatins its respective boundary (identity) by adopting the fusion process of certain cultural traits of other communities. The maintenance of ethnic boundary is in respect of language and culture (Dasgupta: 1997). The Khampti vis a vis Nepalis, Adivasis, Assamese, Bengalis, Biharis and Marwaris speak their respective languages/dialects at homes. Hindi is the common language at the Anula Shagun T.E.

Interestingly, it is also observed from the table 5.2 of the study that the Tamangs of the Nepali community are more closer to the Khampti planter's family. They worship their god along with Khamptis at the Gunanagar Budhist Monastry. The common religious bond may have helped the Tamangs, Thamis and even Gurungs and Mangars to be more closer to the Khampti plantation owner and his family. The Budhist Losar festival has definitely pulled them together in day today socio-cultural life with the dominant Khamptis of the region. But at the micro level, they have maintained their identity in respect of language and other cultural practices. The Nepalis speak Nepali language as their mother tongue at homes and celebrate Dasai(Dashara) and Tihar (Deepawali) festivals which the Khamptis do not do so at their homes. This is the area of fission process. While the fusion process in respect of Dasai and Tihar festivals is that the Khamptis attend the Nepali festivals if they are formally invited at the Nepali households. The same thing is also found in case of Sangken, Spawmg Yawang and Losar festivals of the Khamptis. Next to Tamangs, Thamis and Newars, the Gurungs and Mangars are quite closer to the Khamptis in respect of fusion process as the Mangars and Gurungs have greater tendency to convert themselves into the Budhist religion due to their traditions being borrowed from the Nepal Himalayas. Many Tamangs, Gurungs, Thamis and Mangars have Mit relationship not only among themselves but also with the Khamptis of the region. This Mit relationships may take place between both the sexes or sometimes it is also found to have taken place between the two persons of the same sex (Sharma: 2005). Traditionally, the Mit relationships could take place between or among high and low castes in the Nepali society. Thus, the meaning of Mit connotes a friend. Binding in Mit relationship has been abslutely comprehended with making 'blood' relationship or blood-brotherhood or blood sisterhood. Such relationship can be contacted between men and women of different castes, tribes and communities. The relationship is contacted after observing a ritual cermony by exchanging rings or money or any other things which are to be kept carefully throughout their life, as Mits. The brotherhood or sisterhood extends to every aspect of their life. In any ritual, ceremony or festival, a Mit must be invited in his or her fellow Mit's household. To retain the Mit relationship intact, the sons and daughters of two Mits are to be compulsorly refrained from marrying each other. At the death of a Mit's family members, another Mit has to strictly observe the death ritual as prescribed by his or her respective socio-cultural tradition. The majority of Gurungs, Mangars, Tamangs and Thamis have not only interwoven in Mit relationships among themselves but also with the Khamptis of the region.

If a Mit realationship is violated in regard to marriage or sexual matter then the follwing customary punishment is adjudged to the accused members of Mits' families. First, a kind of social boycott is done to the accused persons. After paying a specific amount as fine in cash or kind as decided by the Samajs (societies), the accused members of Mits' households have to leave the plantation for ever. Such penalty is not only accorded by the Nepali society but also accredited by the plantation management. The Chhetris, Kamis along with Adivasis are at the farthest end of the boundary maintenance system in the poly-ethnic social as well as cultural environment of the plantation.

The table 5.3 of the study shows that the Marwaris are at the close contact in so far as the poly-ethnic class relationship with the Khamptis of the plantation is concerned. They are the suppliers of necessary goods and articles to the Khampti planter. Next to Marwaris, the Biharis are at the desired proximity of the Khamptis. Finally, Biharis, Assamese, Nepalis and Adivasis are there in the poly-ethnic class relationship system of fission process of the plantation industry with the Khamptis.

Let us come to the question of integration as well as differentiation (Bhadra: 1992) processes that are simultaneously emerging at the plantation.

Table 5.3
Poly-Ethnic Fission Process in the Anula Shagun T.E.

A	
N	
U	
L	Adivasis
A	Nepalis
S	Assamese
H	Bengalis
A	Biharis
G	Marwaris
U	Khamptis
N	52 National Highway
T.	Satkilu Village
E.	**Source:** Field Work: 2003.

Source: Field Work : 2003.

Table 5.4
Integration and Differentiation Processes in the Anula Shagun T.E.

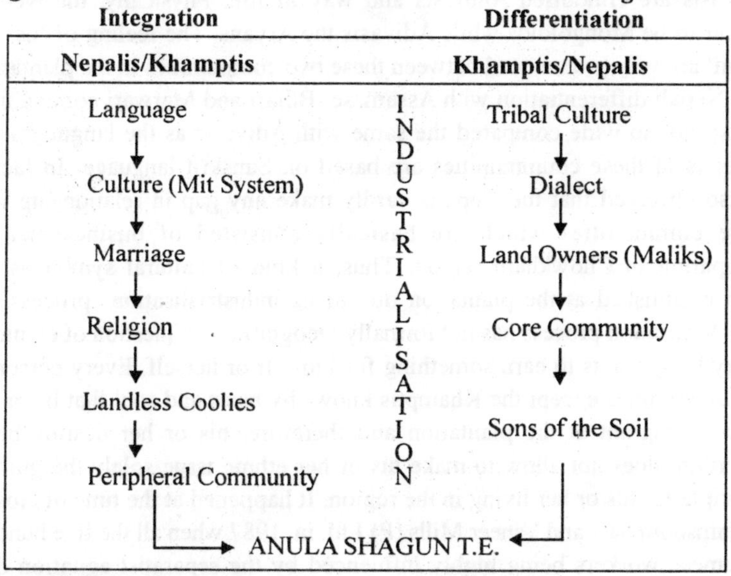

Source: Field Work : 2003.

It is very transparent from the table 5.4 of the study that the extent of integration is on the higher side than differentiation in the plantation. The Sociological parameters like marriage, religion, language etc., have made the plantation community an industrial entity. The difference between 'us' and 'them' as brought about by the concept of "ethnicity" is not so much effective in the plantation. In the simplest term, it can be safely said that all the people of various communities are the immigrants here to earn their livelihood. Being a minor group, the Nepalis belong to a peripheral community in the sense that the major or core community of the region (Gunanagar, Chowkham) is Khampti by ethnicity. The intermingling process in the plantation in respect of their socio-economic relationships, however, at times, has reflected some differentiations in Chowkham- the land of Khamptis. So, the degree of differentiation between the Khamptis and Adivasis is quite high.

At the social parlence, it can also be analysed from the responses of workers that the marriage alliances, if take place, between the Nepalis and Khamptis that ninety percent of the Nepalis, except the Chhertris, stated that marriage is optional for their children. It is upto the desires of their offspring to choose their marital partners. Therefore, it is absolutely taken for granted by all concerned that marriages take place on the desires of marrying couples only. While the differentiation between the Nepalis and Adivasis is cent percent because of their separate habitation, dialect, religion as most Adivasis are Hinduised Animists and way of life. Physically, the Nepalis appear to be Mongoloids while Adivasis the Aryans. The feeling of 'us' and 'them' are very pronounced between these two communities in the plantation. The Nepali differentiation with Assamese, Bihari and Marwari communities is also not so wide compared the same with Adivasis as the languages and dialetcts of these coummunities are based on Sanskrit language. In fact, it is also observed that the Nepalis hardly make any gap in relationship with these communities which are basically consisted of businessmen by occupation in Chowkham region. Thus, a kind of cultural symbiosis has been established at the plantation due to its industrialisation process.The industrialisation process has not formally recognised the question of ethnicity. Every body wants to earn something for himself or herself. Every person of all communities except the Khamptis knows by heart and soul that he or she is an immigrant at the plantation and therefore, his or her destiny being uncertain, does not allow to make his or her ethnic issue solely the guiding principle for his or her living in the region. It happened at the time of closure of Namsoom Saw and Veneer Mills (P) Ltd. in 1987 when all the five hundred Assamese workers being highly influenced by the separatist agitation duly launched by All Assam Students Union (AASU) on ethnic issues, had to left Gunanagar under the directives of Government of Arunachal Pradesh for elsewhere in search of their bread and butter. While the Nepalis who were then working in Gunanagar did not have to face the problem of eviction as of the Assamese workers. The foregone description has therefore amply highlighted the fact that "ethnicity" is just at the cultural parlance only as every community normally has the feeling for respective ethnic identity. For instance, a Nepali always introduces himself as a Nepali if any one asks him about the ethnic group that he belongs to. The same thing is also found with other communities of the plantation. Here, we can say that the basic differentiation is noted at the identity level only. This is because of the bare fact that even if a Nepali wants to transform his ethnic identity at the plantation into a Khampti, no Khampti accepts it overtly though it may so happened covertly due to the reason that the Nepali guy have married a Khampti woman.

However, it is also observed that there is a difference between "we" and "they". By "they" , they mean the people other than the plantation dwellers and by "we", they mean the fellow plantation dwellers. Thus, the theoretical dimension as drawn by Federick Barth (1969) has a wide application here in case of the study under reference as "a group of population" for self supporting industrial environment of capitalist economy (Das: 1995). But this situation is the concomitant result of the cohesion brought about by the plural society of Master-Servant relationship (Bhowmik:1981) of the region which has categorised the Nepali as a minority group. The inter-community boundary maintenance among the Nepalis, Khamptis, Bengalis, Biharis, Assamese and Marwaris is very narrow at Chowkham as well as the Anula Shagun T.E. The segregation paradigm or theoretical Sociological dimension has of course temporal or informal effects among the communities simply on the ground that each and every community has its own feeling for community affiliation. The segregation concept itself connotes a solidarity but it may be in negative form also that lasts long even in the conflicting situation (Weibe and Marriappan:1979) also. Such a negative solidarity appears to have been emerged today at the plantation. Though every community tries to survive unilaterally, their neighbourhood makes their survital bilateral in nature.

The Borrowing: Thread of Integration

At times, on emergency, every household has to depend on the immediate neighbourhood due to the isolated location of the plantation. The emergency calls for borrowing and other types of support from the immediate neighbours. Thus, borrowings have created a broader social neighbourhood. For the Anula Shagun T.E. dwellers, Chowkham as a whole is their neighbourhood which is consisting of almost two thousand households. Each and every person knows others personally. So, borrowing takes place with any community. What is important is to overcome the problem arises due to illness, Pujas, rituals etc. Therefore, borrowing does not count upon the community background of the persons from whom one is borrowing money or other things. The moral supports at oad times from the immediate neighbours irrespective of caste or community background have therefore helped to establish a cross cultural symbiosis-Integration-Unity in Diversity at the Anula Shagun T.E. among all the ethnic communities.

The integration development thesis duly introduced and developed through the state industrialisation process of Arunachal Pradesh calls for a cultural symbiosis. It is one of the non–traditional tea growing/producing areas (Niches) of the country that appears to have been the appropriate place for establishing the Anula Shagun T.E. and the plantation is a model plantation for the Government of Arunachal Pradesh where every ethnic community is simply considered as part and parcel of working class. It can be supported the the statement of Mr. Chowkhamoon Gohain who once said that he is, in the eyes of Government of Arunachal Pradesh , an industrialist and then a Khampti by ethnicity. He also told us while we were conducting field survey in the plantation during 2002 to 2003. Further, he sated that he can develop tea industry by restoring the ecology of the region at par with the government scheme for establishing environmental balance of the state. Thus, today the ethnic issue in social relationship is very vague in the Anula Shagun T.E.

6

SUMMARY AND CONCLUSION

As the title suggests, this is a Sociological study of tea plantation workers in the state of Arunachal Pradesh of North East India. Till the date, hardly any empirical study has been conducted regarding the agonies of the tea plantation workers of the State. The Arunachal Pradesh along with Meghalaya, Nagaland, Mizoram and Manipur are non-traditional tea growing states (CCPA: 1996) of North East India. Prior to 1981, there was not a single tea plantation in Arunachal Pradesh. By and large, tea industry was started in Arunachal Pradesh only after its formation into a full fledged state in 1987.

The State Sponsored Industrialisation

The establishment of tea industry in the state of Arunachal Pradesh was the concomitant outcome of the state process of industrialisation in full fledged form. Prior to 1981, the Government of Arunachal Pradesh had established the Arunachal Pradesh Forest Development Corporation Ltd. (1977) just to streamline the process of wood cutting and then continue the then forest (wood) based industries of the state. However, in the meantime, the corporation introduced tea industry, in the light of reports duly submitted to the government by various expert committees on tea industry appointed earlier during the seventies of 19 th century for the purpose, at Kanubari and Medo of Tirap and Lohit districts respectively. In 1987, two private tea estates were also established, viz, M/S Namsoom Tea Industries (P) Ltd. and M/S Siyang Tea Industries (P) Ltd. in Lohit and East Siyang districts respectively. The favourable climatic conditions of these districts of the state enabled the private tribal planters to introduce and expand the area under tea cultivation. However, it was also observed that tea industry had to face the problem of labour shortage as the local tribes of the region did not accept the tea garden jobs. So, in order to solve the problem of labour shortage, outside labours were started to import at the plantation jobs by providing the temporary Inner Line Permits to the workers. The Government of Arunachal Pradesh felt it much better to encourage the tribal planters to import labour force from outside rather than to welcome the influxion of big tea companies of the country in Arunachal Pradesh so that the local tribal planters could be flourished with the plantation industry in the light of state sponsored tribal integrated process of industrialisation after 1987.

Accordingly, the Jhum (shifting) sites and government vest lands were selected for the introduction and expansion of tea industry in the eastern most enchanted districts of the state so as to have the Arunachal's eastern frontiers safe. At least the government has set an additional target of 8,224 hectares of land that are to be brought under tea cultivation by the year, 2006 A.D. In the process, the Tea Board of India has been reportedly playing a vital role by providing loans with handsome subsidy scheme to the tribal planters. This may also be one of the apparent reasons why now there are more than twenty tea estates, of course of small size in Arunachal Pradesh. Except two private tea estates of 300 and 500 hectares, all other tea estates are of small size in the state.

The North Eastern Frontiers

As stated above, the North Eastern enchanted frontiers of the country were to be made safe enclaves ever since the British days (Elwin:1958) to the post eighties of 19 th century when it emerged as a full fledged state of Arunachal Pradesh. Griffith (1967), the British historian, had also suggested to introduce tea industry to make the Arunachal's eastern frontiers safe. With the introduction of tea industry in the enchanted frontiers, the eastern most belts of the state became closed enclaves being fully barricaded by the plantation society. The enclave formation in the Maynmar and Chinese borders of the state has helped the government to restore permanent safety of the country (Das: 1995). That gave ample opportunity for the tribal tea planters who were the elites of society (Mishra: 1994) to earn good income. The tea industry provides handsome revenue to the government. Compared to other tea plantations of Assam, Tripura, Nagaland, Mizoram, Manipur and Meghalaya, cost of production (Asopa: 2004) of the Arunachal tea is very low of Rs. 20/- only per kilogram of made tea without providing most of the welfare benefits to the workers as of an industrial society. It is found that the government bureaucrats of Arunachal Pradesh along with the management of plantations belong to the sons of soil of Arunachal state while the workers are immigrants from the Assam plains and Nepal Himalayas. Therefore, the immigration of tea plantation labours and the emergence of local tribal owners of tea estates have been found to be the determining variables for the formation of enclave society in Arunachal frontiers. The workers have been deployed at the plantations with temporary Inner Line Permits the renewal period of which in most cases has been already lapsed. So, if any worker challenges the management for poor emoluments or other facilities as per the provisions of labour legislations of Government of India then he will be ousted from the plantation stating him as good as a slave in the plantation of the state. The escalation of such enclave formation would have been apparently possible provided the local tribes of Arunachal Pradesh would have joined the plantation jobs.

Universe of the Study

For the sake of analytical convenience of the study on socio-economic agonies of tea planatation workers in the state of Arunachal Pradesh, the Anula Shagun T.E. of Lohit district was appropriately selected. On the average, the tea estate has accommodated the highest number of Nepali manual workers than any other tea estate of the state. The Nepalis have been recruited by a Khampti tea planter/owner ever since 1987 when the plantation was established at Gunanagar. Tea being an agro-based industry, the Nepalis were recruited for possessing agrarian expertise (Regmi: 1971) of the past. The pull factor for the Nepalis immigration to the plantation industry is permanent settlement with regular industrial job as well as animal husbandry. The study reveals the fact that the Nepalis are preferred much for the plantation jobs due to their perseverance, loyalty to the masters, semi-tribal culture of their places of origin, friendliness, entrepreneurial characteristics and similar physical appearance (Waddel: 1978) as of the local tribes of Arunachal Pradesh. The plantation is located at the distance of 110 kilometres away from the Tinsukia town of Upper Assam. The greatest calibre or expertise possessed by the Nepali people regarding the culture of land terracing in the stiff Himalayas, has also attracted the tribal people of Arunachal Pradesh, to accommodate them in the agrarian belts of the state in general and plantation industry in particular. The Nepalis appeared to have evolved a kind of cosmopolitan culture (Chaube: 1985) that has helped them to integrate themselves with the core culture of the state in general and universe of the study in particular. About sixty five thousand Nepalis are living today in the state of Arunachal Pradesh (Sharma: 2005) while in 1981, there were only 45,508 Nepalis (Subba: 2003) in the state. The cheerful nature, smiling faces and cooperative attitudes of the Nepalis (Northey and Morris: 1976) have attracted the tribal planters to not only employ the Nepalis in the plantations of the state but also to lease out their agrarian belts on share cropping to the Nepalis.

The Hindu-Budhist Contact Zone

The emergence of toiling Hindu work force with tribal ownership and management of the Anula Shagun T.E. appears to support the industrialisation process of tribal Arunachal Government. The lower caste Hindu of Nepal Himalayas (Bista: 1993) along with Hinduised Adivasis of the Assam plains have made the structure of work force really a complex one in the Anula

Shagun T.E. The original Budhist tribal (Animists) background of the Nepali castes like Tamang, Thami, Gurung, Mangar, Newar etc. (Waddel: 1978) has provided them ample stimulus to revert themelves to their original Budhist religion in the truest sense of the term though prior to their immigration to the plantation industry they were nicely tinctured to Hindu way of life in Nepal Himalayas. The immigration has equipped them with ample opportunities to convert themselves into the Budhist religion stating due pretension (reason) for integration with the local Khamptis who are truly the Budhists since time immemorial by religious affiliation. It is further observed that in fact they were fully obsessed with the forceful Hinduisation process in Nepal mainly by Bahuns and Chhetris (Tagadharis). In that venture, the Tagadharis got complete patronage from the then Nepalese Government (Pradhan:1991). This may be the reason why presently the Bahuns and Chhetris are in minority both in Eastern and North Eastern Himalayas. This has been supported by the recent movement for tribalisation (Matwalisation) of all Nepali castes/communities in Darjeeling-Sikkim hills as Tamangs and Limbus among the Matwalis have already been declared as Scheduled tribes. This has resulted into the formation of Tagadhari Samajs in Darjeeling-Sikkim Himalayas. The name of Tagadhari Samaj is known Hitkari Sangathan.

Caste Continuities in the Anula Shagun T.E.

Inspite of emerging integrated society in the plantation, each and every caste and tribe maintains respective caste/tribal inclusiveness in regard to their rituals. They have not been able to erase out their traditions completely in denvo way (Jayraman: 1975). The caste title is still followed strictly while introducing themselves in day today life. A Khampti always calls himself a Khampti and a Nepali introduces himself as a Nepali. The caste-tribe continuities (Srivastava: 1966) are observed in regard to death and marriage ceremonies because their rituals are fully based on their traditions.

Maintenance of Ethnic Boundaries

Every community of the plantation has retained in clear sense its "ethnicity" in regard to language, rituals and culture. Each community observes its own rituals, maintains culture and speak own language at homes. The concept of "we" and "they" become very pronounced at the time of marriage and death ceremonies of respective communities and castes in the plantation industry (Dasgupta: 1997).

Emergence of Integrated Plantation Society

Inspite of having fully exploited society of the plantation, its overt plurality has accommodated (Sarkar: 1987) the divergent cultural traits of all communities. This is amply portrayed at the time of the observance of plantation level festivals like Losar, Sangken, Sapwng Yawng festivals of the

Khamptis, Dasai, Tihar of the Nepalis, Saraswati Puja, Durga Puja of all Hindus, Bihu festival of Assamese community, Mag Sagranti of the Nepalis, X'Mas (Bara Din) of the Christains etc. when all the workers found to have been actively participating with the cultural foods, jester and high emotions (Kar: 1981). The Mit relationship has further sustained well for the emergence of an integrated society at the plantation. The intercaste/community marriages have further sustained the inter-ethnic relationship. They have uncertain future as immigrants to the plantation that has hardly allows or encourages them to expose their anguishness for "ethnicity" issue, while interacting with various communities, as the only means for their livelihood. The plantation management too hardly bothers about the ethnicity issue as they always aspire for earning more and more money from the plantation and around. Borrowing among the communities is still another strong thread for cultural integration at the plantation.

Stratification Over Hierarchy

Aboding at the industrial society of the plantation having the dominant stratified Khampti social system (Mishra: 1994) , the traditional caste hierarchy of Nepali society has been fastly eroding into the plantation-industrial type. A denovo type of social stratification is emerging in which the Marwaris and Biharis are occupying the higher positions and it has also been fully accepted by the plantation system. The owner being the master of the plantation prefers this new type of social stratification than the traditional caste/tribe hierarchy. In the stratified society, the communities of working class are at the bottom or they are the peripherals of the plantation system.

The Exploitation Syndrome

The organised exploitation of working class is the characteristic feature of the Anula Shagun T.E. where not a single labour legislation of Government of India has yet been implemented. The organised exploitation, by merely providing Rs. 35/- as daily wages and house building materials to the workers, is an established industrial philosophy which is being absolutely tolerated by the government process of tribal industrialisation ever since 1987. It is also observed that such organised exploitation is persisting at the plantation due to the absence of trade union organisations of the workers (Bhadra: 1997). Not a single trade union is there in tea estates of the state. Further, there is no appropriate government mechanism of Arunachal Pradesh for restoring harmonious industrial relations in the tea estates. The Department of Industries of Arunachal government hardly bothers about the socio-economic upliftment of tea plantation workers of the state. Therefore, the trade union movement that is prevalent in tea industry of far and wide corners of the country (Sharma: 1991) has not yet been penetrated into the plantation industry of Arunachal Pradesh.

Low Level of Living of the Workers

By and large, the plantation workers are illiterate working folk. So, their level of living is extremely low compared to tea plantation workers of neighbouring states of Assam and West Bengal. They are hardly exposed to the industrial living outside the plantation because they feel themselves as "Sukumbasis" or the recent settlers while the Khamptis called themselves as "Raithanees" or the early settlers in the plantation or Chowkham area of Lohit district of Arunachal Pradesh. Operationally, they can be equated with unorganised agrarian folk of Arunachal Pradesh. The "Unorganisedness" of the workers is nicely supplemented by the fact that most of them remain busy with agriculture and animal husbandry throughout the year. Moreover, their unorganisedness can be understood from the nature of wage revision which has taken place after ten years that too with the whims of the plantation management. So, their destiny is uncertain. Such uncertain destiny has forced them to be in close touch or contact with their places of origin. Normally, they invest their money in Terai belts (adjoining the Indian borders) of Nepal instead of investing the same in Arunachal Pradesh only.

Labour Commitments to Tea Industry

Inspite of having uncertain future, the workers are fully committed to the plantation industry for not a single charge sheet has been issued so far against the Nepali workers for not doing works properly in the plantation ever since its inception (1987). Right from the plucking of tea leaves to packaging of made tea, no work remains pending or undone. This may be the apparent reason why hardly Mr. Gohain visits the tea factory and field except once or twice in a month in course of his morning walk. The workers are given premediated impression that the plantation is theirs' and to copy the way of doing things from the Assam tea plantation workers by forming trade unions means to disobey their master or god father-the owner of Anula Shagun T.E.

Future of the Anula Shagun T.E.

The organisational goal of Anula Shagun T.E. is to expand its planting area from the existing 219 hectares to 700 hectares by the end of 2006 A.D. with thirty lakhs kilograms of made tea per year: The young tea bushes along with cheap immigrant workers of the plantation can fulfill the future plan of the industry. The absence of management bureaucracy having tribal family ownership and management of the plantation may fulfill the organisational goal of the plantation in near future. This is supported by the fact that new tea plantations have been introduced at Medo, Bordumsa and Tengapani areas by the Khampti owner of the Anula Shagun T.E. However, it is found that some inherent problems are noticed among the family members who are the stakeholders of Guna Tea Industries (P) Ltd. Inspite of this, Mr.·Gohain with the help and encouragements of Nepali workers of the Anula Shagun T.E. and also a few Nepalis of Satkilu village, has started new projects on tea. In these new tea projects, all the responsible posts including the manuals are being given to the Nepali people of Satkilu village, the Anula Shagun T.E. and the Bordumsa T.E. In fact, the Nepalis have won the confidence of the tribal tea planter to not only initiate new projects on tea but also they encouraged him morally to practically invest huge amount of money or captial on the projects in various enclaves of the eastern most enchanted frontiers of Arunachal Pradesh of North East India.

Bibliography

Asopa, V.N. : Competitiveness in Global Tea Trade, Oxford University Press and IBH Publishing Company, New Delhi, 2004.

Assam Review and Tea News, Kolkata, 1999-2000.

Balaraman, N. : Technology Transfer in Livestock Sector: Key Issues in Sikkim in M.P. Lama (Ed.) Sikkim: Society, Polity, Economy and Environment, Indus Publishing Company, New Delhi, 1994.

Barreman, G.D. : Hindus of Himalayas: Ethnography and Change, University of California Press, Berkeley, 1972.

Barth, F. : Ethnic Groups and Boundaries: The Social Organisation of Culture Difference, Allan Unwin, London, 1969.

Baruah, Tultul : Mundas in Tea Plantation: A Study of their Health Behaviour, N.L.Publishers, Dibrugarh, Assam, 2000.

Bannet, Synn : "The Dual Role of High Caste Women in Nepal" in James F. Fisher (Ed.) Himalayan Anthropology, Mounton Publishers, Hague, Paris, 1978.

Bhadra, Mita : Ethnicity and Inequality among the Workers of Tea Industry in R.K. Bhadra et. al (Ed.) Plantation labours of North East India, N.L. Publishers, Dibrugarh, Assam, 1997.

Bhadra, Mita : Women Workers of Tea Plantations in India, Heritage Publishers, New Delhi, 1992.

Bhadra, R.K. : Social Dimension of Health of Tea Plantation Workers in India, N.L. Publishers, Dibrugarh, Assam, 1997.

Bhanja, Kamelesh : Mystic Tibet and the Himalaya, Cultural Publishing House, Delhi, 1984.

Bhowmik, Sharit : Class Formation in the Plantation System, People's Publishing House, New Delhi, 1981.

Bhowmik, Sharit : Tea Plantations in West Bengal in Sarath Davala (Ed.) Employment and Unionisation in Indian Industry, Friederick Ebert Stiftung, New Delhi, 1995.

Bhowmik, Sharit : Tea Plantation Labour in India, Friederick Ebert Stiftung, New Delhi, 1996.

Bhuyan, C. : Ahom Buranji, Gauhati, Spectrum Press, 1947.

Bista, D.B. : Fatalism and Development: Nepal's Struggle for Modernisation, Orient longman, Calcutta, 1993.

Borthakur, I.K. : Shifting cultivation and Economic Change in North Eastern Himalayas, in J.S. Lal and A.D. Moddie (Ed.) The Himalaya: Aspects of Change, Oxford University Press, New Delhi, 1981.

Bose, M.L. : History of Arunachal Pradesh, Concept Publishing House, New Delhi, 1997.

Caplan, D. : Land and Social Change in East Nepal:A Study of Hindu-Tribal Relations, Routelege and Kegan Paul Publications, London, 1970.

Chakraborty, Nandini : Changing profiles in Arunachal Pradesh: Role of Women as an instrument of Social Movement in M.N. Karna (Ed.) Social Movements in North East India, Indus Publishing Company, New Delhi, 1998.

Chakraborty, R.N. : Socio– Economic Development of Plantation Workers in North East India, N.L. Publishers, Dibrugarh, Assam, 1997.

Chaube, S.K. : The Himalayas: Profiles of Modernisation and Adaptation, Sterling Piblishers Ltd., New Delhi, 1985.

Choudhury, S.S. : Challenges of Tea Management in Twenty First Century, N.L. Publishers, Dibrugarh, Assam, 2000.

CCPA : Consultative Committe of Plantation Associations, Tea Industry: A Report, Calcutta, 1996.

Das Gurudas : Tribes of Arunachal Pradesh in Transition, Vikas Publishing House, New Delhi, 1995.

Dasgupta, P.K. : Maintenance of Ethnic Boundaries in the Tea Plantations of Assam and West Bengal in R.K. Bhadra et. al. (Ed.) Plantation Labour of North East India, N.L. Publishers, Dibrugarh, Assam, 1997.

Devi, Uma : Plantation Economy in Third World, Vikas Publishing House, New Delhi, 1989.

Dozey, E.C. : A Concise History of the Darjeeling District since 1835 with a complete Itineary of Tours in Sikkim and the District, Jetsun Publishing House, Calcutta, 1989.

Durah, D.K. : Aspects of Women Movement in Arunachal Pradesh in M.N. Karna (Ed.) Social Movements in North East India, Indus Publishing Company, New Delhi, 1998.

Dutta Chowdhary: S. (Ed.) Arunachal Pradesh; District Gazetteers, Lohit District, Govt. of Arunachal Pradesh, Itanagar, 1978.

Dubey, Rameshwar : Privatisation and Its Implications for Trade Unions in C.S. Venkata Ratnam et. al. (Ed.) Labour and Unions in a Period of Transition, Friederick Ebert Stiftung, New Delhi, 1994.

Dubey, S.M. : Modernisation and Elites in Arunachal Pradesh, Government of Arunachal Pradesh, Itanagar, 1978.

Elwin, V. : A Philosophy of NEFA, Advisor to the Government of Assam, Shillong, 1958.

Gogoi, L. : The Tai Khamptis, Namsoom, NEFA, 1971.

Government of India: Anglo– Burmese Relation, 1771–1826, Gauhati, 1947. .... : Plantation Labour Act, 1951.

Government of Arunachal Pradesh : Land Settlement and Record Act (Act No. 10), Itanagar, 2000.

Government of Arunachal Pradesh : Directorate of Industries, Basic Statistics, Onder, Itanagar, 2003.

Greaves, I.C. : "Plantation in World Economy" in Eric Wolf (Ed.) Plantation System in New World, Washington, Pan American, 1957.

Griffith, P. : The History of Indian Tea Industry, Weidenfel and Nicolson, London, 1967.

Guha, A. : Planter's Raj to Swaraj, ICHR, New Delhi, 1977.

Haimendorf, C Von Furer: Anthropology of Nepal, Vikas Publishing House, New Delhi, 1966.

ILO: International Labour Organisation Basic Problems of Plantation Workers, Geneva, 1950.

Jayraman, R. : Caste Continuities in Ceylon:A Study of Social Structure in Three Tea Plantations, Popular Prakashan, Bombay, 1975.

Jones, W.O. : 'Plantation' in David L. Sills (Ed.) International Encyclopedia of Social Sciences, Vol. 8, Macmillan Press, New York, 1968.

Kar, R.K. : Savaras of Mancotta:A Study on the Effects of Tea Industry of the tribal life, Cosmo Publications, New Delhi, 1981.

Kumar, Dr. : Industrial Sociology, Laxmi Narayan Agrawal, Agra, 2001. Legislative Assembly Report of the Government of Arunachal Pradesh, Itanagar, 1987.

Macdonald, A.W. : Preliminary Report on Some Jhankri of Munglan in John T. Hitchock (Ed.) Spirit Possession in the Nepal Himalayas, Vikas Publishing House, New Delhi, 1976.

Mamkottam, Kuriakose : Globalisation and Emerging Labour– Management Relations in C.S. Venkata Ratnam et. al. (Ed.) Labour and Unions in a Period of Transition, Friederick Ebert Stiftung, New Delhi, 1994.

Mishra, K.K. : Tribal Elites and Social Transformation, Inter–India Publications, New Delhi, 1994.

Mishra, S.N. : Arunachal's Tribal Economic Formation and their Dissolution, in Economic and political Weekly, Vol. VIII, No. 43, Oct., 22, New Delhi, 1983.

Myint HLA : Economics of Developing Countries, Hutchinson University Press, London, 1973.

Nepali, G.S. : The Newars: An Ethno – Sociological Study of a Himalayan Community, United Asia Publocations, Bombay, 1965.

Northey, W.B. et.al. (Ed.) : The Gurkhas: Their Manners, Customs and Country, Cosmo Publications, New Delhi, 1976.

O' Malley, L.S.S. : Bengal District Gazetteers "Darjeeling", Logos Press, New Delhi, 1985.

Parmer, P.K. : The Gurkhas, Deep and Deep Publications, New Delhi, 1990.

Pradhan, Kumar : The Gurkha Conquests, Oxford University Press, Calcutta, 1991.

Rai, Lalit Kumar : Forestry and Conservation Issues in the Sikkim in M.P. Lama (Ed.) Sikkim: Society, Polity and Environment, Indus Publishing Company, New Delhi, 1994.

Ramaswamy, E.A. : 'Introduction' in Sarath Davala (Ed.) Employment and Unionisation in Indian Industry, Friederick Ebert Stifung, New Delhi, 1995.

Ratnam, Venkata, C.S. : Globalization and Labour –Management Relations: Dynamics of Change, Response Book (A Division of Sage Publications), New Delhi, 2001.

Regmi, M.C. : A Study of Nepali Economic History (1768–1846), Manjushree Prakashan, New Delhi, 1971.

Sahu, R. : Arunachal Pradesh: Land and People , A Seminar Paper Presented at the Centre for Himalayan Studies, University of North Bengal, Darjeeling, West Bengal, 1986.

Sampath, J.M. : Union–Management Relations in the Changing Scenario in C.S. Venkata Ratnam et.al (Ed.) Labour and Unions in a Period of Transition, Friederick Ebert Stiftung, New Delhi, 1994.

Sarkar, Jayanta : Society, Culture and Ecological Adaptation among the three tribes of Arunachal Pradesh, Anthropological Survey of India. Calcutta, 1987.

Sarkar, R.L. & Lama, M.P. : Tea Plantation Workers in the Eastern Himalayas, Atmaram and Sons Publications, New Delhi, 1986.

Sen, Jahar : Darjeeling: A Favoured Retreat, Indus publishing Company, New Delhi, 1989.

Sengupta, Sarthak : "Preface" in Sarthak Sengupta (Ed.) Health, Healers and Healing: Studies in Medical Anthropology, N.L. Publishers, Dibrugarh, Assam, 1999.

Seth, N.R. : Labour Relations in New Economic Environment in C.S. Venkata Ratnam et.al. (Ed.) Labour and Unions in a Period of Transition, Friederick Ebert Stiftung, New Delhi, 1994.

Sharma, Khemraj, & Das, T.C. : Quality Environment of Tea plantation Workers; A Study in North East India, in V. Parmeswaran and S.K. Ghosh (Ed.) 4 th Indian Congress of Central Board For Workers Education, held at New Delhi on 15–16 December, 2005, Oxford Publishing Company, Jadavpur University, Kolkata, 2005.

Sharma, Khemraj : Sociology of Indian Tea Industry: A Study of Inter–Ethnic Relationship, Mittal Publications, New Delhi, 2005.

Sharma, Khemraj : Tea plantation Workers in a Himalayan Region, Mittal Publications, New Delhi, 2003.

Sharma, Khemraj : The Himalayan Tea Plantation Workers, N.L. Publishers, Dibrugarh, Assam, 2000.

Sharma, Khemraj : Socio–Economic Life of Cinchona Plantation Workers in India, N.L. Publishers, Diburugarh, Assam, 1997.

Sharma, Khemraj : Tea Industry in India: An Introduction, N.L.Publishers, Dibrugarh, Assam, 1999.

Sharma, Khemraj : Impact of Workers Education among the Plantation Workers, Quarterly Journal of Central Board for Workers Education, M.A. Shaligram (Ed.), Nagpur, 1991.

Sharma, Khemraj : Trade Union Movement in Cinchona Plantation of Hill Darjeeling, in R.K. Bhadra et.al. (Ed.) Plantation Labours of North East India, N.L. Publishers, Dibrugarh, Assam, 1997.

Sharma, Khemraj : Caste and Migration in Cinchona Plantations in Hill Darjeeling in R.K. Bhadra et.al. (Ed.) Plantation Labours of North East India, N.L. Publishers, Dibrugarh, Assam, 1997.

Sharma, Khemraj : Socio–Economic Life of Cinchona Plantation Workers in Hill Darjeeling, Thesis approved by the University of North Bengal, Darjeeling, West Bengal, for Ph.D. degree (1994).

Singh,N.B. & Singh, K. : History of All India Gurhkha League (1944–1949), Nirmal Publishers, Distributors, New Delhi, 1987.

Sinha, Pravin : Union in a Period of Transition in C.S.Venkata Ratnam et. al. (Ed.) Labour and Unions in a Period of Transition, Friederick Ebert Stiftung, New Delhi, 1994.

Srivastava, R.P. : Caste–Tribe Mobility and the case of Kumaon Bhutias in C. Von Furer Haimendorf (Ed.) Caste and Kin in Nepal, India and Ceylon, Asia Publishing House, Bombay, 1966.

Subba, Tanka, B. : Ethnicity, State and Development, Har–Anand Publications, New Delhi, 1990.

Subba, Tanka, B. : The Nepalis in North East India: Political Aspirations and Ethnicity in A.C. Sinha and T.B. Subba (Ed.) The Nepalis in North East India, Indus Publishing Company, New Delhi, 2003.

Waddel, I.I.A. : Among the Himalayas, Ratna Pustak Bhandar, Kathmandu, Nepal, 1978.

Weibe, D.& Marriappan, S. : Indian Malaysians: The View from the Plantation, Manohar Publications, New Delhi, 1979.

Wolf, Eric : Specific Aspects of the Plantation System in the New World in Eric Wolf (Ed.) The Plantation System of the New World, University of Washington Press, 1959.

Xaxa, V. : Economic Dualism and Structure of Class, Cosmo Publications, New Delhi, 1997.

SECTION–II : SIKKIM

7

INTRODUCTION

Introduction

The origin of tea industry in Sikkim is a recent phenomenon in the process of industrial development of Sikkim. For the first time in 1960, an attempt had been made by the Government of Sikkim to introduce a tea industry in Kewzing area of South Sikkim to accommodate Tibetan refugees of third world countries. With this singular objective, the Kewzing tea garden started planting tea. But during the next three or four years, the garden could not reap with good harvests. It is known from the people of present Kewzing that soil content of the garden was not favourable for growing rich tea plants. Secondly, the Tibetan refugees could not work successfully at Kewzing as their dress known as *Bhakus, Pangden* with *Hongu* spoiled the small tea plants while working around the small tea plants planted in the initial stages of the plantation. In fact, Kewzing had only 20 acres of land under cultivation on experimental basis.

Thirdly, historically speaking, the Tibetan refugees did not know the terraced cultivation in the Himalayan ecology. Moreover, they were not agriculturists by tradition. This may be the strongest reason why some of the Tibetans shifted their profession from the garden or industrial job to trade and commerce as trade and commerce were their traditional occupation. Still some other among them of Kewzing joined the Indo-Tibetan force of Indian army. Fourthly, the Tibetan refugees, being not agriculturists, failed to adapt to the plantation agricultural environment at Kewzing.

Finally, the garden job requires lot of perseverance of manual type while trade and commerce do not require such perseverance of manual type. Historically, the Tibetan Bhutias were not accustomed to such physical perseverance of manual type. This might be the apparent reason for them to leave the garden job. So, due to the above mentioned reasons, ultimately in 1966, the Kewzing garden had to abandon for ever. Interestingly, following Kewzing instance, a few people of Rolap Busty started planting tea in their respective private land to make handmade tea. This practice of making handmade tea is still found among the villagers of Rolap and the handmade tea is sold at Rangli Bazar of East Sikkim.

The Origin of Tea Industry in Temi

After the abandonment of Kewzing tea garden, the Government of Sikkim started surveying various areas of South Sikkim for employing the financial aids received from the World Bank under the Refugee Rehabilitation Programme of United Nation Organisation in the form of organised employment in tea industry. So, by 27th November, 1968, the then Temi forest area was cleared up and established the present Temi Tea Estate. A section of Temi area was under the rural belt where once upon a time, the Sikkimese Bhutias used to cultivate potato. So, the literary meaning of Temi is Potato *Bagan* (estate) in the Bhutia language. This may be the reason why Temi potato is very famous in Sikkim. After the gestation period of four years, it was found to be ecologically suitable niche for growing tea plants with 20 acres of land under an experimental basis.

Unlike Kewzing tea garden, Temi had different objectives. Firstly, the garden tried to employ the Nepali inhabitants of Temi and surrounding villages. Secondly, the Sherpas who were equivalent to tribe from Nepal and Bhutan were to be employed at that time. During the next ten years, the garden was expanded with 172 hectares or 500 acres of land under tea cultivation. The Temi garden is located at the distance of 22 km. from the Namchi which is the district headquarters of South Sikkim. Presently (2000-2001), it produced 1,12,000 kg. of Orthodox variety of tea having its own brand known as Kanchendzonga and Solja. It has 400 workers. Each worker has the productive capacity of making 231 kg. made tea per year.

There are two divisions of Temi Tea Estate, viz., Upper and Lower divisions. The garden has been encircled by villages and forests in all its boundaries. On the East of it, there is Temi Village/Temi bazar, Damthang village on the west, Ben village in the north and Rambing village in the south. In the east of the garden, there is a forest called Temi-Tarkhu Forest Range which is also locally known as *Gaucharan,* A Tourist bungalow or Tourist Rest House is there in the *Gaucharan* (grazing land).

Since its inception, Temi Tea Estate is a Government enterprise of the Sikkim State. The garden was directly under the control and management of Forest Department of Government of Sikkim till 1974. After 1974, the tea estate is under the Ministry of Industries, Government of Sikkim with a Tea Board known as Tea Board of Sikkim having the representatives from the Department of Industries, Finance, Forest and Agriculture. The Tea Board has a Chairman and members of the tea board hail from the above departments of Government of Sikkim. The Temi Tea Estate is again located at the distance of 35 km. away from the Singtam town which is one of the important trading towns of East Sikkim. The elevation of the garden is from 4800 ft. to 6400 ft. above the sea level and it is a South faced garden.

Labour Recruitment and Migration

Indentured labour, low wages and isolation were the characteristic features of the plantation system in the world (Bhowmik: 1981) in general and Temi in particular. Similar features have been noted in other tea gardens of the Eastern Himalayas (Sharma : 2000). In Temi, the local Bhutia and Lepcha population did not accept the tea garden jobs. In general, the history of labour recruitment in the Eastern Himalayan tea industry is the history of Sardari System. So, is the case with Temi Himalayan plantation. Temi had to follow its own type. Immediately after the opening of the garden, Sardars from different castes and tribes of the neighbouring villages of Temi Tea Estate were appointed. In the initial stage of the plantation, the Sardars had to face lot of troubles in enticing the people around Temi. However, the question of caste and community affiliation of the Sardars having similar caste and tribal background could easily attract their fellow caste and tribal people who in turn were enticed for the garden work (Sharma : 1997). In this way, Sardars used to bring their fellow caste or tribe members as labourers in the plantation. Initially, four Sardars one each from Gurung, Rai, Tamang and Limbu castes were selected by the manager of the tea estate from the neighbouring villages. A Gurung Sardar from Damthang enticed his fellow caste members and made them settled at No. 1 Labour *Dhura* (line) which was latter on named as Gurung *Dhura.* Next to Gurung, a Rai Sardar from Ben village recruited his fellow Rai workers and made them settled in Lamitar *Dhura.* Similarly, a Tamang Sardar from Rambing village recruited his caste fellows and made them settled at Pach *Dhura.* Subsequently, other castes were also recruited as workers by those Sardars and made them settled in other labour lines like 22 *Dhura,* Chaite *Dhura,* 12 *Dhura,* Shyal *Dhura,* Naya *Dhura* and Katwal *Dhura.* Today among the *Dhuras,* only Katwal *Dhura* is consisting of Tagadhari castes (Bahun and Chhetri) as garden workers. Rest of the *Dhuras* are multi-caste or multi-tribal *Dhuras* as these groups are consisting of Matwalis of various Nepali castes. These *Dhuras* are also called Matwali Dhuras. The two groups of Nepali community known as Tagadhari and Matwali have separate socio-cultural history which we will discuss in latter pages of the present book. It is observed that Tagadharis including the Biharis are recent settlers in the garden. Socially, Matwalis claim themselves as *Raithanees* (early settlers) while the *Tagadharis* are called *Sukumbasis* (recent settlers) in the garden. To recruit a caste member as worker in the garden could carry a high dignity in front of management for which a Sardar used to get Rs. 100 at the time of

Puja or Dasai (Dashara) festival as Puja Bonus. So, a kind of competition used to take place for recruiting the workers among the Sardars. Such process of labour recruitment continued in the garden till 1977 after which Mr. Young (Manager) introduced the Badli system of labour recruitment by which a fresh worker is to be recruited in the place of retiring worker of the household. The Sardarship as recruiting institution has been discontinued but Sardars are still found today in Temi Tea Estate as the integral part of supervisory structure of the garden.

After Limbu, a few Chhetris from Tarkhu and Kewzing areas joined the garden as plantation workers. Their migration in Temi Tea Estate had mainly taken place after 1977 when a tea factory was started. After Chhetri, a few mangars from Magarjung area joined the garden job in early 1980's of the last century especially as factory workers. The Bhutia and Sherpa workers were recruited with the help of Bhutia Kajis (landlords) from Tarkhu, Bermoik, Damthang, Kewzing, Ben and Ravangla villages during the early eighties of the 19th century. The other castes or occupational castes of Nepal like Newar (goldsmiths), Kami (Ironsmiths) and Damai (Tailors/Musicians) were recruited in early eighties of last century by the management for technical works of the garden. These castes and tribes are accommodated in various Matwali *Dhuras* of the garden. The pulling factor for their migration to the garden was permanent settlement with regular earnings while pushing factor for migrating to Temi Tea Estate was *Kaji Raj* in agrarian Sikkim and *Kipat Raj* in Nepal (Pradhan : 1991) Himalayas.

The Problem of the Study

This is a Sociological study of tea plantation workers in the Sikkim Himalayas. So far, hardly any study has been done on this aspect of the workers of Temi Tea Estate. The plantation system has dual characteristics—agriculture and industry (Xaxa : 1999). It is known from the above discussion that the Temi garden workers have peasant background of neighbouring villages of Temi and Sikkim state. Once employed in the plantation, they were bracketed into the category of wage labourers (Sharma : 1999). But socially, they are heterogeneous in structure. Historically, the heterogeneous character of Nepali society helps to sustain the isolation of the plantation system as two castes or tribes having two different dialects could not interact together. Another reason for their non-interaction was that a labour line or labour *Dhura* was located at the distance of two to three kilometres. The distance of two to three kilometres in hill terrains is a question of one to two hours journey by foot. The work in the plantation is a continuous process of production relation and it involves certain rules and regulations which are to be obeyed by all. This is a changed situation from that of the past.

The permanent settlement in Temi Tea Estate assures the workers for wages, housing, provident fund etc. So, it is completely a new work situation that gives rise to certain social relationship. Heterogeneity in the economic activity of the past as landless masses to the homogeneous work force by selling their labour in the plantation makes the workers the industrial work force. Most writers, while defining plantation, tend to overlook the socio-economic relations. They have either lucidly explained its production relations or elaborately describe the production unit itself.

The International Labour Organisation notes the term 'plantation' at first as a group of settlers or the political units formed by it, under the British colonialism especially in North America and West Indies (ILO : 1950). Prof. Hla Myint (1973) has distinguished the plantation from peasant agriculture by its large scale enterprise which normally requires more labour per unit of land. Again, William O. Jones (1968) defines a plantation as an economic unit producing agricultural commodities for sale and employing relatively large number of unskilled labourers whose activities are closely supervised.

Therefore, while attempting to conceptualise the plantation, an elucidation of its economic characters alone is not enough. It does not explain the uniqueness of the plantation. The social relations in continuity and change that are taking place in the inter-personal and inter-community level are to be taken into account with thorough caution (Sharma: 1997).

From the above discussion, certain pertinent questions may be drawn as to whether the Tibetan refugees at Kewzing got the same status as 'Sons of the Soil' as given to other communities by 1962 in Sikkim. What happened to the rest of Tibetan refugees after the abandonment of Kewzing Tea Estate? Whether they could not adjust or adapt with the industrial way of life of Temi T.E.? Responding to these questions, the answers received from workers clearly show that only Nepalis are the proponents of terrace cultivation and exponents of industrial development in the Sikkim Himalaya suitable to the Himalayan ecology.

After the introduction of liberalisation, globalisation and privatisation policy for Indian economy, the effect is found equally acute in various government enterprises. It is also seen that ownership of tea gardens with the hands of government has reaped discouraging results all over the country after 1991. Temi Tea Estate is also a Government enterprise. Moreover, due to the Exit Policy of Certified Trade Mark adopted by Darjeeling variety of Orthodox type since August, 2000 it has resulted into the fall of Temi Tea prices from Rs. 800 to Rs. 1000 per kilogram to Rs. 200 to Rs. 100 per kilogram. Option-wise, leaf grade of about 55 per cent attracts the foreign markets and remaining 45 per cent is blended for both internal and external markets at Kolkata Auction Market. But the packet tea of Temi along with other packet tea of the country has been levied with 20% excise duty. Moreover, 2 per cent of the gross profit of Temi garden has to be officially given to unemployed youth forum of the state of Sikkim. Interestingly, it is also observed that though Temi is a Government enterprise, all the cost of production is to be beared by the garden itself. Only the agricultural tax as in other states of the country is not levied to the garden while the sale tax is to be paid to the Government of Sikkim. This is because of the fact that Temi, in the eyes of government, is a unit of government process of industrialisation under the various five year plans instead of production unit of an industrial society. Inspite of the above difficulties, Temi is producing tea of high quality. So, a question may come as to what is the sustaining capacity of Temi Tea Estate in the changed global economic environment. Is it because of low cost of production (Rs. 60 per kilogram of made tea) as the garden does not have the system of paying gratuity to the workers with minimum Bonus (8.33%), non-payment of subsidised rations to the workers, absence of medical facility, fuels, drinking water, other labour welfare facilities, education for the children of workers, electricity facility etc. etc.

Again, is it due to the whole hearted acceptance and cooperation of Nepali castes and tribes of the region with their perseverance, the Temi Tea Garden is sustaining nicely. Their agrarian background helps the workers to accept the tea garden job no matter whether they are Tagadharis or Matwalis. The garden works substantiate agriculture along with animal husbandry because agriculture and animal husbandry go hand in hand in the Nepali society both in the past and today and Temi tea garden economy provides this opportunity (Xaxa : 1997). This is because of fact that Temi Tea Garden has sufficient waste land where cattle fodders are fully available to the agrarian Nepali people.

Another dimension of the study is that there is an interplay of Matwalisation (Tribalisation) and Hinduisation (Srivastava : 1966) process in so far as day-to-day socio-cultural relationship of the workers is concerned. The interactions between Hindu castes and Buddhist tribes, in regard to day-to-day socio-economic activities have shaped to the tune of industrial environment of Temi Tea Estate having specific organisational goals of its own. The ongoing inherent political turmoil between Tagadharis including Newars and Matwalis in Sikkim has definitely affected the Hindu-Tribal relationship at Temi Tea Estate also. The management hierarchy is completely dominated by Matwalis. It has been further noted that the workers don't expect anything especial except the usual wages being fixed up by the Department of Industries, Government of Sikkim which wholly sees the interest of industries first rather than the welfare of workers. This is the reason why the Nepali workers of Temi Tea Estate keep themselves busy with non-plantation agriculture and animal husbandry. This is corroborated by the fact that Temi butter is very popular in Sikkim and hill Darjeeling. It is explored from the observation made on them at Temi that of 400 workers, over 350 workers have animal husbandry along with agriculture.

Although Temi Tea Estate is an agro-based industry, the workers are mostly apathetic to the development process of the industry simply on the ground that Temi is so-called a government garden or government property and workers believe that they have nothing to bother about its future. This occurs in the minds of workers as they have no avenue to ventilate their grievances at their own as they do not have any organisation of their own to do so. In this way, it can be said that they are unorganised workers as of rural belts of Sikkim in the clear sense of the term. To form a trade union means to violate their terms and conditions of services in the garden. Hardly it is found that any worker dares to talk about the formation of workers organisation. This has accelerated by the tempo of state policy of Sikkim that discourages unionisation process in the tea industry in the light of Indian Trade Union Act, 1926. In fact, except the partial implementation of Employees Provident Fund Act and Bonus Act of Government of India, no other labour legislation of Government of India has been adopted in the small-scale industries of Sikkim in general and Temi Tea Estate in particular. It means that whatever the Government of Sikkim provides to them has to be accepted by the workers at Temi. It shows that the workers are still in the colonial system of production relations. Of course, there is no apparent exploitation of the workers to look at in the colonial sense but exploitation of workers exits there in covert form.

In this way, the tea garden workers of Temi of Sikkim Himalaya have been hardly come across by the concept of trade union movement and working class solidarity. They have been bluntly lured by the regional concept of 'Sons of Soil' policy of Government of Sikkim. This may be another reason for their silent exploitation by the management system which is very much organised in the sense that hierarchically there is a manager, an assistant manager, supervisory and clerical staffs who with suggestions of the Ministry of Industries, Government of Sikkim organise the production system of the industry in the modern fashion. Temi being the bastion of regular visit of bureaucrats of Government of Sikkim and outside agencies, manager remains always busy with their visits and he hardly gets time to look after the field and factory operations of the garden.

Operationalisation of the Concept of the Study

As mentioned above, there is hardly any study on Temi Tea Estate, except a few stray reports available at the offices of Tea Board of Sikkim and the Department of Industries, Government of Sikkim. Thus, there is a dearth of published materials on Temi Tea Estate. Mrs. Mamta Desai (1983) has explained in a paragraph regarding the original objectives behind the establishment of the tea garden at Temi. But she has not stated anything about the composition of tea garden workers and their socio-economic conditions. Again, most of the available reports of the Department of Industries, Government of Sikkim and Tea Board of Sikkim have simply reflected the information regarding the tea statistics, target (production), areas, price fluctuation, marketing problems, problems of its extension due to the paucity of land in Temi or due to the existence of villages and reserve forests. Only in 1968, the forest department allowed to clear up the forest of 500 acres for tea plantation due to the pressure of Government of Sikkim to adopt the Rehabilitation programme of International organisation for rehabilitating the Tibetan refugees of third world countries. It is, therefore, transparent from this that the opening of Temi Tea Estate in Sikkim is the noble result of international pressure of United Nations. This is in tune with the birth of tea industry in India during the British Raj. The denial of China to supply tea to the Britishers forced British Government to open tea industry in India. Therefore, Temi Tea Estate emerged not due to the industrial or enterprising attitude of Chowgal (king of Sikkim) but due to the efforts put forwarded by the international agency. Otherwise, the Chowgal was a Bhutia king who had little inclination towards the emergence of an agro-based tea industry in Sikkim because of his cultural affinity to Bhutia community which had has phyobia for agriculture. This might be the apparent reason for having only four Bhutia households today at Temi Tea Estate. The hypothesis has been further testified by the concentration of Bhutia community in urban or semi-urban towns of Eastern District of Sikkim. Even if some Bhutias are found in Southern, Northern and Western districts of Sikkim, they are concentrated mainly in towns like Mangan, Namchi, Gyalshing and Jorethang which provide them with ample opportunity for trade and commerce. Again, even if some Bhutias are found in villages of Sikkim, they are mainly Kajis (Landlords).

In fact, Temi Tea Estate was recognised across the world only after 1981 (much after the merger of Sikkim with Indian Union). Thus, Temi was in experimental phase prior to 1975. Hence, from the evolution point of view, Temi Tea Estate can be classified into three stages of its development since inception (27th November, 1968), viz., Formative (1968-1980), Expansion (1980-1991) and Stagnation phase (1991 onwards). The Formative phase being experimental, there was no clear cut concept of tea industry along with uncertainty of manpower resources. The second phase is characterised by repaid expansion of Tea bushes and manpower supply from the Nepali community of the region with the introduction of a tea factory. The present phase which is a stagnation phase is characterised by the Culture of Uncertainty of industry due to its being outside the Darjeeling Certified Trade Mark or Logo of Orthodox variety in the National and International markets. From price point of view, this is the main reason for the sickness of tea industry in Sikkim (CCPA : 1994) because the other parameters for its sickness like uncertainty of weather, increasing population, apathy of workers of Temi, political interferences, bureaucratic over meanings, fragile Himalayan ecology of Temi etc. have no bearing on the plantation. Above all, the age of tea bushes is very young of hardly three decades of growth along with the higher labour productivity of 231 kilogram of made tea per worker per year. The Labour productivity of Temi Tea Estate is much higher than any other tea gardens of Eastern Himalaya.

The theoretical approach of the study is Social Anthropological one as the Temi Society is neither purely Hindu caste oriented nor purely tribal one in structure. It is in fact a Hindu-Buddhist contact zone of the industrialisation process of Sikkim. It is found that other ecological zones of Sikkim are exclusively meant for specific communities. The three major communities of Sikkim (Sinha : 1975) like Nepali, Lepcha and Bhutia have their specific culture-Ecological zones (Desai : 1988) of respective culture-niches for their habitation. For instance, Lepchas have North zone, Bhutias the East Zone and Nepalese the South and West Zones of Sikkim. The ecological zones of respective community has specific migration history in Sikkim (Caude : 1909). For example, the Nepalis had easy access to Sikkim in early 15th century from South and West Sikkim which happened to be once under the kingdom of Nepal (Coelho : 1970). The Tibetan Bhutia migration to Sikkim taken place mainly from Eastern border attached to Tibet. While the indigenous Lepchas were pushed to Northern Sikkim after the (Risley : 1894) Tibetan Bhutias started converting the Lepchas into Buddhist religion in West and Southern Sikkim in early 16th Century (Percy : 1922). But Temi Tea Estate is found to be the zone of integration or contact between Hinduism and Buddhism as Hindus and Buddhists are simultaneously adapting the same industrial environment.

Some sociological hypothesis have been tested in the present study. The first one is that the industrial environment of tea plantation has transformed the socio-economic life of Nepali castes and tribes of Eastern Himalayas. Secondly, industrialisation process as borrowed from Indian mainland has definitely helped to prosper Hinduisation process in day-to-day socio-economic life of the workers. Thirdly, diffusion and diffision processes are found intermingling in different ways in Temi than as we found in other tea gardens of Eastern Himalayas. Aboding in the same industrial environment, some cultural traits of Hindu, Buddhist and Christian communities are diffused and still some other cultural traits are diffised. Finally the common organisational goal of Temi Tea Estate has shaped the socio-economic life of the workers in a specific direction whether it is apprehensible or comprehensible to the workers in the changed global economic environment.

It is agreed by the Nepali tea plantation workers that the industrialisation process of Government of Sikkim in Temi adds extra impetus to their livelihood, of course optional ones. For them, agriculture minus industry is not a misnomer while industry minus agriculture is completely a myth for their living. This is the inherent reason why inspite of their complete exploitation they have been sticked to the industry. Had there been any other dominant community in Temi like Bhutia or Lepcha than today Temi Tea Estate would be as good as a rural belt as we found surrounding Temi. Thus, the primary objective to open Temi Tea Estate for continuing rehabilitation programme for Tibetan refugees by the Government of Sikkim in the beginning is proved to be a futile exercise today. Rather the second objective of the Government behind the opening of Temi Tea Estate to accommodate the local Nepalis has reaped meaningful justification in the process of industrial development of Sikkim.

In the present study, caste-tribe socio-cultural relationships at Temi Tea Estate have been looked at the close quarters. Besides the general socio-economic aspects of the workers, political economy, health dimension etc. have also been discussed elaborately. The nature of continuity and change in social structure of Nepali and tribal communities is another aspect of the study. Studying the Temi Garden Society, certain social parameters like family, marriage pattern, education level, religious structure, caste-tribe continuum, caste-tribe diffusion and difision processes etc. have also analysed. In regard to the economic life of the workers, occupational structure and mobility, style of life, migration pattern, place of birth, land holdings, animal husbandry etc. have also observed very closely. Again, as there is no trade union organisation in the garden, how the industrial problems are settled ? Who settles the industrial problems ? How the welfare measures of the workers get implemented ? are other aspects of the present study.

Methodology of the Study

In early 2000, a pilot study of the households had been done to acquaint ourselves with the labours, management and other socio-cultural associations. Being Nepali by ethnicity, we were thoroughly accepted by the workers. Another reason for accepting us for the research work by the workers was that. We belong to the Central Board for Workers Education, Ministry of Labour, Government of India as an Education Officer Deputy Director. But in the beginning of our field work, the manager did not supported us stating that he was unable to cooperate officially to is as he was suppose to keep everything of the garden secret under the instructions of the Department of Industries, Government of Sikkim. The pilot study was over by the end of March, 2000.

Data Collection

By June 2000, we started field work with a structured household census and questionnaire. The questionnaire was consisting of sixteen pages with open ended questions for the workers. Besides the questionnaire for workers, separate questionnaires were also prepared for managerial personnel, aged people, portfolio holders of socio-cultural associations, panchayat members, as well as the neighbouring villagers of Temi Tea Estate. Two Kajis of Temi village were also thoroughly interviewed on the historicity of Temi garden, recruitment of workers etc. The field work was over by the end of July, 2001 and after that report writing of the study started along with the literature survey of secondary data available from the libraries of the region and outside. All the 269 households of the workers were covered during the field work period of about one year. All the 400 workers were interviewed thoroughly at homes and work places. The present study does not rely on theoretical sophistication but on the empirical data collected from Temi Tea Estate of Sikkim Himalaya during 2000-2001.

Methods of Data Collection

Considering the problem of the study, the following sample questionnaire had been prepared. The first section deals with household census :

1. Name of the Respondent.
2. Relation with the head of family.
3. Age structure of the family members.
4. Sex structure of the family members.
5. Birth place of the family members.
6. Educational standards of family members.
7. Religious structure of the family.
8. Occupational structure of the family.
9. Landholding pattern of the family.
10. Cattlestock of the family.
11. Modern equipments of the family.
12. Wage structure of the workers.
13. No. of working members of the family.
14. The name of festivals observed in the family.
15. The name of festivals/rituals attended.

These questions were structured one for the household census of the workers. Besides the above questions, the following questions on socio-cultural aspects of the workers of Temi Tea Estate were prepared.

1. Why did you migrated to the plantation?
2. What did you do in your place of origin?
3. Is there any division of roles among your family members? If yes, what are the roles of wife, husband, children and other members of your family?

4. Do you do your duty in the plantation regularly? If yes, how many hours in a day/week?
5. Do you think production/productivity has been increasing or decreasing presently?
6. What are the other job facilities you get from the plantation? (Details)
7. Do you think that your management deposit your Provident Fund regularly?
8. If no, why?
9. What are the main duty you do during 12 months of the year?
10. Do your manager visits your work place?
11. How your management recruit workers in the plantation?
12. Whether you get Bonus? If yes, how much? If no, why?
13. What type of industrial relation is there in your garden between workers and management?
14. Who settles the industrial disputes in the garden?
15. Is there any social organisation in the garden? If yes, what are the names of associations?
16. Who are the executives of these associations? Name them.
17. Which community is most dominant in the plantation?
18. Whether the dominant community is taken in confidence by the management?
19. Whether Panchayat has any role in the plantation? If Yes, why? No and if no, why?
20. What are the functions of socio-cultural associations?
21. What are the relationship among the Nepali castes and tribes?
22. What kind of marriage has taken place in your family?
23. No. of marriage within the caste.
24. No. of marriage with other castes/communities.
25. How would you rank caste/community in your plantation?
26. Whether you invite other communities or castes in marriage, in your house?
27. Do you accept Pucca food from other castes/communities?
28. Do you accept Kuccha food from other castes/ communities?
29. Do your manager or management personnel attend marriage and death rituals in your house if they are called for?
30. Do you sacrifice animals' blood etc., in your household rituals?
31. What are the common festivals in your household?
32. Do you invite other castes in such festivals in your household?

33. What are the major food items you use in celebrating festivals and rituals?
34. Do you offer wine and meat to Brahmin in day today life?
35. If no, why?
36. Do you accept inter-caste/inter-community marriages in your household?
37. If yes, why? If no, why?
38. Who settles the conflicts arising between two families, labour and management and labours and labours?
39. Do you think there is inter-ethnic conflicts in the plantation?
40. Do you celebrate any communal festival? If yes, name? If no, Why?
41. Do you invite Shamen (Jhankri) in celebrating festivals?
42. Do you know the people are converting to other religions?
43. Where do you first go if any of your family member falls sick? Jhankri or Doctor, if to Doctor, Why and if to a Jhankri, Why?
44. Do you have latrine at your home? If yes, Why? If no, Why?
45. What medical facilities are given to you if you fall sick?
46. Is there any creche in the garden?
47. Is there any recreational facility in the garden?
48. Is there any classification of caste/community on the basis of number of years of service in the plantation?
49. Does one community helps others in time of emergency? If yes, how? And if no, Why?
50. Do you think that your plantation will survive for ever?
    If yes, How? And if no, Why?
51. Is there any difference between 'Nak Chhuchees' and 'Nak Thapchees' in the plantation?
52. What do you think about behaviour of your Manager?
54. Do you think that there should be trade union in your garden?
55. Do you believe that 'Sons of the Soil Policy' has helped to raise socio-economic life of workers?
56. Do you think that your garden is really a government enterprise of Sikkim?
57. Who raises the wages of the workers?
58. Are you satisfied with the facilities of the plantation?
59. Which community is most proficient in plantation job?
60. Is there Bhattis in the plantation? If yes, do you go there to drink? If yes, Why? If no, Why?

8

TEMI TEA ESTATE—A PRELUDE TO ITS ECONOMY AND SOCIETY

In the present section, a prelude to the general art of living of workers, political economy of Temi, strings for eco-existence of various castes and tribes, reasons for calling Temi Tea Estate a Hindu-Buddhist contact zone etc. are discussed very precisely.

The tea garden workers of Temi have access to information supplied by the supervisory staff only as they live along with the rank and file workers. The information normally consist of Temi Tea Estate and how management view labours. Being ignorant about the terms and conditions of their services, workers have no idea about the concept and implications of industrial relations in the tea estate. It is observed that due to lack of government mechanisms for restoring industrial relations of harmonious type has helped to keep the workers in darkness and the darkness appears to be their destiny. Such darkness in turn has helped to sustain plantocracy (Devi : 1989) at Temi Tea Estate throughout its development. Interestingly, such plantocracy of its own type has been the democracy in the plantation of its own type as set forth by the management of the garden. To maintain this plantocracy, management always try to discourage workers from going down to Singtam town where they can easily mix up with the people hailing from the wider society. This might be the background why management distributes weekly wages in the morning hours of weekly holiday (Friday) itself so that workers do not have time at their disposal to go down to Singtam town for marketing etc.

In regard to the art of living, the welfare incentives provided by the management like housing, it is observed that workers have to construct their houses on their own. Only the garden land is given. The workers get drinking water from Public Health Engineering of Government of Sikkim which supplies the drinking water for which the bill is to be paid by the workers themselves. As the drinking water from P.H.E. pipes is irregular, the workers have to carry drinking water from *Jhoras* which is locally called *Dharas* coming down from the Temi forest. There is a dispensary but without any doctor or medical practitioner. All the major cases are referred to Gangtok Government hospital and the expenditure incurred on the treatment is to be paid by the workers themselves. A primary school is there in the garden but with insufficient number of teachers and since the school comes under the control of Directorate of Education, Government of Sikkim, the management do not play any role in this respect. This may be the apparent reason why the workers having little bit sound financial condition send their children for higher education to schools and colleges in Gangtok, Darjeeling and Kalimpong towns.

In regard to the general sanitation of the workers of the garden, either workers have constructed their own toilets/urinals or go to *jhoras* for attending toilet and urinals. In regard to the future social security measures, the garden workers do not get gratuity and even the family pension scheme under the Provident Fund Scheme of government of India has not yet been introduced in the garden. It is of the opinion of the management that providing more and more welfare facilities to the workers means to reduce the profit margin of the garden. This may be the reason why during the recent years, trend towards the secondary occupation of the workers is increasing by leaps and bounds and thus non-plantation jobs are much more preferred specially by male workers within and outside the garden. About sixty per cent of workers are females and only forty per cent are males. It shows that main reason why the cost of production per kilogram is only Rs. 60 while Temi is fetching good prices in market (Rs. 100 to Rs. 200). The manager is a government servant and therefore, he bothers least about the socio-economic future of Temi as well as socio-economic development of Temi workers. Since female plantation workers have to encounter with household chores and industrial job simultaneously which has made them double standard in the sense, that they are to be operationally omnipresent in nature. Every morning starts with carrying drinking water from *Dhara* (Jhora-stream) to cooking and then to work at the garden at 7 A.M. The work continues till 11.30 A.M. and at 11.30 A.M. They go for lunch and at 12 Noon they are to resume work till 4 P.M. After 4 P.M., they have to go back home and do household works including cooking till 8 P.M. and then to bed at 9 P.M. This is the regular work schedule of female plantation workers at Temi.

As mentioned above, due to the uncertainty of destiny, the workers always feel of their alienation from the garden (Bhowmik : 1981) on the ground that neither the management nor the Ministry of Industries does really guide them on their life nor the art of living of workers employed in the garden. This has encouraged some of the workers to indulge in anti-social activities like drug addiction, theft, drinking alcohol, double marriages, blue film shows etc. etc. in the garden resulting which the whole lot of incoming generation have been spoiling their lives. To avoid these, some of the workers are sending their children outside the garden. But since the majority of workers are poor, most of the children are going to be the mess of these illegal anti-social activities in the garden.

Operationally, what really happened at Temi is that neither management nor the Government of Sikkim does really feel about the hardship of the workers. The traditional form of Capitalist imperialism has again resumed in the industrial society. The western concept of multi-millionaire liberalisation, as a beautiful hat has to be weared by the eastern poor forcefully, by the government overnight, means just to appease the western industrial world. In this context, an intellectual at Temi said that what is the utility of keeping welfare provisions in the various labour acts and Constitution of India. Whatever the welfare facilities provided to the workers are farse in the sense that the nature of providing these facilities is rather an eye wash to the workers with having merely official justification to government and public at large.

String for Co-existence

On the social parlance, the Hindu-tribal relationship between Nepalis and tribals through marriages across the communities and Nepali language as *lingua franca* (Young husband : 1910) of all castes and tribes are the inherent strings to knit the Hindus and tribals together at Temi. The instances of such knitting are plenty. Here a few instances are being cited to understand the nature of co-existence. If a Nepali boy marries a tribal girl, then both the communities have to accept such cross community marriage. Rather both the communities as per their respective traditions bless the married couples. It is observed that *lingua franca* of Bhutias and Sherpas (Tribals) is Nepali. Though Bhutias and Sherpas have respective languages taught at the schools and colleges in Sikkim, ninety per cent of the tribal students study Nepali as first language. Thus, the artificial classification drawn by the Japanese scholar, Chie Nakane, is wrong as she has stated that there is Nepali, Lepcha and Bhutia in Sikkim having separate way of living. Both in agrarian-industrial as well as urban areas of Sikkim such trinity theory of co-existence as drawn by Chie Nakane is completely wrong as the Sociological factors like marriage, death, other rituals and festivals have so closely interwoven the whole socio-economic fabrics of the society that nobody can really say that without Nepalis, the Lepchas and Bhutias or Sherpas can survive comfortably in the Himalayan ecology. Of course, at the political parlance, there is a covert plurality (Banerjee : 1999) especially among the political leaders and bureaucrats. Otherwise hardly such trinity fever remains in the minds of workers only in election time and once it is over such fever can hardly affects the inter-community relationship at the garden as they all are the sellers of their labour (Bhowmik : 1981). If really the trinity theory could affect the socio-economic life of the workers then by now the whole society would have been banished totally and there would be no more dynamics of Temi society. While the scholars like A.C. Sinha, Mamta Desai and others have vehemently rejected the trinity theory of the Nakane of the Sikkimese society as they have rightly conceptualised the Sikkimese society into Tagadhari and Matwali including Tribal groups.

All the tribals including the Matwalis belong to Mangoloid stocks, while Bahuns and Chhetris belong to Tagadhari or Aryan stock (Sharma: 2000). Tagadhari means those who wear sacred threads and Matwali means those who use wine and meat as compulsory ritual food items. By food habit, Tagadharis are to be vegetarians while Matwalis the non-vegetarians. Rice is very popular stepple food item among the Tagadharis, while millet is very popular food item for Matwalis. The impact of overwhelming tribal way of life in the garden has far reaching consequences in the overall socio-cultural dynamics of all Matwalis and even among the Chhetris from Tagadhari group. The adoption of tribalisation process is however found apprehensive especially among the Bahuns who have been invited for priestly jobs in the households of all castes and tribes. It is because of the fact that priesthood is still considered to be an important social institution among all castes and tribes which has actually debarred Bahuns (those who do priestly jobs) from adopting the tribalisation process in their life in toto.

In relation to participation of Hindus and tribals in socio-economic and cultural activities, both Hindus and tribals participate openly without any hesitation or difference. Among the important cultural rituals, marriages, death and other festivals like Dasai (Dushara), Tihar (Diwali), Makar Sankranti of Hindus and Saga Dawa, Phang Labsol, Lossang, and Lossar of tribals are common areas for their participation. Temi being an isolated enclave, such occasions do really enthusiased the workers to actively involve themselves. The involvement in such occasions help to forget their disparity, animosity and other differences. They participate and enjoy the occasion forgetting their relationship of yesterday's some of which may even be ugly in connotation and meaning. In one way, as workers view, they are the victims of industrialisation process of Sikkim. It is because of the reason that by 'industrial development of Temi', the management feel the 'workers development' while workers sense of development is somewhat different in the sense that they hardly think of the Industries Department of Government of Sikkim. The industry is only trying to stick to the production target being fixed up by the Tea Board of Sikkim in terms of both quality and quantity- workers said.

The garden workers are found on the one hand confused of the present situation and indifference on the other with the regular activities of the garden. A kind of alienation has been noted among the workers especially after August, 2000. But it is also noted that such alienation is the creation of the garden universe itself resulting which the industry in the truest sense of term is 'nobody's headache'. Inspite of continuous downfall of Temi Tea Estate, the Government of Sikkim has been protecting the garden stating it as model tea garden of the Government of Sikkim.

The positive contribution of the tea industry is that it has well adapted the tribals and Nepali castes. The traditional cultural traits of Hindus and Buddhist tribes (Sherpa and Bhutia) have internalised by both the groups. It is interestingly observed that such internalisation of Hindu caste traits with Buddhist way of life in Temi may be due to the impact of Himalayan history and culture in general and Sikkim in particular (Banerjee : 1999). Categorically, to cite an instance in this respect, the Hindu Dasai (Victory day) and Buddhist Losar/Lossang or Christian Bara Din (Xmas day) are common for all the groups as they involve themselves in the observation of these festivals inseparably. The Hindu way of living with Buddhist etho of non-violence and Christian belief on tolerance have helped to sustain the common way of living. Politically, still all the people of Sikkim have some sort of obsessions to be called themselves as Indians (Sujit Chakraborty : North Bengal Plus, *Statesman* : 20th April, 2001).

Culturally, all the people of both Hindus and tribals are skin though some of the cultural practices of each caste and tribe are different on application especially while observing certain specific rituals. Such minor differences are observed even among the Nepali castes also. So, what is important is the participation which is absolutely same among all the three major communities. At home, to certain extent, each community observes respective cultural paraphernalia but once they go out of their doorsteps they behave in holistic manner. No one can really differentiates a Limbu from a Bhutia or Lepcha or Sherpa till he comes closer to the person.

To substantiate the above contention, a few instances are shown here. Mr. Kumar Pradhan has married a Bhutia lady who even cooks Nepali foods in the same efficient way as she prepares Bhutia foods like Thukpa (noodle soup with meat and vegetables) and Momo (steamed dumplings) at her hearth. These two Bhutia food items are not only popular among Bhutias or other tribals but also equally among the Nepalis. The Tibetan Khadas (scarfs) and chewing Churpi (made of fermented milk) are not only popular among Bhutias but also among Nepalis and Lepchas. Similarly, Nepali fermented food like Gundruk, Sinki and Kinema are not only popular among the Nepalis but also among Lepchas and Bhutias. Jnar or Nigar (local made beer) made of fermented millet are popular among all the three major communities of the region.

These days, the inter-community marriages are increasing by leaps and bounds. It is observed that marriageable boys and girls have choice for all communities provided the-would-be couples have sound economic position in the society. This is happening due to the wide spread educational institutions in the state which has made the marriage preferences open. The plausible criteria for marriage is job or other earning sources rather than caste, tribe or community background of the marrying couples.

The Sarau (help in the form of money or kind) system is another string for inter-community participation in death ritual irrespective of caste or tribal background of diseased households. Carrying dead bodies from courtyards to crematorium is open among all the communities.

Because of their tradition, marriage by elopement is most common among the tribals and Matwalis from Nepali community. Only Tagadharis do not prefer to elope girls. Even if formal agreement is arrived at among the Matwalis and tribals on agreement basis, girls are to be eloped a few days earlier to the actual date of marriage ceremony. It is because of the fact that tribals and Matwalis have conventional faith on Gandharva Bibaha (marriage by elopement). The normal course of procedure in regard to marriage ceremony is same among all the communities.

Because of their tradition, marriage by elopement is most common among the tribals and Matwalis from Nepali community. Only Tagadharis do not prefer to elope girls. Even if formal agreement is arrived at among the Matwalis and tribals on agreement basis, girls are to be eloped a few days earlier to the actual date of marriage ceremony.

The tribal way of observing marriages by using wine and meat is common along with the invitation of traditional Shaman (Jhankri) among all the three communities. In fact, tribalisation as a way of life is common feature of Temi Society. Such tribalisation process could be prospered here in the garden because of enclave economy of plantation industry and long association with Bhutia aristocracy and Monarchy in Sikkim along with Lepcha-Bhutia lordship in villages known as Kajidom (Kaji Raj). Under Kaji rule, it is heard from the workers that Hindus had to even forcefully carry compost manure of pigs from the Kaji house to the field. Kajis even tried to convert Nepalis especially Matwalis into Buddhist religion along with Lepchas who were stated by tribals to be the descendents of Rawana and Hindus were in their eyes pure followers of Rama. So, tribals and Matwalis should avoid worshipping Rama. But now due to the industrial way of life at Temi Tea Estate and the participation of workers in the socio-cultural activities have really substantiated the fact that Temi is purely a Hindu-Buddhist contact zone as next door neighbour of a Hindu is a Buddhist or Christian and vice-versa. Had Temi been a rural area having a specific dominant community then today it would not be an industry in real sense of the term.

Tribalisation as way of life is the preference of every community for their overall socio-economic development (Rustomgi: 1971). In this context, let us resume how Nepali Matwali castes are being tribalised. Traditionally, most of the Nepalis belong to Mongoloid stock with animistic/Buddhist religion. This may be the specific reason why most of them have special inclination towards tribal way of life though Matwalis called themselves Nepalis. Most of the outside scholars have failed to understand this reality. The observance of rituals reflects tribalisation process as they sacrifice animals' blood/meat and wine to profitiate their gods and goddesses. In fact, they feel proud to be called themselves as tribes. Aftermath of the merger of Sikkim with Indian Union in 1975, this cultural affinity of Sikkimese Neaplis with Tribals (Lepcha, Bhutia and Sherpa) have discouraged them to come to the mainstream of national life openly. All the castes and tribes call each other with the term 'Daju-Bhai' or 'Didi-Bahini' or with other cultural dignity. Being ruled by totally different races of Indian origin after the merger, all the Sikkimese people in general and Temi workers in particular feel that such cultural dignity have been spoiling. So, they have a kind of obsession towards the Indian Union in Sikkim. This may be the reason why most of the national development projects are not well received by the Sikkimese people. So, is the case of Temi Tea Estate also.

Emerging Problems of Temi Tea Estate

Observing the organisational dynamics of Temi Tea Estate, certain problems have emerged especially after 1991. Among the organisational problems, financial constraint is one. As it is informed by the managerial personnel that no central financial assistance is given to Temi Tea Estate for its development. Only the Department of Industries of Government of Sikkim provides some money for its development. But the amount of money given to it is not sufficient to meet the emerging problems of the industry. The Tea Board of India has no role to play in this respect as Sikkim has her own tea board known as Tea Board of Sikkim. While to the outsiders, Temi Tea Estate has really epitomised the industrial image of the Government of Sikkim in the process of industrial development of the state.

Further, looking at the close quarter, it is observed that the official dialogue between the Tea Board of Sikkim and the Department of industries, Government of Sikkim does not appear to have been any rationale foundation in the direction of industrial development of tea industry at Temi. This can be supported by the question of reorganisation of Temi factory to meet the emerging needs of customers. Here in this respect, Tea Board of Sikkim did not feel it appropriate to initiate the matter to the Government level. This fact became clear when Temi tea was ousted from Darjeeling category of orthodox variety after August, 2000 A.D.

The manpower resource of the garden have specific problems. Being little exposed to outside world, the workers do not know how their legitimate rights are to be realised. How their wages are revised? Who revises the wages? What are the official criteria for their wage revision? etc. are not known to them. Simply they know that the Government of Sikkim revises their wages. Every right to recruit new people in new jobs is left to the manager. So, this right has empowered the manager to appoint people according to his own whims. This is possible for him to do so as there is no trade union. In this way, the one man-show stretches over each and every matter of the garden. Even sometimes, manager does not reply Government correspondences if he feels like. He is the master of the Tea estate. The relationship between workers and management is the relationship of *Sahib-Coolie Raj*. This has become possible due to the lack of operational amalgamation among various departments involved in it. Another reason is that there is no unanimous development package for Temi Tea Estate especially regarding extension of garden area. While the relationship between management and government is cordial till the interests of manager are not encroached upon by the Government. To tame coolies by appeasing government is the only technique of running the tea industry at Temi. Normally, the manager belongs to the same community which the Chief Minister of the Sikkim state belongs to. For instance, Mr. H.P. Bists was the manager in the garden since last two decades till Mr. Nar Bahadur Bhandari was their Chief Minister or influential opposition leader in Sikkim State Assembly. Mr. Bhandari belongs to Bista Caste Group. As soon as Mr. P.K. Chamling became the Chief Minister of the State, Shri Mohan Prasad Chamling who belongs to the same caste group of Chief Minister became the manager of the tea estate. It shows that the sociology of caste system has played a dominant role in the formation of management authority in the tea estate. This has been substantiated by the views of the workers also. Mr. Bista resigned from the garden as soon as Mr. P.K. Chamling became the Chief Minister of the state. This may be the apparent reason why Rai workers talk high about the present manager who is also by caste a Rai. While other castes especially Tagadharis and Newars have poor views on the manager. It proves that the industrial economic development through the introduction of tea industry appears to be a myth because the industrialisation process does not allow the traditional ethos to play any role in the functional sphere of the industry. Thus, the concept of industrialisation as considered to be a means for social development has not yet reached to Temi Tea Estate of Sikkim.

Discussing the problems of participation of workers in the garden affairs, it is found that management feel that workers do not understand the nerves of industrial goals of the organisation. On the other hand, argument launched by the workers is that their participation in the various level of activities of the garden is complete in the sense that no work is pending so far. Again, it is of the opinion of the workers that had they not worked properly, how Temi is sustaining its existence. Right from plucking to packing of tea, it is the workers who do these jobs meticulously. This can be supported by the fact that Temi is having mostly female plantation workers as the major chunk of working population.

Among the workers, another serious problem has been noted during the last five years. The ongoing struggle for overall supremacy between

Tagadharis and Matwalis in the state has clearly distinguished the people at Temi Tea Estate also into two rival groups in day to day industrial life on the garden matters. This has adversely affected the normal functioning of the garden today resulting which the productivity is decreasing day by day.

Thus, the industry has to adopt double standards in putting its actions in tact for achieving the organisational goal along with the interests of the groups. To syncronise the organisational goals with the interests of workers is a gigantic task before the management. The viable alternative appeared to be adopted by the management is to motivate the manpower resources in right direction. Temi Tea Estate is very poor in this respect. Very recently, the Department of Industries has asked the management to launch motivational programmes for the workers of Temi Tea Estate. But it has not guided with details of the motivational programmes. Of course, it has suggested to seek the help of government Organisations, voluntary organisations and other non-governmental organisations in this aspect. Thus, options left to Temi Tea Estate are to follow either of two paths viz to close down the garden for ever or to motivate the people for the organisational development. Doing this, a holistic approach is needed to be adopted by the management. It is, therefore, suggested that the management must leave the existing partisan approach to make the motivational project successful one. In this way, Temi can adopt "Social Impact Motive Model" to sustain the tea industry in future.

9

INDUSTRIAL RELATIONS IN TEMI TEA ESTATE

By 'Industrial Relations', we mean the relationship between labour and management, labour and labour, labour and government and management and government. Since Temi Tea Estate is exclusively an isolated enclave, the labour and government relationship is very thin or unknown. In the present section, we will deal with the dynamics of labour relations in Temi Tea Estate. Discussing the dynamics, various socio-economic, political and issues related to industrial constraints are incorporated. The concept of industrial relation is basically related to human relations. It is human beings who really do everything in the industry. Temi Tea Estate and its industrial relation is of pre-industrial type. The workforce once under the Sikkimese theocracy have been exploited in the colonial form of tea industry. So, this happens in Temi Tea Estate because of the lack of trade union in the garden. To solve the various industrial problems, some efforts have been made to form organisation of the workers.

Employees Association of Temi Tea Estate

Recently, Temi Employees Association has been formed at Temi Tea Estate. It is consisting of supervisory employees and some of the office Babus. The cardinal feature of this association is to look after the interests of the employees. The association is busy with the incorporation of supervisory staffs and office Babus into the category of pensionable staff of the Government of Sikkim. In September, 2001, they met Mr. Pawan Kumar Chamling, the Chief Minister of Sikkim and discussed to incorporate the employees under the pension scheme of the Government of Sikkim. In responding to the demand, the Chief Minister stated that Temi Tea Estate is not purely a government enterprise rather it is a semi-government enterprise having Tea Board of Sikkim to look after the normal works of the garden. It shows that the industrial relation between labour and government is the relation of merely 'Sons of the Soil' and not purely industrial as all the employees, workers and managerial personnel are purely non-pensionable people of the garden.

This may be the reason why colonial form of taming coolies is the method of functioning the garden. There is no trade union for rank and file workers. The workers have been taught by the management that the formation of the trade union is an Indian concept. So, workers have been scared stating that to form a trade union means to invite a sense of revolution in the garden or involve in Zindabad-Murdabad, Gherao, strike, go-slow, violence etc. by the workers in the garden. The workers have been taught to avoid such organisation. No outsider can penetrate the garden. This is the reason why workers do not even dream to form trade union. In fact, they do not know what is really mean by a trade union. Even if some of them tried to form trade union, they were threaten to terminate from their job. Secondly, they were not allowed for the registration of trade union by the Government of Sikkim.

The above contention makes it clear that the industrial relation between workers and management is of 'Master-Servant' type. Only the workers know their Sardars and Baidars. They do not even know the full name of manager and assistant manager. The garden workers are considered to be illiterate folk and hardly any worker dares to talk with the manager even if he or she is called for. They suspect any new person in the garden. They feel that manager may have sent the person to motivate for the management interests. In this way, the workers do not have fair idea about the industry and trade union in the clear sense of the term. So, the trade union movement developed in other tea industries of the country has not yet penetrated in Temi Tea Estate even today (Sharma : 1991). Another reason for not having trade union in the garden is due to the non-implementation of central labour laws in the Sikkim state. This fact is evident from the non-implementation of Family pension scheme which was suppose to start from 16th November, 1995 for the garden workers. Even it is found that the management was so adamant with the introduction of Provident Fund Scheme that they started the scheme from 1998 only.

Therefore, empirically, the industrial relation between the labour and management is the relation of Mutual Compliant type rather than of Mutual Compliance type (Walton : 1991). Under the relation of Mutual compliant type each group feels the other its enemy. Management views the workers as liabilities of the industry rather than assets. Similarly, workers feel management as the blood suckers of the workers. Thus, the exploitation of workers is complete one due to the absence of recognised or registered trade union in the garden.

Further, the organised exploitation of workers from the government side is also evident from the process of wage revision. In 1999 only the wages of the workers was revised after ten years of last wage revision in 1989 with the marginal increase of Rs. 10 only. This happened in Temi as there is no workers organisation to put up the demands at the regular interval of three years as it happened in other tea gardens of West Bengal and Assam.

The elucidation of non-existence of trade union in Temi Tea Estate has made the workers dual in character as they are industrial workers conceptually but in reality they are as good as agricultural 'daily rated' workers employed on 'regular' basis. It shows that they are not industrial workers of twenty-first century. In order to sustain the industry without industrial infrastructure for workers, some works of the garden are given to the local unemployed youth who can create problems pointing the question of the exploitation of workers in the garden. The youths have formed a local samaj consisting of elder persons and youth leaders. The supply of coal, pesticides, medicines etc. are done by the samaj. In other words, the samaj gets contracts for supplying the materials to the management. In this way, the Samaj which is socially an informal body is also in the grips of the garden management.

Samaj at Temi Tea Estate

Informally speaking, every human being wants to live in Samaj or society. So, human beings want to form or organise their organisations which in Nepali society is known as Samaj. At Temi Tea Estate also such Samaj is there. Looking into the prominence of the Samaj, normally management discourage trade union but it consult Samaj about the common issues of the garden and take decision. Even the members of Temi Gram Panchayat are the members of the Samaj. The Samaj is the traditional form of Gram Panchayat. Even if the Gram Panchayat is formally more powerful than Samaj all the disputes of the Garden are solved by the Temi Samaj.

We can generalise from the above contention that Temi tea garden has a form of exploitation of its own type as garden workers are completely unorganised. Thus, the workers are exploited in an organised way while in other tea gardens, the workers are exploited by own organisations partly by trade union leaders, partly by management and partly by the government mechanisms. The passive role of Sikkim Government for Temi Tea Estate is also responsible for such organised exploitation of Tea garden workers at Temi Tea Estate. This exploitation is lingering in the garden due to the absence of appropriate rank and file leaders. It is, therefore, suggested that workers must be trained in trade union education (Bhowmik : 1995) so that the rank and file leaders may emerge from the garden (Sharma : 2000) itself.

Emergence of Nari Kalyan Samaj

A Nari Kalyan Samaj had been emerged at Temi Tea Estate in 1996 to protect the interest of female plantation workers who are more in number than males. One of the objectives of the Nari Kalyan Samaj is to inform the female plantation workers about the changes taking place for female world. In 2001, they organised a Seminar on Need for Women Empowerment for women workers at the garden on the suspicious occasion of National Women Empowerment year. The immediate cause of its birth at the garden was that the present government was indifferent to the industry due to the existence of maximum females as workers. Neither the management nor government of Sikkim bother about the future of Temi workers —the president of Samaj told us during the field work which we had to do very tactfully as garden management did not allow us to mix up with the workers openly.

Other Facets of Industrial Relations

It is observed that due to the indifferent nature of management and government of Sikkim, the productivity of the garden has been detoriating day by day and thus fetching lower prices at the market.

The industrial relation between labour and management is of pre-industrial type due to the absence of collective bargaining process and absence of workers participation in the affairs of the industry. The organisation of work is very vague as there is no fixed category of supervisory sub-staff in the garden. The placement of sub-staff changes every month so that they do not completely know the lacunas of the various sections of the garden. In every month, staff change from factory to field or office and vice-versa. The nature of selection of supervisory staff depends on the availability of appropriate persons at hand to be deployed for the job of the day. Normally, the supervisory staff hail from male group and number of male workers is lesser in the garden. To keep lesser male workers in the garden is the technique of management as males are a bit educated and stubborn who may create problems for management. So, quite frequently, it is observed that the field work is done by workers alone without any sub-staff or supervisory staff except with the occasional visits of the Assistant Manager of the garden.

The protective apron, shoes and umbrella are not given to the workers. These items are to be procured or purchased by the workers themselves. From health point of view, the garden workers are least bothered. This caused the recurrence of tuberculosis among the workers. At hospital of the garden, only one compounder is there. The nature of supplying medicines is very irregular. Thus, the medicinal facility for the workers is beyond imagination. From health dimension, workers are completely alienated from the industrial way of living. They are cut at the neck relating to the whole fabrics of socio-economic and cultural development resulting which a large number of families have been shifting to their original agrarian habitation of villages. The workers are forced to be loyal to their original agrarian fold in augmenting their adaptation process. The delaying process for realising the workers genuine demands has geometrically multiplied the problems of the workers.

Political Alientation : A Myth

Politically, on the whole, it is observed that most of the people of Sikkim are tilted against Indian union. At the micro-level, almost all the Matwalis and tribals are against Tagadharis and Newars who are originally belonged to Aryan stock of Nepal Himalayas having long nose and broad facial appearance. Of course, these days politicians and bureaucrats do not openly criticise the Indian government as Sikkim gets ample budget from the Central Government of India. Moreover, big developmental projects have been working in the state of the Government of India and such projects have accommodated a large number of unemployed youths who are engaged profitably. Interestingly, it is minutely observed that Tagadharis and Newars have hardly 35 per cent population in the state while remaining 65 per cent are population belonging to Matwalis/tribal group who are by heart anti-Indian Union by attitude and motives. The tribals/Matwalis feel that 'Dhotiwallas', the people wearing Dhotis from mainland of India, are uprooting them politically in regard to socio-economic and cultural life of Sikkimese people.

To generalise the above observation, it can be said that they hardly talk against Indian government while extracting the financial benefits from the Indian Government. But they appear to be the veteran critics of Indian government in rest of the time.

According to the people of Sikkim in general and Temi Tea Estate in particular, Indian Government has betrayed the innocent Sikkimese people by administering tactical method of plebiscite having fool making terms and conditions in the ballot papers in 1974 which had stated that 'I, with all my conscience, would like to cast my valuable vote in favour of the merger of Sikkim with the Indian Union'.

It is also heard from the Bhutias and Lepchas that the year of Merger (1975) was the end of their security specially cultural ones and destiny of freedom in Sikkim. So, whenever, any group of people talks in favour of Indian Government, the other groups make public criticisms from the platform of political parties. This appears to be the political history of Sikkim after being merged with the Indian Union in 1975. In this way, they feel that Sikkim is as good as a colony of Indian Government.

But on the other hand, among the young generation, it is observed that the children of present era want to go for higher educational qualifications/ degrees in other states of India as they have been enjoying with the quota being fixed up for the state of Sikkim by the central government. Therefore, the attitude pattern between old and new generations in regard to nationalism is completely different. The children studying or studied in other states of India have with deep sense of nationalism towards the country due to their socialisation with students hailing from far and wide corners of the country. There are four candidates from Temi Tea Estate studying in various medical colleges of the country with the state quota. Again, it is also found that there are six boys from the garden studying in various engineering colleges of the country. Responding to the reason for accepting such facility from the Indian Government, people stated that India has to keep such quota in various national institutes, colleges and universities because the Indian Government has ruled the state by its repressive measures.

On the other hand, this may be the apparent reason why the stand taken by the Indian Government to Sikkim is correct as it claims Sikkim as the integral part of Indian Union on the ground that crores of rupees have been invested annually in the state of Sikkim ever since 1975 by the government of India.

Dynamics of Labour Relations

The dynamics of labour relations can be discussed from socio-cultural perspectives. The inter-ethnic relationship between Matwalis/Tribals and Tagadharis can be observed in terms of participation and involvement. It is observed that former hardly like to visit latter's households in normal times. The former visit latter's households at the time of death observances, marriage ceremonies and other festive occasions if called for.

The Sikkimese Tagadharis try to keep in isolation because they are comparatively more intelligent than Matwalis/tribals. This may be the apparent reason why present Chief Minister had to play caste politics in winning the last election. The local *Nak Thapchee-flat nose* vs. *Nak-Chuchee-long/sharp nose* distinction was only the plausible criteria for last election campaign. Interestingly, *Nak Chuchee* group belong to the minority section by strength in Sikkim. Thus, by the dynamics of inter-ethnic relation here we mean the relationship between *Nak-Chuchees* and *Nak Thapchees'*. The tea garden workers alongwith the general people of Sikkim in regard to making of Chief Minister, having two groups; appear to have totally different stand. Recently, among the *Nak Thapchees* (Matwalis/tribals), Lepchas and Bhutias have also started raising voice for tribal Chief Ministership on rotation basis in Sikkim. Taking this issue, it can be said that there is an inherent confrontation between tribals and caste people in Sikkim. Every time, one group tries to exert tremendous pressure on the other relating to every issue of the government for the overall development of Sikkim.

Threads of Integration

Inspite of having such inherent tension or unhealthy social relationship between *Nak Chuchees* and *Nak Thapchees* groups, *lingua franca* (Nepali) which all the three communities speak, tolerance and non-violence as brought about and introduced by *Nak Chuchees* are inevitable threads for multicultural integration and co-existence in Sikkim in general and Temi Tea Estate in particular.

Caste/Tribe Polarisation

Another interesting development taking place between Matwalis/Tribals and Tagadharis is that almost all Matwalis are incorporated in the category of either Scheduled Castes or Scheduled Tribes or Other Backward Classes groups and the Tagadharis appear to be little bit insecure in availing incentives to their children as they are outside the reserve category. Still another interesting development is that the government is trying to incorporate Gurung and Tamang castes of Nepali community into the category of scheduled tribes. Reacting to this polarisation, some intellectual Tagadharis are of the opinion that doing this the Matwalis and Tribals have to face tough competition among themselves because the dominant population of the Sikkim state belong to the Matwali and tribal groups. This might be the background behind non-implementation of Mandal Commission report by Shri Nar Bahadur Bhandari, Ex-chief Minister of the state. Some Matwalis were then not happy with the step of Mr. Bhandari. This along with the struggle for recognition of Nepali language in the sixth schedule of Indian Constitution made tribals unhappy. Due to these two reasons, the tribals (Lepchas and Bhutias) who were critics to the recognition of Nepali language in Indian constitution, did not support Mr. Bhandari in the last two elections.

The above development clearly transpired the fact that there is an inherent confrontation between reserved group and Tagadharis - Newars. These reserved group either belong to tribals or Matwalis. The cultural affinity between Lepchas/Bhutias/Sherpas (scheduled tribes) and traditional tribal Nepalis (sub-tribes) from Nepali community like Rai, Limbu, Gurung, Tamang, Bhujel, Thami etc. is prospering in Sikkim over the last two decades with the nomenclature of *Nak Thapchee* group. Reacting to the *Nak Thapchee* dominance in the garden, some of the Tagadharis are of the views that even state census operation is manipulating the caste strength in such way that ample effort is going on to show Tagadhari population lesser than the actual number. This has again exerted tremendous sense of insecurity in the minds of Tagadharis as Tagadharis will be extinct more and more by percentage in near future.

In fact, it is presumed that "Nak Thapchhees" have affinity to tribal way of life of trans-Himalayan belt while "Nak Chuchees" have deep affinity to the Indian way of life. Thus, possibly the tribals and Matwalis have not fully comprehended the development strategy set forth by the Indian government in Sikkim as well as at Temi Tea Estate.

All these developments have proved that a kind of social commotion is prevailing in Sikkim which has also affected the day-to-day industrial relation in Temi among the workers and workers and workers and management.

Technology and Manpower Resources

Temi management being bureaucrats, do not feel to accommodate the feelings of the manpower resources while managing the industry at Temi. The level of human development index is very low at Temi. With the onslaught of technological innovation like Computer, Internet etc., the number of office staff have detailed to factory and field works. In this way, they hardly bother about the workers rather management personnel are of the view that if workers feel uncomfortable with the plantation system, they can leave the garden job any time so that the surplus (numbering about 20) manpower from the office can be diverted to the plantation jobs.

Height of Manpower Alienation

The Temi tea plantation workers are agrarian people who are wholly adapted to the agro-based industry on the rough terraces constructed for growing tea plants. Side by side, other agricultural products like millet, Dal, Makai (maize), quash and other vegetables, Cardamom etc. are produced in the garden. This has made the workers to slick and continue with the agrarian economy. This agrarian economy has been substantiated by the animal husbandry in Temi Tea Estate. Because of the continuity of agrarian economy at the garden and outside land of theirs, the garden workers are of the opinion that it would make no difference to them if at any time Temi Tea Estate is closed down. This may be due to fact that they do not have any social security legislation for their old age from the government. Another reason for their alienation is that workers are treated as greatest liability in the eyes of management. The garden workers are not the integral part of developmental strategy of Temi Tea Estate. These are the reasons why the workers are engaged in their own agriculture and animal husbandry every time. Even some of the workers hardly mind if weekly wages are not paid to them in any week on Thursday.

Industrialisation and Workers

The fundamental objective behind the introduction of tea industry in the process of industrialisation in Sikkim was to make the tea industry technologically sophisticated by the turn of the century. In practice, it is observed that industrialisation process has been boiled down to the agrarian development in Temi Tea Estate. Doing this, workers do not mind to accept the resumption of agrarian development. So, there is no aggrandisement on the part of the workers regarding the negligence of management for industrialisation process of the garden. Similarly, there is no reaction from the Ministry of Industries, Government of Sikkim about the reasons for sickness of the industry in Sikkim.

Very surprisingly, the general public of Temi Tea Estate hardly bother to think about the present miserable conditions of Temi and most probably bleak future to come. To the workers, tea industry of Temi does not provide any benefit rather they think that their agricultural land has been confiscated with the help of the government administration by the management. However, while probing into the actual reason for sustaining the industry to the government officials, it is observed that Temi Tea Estate appears to be a beautiful habitat or landscape of Sikkim that may attract tourists all-over the country, considering the increasing importance of tourism in Sikkim Himalaya. It is so beautiful to look at as every side of the garden is under the umbrella of forest and on one side of it is bordered by Temi river.

Tourism Over Tea Industry

A tourist inspection bungalow is under construction at Temi to encourage tourists and tourism industry over tea. This may be true due to the fact that tourism predominates tea in Eastern Himalayas and it is also important in the eyes of government of India and so also to the Sikkim Government because the tourism industry accrues direct foreign exchange from the international tourists. This is stimulating due to the increasing importance of neighbouring Ravangla, a prominent tourist centre in South Sikkim. Moreover, large number of national and international projects on tourism industry have been sanctioned in Sikkim Himalaya during the recent years.

The widespread introduction of tourism industry in Sikkim has enabled the state government to accommodate a large number of unemployed youths in the state. This may be the strong reason to accord prominence to the spread of tourism industry in Temi area. The concept of eco-friendly tourism industry with full of flora and fauna in the Himalaya is the national priority of the day.

Future Prospects of Temi Tea Estate

Temi can provide such infrastructure as it has eco-friendly properties for origin and growth of tourism industry in future. This is one future prospect for Temi Tea Estate. Another prospect is the possibility for the emergence of hotel industry for tourists, trackers and visitors in Temi. This will help to have opened shops of various kinds which again can engage sizeable unemployed population there.

Another feasible alternative to sustain industrialisation process in Temi Tea Estate and manpower relations of harmonious type is to adopt a denovo approach of sustainable regional development of its own type being fully comprehended by all locals rather than making it apprehensive ones. Doing this, the higher altitude barren lands have to be brought under cultivation or utilisation profitably.

The available developmental agencies are to be fully utilised. For instance, there is an Integrated Development project at Temi Tea Estate. The agency has not been fully able to tap the manpower resources of the garden due to the lack of co-operation from the garden management.

Commitment to the Industry

Inspite of organisational negligence, workers have been able to adjust with the industrial way of life of the plantation industry. So, with full commitment, the workers do jobs. It may be due to the fact that basically Nepali castes and tribes have since generations adjusted with the isolated Himalayan way of life. The change of habitation from peasant/agrarian background to the plantation-industrial has nicely adjusted the workers not only economically but also in socio-cultural aspects. A kind of cultural symbiosis has emerged at Temi between the Tribals/Matwalis and Tagadharis. Thus, at present juncture, the tea garden workers are neither purely agricultural nor industrial but they can be considered as psydo-industrial work force of agro-based industry of Sikkim.

Cultural Alternatives for Workers

The above discussion makes it clear that organisationally workers are in search of cultural alternatives. This is evident from the fact that each caste/ tribe has started forming some kind of animistic form of religion involving traditional shamen like Bongthing (Lepcha), Fedengma (Rai), Jhankris (Nepalis), Lama (Tamang) etc. to resume their traditions. Gurungs are in front in so far as their conversion to their original Buddhist religion and other forms of animistic practices is concerned. The formation of Sai Samity (followers of Sai Baba) helps to train people on moral discipline, ban on alcohol, help poor people with trousers etc. Such socio-cultural alternatives innovated by the workers are uninterrupted by the garden management as they have nothing to loose from such alternatives being adopted by the workers. Such organisations have been formed in Temi Tea Estate to forget the industrial druginess and engage themselves in the cultural alternatives. Ten such socio-cultural/religious organisations are working in Temi Tea Estate. Though these organisations try to work in denovo way, the process of working is tribal or Matwali in nature as sacrificing animals, use of meat and wine are the integral parts of the whole cultural alternatives.

10

ECONOMIC LIFE OF THE WORKERS

The present chapter deals with the economic life of the garden workers. Their migration from neighbouring agrarian economy of Sikkim and Nepal to the plantation industry has definitely affected their socio-economic life. Discussing the economic life of the workers, we shall see the organisational set up, composition of work force, various facilities, nature of work, caste and landholding, caste and traditional occupation, caste and cattle stocks and caste and material life at Temi Tea Estate.

The Organisational Set-up

The Temi Tea Estate has been broadly divided into three sections, viz., plantation, factory and office.

Category : 1

Unlike other tea plantations of India, the organisational set up of Temi Tea Estate is very complex. Being a government enterprise, Temi has an elaborate management hierarchy. This is evident from the following Table 10.1.

Table 10.1

Organisational Structure of Temi Tea Estate

Department of Industries
(Ministry of Industries, Government of Sikkim)
↓
Tea Board of Sikkim
(Agriculture, Industry, Finance and Forest
Departments with a Chairman)
↓
Manager
↓
Assistant Manager
↓
Office Staff ⟷ Supervisory Sub-Staff ⟷ Factory Sub-Staff
Workers (Plantation and Factory)

Source : Field work : 2001.

The Department of Industry, Government of Sikkim is the overall controlling body of the organisation. The Minister of Industries is In-charge of Temi Industry. The Minister-In-Charge of Industries appoints the Chairman of Tea Board of Sikkim. The other members of the tea board are appointed by the Ministry from the department of Agriculture, Industries, Finance and Forests. Normally, they are the heads of the concerned departments. It is the policy making body for Temi Tea Estate.

Below the Tea Board of Sikkim, Manager is there at the top hierarchy of the garden. A manager is appointed by the Tea Board of Sikkim and Assistant Manager is appointed by the manager of Temi Tea Estate. Thus, at the garden level, Manager is the functional head. He also appoints office staffs and supervisory sub-staffs for the plantation and factory.

Category II : Supervisory Sub-Staff

The supervisory Sub-staff look after the day today affairs of the garden and processing factory. They are as good as 'regular' daily rated plantation workers as a whole.

Category III : Office Staff

The Office Babus are the monthly rated staffs of the garden. There is a hierarchy among the office staffs. There are two upper divisional clerks and a lower division clerk. Both the upper divisional clerks are Rai by caste and the lower divisional clerk is a Chhetri by caste. Two Limbu peons, one Chaprasi and two Chowkidars of Gurung caste are there in the office.

Evolution of Top Management

At different point of time, the managers were appointed in different ways. In the beginning of Temi Tea Estate, an experienced English manager named Mr. Tipps (1968-1970) was appointed. Mr. Tipps was replaced by Mr. Dickson (1970-1972). Both the managers established the garden in full fledged form. After Dickson, the sons of the soil like Mr. Moktan (1975-1977), Mr. Luksum (1972-1974) and Mr. Khati (1974-1975), were appointed. But those managers of the sons of the soil (Sikkim) could not work successfully. So, in 1977 again an Englishman named Mr. Young was appointed. He worked at the garden with all sincerity and perseverance as manager. After him, Mr. Topden worked at the garden till 1986. In 1986, Mr. H.P. Bista was appointed as manager and he left the garden in 1999. Finally, the present manager, Mr. M.P. Chamling was appointed in 1999 and still continuing in the post of manager today.

Category IV : The Plantation Workers

By 'workers' we understand both plantation and factory 'regular' daily rated workers. Almost all the factory workers are males while the majority of plantation workers are females. The plantation (agriculture) workers are called unskilled workers and factory the skilled workers.

In the beginning, the Temi Tea Estate workers were divided into three categories, viz. *Marad, Aurat* and *Chokra/Chokri* (Children). A Marad (male) had to work for 10 hours a day, and Aurat had to work for 9 hours a day and child had to work for eight hours a day in the plantation. The three tier classification of plantation workers continued in the garden till 1990 at a stretch since its inception. After 1990 child workers were stopped to be employed as employment of child workers means to get less work and higher cost of production with lesser hour of work than the adult workers do per day.

In the light of above discussion, let us see the composition of work force in Temi Tea Estate. Discussing the composition, special mention is made to see the caste and tribal backgrounds of the workers. If we analyse the Table 10.2 then it can be seen that among the Matwalis, Gurungs are dominant with 34.2% of garden workers. Next to Gurungs, Rai (15.0%) and Tamangs (11.2%) are dominant. Again, next to Tamangs, the percentage of Limbu (10.0%) tea garden workers is also significant. The percentages of other caste workers are more or less similar in strength.

It is also observed from the above table that 34.2% of the plantation workers are from the Gurung caste. It is because of the fact that they were brought from Damthang Village which was in those days fully inhabited by the Gurung community. Similarly, 15.0% of the workers are from the Rai caste. Rai workers were brought from Ben village during those days. Next to Rai, 11.2% of the workers are Tamangs who were brought from Rambing village. Rambing was again predominantly a Tamang Village. Next to Tamang, 7.5% of the workers are from the Chhetri caste. Chhetris were brought from Temi busty (now Temi Bazar). Similarly 10.0% of the workers are Limbus who were brought from Damthang village. As discussed earlier, each caste had a Sardar and Gallawalas (labour recruiters) who recruited their caste members from their villages. The Bhutias (2.0%) as the plantation workers were mainly supplied to Temi by Kaji of Rambing Village. But those Bhutias are not the Tibetan refugee Bhutias. The Sherpas (3.8%) were brought from mainly the Ben village. A Bihari after marrying a Chhetri girl has settled here permanently. The other castes like Manger (2.0%), Newar (1.0%), Kami (5.0%) and Damai (5.0%) were mainly migrated from Nepal and other parts of the country. It shows that basically the tea plantation workers are Matwalis (89.0%). Only 11.0% of the workers are Tangadharis in Temi Tea Estate. It is also reported that around fifty to sixty casual workers are employed during the peak plucking season every year. Among the Matwalis, Sherpas and Bhutias are scheduled tribes and Kami and Damai are scheduled castes. Rest of the Matwalis, except the Newars belong to other backward classes in Sikkim in general and at Temi Tea Estate in particular. Only Bahuns, Newars and Chhetris are general castes.

Table 10.2.

Structure of Work Force

Sl. No.	*Caste/Tribe*	*Worker*	*% tage*	*Household*	*% tage*
	Tagadhari				
	Jharra				
1.	Bahun	10	2.5	05	1.9
	Thimaha				
2.	Chhetri	30	7.5	15	5.6
3.	Bihari	03	0.8	01	0.4
	Matwali Setho				
4.	Gurung	137	34.2	90	33.5
5.	Manger	08	02.0	05	1.9
6.	Newar	04	01.0	02	0.7
7.	Rai	60	15.0	40	14.9
8.	Limbu	40	10.2	30	11.2
9.	Tamang	45	11.2	35	13.0
10.	Sherpa	15	3.8	12	4.5
11.	Bhutia	08	2.0	04	1.5
	Kalo				
12.	Kami	20	5.0	15	5.6
13.	Damai	20	5.0	15	5.6
	Total	400	100%	269	100%

Source : Field Work: 2001.

Sex Composition of Workers

There was a difference in regard to sex composition in Temi Tea Estate till 1990 but after 1990 there is no difference between the two sexes. But till 1990 inspite of having Equal Remuneration Act of Government of India, 1976, there was deep differences in regard to the wages and other facilities in the garden between the two sexes.

It is transparent from the Table 10.2 that 59.5% of Temi tea garden workers are females and only 40.5% are males, though the total number of tea garden workers at Temi are more or less same from all the castes and tribes. Among the Matwalis, 38.7% from Gurung caste, 13.8% from Rai, 9.7% from Tamang are worthy to mention here. Only 27.8% workers are male workers in the plantation. On the whole, the Table 10.3 indicates that Matwalis are toiling class in the plantation. It may be due to their tradition (Sharma : 2000) as they were toiling class both in Nepal and agrarian Sikkim and they became indispensable for tea plantation jobs also.

Table 10.3

Sex Composition of the Workers

Sl. No.	*Caste/Tribe*	*House-hold*	*Male*	*% tage*	*Female*	*% tage*	*Total Workers*
	Tagadhari Jharra						
1.	Bahun	5	4	2.5	6	2.5	10
	Thimaha						
2.	Chhetri	15	15	9.3	15	6.3	30
3.	Bihari	1	2	1.2	1	0.4	03
	Matwali Setho						
4.	Gurung	90	45	27.8	92	38.7	137
5.	Manger	5	3	1.9	5	2.1	08
6.	Newar	2	2	1.2	2	0.8	04
7.	Rai	40	20	12.3	40	16.8	60
8.	Limbu	30	20	12.3	20	8.4	40
9.	Tamang	35	22	13.6	23	9.7	45
10.	Sherpa	12	10	6.2	5	2.1	15
11.	Bhutia	4	4	2.5	4	1.7	8
	Kalo						
12.	Kami	15	5	3.1	15	6.3	20
13.	Damai	15	10	6.2	10	4.2	20
	Total	269	162	40.5	238	59.5	400

Source : Field Work : 2001.

The fingers of females are very sensitive to pluck the qualitative tea leaves (Sharma : 2000). Female are simple minded than males. Generally, it is also observed that females can render similar tender care to tea bushes *(Ibid:* 2000) as they do in case of their children at home.

Structure of Working Persons Among Workers

The working structure of the households of the workers depicts the socio-economic status of the tea plantation workers. The structure will be evident from the table 10.4.

It is transparent from the Table 10.4 (that 47.2% of the households have single earning member, 27.5% of the households have double, 13.0% triple and 12.3% of the households of the workers have four persons as working population in the garden at the micro level analysis. In the same fashion, 24.2% of Tamang and 12.1% of Rai households have on the average four working persons. Interestingly, not a single Tagadhari household has four working persons. It is because of the fact that Tagadharis are considered as *Sukumbasis* (recent settlers) and Matwalis as *Raithanees* (early settlers) in Temi Tea Estate. Among the Matwalis, Gurung, Rai and Tamang households have on the average three working persons. It indicates that the dominant working population of the garden are from Gurung, Rai and Tamang castes of Nepali Community.

Table 10.4

Sex Composition of the Workers

Sl. No.	*Caste/Tribe*	*Single*	*%*	*Two*	*%*	*Three*	*%*	*Four*	*%*
	Tagadhari								
	Jharra								
1.	Bahun = 5	3	2.4	1	1.4	1	2.9	-	-
	Thimaha								
2.	Chhetri = 5	10	7.9	4	5.4	1	2.9	-	-
3.	Bihari = 1	1	0.8	-	-	-	-	-	-
	Matwali Setho								
4.	Gurung = 90	40	31.5	28	37.8	10	28.6	12	36.4
5.	Manger = 5	2	1.6	1	1.4	1	2.9	1	3.0
6.	Rai = 40	18	14.2	12.	16.2	6	17.1	4	12.1
7.	Limbu = 30	17	13.4	9	12.2	3	8.6	1	3.0
8.	Newar = 2	1	0.8	1	1.4	-	-	-	-
9.	Tamang = 35	14	11.0	8	10.8	5	14.3	8	24.2
10.	Sherpa = 12	7	5.5	3	4.1	1	2.9	1	3.0
11.	Bhutia = 4	1	0.8	-	-	2	5.7	1	3.0
	Kalo								
12.	Kami = 15	6	4.7	4	5.4	3	8.6	2	6.1
13.	Damai = 15	7	5.5	3	4.1	2	5.7	3	9.1
	Total = 269	127	47.2	74	27.5	35	13.0	33	12.3

Source : Field Work: 2001.

The Wages of the Workers

When the garden was opened at Temi in November, 1968, there was no concrete rule for the payment of wages to the workers. Whatever the amount of wages management used to decide, the workers had to accept the same. However, after 1977, management decided to have a tentative wage structure for the plantation workers. This had to do because in 1977, a tea factory was started at Temi where the factory workers were considered as skilled type who had to be given a bit higher wages than the plantation workers. Following was then wage structure of the plantation workers at Temi during 1977 to 1984.

The Table 10.5 depicts the fact that *Marad* (male) used to get Rs. 2.75 per day, an *Aurat* (female) used to get Rs. 2.00 and a *Chokra/Chokri* used to get Rs. 1.50 per day. There was no other facility for the garden workers at Temi. *Kuccha Deras* (hut) had to be made by the workers themselves without any help from the management. Today the wage structure is Rs. 50 per worker per day irrespective of sex, nature of work and sections etc. For daily work, a *Thickka* of 8 Kilogram is given to worker to pluck tea leaves. If a worker plucks extra tea leaves, a sum of Rs. 2 per kilogram is given to the worker. Again, if a worker plucks tea leaves on Friday, i.e. weekly holiday or any other closed holiday then a sum of Rs. 3 per kilogram of plucked tea leaves

Table 10.5
Wage Structure of the Workers

Sl. No.	*Category of Worker*	*Wages (Per day in Rs.)*
1.	Marad	2.75
2.	Aurat	2.00
3.	Chokra/Chokri	1.50

Source: Temi garden office: 2001.

is given. The wage structure was revised in 1999 after ten years of last wage revision in 1989-90. A factory worker gets Rs. 52 per day as wage.

The Job Facilities of the Workers

During 1968 to 1977, the tea plantation workers had to contend with the wages only. In 1977, the facility like Maternity benefit and housing were started to be given in a casual way. Even there was no weekly holiday. All the seven days of the week were the working days in the plantation. After 1977, Friday was decided to be the weekly holiday with wages for the workers. Friday is weekly holiday in Temi Tea Estate because the nearby bazar i.e. Singtam Bazar takes place on Friday only. Interestingly, it is also observed that if a worker remains absent on Thursday, then wage cut is done for both Thursday and Friday i.e. weekly holiday. The management pays one month wages or minimum Bonus to the tune of 8.33% to the workers as *Puja* Bonus. They are not given the gratuity as per the payment of Gratuity Act of Government of India. Since 1998 only the Provident Fund scheme of the Government of India has started in the garden. Interestingly, the Family Pension Scheme of 1995 under the Provident Fund Act of Govt. of India has not yet introduced for future social security of the workers.

Probing into the other welfare facilities of the workers in the industrial society, it is found that the workers can attend local dispensary for medical treatment at free of cost. But if a patient is to be taken to Gangtok or Siliguri for treatment, no incentive or benefit is provided to the workers. All the expenses made outside hospitals or nursing homes are to be borned by the workers themselves. There is no creche facility for the children of the worker below 6 years of age. Again no extension programme has been launched for the workers regarding building of houses or Labour *Dhuras*. No repair or white washing of houses of workers is done by the management. All these are to be done by the workers themselves spending money from their own purse.

At the garden, the electricity supply is done by the State Electricity Board of Government of Sikkim to the workers. Thus, the management does not show any interest for the same. All the electricity bills of the workers' houses are to be borned by the workers themselves. Similarly, it is also observed that Public Health Engineering Department of Government of Sikkim provides the drinking water to the workers but drinking water bill is also to be paid by the workers themselves. This may be the reason why many workers do not take the facility from the Government of Sikkim rather they prefer to carry drinking water from the local streams *(Jhora* or *Dhara)*. The education of children of the workers upto the primary level is to be done at the garden only. Here in this respect also, management does not show any interest as the school comes under the Department of Education of Government of Sikkim. No ration, fuel and recreation facility are provided to the workers at Temi Tea Estate from the garden management. No cultural activity is also done here as in this respect, management does not show any interest considering it as unnecessary expenditure.

Thus, altogether if we compare the welfare facilities of the tea garden workers at Temi with other tea plantations of neighbouring West Bengal and Assam, the Temi workers don't appear to be the industrial one rather they can be said agricultural workers of rural areas of Sikkim. Here if we assess the welfare facility in terms of cash in West Bengal and Assam tea gardens, then it comes to Rs. 107 per day per worker while it is only Rs. 50 in case of Temi tea plantation workers.

From the above discussion, it may, therefore, be appropriate to generalise that the mode of production of Temi is pre-industrial in nature and colonial form of production relation is still sustaining in Temi Tea Estate of Sikkim. Under such form of production relation as Bhowmik (1981) observed coercion, low wages and immigrant labour are cardinal features of the plantation system. However, regarding the welfare facilities, Government of Sikkim has adopted some provisions which have favoured the tea planters only at Temi Tea Estate. As mentioned in earlier pages that this system has been sustaining in the garden as the workers are lured by the philosophy of Sikkimese sense of "Sons of the Soil" policy.

Considering the conditions of the workers of Temi it can be said that a kind of 'Plantocracy' has been in vogue (Sharma : 2000) in Temi due to its isolated location (35 km. from Singtam town and 22 km. from Namchi Town) being encircled by remote villages and forests. Contract with outside world is very limited. Even if some workers want to go to Singtam or Namchi, if not Gangtok, they have to spend substantial amount of money from their own purse.

Promotion Facility of the Workers

All the supervisory sub-staffs and office staffs are males. The promotion facility for woman workers who are working in the capacity of daily rated regular category is hardly provided. So, woman workers join the garden as daily rated workers and retire as daily rated workers only.

Hazira Bikri System

There is a *Hazira Bikri* system in the plantation. Under the system, an employed person (worker) sells out his/her *Hazira* (job) to another person who is not formally the employee of the garden. A sum of Rs. 20,000 are charged for a single *Hazira.* It is observed that after selling out the *Hazira,* the employees join agrarian job completely in the neighbouring villages.

Caste/Tribe and Land Holding

In the traditional society, castes and tribes of Nepali community had direct relationship with the land holdings (Sharma : 1997). In the plantation, the workers of various castes and tribes have no land holdings of their own. Temi Tea Estate has given land to the workers and employees since its inception. The distributed garden land to workers is called *Ko-The-Bari* (kitchen garden). However, the various categories of workers are given various amount of land. This will be evident from the following Table 10.6.

Table 10.6

Kitchen Garden for the Workers at Temi Tea Estate

Sl. No.	*Category of Worker*	*Kitchen garden (in Tang)**
1.	Managerial Personnel	25
2.	Supervisory/Office Staffs	20
3.	Worker	10

*1 Tang = 10 sq. feet.

Source : The Garden Office : 2001.

It is observed from the above Table 10.7 that 34.2% of allotted kitchen garden is owned by Gurung workers. Another 15.0% and 11.3% of allotted kitchen garden are owned by Rai and Tamang workers respectively. Still another 10.0% of kitchen land is owned by the Limbu workers. The kitchen garden holding is very thin among Bohuns and Chhetris with 2.5% and 7.5%

respectively. It means that 90.0% of the allotted kitchen garden is owned by the Matwalis.

The ownership of land outside the garden as *Dakhali* is totally different as 29.8% of the land is owned by Bhutias who are the descendents of Kajis (zamindars) of Sikkim. The Kajis used to be the Zamindars or landlords in the

Table 10.7
The Temi Workers and Their Landholding Pattern

Sl. No.	*Caste/Tribe*	*Kitchen Garden (Kothebarie) (in Acre)*	*% tage*	*Dakhali (land outside Garden) (in Acre)*	*% tage*
	Tagadhari				
	Jharra				
1.	Bahun = 10	100	2.5	-	-
	Thimaha				
2.	Chhetri = 30	300	7.5	-	-
3.	Bihari = 30	30	0.8	-	-
	Matwali/Tribals				
	Setho				
4.	Gurung = 137	1370	34.2	10 (Dry)	14.9
5.	Manger = 8	80	2.0	-	-
6.	Newar = 4	40	1.0	2 (Dry)	3.0
7.	Rai = 60	600	15.00	6 (Dry)	9.0
8.	Limbu = 40	400	10.0	3 (Dry)	4.5
9.	Tamang = 45	450	11.3	10 (Dry)	14.9
10.	Sherpa = 15	150	3.7	10 (Dry)	14.9
11.	Bhutia = 8	80	2.0	20 (Dry)	29.8
	Kalo				
12.	Kami = 20	200	5.0	4 (Dry)	6.0
13.	Damai = 20	200	5.0	2 (Dry)	3.0
	Total	**4000**	**100%**	**67**	**100%**

Source : Field Work: 2001.

past. This legacy might have perceptible impacts in the land ownership pattern as the major share of the outside land is owned by Bhutias. Interestingly, it is observed that only Matwalis have land outside the garden which as mentioned above is called *Dakhali land.* The nature of such land is dry as such land is situated at the higher altitudes of Temi. As higher altitude land is very dry, crops like millet, Bajra etc. can be grown here. Growing of millet is enabled by the dry land to the Matwalis. Such land is called *Sukha Kheti.* Millet is important crop for the preparation of *Jhar* or *Nigar* which are indispensible ritual food items for the Matwalis. Tagadharis have no land outside the garden as they prefer wet land *(Pani Kheti}* which are not there. Tagadharis prefer wet land as they prefer rice as main food item both in normal occasion and at the time of observing rituals. Another reason for not holding wet land outside the garden by the Tagadharis is that they are recent settlers *(Sukumbasis)* who can hardly afford to purchase such wet land because they are very poor. The selling price of wet land is above forty thousand per acre in neighbouring villages of Temi Tea Estate.

In the olden days, such kitchen garden was to be given to the worker to grow vegetables as the marketplaces were located in far off places from the garden. During the period, the permanent settlement with landholding right on kitchen garden appeared to be the pushing factor to join the garden jobs for the workers. Having the forest reserve around Temi Tea Estate, planters could easily procure sufficient land from the forest keeping in view the kitchen garden could be reoccupied in future by the plantation for its extension of the area once it is abandoned by the workers due to the non-availability of irrigation water.

With the rampant deforestation of Temi-Tarkhu Forest Range during the late eighties of 19th century, workers occupied many land near the garden. So, now many workers have their own land around the tea plantation. Even *a Dakhali* Busty is here in Temi Tea Estate. *Dakhali* means the land encroachment done by the people. As in other areas of Sikkim, many neighbouring areas of Temi Tea Estate have brought under *Dakhali* for ever. In the light of this discussion, let us see the landholding pattern of the workers of Temi Tea Estate (See Table 10.7).

Cattle Stock and Plantation Workers

The cattle stock and Nepali society are closely interwoven. Without cattle stock, no agrarian caste structure can survive. However, the various castes and tribes have various type of cattle stock as in the past in Temi today. Though the tea garden workers left the agrarian economy long back in the garden but domesticating cattle stock is still continuing in the plantation. The structure of cattle stock population is evident from the Table 10.8.

It is observed from the Table 4.8 that on the average each household has four livestock. It shows that basically in the Temi Himalaya the Bahuns donot have domesticated poultry and piggery in their households while Chhetris have poultry farms at their homes. This happens because of the fact that historically Chhetris were the descendents of *Khas Matwalis* (Sharma: 2000) of Nepal Himalayas who used to sacrifice animals blood in rituals. On the

Table 10.8.
Caste/Tribe and Cattle Stocks in Temi Tea Estate

Sl. No.	*Caste/Tribe*	*Cow*	*%*	*Poul-try*	*%*	*Pig-gery*	*%*	*Sheep*	*%*	*Total*
	Tagadhari *Jharra*									
1.	Bahun = 5	2	1.4	-	-	-	-	-	-	2
	Thimaha									
2.	Chhetri = 15	8	5.7	6	0.8	-	-	7	3.9	21
3.	Bihari = 1	1	0.7	-	-	-	-	-	-	1
	Matwali *Setho*									
4.	Gurung = 90	40	28.4	160	21.6	-	-	45	25.2	245
5.	Mânger = 5	2	1.4	20	2.7	3	2.4	3	1.7	28
6.	Newar = 2	1	0.7	10	1.3	1	0.8	10	5.6	22
7.	Rai = 40	30	21.3	200	27.0	30	24.0	20	11.2	280
8.	Limbu = 30	18	12.8	100	13.5	25	20.2	15	8.4	158
9.	Tamang = 35	19	13.5	130	17.5	25	20.2	40	22.5	214
10.	Sherpa = 12	3	2.1	9	1.2	8	6.5	4	2.2	24
11.	Bhutia = 4	4	2.8	60	8.1	10	8.1	6	3.4	80
	Kalo									
12.	Kami = 15	6	4.3	30	4.1	12	9.7	8	4.5	56
13.	Damai = 15	7	5.0	16	2.2	10	8.1	20	11.2	53
	Total = 269	**141**	**11.9**	**741**	**62.5**	**124**	**10.5**	**178**	**15.2**	**1184**

Source : Field Work: 2001.

other hand, pigs and hens are equally important domesticated animals along with other cattle stocks like cow and bull for Matwalis. Again, Beefs, Chicken and pork are very popular meat both for normal and ceremonial times to the Matwalis than motton. Motton is very popular meat for Tagadharis. This may be the reason why Tagadharis have domesticated sheeps in their homes. The Tibetan foods like Thukpa (noodle soup with meat and vegetables) and Momo (made of beefs and pork as well as motton) are very popular among all Nepali castes and tribes of Darjeeling-Sikkim Himalayas. Even Tagadharis of present generation are fond of Thukpa and Momo, made of motton. Thus cattle stock forms the integral part of the Himalayan society in general and Temi Tea Estate in particular.

The Garden Workers and Style of Life

Another area of economic life of workers is the style of life that they have been leading in the plantation. The style of life can be more clear if we see the following Table 10.9.

Table 10.9. Caste/Tribe and Style of Life of the Workers

Sl. No.	*Caste/Tribe*	*Watch*	*Clock*	*Tele-phone*	*Tele vision*	*Radio*	*Vehicle*	*Sofa sets*
	Tagadhari							
	Jharra							
1.	Bahun = 5	4	1	-	1	1	-	-
	Thimaha							
2.	Chhetri = 15	15	12	2	6	3	-	4
3.	Bihari = 1	2	1	-	1	1	-	1
	Metwali							
	Setho							
4.	Gurung = 90	100	60	5	30	15	2	10
5.	Manger = 5	2	2	1	2	2	2	2
6.	Newar = 2	2	2	1	2	2	2	2
7.	Rai = 40	20	5	2	25	10	5	5
8.	Limbu = 30	18	20	1	28	5	3	5
9.	Tamang = 35	20	15	2	25	12	3	20
10.	Sherpa = 12	8	12	1	12	8	3	8
11.	Bhutia = 4	6	4	2	4	2	2	4
	Kalo							
12.	Kami = 15	8	8	1	4	3	-	2
13.	Damai = 15	3	3	-	10	3	1	8
	Total	**208**	**145**	**18**	**150**	**67**	**23**	**71**

Source : Field Work: 2001.

It is transparent from the Table 10.9 that the style of life of the workers belonging to Matwali group is much better than the Tagadharis in Temi Tea Estate. The style of life having the modern equipment is much more in number among the Matwalis than Tagadharis. This may be due to the fact that Matwalis either belong to scheduled tribes or scheduled castes category or other Backward classes group or status in the society due to the Government schemes which have helped them to lead better style of life since the last five to seven years.

The style of life of Temi workers is predominantly Matwali in the sense that workers are satiated with engaging their offspring in the garden or outside jobs in the state.

Among Tagadharis, Chhetris have better style of life having television sets, sofa sets and telephone connection. All the vehicles numbering about 23 are owned by the Matwalis. These are the only vehicles available at Temi Tea Estate to reach them to the Singtam and Namchi towns. All the vehicles are under the control of unemployed youths of families of the workers. Almost all the workers want to acquire television sets no matter black/white or coloured one. Journey by vehicles to the towns and purchase television sets form the integral part of style of life of the workers in Temi Tea Estate. However, it is observed that the workers must develop thrift habit in order to improve their style of life [Lama : 2001, Lahiri (Ed.) 2001] in the families.

11

SOCIAL LIVING OF THE WORKERS

In the following sections, an attempt has been made to indicate the impact of plantation industry on the social life of the workers which highlight the extent of changes taking place in social institutions of the industrial environment. Here we have conceptualised the changes taking place in the institution of caste system, commensal relations, place of birth, educational structure, marriage pattern, family composition, religious structure, traditional and modern health practices etc.

Prior to their migration to Temi Tea Estate, the Nepalis had caste system as of Nepal. The agrarian caste system of Sikkim had been similar to that of Nepal. This will be evident from the following Table 11.1.

Table 11.1
Traditional Nepali Caste Hierarchy

Sl. No.	*Verna*	*Caste*
1.	Brahman	Upadhya, Kumai, Jaisi, Deb Bha ju
2.	Kshatriya	Thakuri, Chhetri, Khatri
	Double order	Manger, Gurung
3.	Vaisya	Newar High Castes
4.	Shudra	Rai, Limbu, Low Caste Newars, Sherpa, Sunuwar, Murmi, Thamis etc.
5.	Untouchables	Kami, Damai, Sarki, Chyame, Jyapu, Pore etc.

Source : Nepali : 1968.

It is transparent from the above table that excepting the Brahman and Kshatriya (Tagadharis) all other castes of various Varnas are the toiling castes of the Nepali society both in the past and today. Even the castes belonging to double order were as good as the Vaisya, Shudra and untouchables as they did not accept the Hindu caste system in full.

The Nepali caste system of the plantation industry at Temi is quite different from that of agrarian Sikkim. However, in certain situations, the distinct social status of *Nak Chuchees* and *Nak Thapchees* in general and respective caste in particular can be understood. Such situations are the observance of some customs in relation to marriage and death rituals. The difference between a Rai and Limbu can be understood in such situations only when they perform their divergent rituals which are borrowed from their traditions. But broadly one can differentiate between *Nak Thapchees* and *Nak Chuchees* while observing the rituals. In the present study, caste is understood as an endogamous, localised and hereditary ritual group. However, in the present study, our concern is centered around the caste composition, changes taking place in the caste structure at Temi and commensal relations in the plantation. The basis of classification of changing caste system in the plantation is very simple as fully operationalised by the Sikkimese society today into *Nak Chuchees* and *Nak Thapchees* groups. Former are Tagadharis who wear sacred threads and latter the Matwalis who use or to be used wine and meat as compulsory ritual food items. In other situations, consumption of wine and meat is individual phenomenon. A Matwali may not drink wine while a Tagadhari drinks wine in normal times.

Table 11.2
Occupational Structure in Agrarian Sikkim

Sl. No.	*Caste*	*Agrarian Occupation*
1.	Bahun	Priests
2.	Chettri	Warriors
3.	Thakuri	Aristocrats
4.	Newar	Businessman
5.	Rai, Limbu, Yakha, Manger	Agriculturists
6.	Thami, Sunuwar, Gurung	Shepherds
7.	Thamang	Horse Traders/Cavaliers
8.	Bhujel	Beaten Rice Makers
9.	Jogi	Ascetics
10.	Yolmus	Paper Makers
11.	Sherpas	Porters
12.	Lepchas	Shifting (Jhoom) Cultivators
13.	Bhutias	Landlords (Kajis)
14.	Kamis	Ironsmiths
15.	Damais	Tailors/Musicians
16.	Sarki	Cobblers
17.	Biharis	Businessman (Petty)

Source : Field work : 2001.

As in Nepal, the impacts of Hinduism could reach to Sikkim right from the 15th century when Nepalis were warmly invited by the Chowgels (Kings) of Sikkim to exploit agrarian belts of Sikkim to the fullest extent (Das : 1983).

The Bhutias and Lepchas did not accept the agrarian works (Shay : 1965). The same is found in case of tea plantation works also as not a single Lepcha is found as tea plantation worker at Temi Tea Estate. Inspite of their settlement in industrial environment of Temi Tea Estate, the tribals continue with their animistic ritual practices.

The caste hierarchy is not so rigid as we found in agrarian Sikkim. The agrarian Sikkim still maintains to a great extent the caste system through occupation. The agrarian caste system can be evident from the following Table 11.2.

The agrarian caste system of rural Sikkim has undergone drastic changes after the various castes and tribes settled down in tea plantation of Temi. The ascriptive criteria of caste in terms of occupation does not affect the plantation social living though the institution of caste system continues in a loose form. This is apparent from the following Table 11.3.

Table 11.3

Caste Hierarchy in Temi Tea Estate

Sl. No.	*Status*	*Caste*	
I.	Tagadharis (Nak Chuchees) (Non-Backward Class) →	Jharra	Bahun ↓
		Thimaha	Chhetri/Bihari
II.	Matwalis →	Setho →	Rai, Limbu, Manger Gurung, Newar, Thamang ↓
	Tribals (Nak Thapchees) →		Sherpas, Bhutias ↓
	(Backward Classes) (Scheduled Castes) →	Kalo →	Kami, Damai

Source : Field work: 2001.

It is observed from the Table 11.3 that there are two groups, viz., Tagadhari and Matwali. Former has been further divided as found in the Tea and Cinchona plantations of Darjeeling Himalaya (Sharma : 2000) into *Jharra* and *Thimaha* groups. Again, the Matwali Category has been divided into *Setho* and *Kalo* types. The caste like Chhetri and Bihari are *Thimaha* Tagadharis as they are below Bahuns who wear sacred threads of nine strings. *Setho* Matwalis are Mongoloid group while *Kalo* Matwalis resembles with the Aryan stock like Bahun, Chhetri and Bihari castes.

But recent political development in Sikkim has conceptualised the Temi Society into Reserved and Non-Reserved groups. This relates to the occupational stratification of Temi Society. This can be evident from the following Table 11.4. This classification coincides with the concept of *Latto Jats* (innocent castes) like Matwalis and tribals and *Bhatto Jats* (Cunning castes) like Tagadharis. Interestingly, Newars from the Setho group has been excluded from Setho Matwali category. Tagadharis and Newars are unreserved and Matwalis/tribals the reserved groups in the plantation.

Table 11.4.
Social Stratification of the Plantation Workers

Sl. No.	*Status*	*Caste*
I.	Reserved Group (Lotto Jats)	Scheduled Tribes (Sherpas and Bhutias) Scheduled Castes (Kami and Damai) Other Backward Class (Rai, Limbu, Gurung, Mangar, Tamang)
II.	Unreserved Groups (Bhatto Jats)	Bahun, Chhetri, Bihari and Newars

Source : Field work : 2001.

Considering the above social stratification of Temi Tea industry, it is observed that the caste hierarchy is getting lesser importance in application in so far as the day today industrial activities are concerned. It is because of the fact that whenever any promotion prospect arises in the garden this stratification works nicely as new opportunities are to be provided as per quota fixed for the reserved and non-reserved categories of workers. Most of the jobs of the garden are to be given to the reserved group. This polarisation of society at Temi Tea Estate has distinctly portrays the fact that unreserved group has no *locus standi* in the socio-economic life of the garden. This classification has been proved to be more beneficial to the garden management to continue with pre-industrial form of production relations. The reserved group feels that unreserved group is *Sukumbasis* who wanted to have higher or better quality of life within a short time at their cost while unreserved group feels that they are also the integral part of sons of the soil policy of Government of Sikkim. Moreover the reserved group feels that their contribution towards the industry is much more than the unreserved group. Most of the technical jobs are done by the unreserved group. On the other hand, the Matwalis (tribals and Nepali sub-tribes) feel themselves as the real sons of the soil of Sikkim as *Raithanees* since time immemorial of the history of Sikkim. Very recently, efforts are being made to incorporate Gurung and Tamang into the category of scheduled tribes in Sikkim. The Gurungs, Tamangs along with the existing tribes (Bhutias and Sherpas) are basically

Buddhists. Doing this, the existing scheduled tribes do not appear to be happy as the significance of these existing scheduled tribes will be minimised with reduction of tribal quota in various socio-economic and political spheres of Sikkim in general and at Temi Tea Estate in particular. Such feeling has prevailed in the minds of the existing scheduled tribes because their share in occupations or other opportunities will be declined considerably in future. So, a kind of cold war between reserved and unreserved groups is persisting among the garden workers. The unreserved group is equated with migrants from Nepal by the reserved group. Such situation was glaringly experienced at the last state election at Temi Tea Estate when reserved group supported Mr. P.K. Chamling (Matwali) and unreserved group supported Mr. Nar Bahadur Bhandari (Tagadhari). Latter on, this confrontation was subsided due to the cultural affinity of Nepali community as a whole which considers the reserved or unreserved groups as the integral part of the society.

The adaptive mechanism for such cultural affinity is in the area of integration of all castes and tribes in regard to the commensal relation. The traditional agrarian division of Nepali society of Sikkim into *Pani-*

Table 11.5
Caste Relations Regarding Water in Agrarian Sikkim

Pani-Chal-Ne-Jats (Chut)	*Pani-Na-Chal-Ne-Jats (Achut)*
Bahun	Kami
Chhetri	Damai
Bihari	Sarki
Newar, Rai, Limbu, Manger, Gurung, Jogi, Bhujel, Yolmu, Thami, Sunuwar, Sherpa, Lepcha, Bhutia, etc.	

Source : Field work : 2001.

Chal-Ne-Jats (caste from whom water can be taken) and *Pani-Na-Chal-Ne-Jats* (caste from whom water cannot be taken) has been portrayed in the Table 11.5.

It is observed from the table that the commensal relations in regard to water has drastically altered in the garden. However, it is also noted in the Table 11.5 that *Chut* caste (touchables) use to take water from all the castes of Nepali community, Bhutias and Sherpas except from *Acchut* (untouchables) castes like Kami, Damai and Sarki. In Temi Tea Estate, such restriction regarding water undergone considerable changes. This is clear from the Table 11.6.

From the above Table 11.6, it is transparent that all the castes take water from each other in the plantation. A garden *Paniwala* is a Damai lady who distributes water to the workers at the work places every day. People feel proud to take water from the Bhutia families who are considered to be the descendents of Kaji Khandan (families).

Table 11.6
Caste Relations Regarding 'Water' in the Plantation

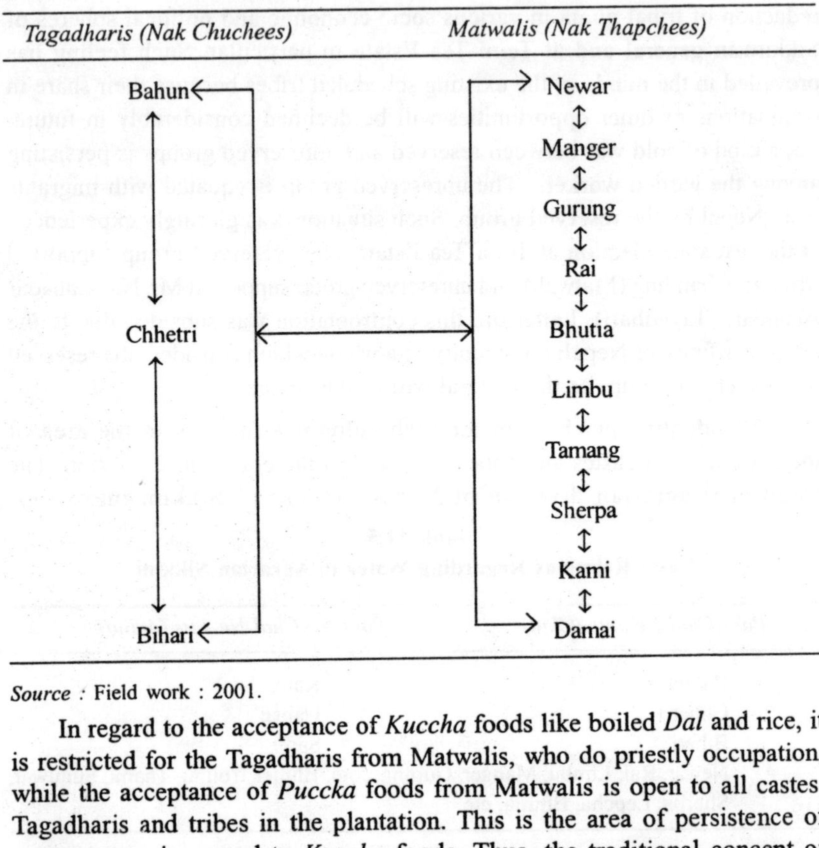

Source : Field work : 2001.

In regard to the acceptance of *Kuccha* foods like boiled *Dal* and rice, it is restricted for the Tagadharis from Matwalis, who do priestly occupation, while the acceptance of *Puccka* foods from Matwalis is open to all castes, Tagadharis and tribes in the plantation. This is the area of persistence of caste system in regard to *Kuccha* foods. Thus, the traditional concept of purity-pollution are still in vogue to some extent especially at the time of observance of rituals and festivals at homes among the castes and tribes. This shows that we do not see the continuity of traditional form of commensal relations among the tea plantation workers at Temi Tea Estate of Sikkim.

Place of Birth of the Workers

In this section, an attempt has been made to observe the place of birth of plantation workers at Temi Tea Estate. The degree of migration from the agrarian Sikkim to the plantation will give us a clear picture about the extent of changes taking place in their overall socio-economic life at the plantation.

The above table indicates that 92.5% of the workers were born in the country. Only 7.5% of them were migrated from Nepal and Bhutan. But they are all at the verge of retirement from the garden jobs. The workers who were born in the Sikkim joined the garden jobs as they were told that it is as good

Table 11.7

Plantation Workers and their Place of Birth

Sl. No.	*Caste/Tribe*	*Born in Garden*	*%*	*Born in neighbouring villages of Sikkim*	*%*	*Outside Sikkim*	*%*	*Outside the country*	*%*
	Tagadhari Jharra								
1.	Bahun = 10	2	0.8	6	6.5	-	-	2	6.7
	Thimaha								
2.	Chhetri = 30	12	4.8	13	14.1	1	3.8	4	13.3
3.	Bihari = 3	1	0.4	-	-	2	7.7	-	-
	Matwali Setho								
4.	Newar = 4	1	0.4	2	2.2	1	3.8	-	-
5.	Manger = 8	4	1.6	3	3.3	1	3.8	-	-
6.	Gurung = 137	118	46.8	10	10.9	5	19.2	4	13.3
7.	Rai = 60	45	17.9	13	14.1	2	7.7	-	-
8.	Limbu = 40	19	7.5	18	19.6	2	7.7	1	3.3
9.	Tamang = 45	20	7.9	15	16.3	5	19.2	5	16.7
10.	Sherpa = 15	8	3.2	3	3.3	1	3.8	3	10.0
11.	Bhutia = 8	1	0.4	2	2.2	-	-	5	16.7
	Kalo								
12.	Kami = 20	10	4.0	3	3.3	3	11.5	4	13.3
13.	Damai = 20	11	4.4	4	4.3	3	11.5	2	6.7
	Total = 400	**252**	**63.0**	**92**	**23.0**	**26**	**6.5**	**30**	**7.5**

Source : Field Work: 2001.

as a government job. But in reality, it is found that it is as good as a private job under Tea Board of Sikkim of the Ministry of Industries, Government of Sikkim. The Matwalis migrated to Sikkim from Nepal during early 16th century as they were beef eaters (Pradhan: 1991). Beef eating was restricted then by the law of land in Nepal. This may be the reason why beef is very-important meat for Matwalis along with tribes. Every Nepali caste like Kami, Damai and Sarki prefers beef most than motton. Six member of Tagadharis were migrated from Nepal and Bhutan in early sixties to Temi Tea Estate to join mainly the clerical jobs. Secondly, some Matwalis had migrated to Sikkim in early 15th century due to poor economic conditions (Sharma : 2000) in Nepal and in early 18th century many Matwalis migrated to Sikkim when Sikkim came under the rule of House of Gorkhas (Pradhan: 1991) till 1816 (O'Malley : 1907). Some

Newars were called upon by the Chowgels (Kings) of Sikkim since early 15th century to mint money as the Newars had rich expertise on minting money. This is a single most reason why not a single Newar of first generation migrant from Nepal or Bhutan is there in the garden . In fact, the question of Nepali migration in the Eastern Himalayas including Sikkim cannot be answered with accuracy due to the absence of authentic documents or records. It is because of the fact that the movement of people in Himalayas hailing from the various parts of Nepal is as old as of human kind—their origin and development

Education of the Workers

On the whole, the education of the workers is every vague as majority of workers are illiterates in the garden. The structure of educational standard among the garden workers is same among all castes and tribes. This can be clear from the Table 11.8.

Table 11.8
Caste/Tribe and Education of the Workers

Sl. No.	*Caste/ Tribe*	*Illiter-ate*	*%*	*Prima-ry*	*%*	*Secon-dary*	*%*
	Tagadhari Jharra						
1.	Bahun = 10	6	2.6	3	2.2	1	2.7
	Thimaha						
2.	Chhetri = 30	19	8.4	9	6.6	2	5.4
3.	Bihari = 3	1	0.4	2	1.5	-	-
	Matwali Setho						
4.	Manger = 8	6	2.6	2	1.5	-	-
5.	Gurung = 137	118	52.0	14	10.3	5	13.5
6.	Rai = 60	20	8.8	30	22.1	10	27.0
7.	Limbu = 40	10	4.4	25	18.4	5	13.5
8.	Newar = 4	1	0.4	3	2.2	-	-
9.	Tamang = 45	20	8.8	20	14.7	5	13.5
10.	Sherpa = 15	5	2.2	7	5.1	3	8.1
11.	Bhutia = 8	2	0.9	4	2.9	2	5.4
	Kalo						
12.	Kami = 20	7	3.1	10	7.4	3	8.1
13.	Damai = 20	12	5.3	7	5.1	1	2.7
	Total = 400	**227**	**56.7**	**136**	**34.0**	**37**	**9.3**

Source : Field Work: 2001.

If we see the Table 11.8, it is found that 56.7% of workers are illiterates and 43.3% of them are literates in the sense that they somehow write their names. Out of 43.3%, it is observed that 34.0% have primary education and 9.3% of them have secondary education. It is also observed from the Table 11.8 that the extent of secondary education is higher among Rai (27.0%), Gurung (13.5%), Limbu (13.5%) and Tamang (13.5%) castes. Next to them, Sherpa (8.1%) and Kami (8.1%) castes have secondary education in the plantation. The percentage of secondary education is more or less same among other castes and tribes also. The percentage of illiteracy is highest (52.0%) among the Gurung. The illiteracy rate among other castes is also more or less same considering their demographic scenario in the garden. This happens because there is no secondary school in the garden. A secondary school is located in Bermoik village which is 15 Kilometers away from Temi Tea Estate. Secondly, garden does not provide educational facility. Only a few well to do families send their children to Gangtok, Darjeeling, Kalimpong and outside in various schools, colleges and universities of the country for higher education.

Family

Traditionally, the peasants and landless agricultural workers had joint families in agrarian Sikkim. The family was patriarchal in nature consisting of a man, his wife, his sons and daughters, married sons, daughter-in-laws, grandsons and grand daughters. Thus, normally, the family used to be of joint type consisting of large number of members. In the present analysis, the term 'family' denotes a group of persons living together in the same house whether related or not. The workers are not allowed to build private houses in the garden. The plantation has provided quarters of 20 × 20 feet size. The workers have to accommodate the family members even if their numbers are more in the households. It is observed in many households, five to seven persons sleep in the Varandha of the households. Considering this, the present study has planned to classify family into Nuclear and Joint types. The Nuclear family denotes a family composed of the parents and unmarried children. Even if a boy or girl who gets a regular job in the plantation, she or he is not provided separate house or kitchen garden till he or she is married. The Joint family denotes a family consisting of parents of a couple, unmarried brothers, sisters, father-in-law, mother-in-law, married sons and daughters-in-laws, grandsons and granddaughters. However, some workers have joint families in the plantation. Some divorced ladies of the garden are engaged in the plantation by the management as females are found more productive, good and sincere in their job. The family structure of Temi Tea Estate will be more clear if we see the following Table 11.9.

It is observed from the above Table 11.9 that the family denotes a group of persons who live together in the same house. Unlike in the traditional society, the structure of family is different in the sense that today it may not be always patriarchal in character. Considering the situation, the family is somewhat different here under the study

Going through the Table 11.9, it is observed that 80% of Tagadhari households are nuclear and only 20% are joint types. It indicates that the settlement in the plantation at Temi has adequately helped to increase the percentage of nuclear families. The percentage of joint family is very high in case of Limbu (25.4%), Newar (16.9), Gurung (16.9%) and Damai (10.2%) castes in the plantation. Next to Damai, 8.5% of Rais and 8.5% of Sherpas have joint families. But by a joint family, here we mean the parents, sons, daughter-in-laws, grandsons and grand daughters who are living together in the same house.

Table 11.9

Family Composition of the Workers

Sl. No.	*Caste/Tribe*	*No. of Household*	*Nucl-ear*	*Perce-ntage*	*Joint*	*Percentage*
	Tagadhari					
	Jharra					
1.	Bahun	5	4	1.9	1	1.7
	Thimaha					
2.	Chhetri	15	12	5.7	3	5.1
3.	Bihari	1	1	0.5	-	-
	Matwali Setho					
4.	Newar	2	2	1.0	-	-
5.	Manger	5	4	1.9	1	1.7
6.	Gurung	90	80	38.1	10	16.9
7.	Rai	40	35	16.7	5	8.5
8.	Limbu	30	15	7.1	15	25.4
9.	Tamang	35	25	11.9	10	16.9
10.	Sherpa	12	7	3.3	5	8.5
11.	Bhutia	4	3	1.4	1	1.7
	Kalo					
12.	Kami	15	13	6.2	2	3.4
13.	Damai	15	9	4.3	6	10.2
	Total	**269**	**210**	**78.1**	**59**	**21.9**

Source : Field Work: 2001.

The percentage of Nuclear family is very high among Gurung (38.1 %), Rai (16.7%), and Tamang (11.9%) and rest of other castes and tribes have more or less similar picture in so far as the structure of family is concerned. It shows that the nuclearisation of family got complete shape in the plantation. Socially, separation of newly married couples from parental home under *Ansa Banda* (Division of ancestral property among the sons) system of the past is a driving force (Sharma : 2000) which has also accepted by the plantation society. On the whole, 78.1 % of families are nuclear and 21.9% are joint in the plantation.

Changing Role of the Family

The Temi Tea Estate society is a patriarchal society. But the authority does not always come from the male folks alone. The male authority is completely different here from agrarian Sikkim. The decision making authority lies with the head of the family relating to the land allocation of parents among brothers, performing rituals and arranging marriages (Berreman : 1972).

The nature of decision-making is different in the plantation as almost 60% of earning members of the family are females. So, whatever the decision is to be taken, it is to be discussed by husbands with their wives first. However, it is also observed that once a man retires from the job his son takes decision and decision taken by the earning son is final. It means that the functional role of family in regard to the authority structure has been changed (Sharma : 1999) considerably.

In the past, daughters were to be considered as liabilities to the parents as daughters were to be given *Daijo* (Dowry) while under the present condition no such *Daijo* is given compulsorily.

Unlike in the past, the elder sister need not to be compulsorily respected by the younger brothers of the family. Even the youngest son of a family can have such authority over all other family members if he is the earning member of the family.

The economic role of male members can be equated with that of female members rather female's role is much above the male members of the family.

With the breakdown of kin-based joint family system, the nuclear families have emerged as an independent self-supporting entities (Bhadra : 1997). Under the situation, all the domestic responsibilities are equally shared by both male and female members. As a matter of fact, in many cases, males contribute a small part of their income to the family purse while females contribute more.

Unlike in the past, female mobility is free or open in respect of attending rituals, marriages, death rituals, shopping at the Bajar etc. Females talk freely at public places. In this way females are not considered subordinates to men in the plantation. However, such openness is a bit restricted among the

Tagadharis. Even Matwalis do not prefer to see their females openly mixed with males specially in sexual matters.

Another drastic change is observed among the workers is that after being married, son moves from parental home and establishes a new family with his wife, sons and daughters. Even if sometimes separate house is not given by the management, separate rooms are to be made in the parental house itself as the new couple want to have an independent living.

The ongoing campaign for Women Empowerment has also touched the plantation where females want to be free from the absolute control of their mother-in-laws, husband's brothers, female affines and kin bonds of the families. Thus, the traditional meaning of family as basic unit to sustain the value of social system has been transformed through the new family unit (Sharma : 1997) mainly run by the young husbands and wives in an independent way.

Marriage

Unlike in the past of agrarian Sikkim, marriage by choice rather than sacrament is most popular among the plantation workers. Even if a marriage takes place by arrangement, the boy and girl have to prefer each other first. This is an established fact known to all that before marriage, the boy and girl meet first due to enclave nature of the plantation. They have no option to go out regularly rather to meet at the plantation itself. Hardly, the consensual marriage has taken place in the plantation till today. Marriage between or among Bhutia, Sherpa and Tamang is considered as intra-caste marriage as they are Buddhists and they have inherited similar traditions. The marriage structure of the plantation workers is depicted in the following Table 11.10.

If we analyse the above Table 11.10, we see that having agrarian belt around Temi Tea Estate, the occurrences of intra-caste marriage is very high (75%) and only 25% of marriages have taken place as inter-caste or inter-community marriages. Caste-wise, Newar and Bihari households have still retained their respective traditions of intra-caste marriage wholly. Similarly, 83.3% of Gurung, 75% of Rai, 83.3% of Limbus, 57.1% of Tamang, 75% of Bhutias, 66.7% of Sherpas, 80% of Kami and 60% of Damais have done intra-caste marriages. Similar picture is also found among other castes and tribes. It shows that the traditional concept of *Jat Bibaha* (marriages within own castes), *Ajat Bibaha* (marriages with lower castes), and *Kujat Bibaha* (marriages with untouchable castes) of the past have little relevance in the industrial society. The marriages among the Matwalis are considered as *Jat Bibaha.* But Newars are found little bit conscious about marriage alliances and do within own caste only. Chhetris, Mangars, Bahuns and Damais are also

Table 11.10
Marriage Pattern of the Workers

Sl. No.	*Caste/Tribe*	*Intra-Caste*	*Percent-age*	*Inter-Caste*	*Perce-ntage*
	Tagadhari				
	Jharra				
1.	Bahun = 5	4	2.0	1	1.5
	Thimaha				
2.	Chhetri = 15	10	4.9	5	7.6
3.	Bihari = 1	1	0.5	-	-
	Matwali Setho				
4.	Manger = 5	4	2.0	1	1.5
5.	Gurung = 90	75	36.9	15	22.7
6.	Rai = 40	30	14.8	10	15.2
7.	Limbu = 30	25	12.3	5	7.6
8.	Newar = 2	2	1.0	-	-
9.	Tamang = 35	20	9.9	15	22.7
10.	Sherpa = 12	8	3.9	4	6.1
11.	Bhutia = 4	3	1.5	1	1.5
	Kalo				
12.	Kami = 15	12	5.9	3	4.5
13.	Damai = 15	9	4.4	6	9.1
	Total	**203**	**75%**	**66**	**25%**

Source : Field Work: 2001.

conscious about the marriage alliances. But inspite of this, the percentage of inter-caste love marriages is increasing. Even among the Chhetris, the percentage of love marriages is very high (33.3%). The present generation opts for love marriages more than *Mangi* (arrange) marriages. The inter-caste marriages take place among all castes and tribes and today all castes and tribes have accepted the love marriages. This happens because the dominant Matwalis do *Chori* (elopement) *Bibaha* only as per the *Matwalisation* (Tribalisation) process of their culture of the society at Temi Tea Estate.

Traditionally, Tagadharis used to maintain a gap of four generations from mother's side and eight generations from father's side before marrying (Sharma : 2000) a girl. But since the plantation is consisting of families emigrated from various parts of Sikkim, North-East India and 7.5% from Nepal, it is not possible to marry within own Gotra (clan) which was restricted or prohibited in the past. The concept of endogamy and exogamy of the past is hardly found to have been affecting the marriage alliances in the plantation today. The *Satto Bibaha* (marriage by bride exchange) among the Tagadharis is not taking place as the garden does not provide jobs to two wives of same person in the plantation. The concept of *Jat Danda* (penalty for breach of endogamy) as found in agrarian Sikkim is no more in vogue in the plantation.

The Religious Practices

Though the religious practices related to Hindu, Buddhist and Christian religions are different, the nature of performing the religious rituals is predominantly tribal or Matwali.

The Table 11.11 portrays the fact that predominantly the Temi Society is Buddhist in nature though 43.1% of Rai, 15.9% of Limbu, 3.5% of Tamang are Hindus by religion, they practice animistic form of rituals and festivals like Lossang, (day three Tibetan Lamas met in Sikkim) and Losar (Tibetan New Year) are more popular than *Dasai* (Dashara) at the plantation. So, practically speaking, excepting Bahun, Chhetri, Manger, Kami, Bihari and Damai, other castes and tribes are as good as Buddhists. Interestingly, 59.8% of Gurungs are Buddhists here by religion. The tribe like Sherpa and Bhutia are purely Buddhists along with Tamangs. Again, 14.5% of households have Christian religion. Among the Kirantis (Rai and Limbu), the percentage of Christian Rai (25.6%) and Limbu (30.8%) is very high as depicted from the Table 11.11. Again, 17.9% of Damais and 12.8% of Kamis are Christians, while Tamang (2.6%), Sherpa (2.6%) and Gurung (7.7%) have been converted into Christianity due to the fact that it appears to be an alternative to survive in the whole Eastern Himalayas and Sikkim also.

Among the Hindus, there are many followers of Sai Baba Dharma. In total, fifty per cent of Hindus are the followers of Sai Baba. The religion like Buddhism, Christianity and Sai Baba Dharma have their own organisational structure. This may be the apparent reason why slowly the Gurungs are reverting to their original Buddhist religion. But Hindus donot have any concrete organisation as this is found among other religions. This is the main reason why they have been the stuant followers of Sai Baba Dharma today at the garden as Sai Dharma mainly reflects the Hindus cult.

Among the Bhutias, Tibetan Refuguees about thirty thousand in Sikkim celebrate Losar while the original Sikkimese Sherpas considered themselves to be pure Buddhists than Bhutias (Refugees and Sikkimese Bhutias) and Lepchas as they are not the followers of lamaist Buddhism. While Bhutias are purely lamaist Buddhists. They first worship lamas headed by Dalai Lama and then Lord Buddha. Inspite of various religious faiths that the workers have at the plantation, the participation in common festivals which we will discuss in the next chapter, like Saga Dawa, Phang, Lobsal, Lossang, Losar,

Table 11.11.
Caste/Tribe and Religions of the Workers

Sl. No.	*Caste/Tribe*	*Hindu*	*% age*	*Budd-hist*	*% age*	*Christ-ian*	*% age*
	Tagadhari Jharra						
1.	Bahun = 5	5	4.4	-	-	-	-
	Thimaha						
2.	Chhetri = 15	15	13.3	-	-	-	-
3.	Bihari = 1	1	0.9	-	-	-	-
	Matwali Setho						
4.	Manger = 5	5	4.4	-	-	-	-
5.	Gurung = 90	17	15.0	70	59.8	3	7.7
6.	Rai = 40	30	26.5	-	-	10	25.6
7.	Limbu = 30	18	15.9	-	-	12	30.8
8.	Newar = 2	-	-	2	1.7	-	-
9.	Tamang = 35	4	3.5	30	25.6	1	2.6
10.	Sherpa = 12	-	-	11	9.4	1	2.6
11.	Bhutia = 4	-	-	4	3.4	-	-
	Kalo						
12.	Kami = 15	10	8.5	-	-	5	12.8
13.	Damai = 15	8	7.1	-	-	7	17.9
	Total = 269	**113**	**42%**	**117**	**43.1%**	**39**	**14.5%**

Source : Field Work : 2001.

Dasai, Tihar, Bhai Tika and Makar Sagranti of the workers are equally important. Even they participate in observing Christmas (Bara Din), if called for. It is the participation of various castes and tribes in festivals of all religions that characterised the Temi Tea Estate a Hindu-Buddhist contact zone (Haimendorf : 1966) of Sikkim Himalaya. The rituals or festivals of all religious groups are the admixture of animism and Hinduism. However, it is revealed from this study that a sort of cultural approximation between tribalism (Matwalisation) and Hinduism with modern processes among Tagadharis and Matwalis is emerging (Sharma : 1999) in the tea industry of Sikkim. Even if a Buddhist does not invite a neighbour Hindu in Lossang or Lossar, *Bhag* or Losar Share consisting of ritual food items like sweet, *Tongba (Chyang)* or in Nepali it is called *Jnar* or *Nigar,* fruits etc. are presented to the Hindu households. Similar process is followed in case of Hindu households to other religious neighbours if not invited at the host households. Observing the *Gaon Puja* (village god festival), all castes and tribes do equally participate no matter they have various religious backgrounds.

It is also observed that a Christian take *Tika* (coloured grinded rice mark at the forehead) from a Hindu girl who is made as good as his own sister by the Christian man. Another issue is the *Rakhi* in the month of September every year when various religious people of male group accept *Rakhi* from ladies and these ladies are treated as their own sisters. Even the Bhutias also accept the *Tika* and *Rakhis* from the Hindu sisters. All castes and tribes of Temi Tea Estate accept *prasad* (food items being propitiated at the pujas) from other religious neighbours. Thus, common neighbourhood has enabled the workers to be the part and parcel of the society at the tea industry of Sikkim.

Health Practices of the Workers

The health practices of the workers at Temi Tea Estate has two facets, viz., concept of Diseases and measures for treatment (Sharma : 1997). Having agrarian background of recent past of the workers, they have ample knowledge about traditional herbal plants to cure the patients. Besides this, they have a deep confidence over the secrets of exorcism duly practice by *Jhankris* or Shamen (Macdonald : 1976). By disease, they use to believe the misfortunes which can be cured through secret Mantras (Prayer of incarnations) of Jhankris (Berreman: 1972) at their homes. But use of the herbal plants is vanishing here due to the rampant deforestation in Sikkim (Hooker : 1855) and at Temi also. These herbal plants are going to extinct and thereby the knowledge of such herbal plant is also decreasing among the present generation of Temi Tea Estate (Rai and Sharma : 1994). This has also caused for the non-existence of adequate number of traditional caste and tribal Jhankris or Shamen. Excepting two Jhankris, there is no other Jhankri in the garden. Thus, the present generation mainly opts for medical doctors for treatment of their diseased family members. But inspite of this change, use of Jhankri is found to a great extent among all castes and tribes. The concept of Satto Ganu (nervous breakdown) of children due to devil attacks is still found among the workers a firm belief. The *Fa-Foo* (prayer of Jhankris) is still done in the households of the workers to evade out the demons (evil spirit) from the body of the diseased members of the households. To do *Sargyam* is to satisfy the evil spirits so that no disturbance takes place at the households of the workers. Again, *Chinta* (Puja by Jhankris) with drum beating is done in the households in black nights. The *Jogis* (ascetics) roam around the households with a horn sound of human bones at nights are presented with rice, money, oil, salt, ginger, a black trouser piece, a piece of iron rod, fruits etc. to satisfy the evils spirits (Bhut Pisach) and to have favourable stars for the members of the households. On the whole, it is seen that health practices are the concern of individual households as the garden management do not bother about it.

The garden workers has altogether ten *Bhatis* (liquor hearths) where at the evenings, most male workers assemble, chatt and drink local *Bhatti* made *Rakshi, Jnar* (nigar) or *Tongba* (Chiyang) made of fermented rice or millets. Almost 50% of the income of male workers are spent for such alcohol in the plantation. Fifty per cent of households attend their toilet/urinals at *Jhora* (rivulets) and *Kholas*. They go to hospitals only on the moment when patients become very serious. Maintenance of good health as an integral part of quality of life is found to be very vague among the workers of all castes and tribes of the plantation. This may be the reason why ninety nine percent of enrolled patients at the garden dispensary is succumbed to Tuberculosis diseases.

12

THE PLANTATION WORKERS—THEIR CUSTOMS AND TRADITIONS

It is observed in the present study that the various castes and tribes intermingle freely in Temi Tea Estate and it appears from the study that they constitute a homogeneous blend. It is also observed that after settlement in the garden, various cultural and economic forces are reshaping the way of life of the workers in different way.

It is also observed that unlike in agrarian Sikkim, the women workers are not confined at home and hearth. In all public places of Temi, the roles of women are equally important as in the garden. In fact, it is observed that women folk carried all their customs, traditions and culture in the society along with males.

As mentioned in earlier chapters, multi-cultural blending are found at Temi in various levels among which foods and drinks is most primordial one. Let us discuss about the main foods and drinks that bind all the castes and tribes at the plantation. All the castes and tribes have internalise these foods and drinks in their daily socio-cultural life.

Basically the plantation workers are rice eaters. Alcoholic drinks are popular equally among the males and females at least at homes. The beef eating is very common due to cold climate and cheap cost. All the castes and tribes are fond of *Momos* and *Thukpas*. A typical type of diet of workers is *dal-bhat* (lentils and rice) with meat for breakfast, a light tiffin and early dinner in the night.

Momo

Momo is very popular Tibetan or Bhutia diet among the plantation workers. It is prepared by stuffing minced meat, vegetables or cheese in flour dough and then moulding them in the form of dumplings. These are then steamed for about half an hour in a three tiered utensils that has bone or tomato soup in the lowest compartment. Steam from the boiling soup rises through the perforations in the containers above and cooks the dumplings. *Momos* are taken alongwith the soup with home made chilly sauce. Momo is found in all the restaurants. Whenever the workers go to bazar, they rush to the restaurants for momos irrespective of caste or tribal background. Even at a party organises at home, people prepare the *Momos*.

Thukpa

It is a noodle soup with meat and vegetables. *Thukpa* is more economical in nature as one *Pela* (full bole of a small vessel) can fill up the stomach of a person. *Thukpa* is more preferred by the workers than *Momo* due to the above mentioned reason.

Phangshas

The *Phangshas* is strips of pork fat stewed with radishes and dried chillies. This meat is very popular among the Matwalis and tribals in the plantation. While Tagadharis do not take *Phangshas* especially who do priestly jobs in the plantation.

Apart from the above food items of Bhutia origin, certain Nepali food items are equally important among the workers of all castes and tribes in the plantation. These food items are delineated below.

Seal Roti

This Nepali cusine is prepared by grinding a mixture of rice and water into a paste. The paste is then poured into hot oil pan and deeply fried. It is normally eaten with potato curry. Normally it is not available in restaurants but widely prepared during festivals and parties. Earlier the Sikkimese tribes did not know to prepare *Seal Roti* but now they have accepted to prepare it due to the Nepali neighbours who prefer *Seal Roti* even in the tribal festivals and at the time of observance of rituals at the houses of tribes. Sharing of *Seal Roti* has become a symbol of integration among castes and tribes in the plantation in general and in rural belts in particular of Sikkim Himalaya.

Niguru with Churpi

The *Niguru* is a local fiddlehead fern and its tendrils when light fried with Churpi (Cheese) form an irresistible dish. In fact, *Niguru* is a Nepali invention while *Churpi* the Bhutia invention. Interestingly both are mingled with and prepared a tasty dish. Thus, eating of this *Niguru-Churpi* by all castes and tribes shows a complete area of cultural coexistence in the plantation. The dish invariably attracts all people of the garden and region.

Gundruk

Gundruk, the Nepali food item are leaves of mustard oil plant that have been allowed to decay for some days and dried in the sun. These dried leaves are then cooked alongwith onions and tomatos and forms a tasty dish.

Gundruk helps the people not only to eat but also to cure gastric troubles. *Gundruk* is very popular among the workers of all castes and tribes. The Bhutia workers are found asking the Nepali neighbours to purchase *Gundruk* in the plantation.

Chang (Thogbas or Nigar/Jnar)

The local made liquor has received top names from Nepali-Bhutia workers. In Nepali it is called *Nigar* or *Jnar* and in Bhutia it is called *Chang.* This drink item has closely integrates the Bhutias, Nepalis and Lepchas in general and in particular at Temi of Sikkim. Without it no ritual or festival is completed. Rather people feel *Khalloo* (sour) if the drink item is not there in the festivals and rituals and other parties in the plantation. It is sipped from bamboo receptacle using a bamboo pipe. The receptacle which has millet in it is topped with warm water a couple of times until the millet loses its potency. *Chang* or *Niger* sometimes be strong and very intoxicating indeed. The *chang* is a must in observing the rituals among the Matwalis and tribals. Without *Jnar* the rituals can not be completed in the households of the Matwalis and tribals. Providing *Chang or Nigar* is a mark of respect for the guests at the Matwali and tribal households.

Besides the above mentioned food and drink items, other cultural items of popularity among the workers are *Sinki* (dried fermented vegetables), *Kinema* (fermented soya beans), *Taava* (bamboo fermented shots), *Rayo Sag* (Mustard leaves) etc. are common foods of integration among the workers of various castes and tribes of the plantation. *Rayo Sag* (mustard oil), *Daloo-Khorsani* (Royal Chilli), *Kalo Dal* (Black Lentil), *Simrayo* (Marshy vegetables) are also common vegetables for all castes and tribes.

Cultural Games and Amusement

There are many cultural games which have really bind all the communities. Though in the origin, specific castes and tribes had their own games and amusement but now they have all become the integral part of the games and amusements of the workers as a whole in the plantation. Following are main sports and games of the workers.

Archery

The archery was purely a tribal game in the past. The archery is found to be very popular among the Lepchas and Bhutias of the plantation. But these days, Nepalis also participate in the archary competition. This is a much loved outdoor game and played during the festival months of December and January by Lepchas and Bhutias. The archary is made of bows and arrows of bamboos and the target each measuring about 39 by 100 metres length. Altogether 11 archers constitute each team with each participant shooting with 2 arrows. The method of calculation scores is quite complex as arrows that land close to the target also win points. The team that first scores 33 points wins the match. Spectators and team members stand along the range and dodge misfired arrow with dexterity. During the break, the spectators and team members stand along with the range and partake to the local beer (Jnar) and snaks in the lawns. The whole atmosphere is that of festivity. Archery competitions are held in which not only the plantation workers but also outsiders do participate actively. Unlike in the past, it is found today that the team for archery is consisting of all castes or tribes in toto who do freely participate. This is another area of cultural integration in Sikkim in general and Temi Tea Estate in particular.

Majog

It is essentially a Chinese game being brought by the Bhutias in Temi. It is something like a dice game. During festivals this game is played by all the castes and tribes in the plantation.

Chawri or Dice

This is very popular dice game and is played using two dices which are snaken in wooden bowl which is then upturned on a leather starp with a loud thump and a shout. The score is kept using small sea shells which are known as *Chawris*. The workers are fond of playing the dice game.

The Folk Dances of the Workers

Another area of workers participation in the multicultural universe of Temi Tea Estate is folk dances of various tribes and castes. The folk dances and songs are an ingrained part of the workers. Most of the dances relate to the beauty of natural surroundings, some depict the harvest season and others are performed for goodluck and prosperity. Many of the musical instruments that accompany the dances are unique to Temi. Some of the popular dances of Temi are described below where the participation of workers is uniform as these dances are performed by all castes and tribes. Let us first start with the Nepali folk dances.

Maruni Dance

Although the Maruni dance is closely associated with the festival of Tihar meaning thereby the 'Festival of Light'. Because of its popularity, it is performed even in occasion like marriages. Tihar is celebrated in the memory of return of Rama from exile. During this festival *Maruni* dancers nicely dressed in colourful dresses and respond with rich ornaments and nosering called 'dungris' go on a house to house visit. The dances are usually accompanied by a clown called *Dhatu-Waray.* Sometimes the *Maruni* dances are performed with accompaniment of nine instruments orchestra known as 'Naumati Baja'. Like participating in games and other amusements, workers of all castes and tribes participate in the *Maruni* dances. Even some people participate in the *Maruni* team, others of all castes and tribes become the close observers of the dance and enjoy equally on the moments. The *Maruni* dance was inherited from the Mangers and Gurungs of Nepal and from agrarian Sikkim.

Tamang Selo

The *Tamang Selo* is associated with the Tamang caste of Nepali community. In olden days, only Tamangs used to have *Tamang Selo* dance. But now it is a part and parcel of culture of Nepali as well as other tribes of the plantation. The *Tanmang Selo* dance is performed to the rhythmic sound of *Damphu* (a musical instrument) and therefore, also called 'Damphu Dance'. The Nepali *Jhaure* Songs and *Tamang Selo* are important folk songs and dances for the plantation society today. All the castes and tribes treat *Tamang Selo* as common dance of the Himalayan society.

Tibetan Folk Dance—Tashi Sabdo

This dance is perform to honour the yak, an animal on which man is completely dependent upon for survival in the higher altitudes of the Himalayas.

Tibetan Yak Dance

This dance is performed by all the castes and tribes of the plantation especially in winter seasons.

Apart from the above mentioned dances, other dances like Subba Chebrung dance, Bhutia Talachi, Tibetan Singhi Chamm, Sherpa Sebru Naach, Gurung Sorathi, Bhutia Lu-Kharig Thamo, Lepcha Kar Gnpk, Bhutia Gna-to-Kiti, Lepcha Dharma Jo, Bhutia Be-Yul-mista, Lepcha Mon-Dyak-Lok, Nepali *Dhann Naach,* Bhutia *Chi Rimu* etc. are also known to each and every caste and tribe of the plantation.

Festivals in the Hindu-Buddhist Contact Zone : Temi Tea Estate

In the following section of the study, we will see the various festivals of Hindus and Buddhists of the plantation. Let us start with the Hindu festivals.

Dasain

The fortnight long festival usually falls in the month of September or October every year. The festival is also understood the festival on the triumph of Durga Ma over the evil forces. On the first day barley seeds are sown in the soil and their growth a few inches foretells a good harvest. The next important day a week latter is *Fulpati* meaning the day of flowers. *Maha Astami* and *Kal Ratri* follow *Fulpati* festival. The next day is *Nawami* and also marks the victory of Rama over Rawana. During next day, people smear their foreheads with coloured rice and barley sprouts which were sown on the first day of *Dasain* and picked and placed over ears. It is observed that on this day (Dasami) youngers get the coloured *Tika* from elders and respected persons irrespective of castes or tribal backgrounds. The non-Hindus neighbours are invited for parties. *Bhoj* is given to the non-Hindu neighbours of the plantation as *Gaulees* (Co-inhabitants) of the same habitation i.e. plantation. A *Sarwajanik Durga Puja* was held in the plantation where all the people of the garden participated. Interestingly, even the Christians also participate in such *Sarwajanik Puja* done in the plantation.

Tihar

This is the festival of lights and it symbolises the return of Rama from his exile. During the festival, animals are honoured on successive days. The first day is *Kag Tiwar* which is dedicated to crows and they are offered rice and some of crows are even garlanded. On the second day, which is known as 'Kukkur Tihar' when dogs are garlanded and given rice. On the third day i.e. *Gai Tihar,* the cows are garlanded and their horns are painted with bright colour. Now it is the turn of bullocks on the next day. The *Depawali* which falls on the third day is considered to be most important day as believed by the workers that on that day goddess Laxmi comes for visiting the home. Every home is lit bright with candles and electric lights. The fifth day is also known as *Bhai Tika* in which the brothers visit the sisters' houses and they apply *Tika* (vermillion powder) to each others' foreheads. It is also an occasion for exchanging gifts. During *Tihar,* traditional carol known *Deusi* and *Bailo* are sung from one house to another in which a group of youngsters (mainly) form a team and do *deusi* and *bailo* with gale and giety. Even if the Christians do not celebrate the Tihar, they participate in *Deusi* and *Bailo.* All other religious people also respect the *Tihar* festival equally with their own festival and attend the Hindu households if called for. Even some of the people participate in *Deusi* and *Bailo* groups of Hindus.

Saraswati Puja

This puja is held at the plantation level in which all participate freely without any hesitation. Even the management personnel have seen participating in the Puja day.

Magh Sankranti

This festival takes place in January every year. Fairs are held in the banks of rivers or confluence of two rivers. In such festival, the workers of all castes and tribes assemble and enjoy with foods, Seal-Roti, ground- nuts etc.

From the above, it can be said that unlike other caste ridden society of the country or agrarian Sikkim, the festivals have embraced all the religious groups into one homogeneous team of the plantation. In fact, these festivals have become the cultural alternatives rather than religious dogmatism as we found in other parts of the country, as Hindu festivals there are observed only by the Hindus. Similar is the case with other religious festivals.

Saga Dawa

This is the Triple Blessed Festivals and is considered as the holiest of the holy Buddhist festivals. On this day in different years of his life Buddha took birth, achieved enlightenment and passed away attaining Nirvana. Interestingly in this festival, all are found participating with foods, profession and liquors in the organised ways by the Bhutias.

Lhabab Dhucchen

This festival symbolises the descent of Buddha from the heaven with thirty-three gods after visiting his mother. Dhucchen means festival, Lha means heaven and Bab means descent. All the castes and tribes participate in this festival in the plantation.

Drukpa Teshi

This festival is celebrated in the memory of Buddha's first preaching of Buddhism at Sarnath with his five disciples, on nobel truths of human life like suffering, origin of suffering, cessation of suffering, Nirvana etc. This festival comes in the month of August when all the people participate if called for in the Buddhist households.

Phang Labsol

In this festival, the snowy range of Kanchangunga is worshipped. This festival is marked the signing of treaty of brotherhood between Bhutia and Lepcha. Phang means witness. This festival is also celebrated in the month of August. Like other festivals, all the people participate in this festival also freely if called for.

Lossong Festival

Lossong marks the end of harvest season and also the end of the Tibetan tenth month of the Tibetan year. In this occasion, Chaam dances are done in which evil spirits are evaded and good spirits are invited. In this festival normally the non-Buddhists attend the dance and share with foods and drinks as the mark of respect to the festival.

Lossar

It is the Tibetan New Year in the month of February every year. All the people of the plantation are invited with foods and drinks along with meat and *Chaang* (Tongba) prepared since couple of months in the households of the Bhutias.

Bumchu

This festival is celebrated in the month of January every year. In the festival, the holy water given by Lama is given to all the people as festival water which is accepted by all castes and tribes of the plantation.

The Kalchakra Puja

This festival is done in the memory of mystic aspects of the Buddhism. The Kalchakra is considered another form of Viswamata. Like other Buddhist festivals, this festival is also attended by all people with warm greetings to the Buddhist host households.

From the above discussion, it is understood that Hinduism and Buddhism co-exists at Temi Tea Estate though people donot bother the real meaning of the festivals rather they are concerned with the neighbours. The participation is accentuated by their acceptance for co-existence of all religions and people believing various religious faiths in the plantation.

The Mit System

Another string for restoring or sustaining the Hindu-Buddhist contact zone in Temi Tea Estate is the institution of *Mit* System in the plantation industry. The *Mit* system may take place between both sexes or sometimes the two persons of the same sex. All the Nepalis, Bhutias or Sherpas and even between the high castes and low castes of Nepali community may have *Mit* relationship. The meaning of *Mit* is friend. The *Mit* relationship takes place among the bosom friends also. Thus, the meaning of *Mit* connotes friend which has been compared with making a 'Blood relationship or blood brotherhood/blood sisterhood'. This relationship can be contacted between men or women of different castes, tribes and community who are already related with one another for a pretty long time. Once contacted, the new relationship thus formed holds good on marriages and other ceremonies. In any ritual or ceremony the *Mits* must be invited in the host *Mit* households.

No marriage takes place between the sons and daughters of two *Mits*. At the death of a *Mit* family members another *Mit* has to strictly observe the ritual. The majority of the Matwalis have *Mit* relationship among themselves in the plantation. It is also observed that Bahun-Chhetri-Manger workers have *Mit* relationship among themselves. Many Buddhist Bhutias Sherpas and Tamangs in the plantation have *Mits*. It is because of the fact that *Mit* was there among the Kings of Nepal and in Sikkim by the Bhutia Chowgels with the people of Nepal and North-East India to exploit the agrarian resources of Sikkim. However, now the *Mit* system has became very effective instrument for social cohesion among the various castes and tribes in the plantation of Temi. If the *Mit* relationship is violated in regard to marriage or other rituals then following customary punishment is given to the accused persons.

As per the old laws of *Mit* System it is applied in the way that if any one takes a *Mit's* daughter or wife, he is punished; have his hands cut off or his penis cut off, of course, secretly in the jungle. He may also have to pay a weight in kind equal to his penis and testicles. If the wife of a *Mit* goes with his *Mit* then the same rule is applied to the absconded women. In other words, should one *Mit's* wife entice by another *Mit* or sons of the *Mit* then she has to pay seven things to her original husband.

After paying the fines the new couple is asked to leave the plantation within twenty four hours. So, it is hardly found any people violating the *Mit* rules in the plantation during the last thirty years of its establishment. It is also found that even management is very particular with the question of *Mit* relationship.

Another interesting string to integrate the plantation workers is the concept of *Afno Manchees* (own men) and *Arka Manchees,* (not related persons). This concept appears to be very important for sustaining the pre-industrial form of industrial (production) relation in the plantation. Though they are completely exploited they do not openly talk against the management as the management personnel are their *Afno Machees.* This concept is ingrained in the minds of the workers that hardly allow them to talk against the management.

The above customs and traditions of the Himalayan culture and history have helped the plantation to somehow stretch forward in the Hindu-Buddhist contact zone of Sikkim Himalaya amid the changes brought about by the liberalisation, privatisation and globalisation policy of Government of India.

SUMMARY AND CONCLUSION

The Sociological study on Temi Tea Estate is a denovo effort in the literature of plantation society in India. Hardly any study has been done on Temi Tea Estate so far. The present study is an addition to the literature of plantation workers in India. More specifically, the present study is a piece of research work done to comprehend the changing socio-economic development of Temi Tea Plantation Workers in Sikkim and also to see the nature of socio-cultural existence of various castes and tribes in the industrial environment after their settlement in the garden from the agrarian background of Sikkim and Nepal.

I

The Temi plantation was started in 1968 by the Government of Sikkim after it failed to grow tea plants at Kewzing area of South Sikkim. The Temi garden was started on an experimental basis in 1968 with 20 acres of land from the Forest Department of Government of Sikkim. Aftermath, due to the favourable ecology and adequate manpower supply from Nepali community, the garden was expanded to 172 hectares or 500 acres of land under cultivation.

The Temi garden is located at the distance of 22 km. from Namchi, the district headquarters of South Sikkim and 35 km. from Singtam town of East Sikkim. In 1977, a factory was started at Temi for manufacturing tea at the commercial basis.

The elevation of the garden is from 4,800 ft. to 6,200 ft. above the sea level and it is a South faced garden. The twin objectives behind the opening of Temi garden at South Sikkim by the Government of Sikkim were to: (*a*) provide employment for local Sikkimese Nepalis, and (*b*) rehabilitate the Tibetan refugees. It shows that the garden workers were to be recruited from among the Tibetan Refugees and local Nepalis. It is transparent from this study that Tibetan migration had still been continuing then in Sikkim from the main land of Tibetans. The study found that Sikkim Government had given the refugees with the status of 'sons of the soil' till 1968.

From the study, it is found that 98% of workers are Nepalis and 2% are tribes at Temi Tea Estate. Among the existing 400 workers, only 80 are tribes from Sherpa, Bhutia and Tamang tribes. Not a single Lepcha worker is there at the garden. Nepalis were preferred in the garden as workers by the management due to their agrarian legacy supported by the culture of terraced cultivation in the entire Himalayas. So, Nepalis appeared not only the proponents of terraced cultivation in the Himalayas but also the exponents of industrial development suitable to the Sikkimese ecology.

II

It is observed in the study that the Hindu-Tribal socio-cultural relations at Temi being the Hindu-Buddhist contact zone is apparently a symbiotic one. The present Nepali workers used to do divergent agrarian works prior to their migration to Temi Tea Estate.

Looking at the sustainable capacity of Temi Tea Estate, it is observed that generally the ownership of tea garden with the hands of government has reaped discouraging results all over the country. But Temi is a government enterprise having Tea Board of Sikkim at the top of management hierarchy under the Ministry of Industries, Government of Sikkim. The changes of ownership of the garden from the department of Forest till 1974 to Industries to date gathered a lot of successful experiences and visions for the development of tea industry in Sikkim. Again, the industry is supervised by the head of department of Industries, Forest, Agriculture and Finance corporately under the banner of Tea Board of Sikkim. Exploring the reasons for its sustenance, it is found that the following factors have contributed a lot, (a) Low cost of production, (b) Non-payment of Gratuity, (c) Minimum Bonus, (d) Non-payment for educational facility to the children of the workers, electricity, drinking water, recreation facility etc. Only Rs. 50 as daily wages are given to the workers of the garden. Even the housing facility in regard to materials and building cost of houses are not given to the workers. Recently after 1998, the provident fund scheme has been launched in the garden. The family pension scheme under the Provident Fund is a remote dream for the garden workers. All the employees are non-pensionable work force in the garden. Again, creche facility as well as toilet and urinals are not provided in the garden for the workers.

Many problems started since its inception (1968) became more precarious after 2000 August when Temi tea was ousted from Darjeeling Logo in the national and international markets. After August, 2000, the prices of Temi tea is continuously falling from Rs. 800 to Rs. 1000 to Rs. 100 to Rs. 200 per kilogram. Even the packet tea made at Temi having its own brand named as 'Kanchendzonga' and 'Solja' have hardly fetching the price of Rs. 94 per kg. However, 55% of leaf grade of the garden attracts the international market and remaining 45% is blended for the internal market at Kolkata Auction Centre.

It is also found that the workers buy necessary things at Temi Bazar where mostly the shopkeepers are Bhutias of Tibet background. So, Bhutias have shifted their profession from industrial (Kewzing) to petty trade and business which is their traditional occupation in the entire Himalayas and in Tibet also. This is the reason why only the Nepalis have accepted the tea garden jobs wholeheartedly whether they are Tagadharis or Matwalis. The garden works have substantiated agriculture with animal husbandry as both go hand in hand in the Nepali society in the past and also today in the tea garden economy which provides this opportunity. This is because of the fact that Temi Tea Estate has sufficient waste land where the cattle fodders are easily available to the Nepali agrarian people. This might be one of plausible reasons why Tibetan refugees not being agriculturists, failed to adapt with the plantation-agricultural environment of Temi. Still another reason as observed in Temi is that the garden job required lot of perseverance of manual type while the petty trade and business do not required such physical perseverance as historically Tibetan refugees were not accustomed to such physical perseverance of manual type. This is the actual reason why the Tibetan refugees left tea garden job.

III

The interactions between the Hindus and Tribals at Temi have been shaped to the tune of industrial environment having specific objectives in the changed global economy. The ongoing political turmoil between the *Nakchuchees* and *Nak Thapchees* in Sikkim has also affected the Hindu-Tribal relationship at Temi. The management hierarchy is completely dominated by the *Nak Thapchees.*

At the garden level, it has been further noted that the workers do not expect anything extra than normal wages that they get for their labour as being fixed by the Department of Industries of Government of Sikkim which wholly considers the interest of industry first than the welfare of the workers.

It is, therefore, explored from the study that the workers keep themselves busy with non-plantation agriculture and animal husbandry. This is widely supported by the fact that Temi butter is very famous in Sikkim and even in the hill areas of Darjeeling District. It is observed that off 400 workers of the garden, 350 have animal husbandry along with agriculture economy.

It is also explored in the study that Temi Tea Estate is passing through a tough time to survive amid the challenges brought about by the liberalisation of Indian economy. The garden management remains busy attending the bureaucrats of the government of Sikkim and outside agencies. This made the garden workers apathetic to the development process of the industry on the ground that Temi is a government garden or government property and workers have nothing to bother about its future. Of course, this pinches the mind of the workers because they have no avenue to ventilate their ideas or grievances as they do not have organisation of their own. In these ways, it can be said that they are unorganised workers in the clear sense of the term. To form a trade union at Temi means to violate the terms and conditions of service in the garden. It is equally observed that hardly any worker dares to talk about the formation of workers organisation. This has accelerated by the tempo of state anti-labour policy which discourages the unionisation process in the industry, in the light of Indian Trade Union Act, 1926. In fact, most of the labour legislations of Government of India have not been so far adopted at the small scale industries of Sikkim and in Temi Tea Estate also. It means that whatever the welfare facilities provided to them have to be accepted by the workers at the garden. It indicates that the workers are still in colonial system of production relation. The management is management by profession. Even if a manager wants to be the well wisher of the workers he cannot simply do it on his own for the workers. In this way, workers are exploited. Of course, no apparent exploitation of workers is found here but it exists in covert form as prevalent in the unorganised sector of the State of Sikkim.

The garden workers of Sikkim Himalaya have been hardly come across by the concept of trade union movement and working class solidarity. They have been overshadowed and overwhelmed by the regional concept of 'Sons of the Soil' policy of the Government of Sikkim (Basnet : 1974). This is found to be the main reason for their silent exploitation by the management system which is very much organised in the sense that hierarchically there is a manager, assistant managers, supervisory and clerical staffs who with the suggestions of the Ministry of Industries, Government of Sikkim organise the activities of the industry in the modern fashion.

The tea industry instead of being a production unit is considered as an unit of government process of industrialisation under the various five year plans. Thus, the organisational goals of Temi Tea Estate and of the government appear to be polar opposites resulting which the strategy for Temi development is contradictory to each other. This fact has been nicely supported by the resignation of a manager having two decades of his rich experience in Temi Tea Estate. The irony of the fact is that everybody speaks high about the Temi tea but nobody speaks about the organisational hardship that has to be judiciously overcome by the working people involved in day-to-day production activities of the garden.

IV

The Nepali tea garden-workers in the Himalayan niche are found to be the custodials of agricultural environment through which their industrialisation process has added extra stimulus for their better livelihood, of course, an optional one. For garden workers, agriculture minus industry is not a misnomer while industry minus agriculture is either unrealistic or unpractical. This is the reason why inspite of having organised exploitation they have been sticked to the tea industry job. Had there been any other community of the region like Bhutia and Lepcha, then today Temi Tea Estate would be as good as rural belt as we found surrounding Temi. As mentioned above, the primary objective for opening Temi Tea Estate to rehabilitate the Tibetan refugees by the Government of Sikkim is proved to be a futile exercise today. Rather the second objective of its original strategy to accommodate the local Nepalis has reaped a meaningful justification for the process of industrial development of Sikkim. Regarding the preference for tea garden job, it is found that almost all the workers give secondary importance to it. This is a different story in Temi than in other tea gardens of West Bengal and Assam where more and more people want to get the tea garden jobs.

The Temi Tea Estate is found to be a purely Hindu-Buddhist contact zone of the industrialisation process of Sikkim. It is found that other ecological zones of Sikkim are exclusively meant for specific communities (Sengupta: 1970). The three major communities of Sikkim like Nepali, Bhutia and Lepcha have respective culturo-ecological zones or cultural niches (Desai : 1983) of their own. For instance, Lepchas have North zone, Bhutias the East zone and Nepalis the West and South zones of Sikkim. As it is observed that such ecological niche of respective community have associated with the specific migration history in Sikkim in general and Temi Tea Estate in particular. Take for instance, Nepalis had easy access to Sikkim in early 15th century from South and West Sikkim which once happened to be under the kingdom of Nepal. The Tibetan migration taken place in Sikkim mainly from adjoining Gangtok (East), while Lepchas pushed to the Northern Sikkim after the Bhutias started to convert them into Buddhist religion in early 16th century. Thus, Temi is found to be a zone of integration as Nepalis and Bhutias/tribals are simultaneously living in the same industrial habitation (environment).

V

Studying the garden workers, it is found that they get information regarding Temi and labour-management relations from the supervisory staffs. Being ignorant about the terms and conditions of their service, workers have no idea about the concept and implication of industrial relations in the tea estate. Lack of government mechanisms for restoring harmonious industrial relations has also helped to keep the workers in darkness and therefore, the darkness is appeared to be their destiny. The darkness has helped the workers to be apathetic to the industry. Such apathy could sustain the 'Plantocracy' at Temi throughout its period of development. The 'plantocracy' means the democracy in the plantation of its own type as set forth by the management of the garden. Management always try to discourage the workers from going down to Singtam or Namchi towns where they can easily mix up with the people hailing from the wider society. This might be the background why management distributes weekly wages in the morning hours of weekly holiday itself so that the workers donot get time to go down to Singtam or Namchi towns for marketing etc.

All these developments have created a kind of uncertainty in the minds of the workers. The workers always feel of their alienation from the garden on the ground that neither the management nor government of Sikkim really guide them on right perspectives. This has encouraged some of the workers to involve themselves in anti-social activities like drug addiction, theft, drinking alcohol, double marriages, blue film shows etc. etc. in the garden resulting which the whole lot of incoming generation have been spoiling their lives. This might be the reason why some workers who have better financial position send their children outside for education and better exposure. This is limited among the rich families only.

In fact, what really happened at Temi is that neither management nor government do really feel the hardship of the workers. In the name of organisational development, the workers are messed in the garden today as the socio-economic development of workers has adversely affected today. This has resulted into the total deadluck of working class in the industry. An intellectual said at Temi that what is the utility of keeping welfare provisions in the Department of Industries of Government of Sikkim or in Indian constitution. Whatever the welfare facilities are provided is farse in the sense that nature of providing the benefits is rather an eye wash to the workers.

VI

Again, studying the Hindu-Tribal relationship between *Nak Chuchees* and *Nak Thapchees,* it is found that marriages across the castes of each group and Nepali language as *lingua franca* are two important inherent strings to knit the Hindus and tribals together at Temi. If a Nepali boy marries a tribal girl, both communities accept such marriage and as per their respective traditions bless the married couples with *Tika-Talo* (Coloured rice at the forehead with blessings for happy and prosperous life). It is also found that the *Lingua Franca* of Bhutias, Sherpas, Tamangs and Bihari is Nepali. Though Lepchas, Limbus, Bhutias (tribals) have their respective languages being taught at the schools and colleges, ninety percent of the tribal students study Nepali as first language in Temi Tea Estate.

In regard to their participation in socio-economic and cultural activities, both Hindus and tribals participate freely without any difference. The involvement of workers in cultural festivals like Durga Puja, Tihar, Saga Dawa, Lhabsols, Dhueechen, Drukpa Teshi, Phang Lhabsol, Losoong, Lossar, Bumchu, Bhai Tika, Rakhi, Makar Sankranti etc. in the isolated enclave help to forget their disparity, animosity and unequal political mileage created by the politicians and bureaucrats of Sikkim (Chakraborty: 2001) during elections.

The industrial development of Temi has been unfortunately sensed to be the workers' development by the management while workers' sense of development is somewhat different in the sense that they hardly think of industry as the primary source of their development. The rise and fall of Temi Tea Estate is due to the indifferent attitude of management. The survival question of Temi Tea Estate had hardly felt by the management and government till 1999 or 2000. The over bureaucratic outlook of Tea Board of Sikkim is responsible factor for the sickness of the garden. The garden appears to be nobody's headache. Inspite of detoriation of the garden in terms of productivity, the garden is still sustaining under the protective umbrella of Government of Sikkim.

The Tea industry has adapted the tribals, Matwalis and Hindus to internalise the cultural traits of diffused types among themselves. The Hindu way of Matwalisation with Buddhist etho of tolerance and non-violence have helped to sustain the common living. Politically, still both groups have some sort of obsession to be called themselves as Indians.

VII

Culturally, all the three major communities are akin though some of the cultural practices of each community are different in application especially while observing specific rituals. But if we see the observance of rituals closely, such differences are also found even among the various castes of Nepali community. What is pertinent is their participation which is absolutely same among all the three major communities (Salisbury : 1972). At home, to certain extent, each community observes their respective cultural paraphernalia but once they go out of their doorsteps they behave in a holistic manner. No one can really differentiates a Limbu from a Bhutia or a Lepcha unless he comes closer to the person. The Bhutia food items like Thukpa, Momo, Tongba (Chiang), Khadas, Churpi etc. and Nepali fermented food like Gundruk, Sinki, Kinema, Jnar or Nigar are equally popular among all castes and tribes of the plantation. The most common criteria for marriage alliances is job or other earning source rather than caste, tribe or community background. Thus, instead of caste hierarchy, a social stratification is fastly emerging in Sikkim in general and at Temi Tea Estate in particular. At the time of observing death rituals, *Sarau* (help in the form of kind) is common to all irrespective of caste or tribal backgrounds of the diseased households. Similarly, carrying dead bodies from the courtyard to the crematorium is open to all among three communities in the plantation.

Because of their traditions, marriage by *elopement* is most common among tribals and Matwalis from Nepali community. Though consensus arrived (Bedi : 1989) among the Matwalis and Tribals on arrangement basis, girl has to be eloped a few days earlier to the actual day of marriage ceremony. In fact, tribalisation process could be prospered at Temi due to the enclave nature of the plantation.

Observing the background as to how the Nepali Matwali castes are being tribalised, it is found that traditionally most of the Nepali castes belonged to Mangoloid Tibeto Burman group (Gawler : 1873). The Bhutia, Sherpa and Tamang have tried to retain such tradition intact while others have intermingled with the Hindu castes and tribes. Due to this reason, Matwalis have special inclination towards the tribal way of life. The other castes like Manger, Gurung, Sunuwar, Thami, Rai, Limbu and Lepcha were also intermingled with Hindu castes in terms of acculturation process along with animistic practices (Waddel : 1899). This might be the reason why Matwalis feel proud to be called themselves tribals or behave in tribal way by sacrificing animal blood, meat and wine in rituals and festivals. If such items are not there than the whole rituals or festivals become *Khallo* (sour) rather than *Rashiloo* (joyous) in the plantation. This is taking place due to their long association with Chowgel kings as well as having Lepcha and Bhutia neighbours. While in normal times, use of wine is very much restricted by Buddhist, Kiranti, Tamang and other social organisations. If anybody of the respective organisation as member is found drunked then he or she will be fined and even social boycot is done for one year.

It is learnt from the manager of the garden that no financial assistance is given from the Central Government of India. Whatever the assistance is received from the Tea Board of Sikkim is not sufficient to meet the emerging problems of the garden. Being a model garden of the Government of Sikkim, at the outset, it has epitomised the industrial image of the Government.

The question of reorganisation of Temi factory during 1995-2000 remained in paper only. It is reported by the managerial personnel that the reorganisation question to meet the changing needs of the customers had to be realised by the tea board. The caste system has been playing a dominant role in the formation of top management hierarchy in the garden. It proves that the industrial development through the introduction of tea industry at Temi by the Government is a half-hearted reality or a myth rather than absolute reality because the industrialisation process does not allow the traditional etho to dominate the functional sphere of the industry.

VIII

Under the situation, Temi Tea Estate has no way out except to motivate the people for organisational development or wipe it out for ever. To motivate the people is only the alternative than to close it down for ever. Motivation needs holistic approach in which all concerned departments of the Government of Sikkim have to put forward the management of the garden with concrete project package. Doing this, the confidence of the workers is to be taken into account. It is, therefore, suggested that the management must leave the existing partisan approach to partnership one. The challenges brought about by the market economy for Temi tea have to be sorted out by the Government of Sikkim at the appropriate level. The existing system of brokers Raj for Temi tea is to be overcome by the Government of Sikkim.

The issue regarding the problem of its extension is another area of government intervention with the Ministry of Forests. Unless and until the Forest Department of Government of Sikkim gives clearance certificate of 100 acres of forest land to Temi Tea Estate, there is a remotest chance of its extension. The adjoining rural belts cannot be brought under tea cultivation as per Rural Land Reforms Act of Government of Sikkim. Thus, from this, it can be said that government has to take it as a gigantic task. From the labour front, these problems appear to be uncompromising as so far nobody has endeavoured to make them explained in clear way. Whoever has heard about it is reacting with apprehensive gesture rather than in comprehensive dimension. Under such situation, the industrial development of Temi Tea Estate through the Tea Board of Sikkim requires serious thought to put at the policy making forum.

Finally, the *Sahib-Coolie Raj* in colonial form of production relation is to be erased out. The apathy of the workers and, therefore, their apparent sense of alienation to the industry is to be omitted first so that the workers can stop saying that closure of Temi garden cannot create any damage to their economy. The emerging tourism industry around Temi cannot ensure permanent 'regular' jobs to the workers. The vibrant vision for economic development of Sikkim by the Government through North-East Development

Council has to be taped as viable alternative for Temi survival. To make it materialised, the culture of trust is to be established between workers and management. Otherwise, the whole fabrics of industrial development of Temi may be jeopardised in future. The concept of industrial cohesion between labour and management is only ultimate alternative for the survival of Temi Tea Estate in near future.

Bibliography

1. *Sikkim and Bhutan,* 1909 by J. Caude White.
2. *Sikkim and Bhutan,* 1970 by V.H. Coelho.
3. *Himalayan Journal,* 1955 by John Hooker.
4. *Gazetteer of Sikkim,* 1894 by H.H. Risley.
5. *Enchanted Frontier,* 1971 by Nari Rustomji.
6. *India and Tibet,* 1910 by Col. Younghusband.
7. *Tours in Sikkim,* 1922 by Brown Percy.
8. *Sikkim and Mountain Kingdom,* 1972 by C.Y. Salisbury.
9. *Sikkim,* 1873 by J.C. Gawler.
10. *An Expedition to Lasha*, 1906 by Col. Younghusband.
11. *Report of a Mission to a Sikkim,* 1885 by Colman Macaulay.
12. *Among the Himalayas,* 1899 by L.A. Waddel.
13. *Lands of Thundervolt,* 1865 by Ronald Shay.
14. *Sikkim Saga,* 1983 by B.S. Das.
15. *Sikkim : A Short Political History* by L,B. Basnet, 1774.
16. *Politics of Sikkim,* 1975 by A.C. Sinha
17. *State Government and Politics : Sikkim* by N. Sengupta, 1970.
18. *Sikkim,* 1989 by R. Bedi.
19. *Medicinal Plants of Sikkim,* 1994 by L. Rai and E. Sharma.
20. *Socio-Economic Life of Cinchona Plantation Workers in India* by Khemraj Sharma, 1997.
21. *Tea Industry in India : An Introduction,* 1999 by Khemraj Sharma.
22. *The Himalayan Tea Plantation Workers,* 2000 by Khemraj Sharma.
23. *Impact of Workers Education Among the Plantation Workers,* 1991 by Khemraj Sharma.
24. *Eco-system and Ethnic Constellation of Sikkim,* 1988 by Mamta Desai.
25. Sharit Bhowmik on *Class Formation in the Plantation System*, 1981.
26. *Plantation Labourers of North-East India* by R.K. Bhadra, *et. al.*, 1997 an article by Dr. Khemraj Sharma on *Caste and Migration in Cinchona Plantation of Hill Darjeeling.*

27. *Economics of Developing Countries*, 1973 by H.L. Myint.
28. G.S. Nepali, *The Newars : An Ethno-Sociological Study of Himalayan Community*, 1965.
29. O'Malley, L.S.S., Bengal District Gazetteers 'Darjeeling', 1907.
30. Kumar Pradhan, the *Gurkha Conquests*, 1991.
31. W.O. Jones, "Plantation in International Encyclopaedia of Social Sciences", 1968.
32. ILO : International Labour Organisation, "Basic Problems of Plantation Labour", 1950.
33. W.B. Northey and C.J. Morris, *The Gurkhas : Their Customs and Manners*, 1976.
34. Macdonald, A.W., 'Preliminary Note on Some Jhankris of Munglan' in John T. Hitchock, (Ed.), *Spirit Possession in the Nepal Himalaya*, 1976.
35. Srivastava, Ram P., 'Tribe-Caste Mobility in India and the Case of Kumaon Bhotias' in Christoph Von Furer Haimendorf (Ed.) *Caste and Kin in Nepal, India and Ceylon*, 1966.
36. Walton, R.E., 'Managing New Technology and Labour Relations : An Opportunity for Mutual Influence' in Erhman J., (Ed.), *American Labour Supplement*, 1991.
37. Haimendof, V.F., *Anthropology of Nepal*, 1975.
38. *Tea Board of Sikkim, 2000 : A Report.*
39. Uma Devi, *Plantation Economy in the Third World*, 1989.
40. *Department of Industries, Government of Sikkim 2000: A Report.*
41. Berreman, G.D., *Hindus of Himalayas: Ethnography and Change*, 1972.
42. V. Xaxa, *Economic Dualism and Structure of Class*, 1997.
43. Sujit Chakraborty, Statesman 2001 an article on *Sikkim Merger, Union and Society (N.B.* Plus *Statesman).*
44. S. Banerjee, 1999, An Article on *Ethnic Politics in Sikkim, N.B.* Plus, *Statesman.*
45. *Consultative Committee of Plantation Associations*, Calcutta, 1994.
46. Government of Sikkim, Rural Land Reforms Act, 1980, Gangtok, Sikkim.
47. Government of India : *Payment of Bonus Act*, 1965, *Provident Fund Act*, 1952, *Payment of Gratuity Act*, 1972, *Family Pension Scheme under the Provident Fund Act*, 1995, *Payment of Wages Act*, 1936, Plantation Labour Act, 1951.
48. Khemraj Sharma on 'Trade Union Movement in India with Particular reference to Cinchona Plantation' in R.K Bhadra, *et al. Plantation Labours of North-East India*, 1997.
49. *Tea Plantation Labours in India*, 1995, Frederick Ebert Stiftung, New Delhi by Sharit Bhowmik.
50. Assessment of Tourism in Sikkim by Pranab Kumar Chakraborty in Mahendra P. Lama, (Ed.), *Sikkim : Society, Polity, Economy and Environment*, 1994.
51. *Sikkim Human Development Report, 2001* by Mahendra P. Lama.
52. *Sikkim : The People's Vision, 2001*, by Ashok Kumar Lahiri, *et al.*

SECTION–III : DARJEELING

13

BACKGROUND AND SCOPE

The 18th century came to a close turn with the British drinking more tea than ever. It had truely become their cup of tea, a cup that rejuvinated and cheered. By the year 1720, the British had acquired such an appetite that the East India Company imported one million pounds of tea in that year from China. The demand for the beverage grew so phenomenal height that five years later five million tons of tea were imported, once again in just one year. In 1773, the company had 17 million tons of tea in their warehouses and it gives an idea to us that Boston Tea Party fired the imagination that tea should be imported to Britain even from America.

In 1773 itself, the British Parliament passed the Tea Act that gave the East India Company a total monopoly of the tea trade with China. The monopoly had undreamed of advantage since China was the only known tea producing country and the Company the only importer in the world. Theoretically, the Company or the Chinese government could manipulate the tea trade to any extent and if any conflict took place, it would be the two parties only to manipulate the case. This practice came to an end in 1813 when a Charter was passed which handed over the tea trade to the Crown in England which end the monopoly of East India Company in this respect. This gave extra courage to import 36 million pounds in 1816. However, in the meantime, in 1790, a halfhearted interest had been shown to understand the plant when the Company asked a Calcutta based businessman named Purangiri Gossain who had a good rapport with Tibetans to procure tea plants and seeds from the Tibet. Tibetans drink tea the whole day and it seemed logical to get the plants from Tibet especially when China was refusing to part with anything regarding tea. Some historians conjuctured Tibet-Nepal war in the meantime prevented Mr. Gossain from procuring the samples of tea from Tibet. In 1833, the Company's lukewarm interest in tea cultivation metamorphosed into a priority. In the same year, China openly refused to supply tea to British government which gave a jolt to tea habituated British people. In January, 1834, Lord William Bentick, the then Governor-General of India appointed a committee to enquire into the prospect of tea cultivation in India, to consider the question of importing tea seeds and plants from China and to decide upon the most favourable localities for growing tea in India. The tea committee recommended that the most suitable locations were as follows :

1. The lower hills and valleys of the Himalayan range ;
2. Eastern Frontier of British India ;
3. In the Nilgiris.

Unfortunately, the government overlooked some of the reports which were lying with the government especially for the Assam Tea areas. Robert Bruce and his brother C.A. Bruce had found that the plants were growing wild in Assam and by 1825 they brought some samples of the plants along with the seeds to Calcutta. In another finding the Commissioner of Assam in 1824 and Captain F. Jenkins reported the Government about the economic viability of Assam in which they mentioned about the prospect of the tea cultivation in Assam. Later on the species which were sent to Government were proved to be the samples of China variety. The plants were reserved nicely in Botanic Gardens. In 1835, thus actually the British government showed serious interest to start the tea cultivation in India. By 1835, Darjeeling was ceeded from the Sikkim Raja and Mr. Campbell became the Superintendent of Darjeeling.

It is rightly pointed out by O'Malley (1947) that the establishment of tea industry in Darjeeling is due to the enterprises of Dr. Campbell. He and Major Crommelin at Lebong started an experimental nursery of tea with the tea plants brought from Kumaon hills. The experiment proved highly successful and encouraged nicely to begin the plantations at an extensive scale. Similarly, Mr. Martin started plantations at Kurseong range. After the total takeover of the Darjeeling and Kurseong from the Sikkim Raja in 1854, the Darjeeling Tea industry got the actual shape of an industry in the truest sense of the term. In 1854, Kurseong and Darjeeling company opened Alubari Tea Estate. The Emperial Gazetteer of India has noted Pandam and Stenthal gardens were established in the same year. The Land Mortgage Bank established Davai-Pani T. E. Along with these gardens, other gardens like Ambotia, Ging, Takda and Phobseering Tea Estates were also established. In 1859, Dhuteria T. E. was established. Again, in 1864, Takvar, Badamtam and Makaibari Tea Estates were established. In the end of 1864, altogether 113 gardens were established in hill Darjeeling. In 1891 there were 117 gardens. After this the number of gardens started declining due to merger and acquisitions, the actual land under the cultivation went on increasing. By this time, tea trade became the staple means of livelihood of the people. The following table 13.1 will show an important picture of the industry in the period.

Table 13.1
Number of Garden, Area under Cultivation, Outturn and Employment (1866-1905)

Year	*No. of Garden*	*Area under Cultivation*	*Outturn*	*No. of Labourers Employed*
1866	39	10,392	4,33,715	N.A.
1867	40	9,214	5,82,640	N.A.
1868	44	10,067	8,51,549	6,859
1869	55	10,769	12,78,869	7,445
1870	56	11,046	16,89,186	8,347
1872	74	14,503	29,38,626	12,361
1873	87	15,695	29,56,710	14,019
1874	113	18,888	39,27,911	19,424
1885	175	38,499	90,90,298	N.A.
1895	186	48,692	1,17,14,551	N.A.
1905	148	50,618	1,24,47,471	N.A.

Source : W.W. Hunter: A Statistical Account of Bengal (for 1866-1874 figure) 1874 and for 1885 to 1905 (O'Malley 1907) Darjeeling District Gazetteer (Darjeeling), West Bengal.

If we analyse the above Table 13.1 we see that by 1905 the number of tea plantations started decreasing but the production went on increasing. This was because of the fact that the number of gardens were merged together while the production was not affected adversely. Interestingly, from the above table it transpires the fact that after 1885 the workers were not taken into account on the ground that by then the industry did not require more labourers as they started to get sufficient workers from the local areas also. Secondly, the planters started introducing the system of *Hatta Bahira* (to oust the workers after their supperanuation). Since Darjeeling tea was meant for the quality, more stress used to be given on quality than quantity since then to present day. Now, the tea production has come to ten million kilograms, in existing 70 tea gardens in 1999. During the eighties of the last century, the production went upto 13 million kilograms. Over the years, due to the deforestation, increasing population density, soil erosion and political commotion, Darjeeling tea industry is facing problems of different types today. The number of workers increased to 48,116 in 1990 (Tea Board: 1990) with 2,00,065 hectares of land under tea cultivation and having the labour productivity to 301 kg. per year of made tea which is the lowest one in West Bengal (Chhetry: 1999) as well as in India. Still another problem of the industry is the shifting nature of ownership and changing managerial cadres which have redoubled the problems. Again, poor work culture and over politicisation of the workers have also deteoriorated the economy of the industry.

Recruitment of Workers

Rai, while delivering a talk in a seminar at Darjeeling on "Operation 15 Quintals" observed that in the beginning, the planters had the problem of getting workers. By 1839, one nobleman, named Shri Dakman Rai had come to Darjeeling with a caravan of twenty pack ponies loaded with foodstuff and other essentials for his visit to Mahakal Dara temple. Dr. Campbell requested him to help with the supply of workers. By the end of the year, Dakman Rai brought thousands of Rai labourers from Nepal and Sikkim. For this, he was given a free grant land at Soureni, Phugiri and Simrikpani areas. At times because of ill sanitation, improper water supply and inadequate medical treatment, whole plantation workers used to run away from the gardens and managers used to go round the villages with money in bags to allure the workers and to discourage them from running away from the gardens. This was the annual occurances during the winter months as then having no bridges in the rivers, workers used to run away in winter times from the gardens and managers used to be frustrated. The Darjeeling Planters Association had standing order not to entice workers of one garden for another garden. Each garden had a team of Sardars and Gallawalas (labour recruiters) who used to go Nepal and Sikkim to recruit labourers in winter times. The recruiters used to get Rs. 10/- each respectively as recruiting Bonus. At first, the Gurkha labour force refused to accept the coins the then known as 'Company Paisa' and wanted to have coins similar in the circulation in Nepal and Sikkim which was known as 'Chaptay Paisa' (flat paisa). Hence Newars had to be brought from Nepal to mint this type of coins which remained in circulation for a short while. Thus, the history of labour recruitment in Darjeeling is the history of Sardari System. After being brought at the gardens, the workers were tight down in such a way that they become almost bonded labour. To do this, even a para military force known as North Bengal Mounted Rifles were kept at the plantations (Sarkar and Lama: 1986).

Unlike the labour recruitment policy which had been adopted in tea plantations of Assam, Terai and Dooars areas of India, the various acts of British government would not be applied in hill plantations as the areas were outside the administration of Bengal (Sharma: 1999). The sardars first tried to entice the local tribe known as Lepcha who refused to work in the plantations as they were completely shifting cultivators in the region. Recruiting workers was a tough business as both Nepal and Sikkim were two separate foreign countries. In this respect, Sardars played a predominant role though they had to face lot of troubles to entice the people in Nepal and Sikkim which had strongly condemned for such recruitment of their nationals in *Munglan* (India) plantations. Here the question of caste and community feeling of *Sardars* played a significant role to recruit the workers. Each *Sardar* having a caste background could easily attract his fellow kins. In this way, *Sardars* used to bring plantation workers from Nepal and Sikkim in Darjeeling hills (Ibid).

In the process, the *Sardars* ware assisted by the *Gallawalas* who were deputed at the various places in Nepal and Sikkim from October to February every year for recruiting, enticing and even indenturing labourers. A sort of competition could place among the *Sardars* in respect of commission known as Recruiting Bonus from the management just before Pujas. To induce more and more workers in the plantations by showing all the bogus advantages of thc industry including the permanent settlement could carry high dignity to the *Sardars* (Mukherjee: 1945) in front of the management. Only some immigrants came from Nepal who wanted to join the plantation jobs as they had relatives there before they came (Sen: 1977). The *Sardars* had to do this so as to please the planters who were very keen to do so by securing groups of married couples who were proved more promising than to get unmarried ones. To do this, very often *Sardars* even used to intoxicate the people and forced them to marry on the way before reaching gardens from Nepal and Sikkim. In this process, they even asked kins to marry there in Nepal and for such act they were escalated from the villages resulting which they were forced to migrate to *Munglann* (India). Such people were known as *Pataki/Chutaki* (untouchables) in Nepal. It was known from the elders of the gardens that many families had such *Pataki/Chutaki* background from Nepal.

A large number of Matwalis mainly *Rai, Limbu, Tamang, Gurung, Thami* and *Mangars* were recruited from Eastern Nepal due to their exploitation there by Tagadharis who emmigrated from Western Nepal (Pradhan: 1991). Virtually, the *Sardari* system persisted as the only agency of labour recruitment in tea plantations of Darjeeling hills.

At the turn of the century, the situation changed in the plantations as there appeared to have been the surplus population. To meet the situation, the planters started implementing 'Contract Clause' of Bengal Act III of 1915 which provided not only for the recruitment of labourers but also incorporated provisions of labour retrechment. Thus from 1930 onwards, many workers were retrenched from tea plantations in the name of *Hatta Bahira* system.

Under the Sardari system, a worker used to be known to another worker by the name of the *Sardar* under whom he or she was working in the plantation. A *Sardar* used to make his own caste Dhura (labour line) consisting of workers of his own caste from Nepal and Sikkim. The same thing used to do by the other *Sardars* of various castes and in this way various caste

Dhuras came into existance in Darjeeling gardens. The Sardarship as the only means of labour recruitment persisted in the plantations till the enactment of Plantation Labour Act, 1951. With the passing of the Act, the workers had been started to be recruited from among the local people of Darjeeling hills (Sen: 1977). After 1964, the *Hatta Bahira* system was abolished and after that the labourers are recruited on the *Badli* (substitute) basis by which the dependent members of working workers would be given the jobs in the plantations on the basis of Hardship Theory by which an annual survey is made for the workers households and given jobs to those who are dependent members of the needy households.

This may be the reason why there are thirty thousands casual workers in the Himalayan tea plantations today. Even the supervisory jobs are given to the local unemployed youths who have minimum educational qualification. Comparatively, it is observed that *Tagadharis* are recent settlers in the plantations who are engaged mainly as office staff of the plantations. This may be the reason why socially *Tagadharis* are called *SUKUMBASIS* (recent settlers) and Matwalis called themselves as *"Raithanees"* (early settlers) in tea plantations of Darjeeling Himalaya.

With this background of the recruitment of the workers let us see the structure of workers in different periods of history of tea plantations. As it is already mentioned that there were sixty four thousand tea plantation workers in Darjeeling Himalaya in 1905, the number of workers decreased from 1951. It is seen from the report of O'Malley (1947) District Gazetteer, "Darjeeling" that after 1947 there has been steady decline in the labour force in tea plantations all over India (Dasgupta: 1986). The average daily employment feel from 10.18 lakhs in 1951 to 8.19 lakhs in 1964. The following Table 13.2 will show the structure of labour force in Darjeeling hills.

Table 13.2

Structure of Labour Force in 1961, 1971, 1976, 1980 and 1999

1961	1971	1976	1980	1999
60,979	56,990	45,790	45,987	52,913

Source : Dasgupta 1986 and Labour in West Bengal 1994. Field Work 1999.

The Table 13.2 shows that the number of workers increased in 1999 from 1980 because of the fact that area of tea plantations increased on the one hand and demand of the Himalayan Plantation Workers Union which urged for utilising more and more number of workers in the plantations because of difficult terrains of the hills This may be the reason why today there are 1:4 land-man-ratio in most of the plantations of the region. Here, management appears to be right when they said that the cost of production is very high in the hill tea gardens.

Operationalisation of Concept of the Study

This is a Sociological study of tea plantation workers of Darjeeling Himalaya. So far, hardly any study has been done on this aspect of the workers. It is known from this study that the workers were emmigrated either from Nepal and Sikkim from their agrarian background to industrial environment. Once employed in the plantations, they were bracketed in the category of wage labourers. But socially they are heterogeneous in structure. Historically, the heterogeneous character of Nepali society helps to sustain the isolation of the plantations as two castes having two different dialects could not interact together in day-to-day life. Such thing continued in the plantations till 1947. Interestingly, it is found that inspite of settlement in the plantations, the workers remained isolated even after 1947 because socially the wider society of the Himalaya still called them *Kamanees* (garden) backward people. However, after 1947 trade unions started penetrating the gardens and helping mobilising the workers for separate ethnic consciusness of the working class. In this study, the working class of the plantation workers has been viewed from the ethnic dimension in order to give a realistic explanation. Trade union movement, unlike in other industries or areas is not exactly the movement of working class alone here rather it is the movement of people as a whole living in the plantations. So, the present study shall show the nature of trade union movement in the plantations. Further, it also highlights the ethnic dimension of trade union movement, workers participation in trade union movement of the region. Discussing the workers participation in union activities, socio-economic as well as cultural factors playing in their participation in the unions are also taken care of Ideology of trade unions has studied in detail in order to understand the distinct nature of movement in the plantations. The socio-economic life of the workers has formed the basis of unionisation of the workers. Thus, their socio-economic conditions have also been added in the study to explore into the fact that whether really the plantations can sustain the workers families as a whole or not.

Data Collection

In the initial stage of the study, all the trade union leaders were contacted and visited their union offices and discussed the problem of study at Darjeeling. That along with our personal visits to about 45 gardens off 70 in Darjeeling hills, a questionnaire was prepared along with the household census and sent to the union offices at Darjeeling in 1996. In the next six months the responses were very thin. After six months, again we made a thorough persuassion with the union leaders at Darjeeling and started getting the questionnaire duly filled up with the observations of union leaders. Thus, altogether, it took another one year to collect the complete data. After that we personally visited to the various tea gardens of the Himalaya and able to cross-checked the data. The data collection work was finally over by the end of 1998. After that the report writing work could be started and completed the report writing in the middle of 1999. Separate questionaire were sent to union leaders, leader at the unit level and workers who collected the data and sent to us for the analysis. The theoretical approach in the study is the social anthropological one as basically the Nepali society of the plantations can be compared as good as any other tribal society of the Himalaya. Being tribal in nature, the trade union movement of trade union organisations have also formed in different dimension than we found in other industries of the country. Hailing from the same community, we were thoroughly accepted by the community of the region for the study.

Method of Data Collection

Considering the problem of the study, following questionnaire was prepared in regard to the workers participation in trade union movement in the Himalayan industry. Preparing the questionnaire, special conjucture had been labelled to consider the socio-economic dimensions of the workers and society as a whole. Unlike other industries and regions of the country, socio-cultural aspects matter much here if we see the history of society in toto. The isolated economy of inaccessible environs have definitely shaped the destiny of various organisations including trade union organisations. Here, trade unions are frontal organisations of political parties while in other areas, they are peripheral organisations of political parties. The trade unions are frontal organisations in the sense that all the ethnic issues of the political organisations have come up from the tea gardens and almost all the ethnic movement had been germinated from the plantations only. Trade unions appear to be the social organisation rather than purely the economic organisations or means to protect the economic interests of the workers. In fact, the trade unions are via-media of the local *Samajs* and political parties in the plantation industry in particular and society in general.

By nature, the plantation workers appear to be the custodians of all whims, aspirations, pains, sorrow, and means to really make known to the society of the community. Why this happens here is due to the negligence of government by making the region and the society merely a pawn of betrayal with lofty momental guarantees for their overall development. This is the actual reason that government has lost the confidence of the people in the plantations. To study all these, the following sample questionnaire had been made. The first section deals with household census.

1. Name of Respondent.
2. Relation with the head of the family.

3. Sex of the Family members.
4. Age structure of the Family members.
5. Education structure of the family members.
6. Occupation of family members of the workers.
7. Place of birth of the family members.
8. House type of the workers.
9. Present and past trade union membership of the workers.
10. Land holding pattern of the workers.
11. Reasons for leaving the previous trade unions.
12. Members of political parties.
13. Length of service of the workers.
14. Types of works done in the plantations and outside.
15. Participation of the workers in union activities like meeting, strikes, membership drive, casting votes, canvassing, for the union, reading the union notice board etc.
16. Awareness about the trade union activities etc.
17. Factors responsible for the success in negotiations.
18. Factors responsible for the failure in negotiations.
19. Reasons for joining unions.
20. Reasons for not joining unions.

These questionnaire were structured one for the households census of the workers. Besides, the following questions were incorporate in questionnaire of the study in again structured manner in order to analyse the nature of workers participation in trade union movement of the industry of the Himalayan region.

1. Do you know the leaders of your union?
2. Where they stay and work?
3. Do you pay Puja subscription to your union?
4. Do you have any idea about the difference between union and political subscription?
5. What is the caste and community background of your union leaders?
6. To which political party or federation your union is affiliated?
7. Do you know the name of the other unions and their leaders?
8. Do you think that all castes and communities are given equal chance for the union leadership in the plantation?

9. Which aspect of the workers are given top priority by your union?
10. Is there any female union leader in your union?
11. What is the party ideology of your union?
12. Does your management people participate or show interest in union elections?
13. Does your management declare holiday in the union election day?
14. Whether political party leaders visit to your garden in the election day of the union?
15. Do the leaders of various unions sit together and drink tea, snacks etc. and gossip in festivals and rituals etc.?
16. Who settle the conflicts arising between two families, trade unions and management, trade union and trade union and workers and workers?
17. In times of emergency, which union leaders are invited by your management?
18. Does your union issues the receipts of the subscription to you?
19. Do you know your union has to send annual returns to the Assistant Labour Commissioner?
20. Does your union takes part in Bonus meeting at Calcutta?
21. Does your union represents in Wage Revision Board?
22. What type of work is done by union regarding productivity raising, population control, quality of life of workers, and creation of additional employment potentialities?
23. Do you believe to your union leaders regarding proper utilisation of union fund?
24. Does your union informs members about the proceedings of the meetings, conciliations and agreements done with the management in toto?
25. Have you ever gone through the proceedings of meetings, and agreements from the records of the union offices?
26. Does your union discusses with members about the memorandums (Charter of Demands) to be submitted to the management or govt.?
27. Do you have caste or community panchayat?
28. What are the functions of caste/community panchayat, if there is any in the plantation?
29. Is your union a recognised union?
30. Are you satisfied with the method of recognition?
31. Do you agree that the unions are necessary to protect the interests of the workers?
32. Do you agree that the unions fulfil the interests of political parties?

33. If your union gets double benefits for you, are you ready to contribute more to your union purse?
34. All the leaders of your union are workers?
35. Do you agree that there should be one union in one plantation?
36. Are you satisfied with the functioning of your union?
37. Are you ready to sacrifice to your union?
38. Do you feel that it is necessary to have non-worker leaders in your garden unit union?
39. Are you in favour of political affiliation of your union?
40. Are you satisfied with the union registration?
41. Are you satisfied with the introduction of Panchayat system in the plantation industry?
42. Who is more powerful - T.U. leader or Panchayat leader?
43. Who is given more recognition by your management?
44. What is in your view about the causes of work stoppages, strikes etc.?
45. Why the workers participate in strikes?
46. Why in your view workers do not participate in strikes?
47. Are you satisfied with dispute settlement machineries?
48. Are you satisfied with grievance handling proceedure of your garden?
49. Do you agree that strike helps to raise wages?
50. Do you agree that strike help realise the management that workers are also a big power?
51. Do you prefer Gherao, go-slow, tool down strike or work to rule the day in the changing context?

Literature Survey on the Problem of the Study

Till the date, the study of workers participation in trade union movement in tea industry is unheard of. Whatever the study has been done here is rather either on economics of tea industry or production or productivity problems of the Himalayan tea industry. The plantation workers unlike in Dooars and Terai areas of West Bengal are semi-literates. Secondly, the trade union leaders though mostly hailing from the office Babus (clerks) category belong to the same community while in Dooars and Terai gardens they are mainly *Bengali Babus* in the plantations. Thirdly, the workers and leaders of the unions being the members of the same community, workers are not entirely apathetic (Ramaswamy. 1977) to the unions. Given always the interested rank and file workers, they pressurise the leaders to confirm the members interests and wishes on the unions. In fact, as Ramaswamy (Ibid) observed 'there may be something in the union itself or its social conditions which induces the high participation of the workers' may be correct in the area under study. Another dimension for the participation of workers in unions is due to the management hostility to the workers. This is because of the fact that as mentioned at earlier paragraphs management are as good as colonial planters in the region who have nothing to do with socio-economic upliftment of the workers. Here, the unions are cohesive groups of the workers as they assured for sustained participation in the union activities in order to endure unionisation for more than the mere job interests. The workers are found to be ideological unionists rather than work oriented one. Here ideology is one which has been shaped since generations together and this ideology is the sum total of values, believes etc. of the *Gurkha* community. Such ideology is the creation of socio-cultural as well as political history of the industry and government. Dasgupta (1986) observes that Overstreet and Windwillar stated that regional particularism has been the potent of strength of Indian communists. Indian communists consider themselves custodians of regional separatism. According to these the communities have unquestionably gained by championing the cause of underprivileged linguistic minorities. By utilising the regional grievances as well as socio-economic discontent it could evoke a greater response in its areas of influence. The ideology of the dominant unions of the plantations is shaped by the concept of *Gurkha* ideology for the restoration of separate identity. The demand for *Gurkha* homeland was supported by communists at Darjeeling at times with the idea of national identity in the form of separate state or separate autonomy for the region. The constant reiteration of demand for autonomy by the communists in the hills kept hopes alive the *Gurkah* consciousness. It is very often presumed that the undivided communists party of India used the demand for Gorkhasthan and *Gurkha* autonomy in 1940's to create a popular base in the hill areas especially in the formation of trade unions in tea plantations. In any case the union is part of social environment and it attracts the attitudes of individuals. The ideological members of the unions have additional love for the union's existence as powerful instrument of workers identity. This study shall highlight on nature of workers participation in union activities due to multiple reasons among which separate ethnic identity is one. Till now, most of the scholars have concentrated on the study of national federations or unions and on the top leaders. But it is found that top leaders do not enroll new members, negotiate with management or do entertain conflicts with the rival unions. The top leaders are only policy makers. Similarly here in the present study also, national unions like NUPW, CITU, AITUC etc. do not involve the grassroot level unionism. It is the local leaders and unions which have the complete role to play in such spheres. Of late the workers have also realise this fact in the Himalayan tea plantation industry. It is therefore viewed that humble down to earth empericism is the need of the hour in studying the tea plantation workers. This is the open reality that workers of the plantations have preferred the unions which are the creation of local situations rather than the imported phenomenon.

14

SOCIO-ECONOMIC CONDITIONS OF THE WORKERS

In this section of the study, we will see the socio-economic conditions of the workers. In social parlance, caste, family, household and marriages have taken for the study.

Studying the caste system in the Nepali society, Haimendorf (1978) has classified it into three groups, viz, Tagadhari (those who wear sacred threads), Matwali (wine eaters) and Untouchable. The castes like Bahun, Chhetri and Thakuri form the Tagadhari group while the Matwalis like Rai, Limbu, Tamang, Gurung, Mangar, Thami, Bhujel, Newar, Sherpa, Sunuwar, Lepcha etc. form the Matwali group who occupy the middle stratum of the hierarchy and Kami, Damai and Sarki occupy the bottom stratum of the hierarchy. Caplan (1970) has conceptualised the Nepali society into Tagadhari, Matwali and Untouchable groups. The twice-born Bahun, Chhetri and Thakuri form the Tagadhri group while the Mongoloid castes form the Matwali group and Kami, Damai and Sarki form the untouchable group. However, Haimendorf (1966) has classified the Nepali society into Tagadhri and Matwali groups considering the changes taking place in Nepal after 1926 after which the slavery system was abolished. Similarly, Caplan (1970) also states that such three tier classification of Nepali society had more meaning in the society till 1963 when the Panchayati system was introduced fully in Nepal. Again, Caplan said that such three tier system of Nepali society could not be sustained due to the advent of modernisation in Nepal after 1980. Similar view is also shared by Bista (1991). The traditional untouchable castes cannot be called untouchables both in Nepal and India today. In the present study, the Nepali society has been conceptualised into two tier classification, viz. Tagadhri and Matwali considering the industrial environment of tea plantation industry of the Himalaya. The Tagadhari has been further sub-divided into *Jharra* (pure) and *Thimaha* (non-*jharra*). Similarly, the Matwali has been sub-divided into *Setho* (White) and *Kalo* (black) types. The caste like Chhatri and Thakuri of Tagadhari group are below Bahuns as they are Kshatriyas. Secondly, they are quite closer to the Matwali way of life as they sacrifice some animals' blood in rituals and pujas and thirdly they donot wear sacred threads of nine strings as wear by Jharra Tagadhari. In fact, conventionally, Chhetri and Thakuri can wear secred threads of six strings only. While Jharra Tagadharis are to be purely vegetarians while observing the rituals and pujas. The caste like Rai, Limbu, Gurung, Mangar, Tamang, Newar, Sunuwar, Thami, Sherpa, Lepcha etc. having purely Mongoloid characters are operationalised as Setho Matwalis and castes like Kami, Damai and Sarki are conceptualised as Kalo Matwalis as they along with Setho Matwalis use wine in their rituals. Similarly, their rituals cannot be complete without wine/meat. Socially, Tagadharis are called *Batho Jats* (Cunning castes) while Metwalis as *Latto Jats* (innocent castes). Further, all the Matwalis are more or less have declared as schedule castes, tribes and other backward castes in the region. Such classification of Nepali society of the plantation industry into Tagadhari-Matwali remains meaningful in so far as the day today social life of the workers are concerned. Apparently, any stranger can distinguish a Tagadhari from a Matwali while it is very difficult to distinguish between a Rai and Limbu unless the stranger becomes close to them. In fact, it is also observed that almost all the castes including the Thimahas have been nicely adapted to the Matwali way of life. The Brahmins are the exception perhaps due to priestly character of the caste which they have not been completely abandoned here like Nepal and Sikkim. Another reason is that all Nepali castes called them *Bajees* (Priests) which stands something deregatory to the Brahmins especially who donot do Pujas in their day to day life as a profession. Secondly, as *Bajees* they are often called to do religious rites both at homes and at plantations and even at the houses of Kalo Matwalis. While Chhetris and Thakuris being Thimaha Tagadharis are not called to do such Pujas. This is the reason why Jharra Tagadharis are not able to completely assimilated into the Matwali way of life even if some of them wanted to do so. Interestingly, these days such Tagadharis have to visit to the funeral rites of Kalo Matwalis and this is accepted by all Setho Matwalis. This might be the reason why these days both Kalo and Setho Matwalis have form a corporate group in tea plantations of Darjeeling hills.

In the present study, as mentioned earlier, family is one of aspect of study. The term 'Family' denotes a group of persons who live together in the same house. Unlike in the traditional society, the structure of the family is different in the sense that today it may not be always patriarchal in character. Considering the tea plantation situation, the family is somewhat different.

Table 14.1
Family Structure

Sl. No.	*Caste*	*Joint*	*Percentage*	*Nuclear*	*Percentage*
1.	Bahun = 125	25	0.3	100	0.3
2.	Chhetri = 879	153	2.2	716	2.1
3.	Thakuri = 125	24	0.3	101	0.3
4.	Newar = 1030	412	5.6	618	1.8
5.	Rai = 21290	2219	30.4	18971	55.3
6.	Limbu = 2830	842	11.5	1988	5.8
7.	Mangar = 1899	569	7.8	1330	3.9
8.	Gurung = 968	290	0.7	678	2.0
9.	Bhujel = 244	73	1.0	171	0.5
10.	Tamang = 9745	1915	26.3	7830	22.8
11.	Thami = 300	90	1.2	210	0.6
12.	Sunuwar = 307	92	1.3	215	0.6
13.	Lepcha = 273	218	3.0	55	0.2
14.	Sherpa = 258	78	1.1	180	0.5
15.	Kami = 895	179	2.5	716	2.5
16.	Damai = 290	58	0.8	232	0.7
17.	Sarki = 230	46	0.6	184	0.5
	Total = 41588	**7293**	**17.5**	**34295**	**82.5**

It is observed from the above Table 14.1 that 2.8% of Tagadharis have joint families while 2.7% of their families have nuclear families. This shows that the settlement in the tea industry has helped to increase the percentage of nuclear families or the percentages of joint families declined considerably than of the past in the agrarian society of Nepal and Sikkim. The percentage of joint family is very high in case of Rai (30.4%) and Tamang? (26.3%) castes in the plantations. Next to Tamang, 11.5% of Limbus have joint families. Similarly, the percentage of joint family is 7.8% in case of Mangars and Newars have 5.6% of joint family. By joint family, here we mean the parents, sons, daughter-in-laws, grandsons and granddaughters living in a house.

The percentage of nuclear family is highest in case of Rai with 55.3% and it is followed by Tamang with 22.8% but rest of the other caste have more or less similar picture in so far as the nuclear family structure is concerned in the plantations. It happens because normally after the marriages of sons, separate houses are given to them provided they are working in the plantations, by the management as per the principle of tea plantation industry in the region in order to fulfil the terms of agreement for 8% new housing to be made per year. Socially, separation of newly married couples from the parental house under *Ansa-Banda* (division of ancestral property among the sons) system is a driving force behind the separation which has also accepted by the plantation system while incorporating the cultural value of the society. It shows that the nuclearisation of family got complete shape here also which is not found in any other industries of the country. On the whole, 82.5% of tea plantation workers in the Himalayan plantation industry have nuclear families with mostly the separate households of their own.

As it is already mentioned that there are 41588 households of the workers in tea industry of the region. Here an attempt has been made to see the nature of house types of the workers of various castes and tribes of the plantations.

It is transparent from the Table 14.2 that 21.3% of the houses of the workers are of *Kuccha* type made of Bamboo frame with thatched roof while 78.7% of the houses are of *Puckka* type in the plantations. Comparatively, Tagadharis have more *Kuccha* houses. For instance, 64.8% of Bahuns, 51.1% of Chhetris and 48.2% of Thakuris have *Kuccha* houses. It is also observed from the table that almost all the Matwalis have houses of *Puckka* type. It is because of the fact that Tagadharis are Sukumbasis (*recent settlers*) *while Matwalis are called themselves as Raithanees* (*early settlers*) in the plantations. So, the Tagadharis have to contend with the *Kuccha* type of houses for preety long time. From the discussion that follows here is that it is confirmed that the assurances of the planters to construct 8% new houses of the workers every year in the light of Plantation Labour Act, 1951 is in paper only. Had it been done in reality than by 1969 all the houses of the workers would have been completed into *Puckka* types. Discussing this problem with the planters, it is known that the owners of the gardens donot want to invest substantial amount of money at a time in this aspect only. To them, 8% investment means the eight percent in total tea industry of the region. This view has also been coroborated adequately by the annual report of the Darjeeling Planters association since 1985. Interestingly, during Gurkha National Liberation Front movement in the hills, not a single house was constructed for the workers pretending that a huge loss had to incure by the plantations in terms of production and productivity and profit. Again, it is also observed from the present study that majority of new houses are made for staff and sub-staff of the industry as the demands incorporated in Charter of Demands of the unions. Thus, on an average, 53% of Tagadharis households are of *Kuccha* type and only 47% of them have *Puckka* houses. Off this 47% of houses, 32% of Tagadharis belong to the category of office Babus. Interestingly, 79.9% of Matwalis have *Puckka* houses and only 20.1% of them have *Kuccha* type of houses. Of 20.1% of Matwalis, 17.7% of them donot have working members outside the gardens. It means that both male, and females of this 17.7% of Matwalis are working inside the plantations and hence they have no supplimentary source of income generation. It is also observed that normally the workers themselves very often made their houses uptodate with the money earned by the members who are working outside the gardens. Thus, money earned by family members from outside the gardens makes a lot of difference in the living conditions of the workers in Darjeeling hill plantations.

Table 14.2
Caste and Type of Houses of the Workers

Sl. No.	*Caste*	*Total Households*	*Kuccha*	*Percentage*	*Puckka*	*Percentage*
1.	Bahun	310	201	64.8	109	35.2
2.	Chhetri	789	449	51.1	430	48.9
3.	Thakuri	400	193	48.2	207	51.8
4.	Newar	1030	120	11.7	910	88.3
5.	Rai	20730	2090	10.1	18640	89.9
6.	Limbu	2830	1050	37.1	1780	62.9
7.	Managar	1899	726	38.2	1173	61.8
8.	Gurung	968	238	24.6	730	75.4
9.	Sunuwar	307	108	35.2	199	64.8
10.	Bhujel	244	77	31.6	167	68.4
11.	Thami	300	23	7.7	277	92.3
12.	Sherpa	258	63	24.4	195	75.6
13.	Lepcha	273	75	27.5	198	72.5
14.	Tamang	9745	3003	30.8	6742	69.2
15.	Kami	895	212	23.7	683	76.3
16.	Damai	290	145	50.0	145	50.0
17.	Sarki	230	95	41.3	135	58.7
	Total	**41588**	**8868**	**21.3**	**32720**	**78.7**

Another dimension of the social life of the workers was selected for the study was the marriage structure in order to understand their social living.

If we analyse the above Table 14.3, it is seen that occurences of intra-caste marriages and inter-caste marriages is more or less same (46.8% intra-caste and 53.2% inter-caste) in the plantations. Castewise, Tamangs have still retained their traditions of intra-caste marriages with 93.0%. Similarly, 80.0% of Kamis, 80.0% of Newars, 75.8% of Bahuns, 59.8% of Damais, 55.4% of Limbus and 49.9% of Chhetris have done intra-caste marriages. On the other

Table 14.3
Caste and Marriages of the Workers

Sl. No.	*Caste*	*Intra-Caste*	*Percentage*	*Inter-Caste*	*Percentage*
1.	Bahun	200	75.8	64	24.2
2.	Chhetri	264	49.9	265	50.1
3.	Thakuri	70	29.9	185	70.1
4.	Newar	423	80.0	106	20.0
5.	Mangar	397	30.0	926	70.0
6.	Gurung	80	10.1	714	89.9
7.	Rai	3973	30.0	9256	70.0
8.	Limbu	1026	55.4	826	44.6
9.	Tamang	4921	93.0	371	07.0
10.	Sunuwar	78	29.5	186	70.0
11.	Bhujel	79	29.9	185	70.1
12.	Thani	80	30.3	184	69.7
13.	Sherpa	80	30.3	184	69.7
14.	Lepcha	27	10.2	237	89.8
15.	Kami	423	80.0	106	20.0
16.	Damai	158	59.8	106	40.2
17.	Sarki	79	29.9	185	70.1
	Total	**12,367**	**46.8**	**14,086**	**53.2**

hand, 89.9% of marriages among the Gurungs, are intra-castes. Again, 70.0% of Mangar, 70.0% of Rais, 70.0% of Bhujels, 89.8% of Lepchas, 70.1 % of Sarki, 69.7% of Sherpas, 69.7% of Thamis and 70.1% of Thakuris have done inter-caste marriages. It shows the concept of *Jat Bibaha* (marriages within own castes). *Ajat Bibaha* (marriages with lower castes) and *Kujat Bibaha* (marriages with untouchable castes) of the past have no relevence here in the industrial society. Again, marriages between Kirantis (Rai, Limbu and Lepcha) are considered as *Jat Bibaha.* Further, the marriages among Gurungs, Mangars, Bhujels, Sunuwars etc. are also considered as *Jat Bibaha*. But Newars are found little bit conscious about the marriage alliances and normally they do marriages within the Newars only. Similar picture is also found among the Kamis as they are much conscious about it as they are very progressive than Damai and Sarkis. Tamangs are very conscious in this respect as 93.0% of their marriages have taken place among the Tamangs only. Among the Tagadharis, Bahuns have married with Bahuns only. It shows that still hardly Bahuns want to do inter-caste marriages with Thakuris and Chhetris. While

Chhetris and Thakuris have higher percentages of inter-caste marriages as they are more and more atuned with the process of Matwalisation (Tribalistion) in the plantations. Among the other Matwali castes, Lepchas (89.8%) and Gurungs (89.9%) have more and more number of inter-caste marriages. Lepchas, as often called *Pittalle Varas* (condemned vessels) and Gurungs (over humble) could not stick to have only intra-caste marriages. Secondly, their percentages of population is also insignificant. Similar, picture is found among the Rais, Mangars and Bhujels also though Rai is the most dominant caste in the plantations. Sherpa, Thami and Sarki population is also very thin in the region under study. So, they have to adjust with other castes in this respect.

Like social aspect of the workers, certain economic variables had also taken for the study. Among the economic variables, occupations of the workers is very important. Unlike in the traditional society of Nepalis, all are the workers today some in the plantations and rest outside. Here, the question is not concerned with the occupational structure but with the number of working population of the workers.

Table 14.4

Caste and Number of Working Persons in the Families

Sl.No.	*Caste*	*Single*	*%*	*Two*	*%*	*Three*	*%*	*Four*	*%*	*Five*	*%*
1.	Rai	4700	55.5	14,521	50.2	1,244	49.9	208	17.3	57	11.5
2.	Limbu	501	5.9	1,981	6.8	170	6.8	136	11.3	42	8.5
3.	Tamang	1771	20.9	6,822	23.6	585	23.5	468	39.1	99	19.9
4.	Mangar	285	3.4	1,329	4.9	114	4.6	92	7.7	79	15.9
5.	Gurung	175	2.1	671	2.3	59	2.4	48	4.0	15	3.1
6.	Sunuwar	50	0.6	215	0.7	19	0.8	15	1.3	08	1.6
7.	Kami	150	1.8	627	2.2	54	2.2	43	3.6	21	4.2
8.	Damai	30	0.4	203	0.7	18	0.7	14	1.2	25	5.1
9.	Sarki	32	0.4	161	0.6	14	0.6	11	0.9	12	2.4
10.	Sherpa	35	0.4	181	0.6	16	0.6	07	0.6	19	3.8
11.	Bhujal	32	0.4	171	0.6	15	0.6	12	1.0	14	2.8
12.	Lepcha	42	0.4	191	0.7	17	0.7	13	1.1	10	2.1
13.	Chhetri	301	3.6	527	1.8	24	1.0	27	1.4	10	2.1
14.	Bahun	48	0.6	217	0.8	19	0.8	15	1.3	11	2.2
15.	Thakuri	67	0.8	280	1.0	24	1.0	19	1.6	10	2.1
16.	Newar	24	2.5	618	2.1	82	3.3	66	5.5	53	10.7
17.	Thami	45	0.9	210	0.7	18	0.7	15	1.3	12	2.4
	Total	**8,475**	**20.4**	**28,925**	**69.6**	**2,492**	**6.0**	**1,199**	**2.9**	**497**	**1.2**

It is observed from the above Table 14.4 that 69.6% of households have double earning members, 6.0% of the households have three working members and 2.9% of the households have four working members in the plantations. Interestingly, 1.2% of the households have five working members. Only 20.4% of the households have single earning members. Castewise, 19.9% of Tamang households have five earning members. Tamangs are followed by Mangars households having 15.9% of five earning members. In the third place, 11.5% of the households of Rais have five working members. Again, 10.7% of Newars households have five working members. Rest of the castes have comparatively less number of working members in their households. Again, 39.1% of Tamangs have four working members, 17.3% of Rais and 11.3% of Limbus have four working members. Surprisingly, 49.9% of Rai households have three earning members. Rai is followed by Tamangs in this respect having 23.5%. Similarly, 50.2% of Rai and 23.6% of Tamang households have double working members. Single earning members among the Rais is 55.5% and 20.9% among the Tamangs. On the whole, it is observed from the table that Tamang, Rai, Limbu Mangar, and Gurung households have better socio-economic

Table 14.5
Caste and Land Holding Pattern of the Workers

Sl. No.	*Caste*	*Total Land*	*In the Garden*	*%*	*Outside the Garden*	*%*
1.	Bahun	13	3	0.8	10 (Wet)	0.8
2.	Chhetri	13	8	2.2	5 (Wet)	0.8
3.	Thakuri	7	5	1.4	2 (Wet)	0.8
4.	Newar	75	15	4.1	60 (Dry)	9.6
5.	Rai	195	40	11.0	155 (Dry)	24.9
6.	Limbu	63	28	7.7	35 (Dry)	5.6
7.	Mangar	37	19	5.2	18 (Wet)	2.9
8.	Gurung	20	10	2.7	10 (Wet)	1.6
9.	Bhujel	9	3	0.8	6 (Dry)	1.0
10.	Tamang	297	97	26.5	200 (Dry)	32.2
11.	Thami	55	30	8.2	25 (Dry)	4.0
12.	Sunuwar	44	31	8.5	13 (Dry)	1.1
13.	Lepcha	55	27	7.4	28 (Dry)	4.5
14.	Sherpa	40	25	6.9	15 (Dry)	2.4
15.	Kami	30	10	2.7	20 (Dry)	3.2
16.	Damai	30	5	1.4	25 (Dry)	4.1
17.	Sarki	13	8	2.2	05 (Dry)	0.8
	Total	**996**	**364**	**36.5**	**622**	**62.4**

conditions than the other castes of Matwali group. Among the Tagadharis, Chetris have better socio-economic conditions than Bahuns and Thakuris. In the same fashion, among the Matwalis, Tamangs have much better socio-economic condition than others. Most of the Newars prefer business than working in the plantations or outside as manual labour. Rest of the population of the households work outside the gardens.

It is apparent from the above discussion that Matwalis (Rai, Limbu, Tamang, Gurung, Mangar, Bhujel, Sunuwar, Thami, Lepcha, Sherpa, Damai, Kami and Sarki) prefer the manual jobs in the plantations. This may be due to their legacy of the past that harps them to be the toiling castes (Pradhan: 1991) in Nepal and Sikkim. This has characterised the Nepali community as *Khati Khanee Jat* (labourious community) in the world and their culture is a culture of hard work. Even cutside the plantations, they have to put hard work no matter whether it is a private or public job.

Another dimension of economic life of the workers is the land holding pattern among the castes and tribes. Land holding indicates the status of the family of the workers in the plantations.

If we analyse the land holding pattern of the workers, it is found from the above table that 26.6% of land is owned by Tamangs in the gardens and same is found in case of their land holding outside (32.2%) the gardens. Next to Tamangs, 11.0% of garden land and 24.9% of outside land is owned by Rais. Among the Tagadharis, Chhetris have better land holding ownership than both Bahuns and Thakuris with 2.2% (inside the gardens) and 0.8% outside the gardens. Next to Tamangs, Rai and Limbu, Newars have better land holding patterns. Interestingly, 62.4% of land is owned by the workers outside the gardens and only 36.5% of total land holding is inside the gardens.

The type of outside land owned by Tagadharis is mainly wet type while excepting Mangars and Gurungs, all Matwalis have dry land outside the gardens. Here again, it is observed that Tagadharis prefer wet land due to their food habit in which rice is most important staple food while by food habit, Matwalis prefer dry land where millet can be cultivated. By tradition, Matwalis (drinking castes) must have *Jnar* or *Nigar* (local made beer) to complete their rituals and preparing *Jnar* or *Nigar*, millet is a must. It shows that the nature of land holding between Tagadharis and Matwalis is guided by their respective traditions of the past. Most of the Tagadharis reported to have their wet land in Bijanbari. Mirrik, Bongkulong (Soureni area of Mirrik) and Kalimpong while most of the Matwalis have dray land in nearby villages. Ownership of land in higher altitude villages of the workers is thin compared to lower altitude villages due to thin density of population, meagre scope for terracing the land and water resources. Due to stiff hill terrains the higher altitude land is difficult to bring under cultivation.

Another area of economic life of the workers is the quality of life that they have been leading in the plantations. Sometimes, the quality of life is supplemented by the style of life in the households of the workers.

Table 14.6

Caste and Quality of Life of the Workers

Sl. No.	Caste	Vehicle	T.V.	Radio	Watch	Telephone	Sofa Seat
1.	Bahun	2	170	200	310	1	35
2.	Chhetri	3	490	300	768	10	252
3.	Thakuri	6	310	328	391	20	600
4.	Newar	25	1,000	400	1,020	52	780
5.	Rai	10	10,000	700	10,275	30	888
6.	Limbu	12	2,500	960	2,800	25	1,000
7.	Mangar	6	1,200	700	1,800	18	300
8.	Gurung	4	726	600	956	7	630
9.	Bhujel	1	40	230	236	1	300
10.	Tamang	18	9,730	9,000	9,780	40	680
11.	Thami	2	199	200	300	6	350
12.	Sunuwar	4	302	235	308	1	140
13.	Lepcha	10	209	167	245	15	280
14.	Sherpa	12	230	200	250	10	260
15.	Kami	8	780	713	800	3	687
16.	Damai	8	260	230	280	3	240
17.	Sarki	10	210	210	220	2	240

It is observed from the above Table 14.6 that the life style or quality of life of the workers belonging to the Matwali group is much better than the Tagadharis in the plantations The quality of life having the modern equipments is much more in number among the Matwalis than Tagadharis. This may be due to the fact that almost all the Matwalis have either schedule caste, schedule tribe or other backward caste status in the society due to the policy of government. The reservation of Matwalis in the government and other schemes help them to lead better quality of life since the last two decades in the society in general and plantation industry in particular. It is also observed from the above table that access to better economic resources are monopolised by the Matwalis. This has lead Tagadharis either to totally merged with Matwalis or to migrate from the plantations to elsewhere in the hills or outside. The outmigration of Tagadharis was more rampant during the G.N.L.F. agitation, many Tagadharis left plantations for Nepal or Siliguri during the period.'

The quality of life of the workers in the plantations is predominantly Matwali in the sense that workers are satiated merely with engaging their offsprings in gardens or nearby gardens. It is rather observed to be a temporary phenomenon while in reality, quality of life of the workers is a permanent phenomenon for continuous progress of a society as a whole. Rendering quality issues that can go a long way is very limited among the workers. So, what is needed to do by the workers is to copy the thing that are good for the society from neighbouring communities like Bengali, Marwari, Bihari and others that can help to have better quality of life or life style for the coming generations in regard to money, education and savings. Basically, the extravagant nature of the workers must be stopped in order to bring about a change in the quality of the people in the plantations.

In order to understand the socio-economic conditions of tea plantation workers in the region under study, it is very much essential to know the West Bengal Plantation Labour Rules, 1956 which is framed in the light of Plantation Labour Act, 1951. The West Bengal Plantation Labour Rules, have VII chapters with 79 articles. Let us see the details of the Rules which are to be equally implemented in the plantations of Darjeeling Himalaya.

The chapter I has provided certain definitions of the Plantation Labour Act, 1951. Chapter II, III, IV, VI and VII are very important for us to know the plantation workers in West Bengal including the Himalayan plantations and their workers. The chapter I has describes the powers and functions of Inspecting Officer. It states that an Inspector shall for the purpose of giving effect to the provisions of the Act have power to do all or any of the following things :

(1) to photograph any non-adult workers.

(2) to inspect, examine, measure, copy, photograph, sketch or test as the case may be any house, building or rooms, register document maintained under the Plantation Labour Act, 1951 or anything provided for the purpose of securing the health or welfare of the workers employed in a plantation.

(3) to prosecute, conduct or defend before a court any complaint or other proceeding arising under the Act.

(4) to require an employer to supply or send any return or information relating to the provisions of the Act.

(5) to satisfy himself at each inspection that the provisions of the Act and Rules regarding the health and welfare of the workers employed in the plantation are observed, the adolescent and children employed in the plantations have been granted certificates of fitness and that no adolescent or child is employed who is unfit, the

prescribed registers are properly maintained, the periods of rest and holidays provided by the Act are granted and that the limits of hours of work (eight hours) laid down herein are not exceeded; the notice of period of work required it duly affixed; leave with wages of workers sickness leave and maternity benefits are granted in accordance to the provisions of the Act, to note how far the defects pointed in previous inspections are overcome or removed and how far orders previously issued is maintained or complied with; to point out all such defects pointed out or irregularities as he may have observed and to give orders for their removal and to record and furnish to the employer a summary of defects or irregularities and of his orders.

The plantation Inspector will be the Labour Commissioner. If the Labour Commissioner is in leave or the post is vacant, the Additional Labour Commissioner shall act as the Chief Inspector of Plantations. Again, the officers of the Government of West Bengal who are appointed as Deputy Labour Commissioner or Labour Officer, Assistant Labour Commissioner or Inspector of Factories or Medical Officer of Factories may be appointed as the Inspector of Plantations. Every order passed from time to time by the government shall be applicable to the employer and the new order passed by the government shall be sent to the employer personally or at his office or by registered post.

The role of plantation inspector has been critically observed in the present section. Normally, workers do not know the inspector of plantation as they do not keep liaison with the workers. Secondly, some inspectors inspite of having sense of duty cannot do it properly due to pressure from the top, both politically or otherwise. Thirdly, the plantation inspectors being the labour administrators in the plantations have their inherent problems. To know their inherent problems, let us see the nature of their work. Functionally, the labour administrators have two main roles, viz., (a) enforcement of Labour Legislations and (b) prevention and settlement of industrial disputes through the collective bargaining, conciliation, arbitration and adjudication. But doing these works, they are to note the fact that these duties are based on the principle of Directive Principles of State Policy of Constitution of India. The spirit of the state policy is to establish an egalitarian society and therefore the restoration of social justice is the motto of these state policy and therefore the role of labour administrator in the industry also. The principle of social justice has been used in different fashion in developed and developing countries as per their social systems. In our plantations, 40% of labour disputes are found over non-implementation of statutory provisions like working hours, intervals for rest, maintenance of registers and records, non-submission of returns, non-payment of wages in time, leave and holidays, welfare, safety and health measures and all these are enforceable under the law. Out of 100%, 35% of the disputes arise out of grievances such as denial of promotion, upgradation, union recognition termination of employment, lay off, closure, retrenchment, transfer etc., and these are also enforceable on violations of settlement or agreement etc. (Karan: 1999). In the absence of a separate regulatory mechanisms to tackle all these disputes, failure of enforcement machinery to secure its implementations and due to wide connotation of definition of the industry and industrial disputes given in the Industrial Act, 1947, these disputes are presently tackled by conciliation officers. It is seen that 70% of industrial disputes of the gardens are done by conciliation method only. The reason may be due to the excessive delay in adjudication which force the workers and management to seek the help of court. However, it is noted through the various agreements that lack of understanding and little knowledge of sociology of conflicts among the unions and management, the agreements do not last long.

Rest of the industrial disputes are observed on the issue like determination of wage structure, fringe benefits and other conditions of employment. For instance, now Coordination Committee of Tea Plantation Workers Union is demanding for wage structure on monthly basis. It is revealed from the experience from the plantations, 22% of these disputes are settled by collective bargainings and 78% of them are settled through conciliation. Due to the constant threat of using industrial action by the parties (Unions and management), the conciliation officers are eventually called upon to intervene and assist the parties. This has to be done by the conciliation officer in order to maintain peace and harmonious industrial relations in the plantations.

However, it is also noted that after 1991, the protectionism in trade (tea industry) has either been substantially diluted or even abolished. Like other industries, tea is also facing difficulties to maintain its efficiency for their survival. Their bargaining areas have been squeezed to such an extent that they cannot afford to permit adverse labour management relations beyond a limit. Now, the past appeasement policy of government in industrial relation field is totally decreasing. So, on the side of industry, mutual trust, participative culture, effective communication and information sharing are needed. And on the side of conciliation officer also certain changes are to be brought by the government.

Globalisation, Liberalisation and Privatisation stress on the training, educating and retraining of all concerned of the industry. Firstly, the status of conciliation officer as well as their terms of employment must be attractive in order to inspire sufficient confidence in parties. Secondly, the career development of the officers is very essential. Thirdly, recognition for good jobs done by the officers is to be taken into account. The attitudinal and environment changes are to be brought in the organisation. Again, the infrastructural and informational facilities are to be provided to them, for instance, not a single plantation inspector has government vehicle to go far and inaccessible areas of tea plantations. Finally, in-service training and retrainings are to be given at regular interval. The empowerment of conciliation officers are very important so that they can follow 'fire fighting' approach in labour administration in tea industry where almost all the workers are illiterates and all the management are highly educated. Further, the officers are well equipped with information which normally they are ignorant from the higher ups. A good hierarchy is to be maintained between the inspector and conciliation officer who is to have sufficient knowledge of the tea plantation industry and workers, skill, human resource orientation, and other qualities like credibility, clarity, conscience, courage, character and compassion to the workers. To do this Section of 7 and 7A of Industrial Disputes Act. are to be ammended. If these works are done then the role of labour inspector or plantation inspectors can be improved to a great extent. 'Hiring and purchasing philosophy' of the industry is to be made redundant if tea industry is to prosper and compete the other tea producing countries of the world.

The Duties of the Certifying Surgeon

For the purposes of the examination and certification of young persons who wish to obtain certificates of fitness, the certifying surgeons shall fix a suitable time and place in consultation with the employer for the attendance of such persons before the expiry of one month from the date of application, suited within the local limits assigned to him. Again, every certifying surgeon shall keep bound books containing certificates respectively in foil and counterfoil. In each book, the form shall be numbered consecutively and shall be printed on cloth-backed or other durable paper. The foil and counterfoil shall be filled in and either the signature or the left thumb mark of the person to whom the certificate is granted shall be taken on them. On being satisfied as to the correctness of entries made therein and of fitness of the person examined, the certifying surgeon shall sign the foil and initial in the foil and shall deliver the foil to the person examined. The foil will be the certificate of fitness. All the counterfoils in the book shall be preserved by the certifying surgeon for a period of at least two years after the issue of the last certificate in that book.

A person who loses a certificate of fitness which has been granted to him may apply to the certifying surgeon who granted it for a copy of the certificate and the said may grant a duplicate of the lost certificate. The 'Duplicate' shall clearly written in red ink across the duplicate certificate. The counterfoil in the bound book of forms shall be similarly marked 'Duplicate' and initiated by the initial of the surgeon. For every copy of a duplicate certificate granted, a fee of eight annas shall be charged from the person concerned which shall be credited to the government. The certifying surgeon shall maintain a register of all fees paid for the issue of duplicate certificates and shall initiate each entry therein. No duplicate certificate shall be granted to any person otherwise than in accordance with the provisions of this rule. The certifying surgeon at his periodical visit shall satisfy himself as to the fitness of all the adolescent and children employed in the plantation and shall revoke the certificate of fitness of any adolescent or child whom he deems to be fit.

The certifying surgeon shall hand over to the employer and chief inspector of factories and plantations a note detailing the result of each visit to the plantation. The certifying surgeon shall upon request of the chief inspector carry out such examination for any plantation or class of plantations where young persons are or are to be employed in any work which is likely to cause injury to their health. The employer shall provide for the purpose of any medical examination which the certifying surgeon wishes to conduct at the plantation a room which shall be properly cleaned and adequately ventilated and furnished with a screen, a table with writing materials and chairs. If a disqualified medical practitioner is employed in a garden or group hospital as certifying surgeon, an appeal shall lie against his findings to the Civil Surgeon of the area in which the plantation is situated.

The certifying Surgeon should have the following qualifications:-

(A) A certificate granted by authority specified in the schedule to the Indian Medical Degrees Act, 1916;

(B) A certificate granted by an authority specified in the schedules to the Indian Medical Council Act, 1963;

(C) A certificate granted under any State Law relating to the medical councils.

The chapter III of West Bengal Plantation Rules deals with health aspect of the workers. Drinking water is the most important dimension of health. It is stated in the Rules that an adequate supply of wholesome drinking water shall be made available in every plantation at work sites, at all times during the working hours. The water provided for drinking shall be supplied from the tap connected with a public water supply system or from any other source approved by the Chief Inspector of Plantations. If the drinking water supply is not supplied from the taps connected with the public supply system, it shall kept in suitable vessels and shall he renewed at least daily. All practicable steps shall be taken to protect the water and vessels from contamination and to keep vessels scrupulously, clean. Drinking water shall not be supplied from any open well or reservoir unless it is so constructed, suited in proper place, protected and maintained as to be free from the possibility of pollution by chemical, bacterial or other extraneous impurities. Where drinking water is supplied from such well or reservoir, the water in it shall be examined at such periodical intervals as may be directed by the Inspector by written order to determine if it is free from impurity and safe for consumption and shall be sterilised, if necessary. In every such case, the dates on which examination and sterilisation are carried out shall be recorded.

Report of the Health Officer

The Inspector may by order in writing, direct the employer to obtain at such time or at such intervals as he may deem fit, a report from the nearest laboratory to be specified by the Inspector about fitness for human consumption of the water supplied to workers and decision shall be taken on the opinion of Health Officer or certifying surgeon, if the former is not available. In every case the employer shall submit to the Inspector a copy of such report as soon as it is received.

Distribution of Water

Drinking water shall be supplied at work sites, at conveniently accessible points through the Paniwallas or by the tankers etc.

Latrine Accommodation

Latrine accommodation shall be provided in every plantation on the scale of one latrine for even fifty acres of the area under cultivation or part thereof provided that there shall be at least one latrine for males and at least one separate Latrine for females. The latrines shall be conveniently situated and shall be readily accessible to the workers employed in the plantation. The latrines should confirm to public health requirements and latrines other than those connected with an efficient water borne sewage system, shall comply with the requirement of the public health authorities. The employer shall make necessary arrangement for daily clearing of the latrines. Every latrine shall be under the cover and so partitioned off as to secure privacy and shall have a proper door and fastenings. Where workers of both sexes are employed there shall be displayed outside each latrine or latrine block, a notice in Hindi and also in the language understood by the majority of workers, signifying that the latrine is intended for use of men only or women only as the case may be. The notice shall also bear the figure of a man or a woman as the case may be. Where the pipe water supply is available with a sufficient number of water taps, conveniently accessible shall be provided in or near such latrine accommodation. If pipe water supply is not available, sufficient quantity of water shall be kept stored by the employer, in suitable receptacles near the latrines.

Construction and Maintenance of Drains

All drains carrying waste or sullage water shall be constructed in masonary or other impermeable materials and shall be regularly flushed and the effluent disposed of by connecting such drains with a suitable drainage line. Where there is no drainage line, the effluent shall be decodorised and rendered innocuous and then disposed off in suitable manner to the satisfaction of the Health Officer.

Another aspect of health is medical facilities or amenities provided to the workers of the plantations. The Rules states that there shall be two types of hospitals in the plantations, viz, garden hospitals and group hospitals. The garden hospitals will deal with out-patients, infectious cases, midwafery, simple pre-natal and post-natal care, care for infants and children and periodical inspection of all types of cases. Admission to group hospitals shall be done only when the employer shall not provide the facilities in the garden hospitals. The group hospitals shall be capable of dealing efficiently with all types of cases normally encountered but will not used for routine treatment. Again, admission to group hospitals will be done only on the recommendation of garden hospital medical practitioner or doctor. So, here every garden employer shall provide a garden hospital in his plantation according to the standards laid down in these Rules or the employer may have lied on beds in such hospital in a neighbouring plantation or other hospitals according to the scale of 15 beds per 1,000 workers as may be approved by the Chief Inspector. Further, the Rules also states that a plantation or group plantations may provide a dispensary with a qualified medical practitioner assisted by at least a full time trained nurse and such other staff as the Chief Inspector may consider necessary with corresponding reduction in the number of beds on which the plantation or group of plantations shall have a lien. A plantation employing 1,000 or more workers shall run its own garden hospital whereever possible while the plantations employing less than 1,000 workers which are situated within reasonable distances from another may with the approval of Chief Inspector combine and provide joint hospitals, dispensaries and share their expenses including the expenses of transport of patients. For the purpose, the plantations concerned shall submit to the Chief Inspector particulars of the scale of staff proposed to be employed, the equipment proposed to be provided, the location of joint hospitals, dispensaries, areas of plantations served, the distances of plantations from one another, the number of workers employed and all other relevant informations. In case of combined hospitals, plantations employing more than 200 workers shall whereever possible run their own dispensaries referred to in provisions of the Act of 1951. In the plantations where a garden hospital, dispensary or, a combined garden hospital or dispensary or a combined garden is not provided then it should maintain immediately by providing a first-aid box or cupboard equipped with such contents as may be specified by the Chief Inspector. The first-aid box or Cupboard shall be kept in charge of a responsible person trained in first aid box treatment whose services shall be readily available during all hours to render the first aid.

Again, the plantations having 350 or less workers should have dispensaries as per the specification given by the Inspector of Plantations having five detention beds under the full time care of a qualified compounder to be supervised by regular doctor from the nearest plantation.

Every garden hospital shall be under a qualified medical practitioner assisted by at least one trained Dhai, one trained midwife, a qualified compounder and a trained health assistant. The services of the staff shall be readily available during all hours. The Act also prescribed that there shall be one qualified medical practitioner for every 1,750 workers, there shall be one midwife for every 700 workers and there shall be one health assistant for every 2,100 workers. Where more than one medical practitioner is appointed, attempt shall be made to appoint at least one lady doctor.

A minimum of 15 beds shall be provided in every garden hospital per 1,000 workers served and each bed shall be allowed at least 60 square feet of floor space. Every hospital shall be of sound permanent construction with impermeable washable walls to a height of at least 5 feet on the inside and floor with proper water supply and efficient sanitary arrangements. Every hospital shall have pure piped water-supply and wards consulting room, operation theatre and dispensary each shall have a water point over a suitable glazed sink. The following departments shall be provided in the hospitals :-

1. General ward for males,
2. General ward for females,
3. Matennity with separate labour room,
4. Family Planning Centre,
5. Infectious ward with separate sanitary arrangements,
6. Out-patient department (with sufficient space for patients to wait under covers) preferably suited in a separate block from general wards,
7. Consulting room so arranged that patients can be examined in privacy.
8. Minor operation and dressing room,
9. Dispensary and drug store,
10. General store,
11. Kitchen for cooking (fly-proofed),
12. Staff quarters.

Group Hospitals

The plans for establishment of group hospitals containing details as regards their location and size, areas of plantations served, the number of workers employed therein etc. shall be approved by the state government. Every group hospital should have a minimum of 100 beds and there shall be at least three beds for 700 workers, every bed having 80 square feet of floor space. However, the government can relax the number of beds considering the alternative arrangement if exists for treatment of patients. The hospitals shall build according to the specifications of the State Government. There shall be the provisions of piped water supply of pure water, electricity, modern methods of sanitation and waterflushed closets. Each ward, labour room, surgical dressing room, consulting room and dispensary shall have a water point over a suitable glazed sink.

Each hospital shall have the provision for the following sections:

1. Operation theatre block,
2. X-ray block, Physical Therapy block,
3. Labour room,
4. T B. and V. D. Clinics,
5. Consulting and examination room,
6. Clinical laboratory room,
7. Dispensary,
8. Administrative block and office block,
9. Kitchen and Laundry blocks,
10. Stores,
11. Lavatories and bathrooms,
12. Mortary and Post Mortem rooms and
13. Out-patients block which should preferably be at some distance from the wards.

It is also specified by the Rules that there should be separate wards for males and females, maternity wards and isolated wards for infectious diseases. Similarly, X-ray and physical therapy blocks if not there, separate arrangement has to be made by the employer in some other hospitals. Every group hospital shall have such medical and other staff. All doctors in group hospitals should be qualified medical practitioners. There shall be 15 nurses for 100 beded hospitals of whom one shall be senior trained, five junior trained and nine assistant nurses. Such classification may be made according to their qualifications and experience. There shall be trained Health Visitor for supervision of mid-wives and Dhais and of the quality of such welfare work.

A properly equipped ambulance shall have to be maintained in every group hospital. Every dispensary, garden hospital and group hospital shall maintain such equipment and drugs etc. as may be specified by the government. The medical officer in-charge of each dispensary of garden hospital and group hospital shall maintain such registers, books, accounts and medical record in respect of every patient, as may be prescribed by the State Government. He may also comply with such regulations as may be by the State Government in respect of medical stores.

The out-patients department shall include the detention for observation and treatment, preventive treatment, such as vaccination of all drugs including those needed for injections and dressing and appliances that may be considered necessary, ante-natal and post-natal advice, provisions of certificates, free of cost in respect of maternity and sickness benefit claims under the Act. For inpatient treatment, the hospitals shall have provisions for food and medicine including such treatment at confinement as may be available at the hospital. If necessary, the government may fix the charge of food supplied to the patients while they are in the hospital.

It is also prescribed in the Rules that employer shall within six months of the effect of the Rules has to submit to the Central as well as State Governments regarding the facilities rendered to the patients. If any employer does not provide and maintain the medical facilities as required by the Rules to the satisfaction of Chief Inspector, then he may be fined with half of the estimated cost in advance. Further, the defaulting employer shall be liable to pay full cost of such medical facilities including charges in respect of a medical officer's visit to the plantation for the purpose of attendance on any sick worker or workers, the maintenance of sick worker in a hospital or dispensary for each day's maintenance and transport to and for provided to the sick worker or workers. When such fine is due, then the Chief Inspector shall give him notice in writing requiring the payment of amounts to the collector who may recover the same as an arrear of land revenue.

The State Government, by Gazettee Notification shall constitute a Medical Advisory Board for consultation in regard to matters connected with the provisions of medical facilities. The Board shall consists of three persons of whom one shall be notified as Chairman, two representatives each from employer and workers and a representative of the Indian Medical Association. The Board advises the State Government regarding the standard of medicines or medical facilities, scrutinize the yearly progress of the employer in this field and issue reports about the medical facilities of the workers to the State Government.

Another area of the Rules is welfare of the workers. It is prescribed by the Rules that in every plantation where one hundred and fifty or more workers work, there should be a canteen with facilities for sale of tea and snacks to the workers. The tea and snacks in every canteen shall be sold to the workers on a "non-profit-non-loss basis". The prices of the items served in the canteen shall be conspicuously displayed in every canteen notice board.

In every plantation where there are fifty or more workers in any day of the preceding twelve months, the employer should provide and maintain a creche or creches for the use of the children of the women workers who are below the age of six years, according to the standard laid down in the Rules. Every creche shall be conveniently accessible to the mothers of the children accommodated therein with 15 square feet of floor area for each child. Again, there should be the provision for sound construction of the creche with a good plinth as approved by the Chief Inspector. The creche must have good furniture and cradle for each child below the age of two years with a woman as creche in-charge The Dhai must be there as trained ones. In every creche there should be a washing room for the children. In every creche, there should be the provision for supplying clean and pure milk for the children upto the age of two years. For children above two years, there should be adequate supply of wholesome refreshment. The mother of each child accommodated in the creche shall be allowed to nurse her child at least twice a day. The creche staff should be provided a suitable cloth for use while on duty in the creche with the children.

The Rules also provide that every employer should provide recreational facilities to the workers such as indoor games suitable for adults and child workers, play ground for adult and children of the workers should be there in every plantation as well as the equipments for the sports and games etc. Again, a group of employers may maintain joint recreation centres and play-grounds near the workers' quarters.

Educational Facilities for Workers' Children

Every employer shall, if the number of workers' children between the ages of six years and twelve years in his plantation exceeds 25, provide and maintain a primary school or schools for imparting primary education to the children. If the employer may not provide and maintain primary school if there is one under the direct control of and management of State Government or of any local body for imparting free education to the children upto the primary or higher standard, with enough seats to admit the children between the ages of six and twelve years of workers in his plantation and within a distance of one mile from the place where workers reside in their plantation or if under any other law, he is required to pay a cess or tax for primary education. It is also stated in the Rules that a group of employers may maintain a joint school in a reasonable distance, from the houses of the workers. Along with school, there should be open play ground for the children who attend the school.

The employer or employers should appoint one teacher for every forty children. The teacher must have requisite qualification prescribed by the State Government laws. The curriculum, duration, standard and syllabus of the course of instruction to be imparted in the primary school shall be such as may be approved by the State Government. No fees should be taken from the children who attend the primary schools.

Housing Accommodation for the Workers

Every employer shall provide and maintain for every worker and his family residing in a plantation, housing accommodation as near as possible to the place of work. It shall be open to an employer to provide such accommodation in the course of several years provided that houses shall be built for at least eight percent of the resident workers every year.

All housing accommodation for the workers in a plantation shall conform to such standards and specifications as may be approved by the State Government on the recommendations of the West Bengal Housing Board. If there is no standard plan provided by the government housing board, then in that case the houses are to be made as per the specifications given by the Chief Inspector of the plantations. The housing accommodation should be provided on dry well-drained land, which has consistent of the wholesome drinking water within the reasonable distance for the plantation. In material tracts, the houses shall be built at a safe distance from the swamps and marshes and above the highest flooded level. The size of the plot selected for preparation of the sites for the construction of houses shall be determined subject to the previous approval of the State Government. Again, adequate lighting arrangement shall be provided in and around the areas in which housing accommodation is provided. The employer shall maintain a good condition of approach road to the workers where they are accommodated. The employer shall keep vicinity of the accommodation clean. The latrines and wastes should be cleaned; drains should be cleaned. All the houses will be built in accordance of the Housing Scheme of the Government of West Bengal for the workers. Every employer shall submit the report of the houses provided to the workers annually to the Chief Inspector. The house of the workers is to be repaired at the expenses of the employer time to time considering the conditions of the houses. The worker should bring to the notice of employer regarding defects etc. Here the Inspector should report the conditions of workers' houses to the employer and then it is the duty of employer to overcome the defects of the houses. The employer shall get all the houses limed-washed at least once every year and all the doors, windows and other wooden structure varnished or painted once in every three years. A record of dates which the lime-washed or painting was carried shall be maintained in the register. No rent shall be charged by an employer for housing accommodation provided to the workers and their families, residing in the plantation. The houses shall be allotted on the basis of one house for a worker having a family for the use of the worker and his family. If there are two more workers in a family, one house shall be allotted in respect of any such family in the name of any worker of the family. In the termination of service of a worker in whose name the house is allotted under the proceeding previously, the house be shall allotted in the name of any other member of his family who is a worker. It is also prescribed in the Rules that the employer may allot houses to workers not having families at the rate of one worker for not more than four such workers. The occupant of the house shall not make any unauthorised additions to or alteration in the house. Further, the occupant cannot exchange the house with the occupant of another house except with written permission of the employer. The occupant shall not let the house or any part of it to any other person without the permission of the employer. No goat or cattle shall be kept in the house or in the varandah etc.

Occupation of Accommodation after Termination of Employment

When the worker dies in the service of the employer or retires or goes on transfer or resigns or goes on leave or when his services are terminated, he or she or his or her family retains the house upto the period as detailed below :

1. In case of death, transfer or termination of services, a period of not exceeding two months;
2. In case of retirement or resignation, a period of not exceeding one month;
3. In case of leave for the period of leave and;
4. In case of where the discharge or dismissal of a worker is disputed and the matter has been referred for conciliation or has been taken to an industrial tribunal or court, for so long as the case is not finally disposed of.

If the competent authority is satisfied that a worker or any other member of his family refuses to vacate the house allotted to such worker after the expiry of the period he or she may be served with a notice of vacant by post or by affixing a copy of it on the outer door or some other conspicious part of the house or by such other manner which he deem fit for doing the same. In the event of the failure of worker to vacate the house than in that case the competent authority may evict the worker from the house. But before the eviction of the worker, the eviction notice is to be given to the worker. In case of termination of his services, an employee, where possible be given reasonable facilities to harvest the standing crops in his garden plot or in the alternative, he shall be paid adequate compensation in lieu of the standing crops.

The Chapter V of West Bengal Plantation Labour Rules deals with hours and limitation of employment. Every worker has to work for eight hours work in the plantation. The Rules provides for weekly holiday. It states that no worker shall be required to work on the plantation on a Sunday except when he has had or will have a day of rest on one of the three days immediately preceding or succeeding that Sunday, if the weekly holiday is substituted by any other day. Even if the worker may be asked to work in the closed holiday but in so doing he shall not work for more than ten days consequatively without having holiday for full one day. Every worker shall be paid for work on the day of rest at the overtime rate prevailing in a particular area as fixed under the Minimum Wages Act, 1948 and where there is no such rate, at double the ordinary rate. The notice regarding the period of work should be written in English and in language understood by the majority of workers in the plantation which should display notice at the convenient place for the workers.

Another aspect of the Rules is that it provides provisions for sickness and maternity benefits as per its Chapter VI. It states that every worker shall be entitled to obtain sickness allowances from his employer or each day of certified sickness from his employer for the total period of 14 days in a year at the rate of two-thirds of his daily wages or of the average daily earnings if he is employed on piece wages subject to a minimum of rupee one per day for an adult worker and a minimum of seventy paise per day for a child worker. The sickness benefit shall be paid at the option of the worker either at the time of payment of weekly advances on account of wages or along with the first instalment or wages payable to the workers after he resumes his work on recovery from certified sickness leave.

Every employer shall pay to the worker sickness allowance due to him on presentation of such certificate in accordance with the provision of Act. If a worker has to pay any fee for obtaining sickness certificate, the employer shall bear the cost.

The Rules also stated that if a worker does not take any sickness benefit in a year then in that case his leave should be allowed to take in the succeeding year provided the number of days shall not in any case exceed thirty days. In addition to this, the worker shall in case of certified sickness be allowed to have leave with wages on the leave not taken for medical purpose. But the leave should be genuine on the production of certificate obtained from the Chief Medical Officer of plantation, a government doctor not below the rank of an Assistant Surgeon.

Further, the Act also states that every woman employed in a plantation shall be entitled to and her employer shall be liable for the payment of maternity benefits as per the provisions of Maternity Benefit Act, 1961.

The Chapter VII deals with the Miscellaneous provisions of the Rules deals on the Appeal Procedure to the worker. After the thorough enquiry of the cases, the worker shall be given award in the penalty to the employer by the District Magistrate from the revenue of the plantations.

If we analyse the provisions of West Bengal Plantation Labour Rules, 1956 as modified in 1959 and 1972, it is seen that the Rules is mainly concerned with the workers and not with the family members of the workers. Secondly, the elaborate Rules of the government is uncomprehensible to the rank and file workers who are mainly illiterate and semi-literate in the plantations. These may be the apparent reasons why lot of outside leaders of middle class educated have taken upper hand in trade unions and trade union movement in the plantation industry. Thirdly, the plantation Rules is based on the welfare legislation (Plantation Labour Act, 1951) and hence very often over the period of fifty years of independence, the plantation workers are sorry subject for the academicians and politicians as well as policy makers who consider the workers as backward or isolated class of working class in the country. Further, the plantation Rules are not as a whole be applied in the Himalayan Plantation Industry as it does not reflect the distinct problems of the region and workers. The socio-economic upliftment of the workers in the light of the Rules is appeared to be half-hearted effort in the sense that the workers are not the same type of workers as we find in Terai and Dooars areas of the State. It may be the holistic approach for the Government of West Bengal but not for the workers working in the Himalayan plantations as they feel the Rules being alien to the workers and these Rules may be beneficial to the management to twist the provisions to their own biased interpretations. Of course, for example, housing is given to the workers but nobody knows the nature and type of houses there. During the rainy season, water pours from the roof of the houses and workers have to sit under umbrellas throughout the night. Medicines for fever, headache and stomache pains are same at the hospitals of the plantations for the workers and if any intelligent person asks the doctor about the fault then the doctor's responses say that he has nothing to do as such medicines are provided by the management. Talking of wage structure of the workers which is 34.80 today, it is observed that what is the logic to get twelve to fourteen thousands rupees per month by a manager when a worker hardly gets seven hundred rupees per month. Similarly, from the social upliftment point of view, there has no change of the workers since the last 150 years as workers were Coolies and today also they are still 'Coolies'. They are made Coolies for ever.

15

TRADE UNION MOVEMENT IN TEA INDUSTRY

Prior to 1947, it is seen from the study that socio-economic life of tea plantation workers was totally a life of slaves. In 1945, during the war period, a trouble cropped in Dhajia T.E. taking the issue of rations of the workers. Management even told the workers to go to Nepal for rations and other necessary things. This created a sense of deprivation in the minds of the workers. Similar picture was there in other gardens of the hills where even young beautiful girls were the private property of management. However, such grievances were accumulating in the minds of workers. By this time, some local leaders like Ratanlal Brahmin, Janaklal Subba, B.B. Hamal, B.B. Chettri, Susil Chatterjee etc. were trying to mobilise workers by holding meetings in the labour lines secretly at nights. So, no trade union movement in the clear sense of the term could take place in the Himalayan tea industry as union was considered as an illegal organisation by management and government or local administration in Darjeeling.

Origin of Trade Union Movement

Discussing the origin the trade union movement in his book 'A History of Indian Tea Industry' (1967) Sir Percival Griffith states that 'In Darjeeling trouble began with the election of a communist candidate to the Bengal Legislative Assembly in 1946, after which the communist party of India organised a tea garden workers union in the Darjeeling District and then proceeded to serve strike notices in 17 tea estates. Lack of uniformity in wages and other forms of remuneration between one garden and the other played into the hands of mischief makers. The Darjeeling planter has always been a sturdy individualist and independent tradition of old proprietory gardens still lingered. It was easy therefore, for the communists to pick up gardens, where conditions either were or seemed less favourable to labour and they exploited this technique with considerable skill. It was at one time hoped that the non-communist body known as Gorkha League would have a steadying effect on labour in Darjeeling, but the league at this time was badly led. It showed no sense of responsibility and it was often concerned to outfit the communists in its demands. The Darjeeling Planters' Association took steps to secure greater uniformity of conditions, but the situation remained uneasy.

Trouble developed in an acute form in Mundakotee T.E. in the second half of 1946. The CPI had secured a firm footing in that garden and had for some months deliberately encouraged indiscipline and fostered a go-slow movement. Disciplinary action was taken in December, 1946 and 11 of the ring leaders signed a declaration that they would be amenable to garden discipline and refrain from subversive activity. The Chairman of the Industrial Tribunal inquired into these matters the promise was in words only and never followed in action. Matters went from bad to worse and in April 1947 the garden authority felt thereby obliged to declare a lock-out. The instigatiors of the trouble were dismissed and eviction orders were served against 11 of them. The lockout continued till January 26, 1948 and it was perhaps the most prolonged one ever known in the North-East India.

The strong action taken by the authorities of Mundakotee T.E. and unequivocal report of the Industrial Tribunal and a salutary effect for a time, but inspite of West Bengal Government's ban on the CPI, the communist union continued actively, again broke up in the same garden, but strong action by the police, followed by arrests of some ring leaders seemed to have convinced the labour that they were being led astray. Other estates were also affected by the general unrest created by CPI. In Margaret's Hope T.E., for example, an estate employee set himself out to make work impossible. In the words of the Chief Labour Advisor, 'he organised a reign of terror in the garden. By day all appeared to be quiet, but at night employees were forced to join the CPI and to pay subscriptions and were assaulted if they refused'. It is believed on reliable evidence, that a plot to kill manager and his head clerk was hatched and on 27th March, 1950 an assault was made on a garden employee who had refused to join CPI. The manager took strong action against subversive activities subsequently approved by the Assistant Labour Commissioner and the prime mover of these troubles was arrested. Conditions gradually returned to normal.

These incidents at Mundakotee and Margaret's Hope were typical of the spirit which persisted in many parts of the districts at that time. The mood lasted for a considerable time and at the end of his tour in the district, Griffith recorded a note to the effect that government lapsed the bonds of discipline, the frequent meetings of CPI at local Bazars were the starting point of disorder on the gardens and that in some time in some areas, intimidation of staff was going on all the time. Planters were in a continued state of nervous tensions. Since that time a gradual improvement has taken place and at the end of our period, relations between management and labour in Darjeeling are reasonably good.

It is noted however, Griffith could not understood that the landmark of trade union movement in Darjeeling hill gardens had already started before in 1946. Prior to this (Lama and Sarkar : 1986) starting years of trade union movement any sort of freedom movement, prolonged management by British planters under the British Raj, critically long period of Second World War and its harmful effects on the economy, the depression of 1930's, the passing of Trade Union Act, 1926 granting the right to organise the trade unions, all these did not have any effect on the tea plantation workers in Darjeeling till 1946-47, in terms of motivation and consciousness for collective bargaining for improving living condition of workers. The British Economic Historian, Griffith also without knowing the local living condition commented as 'Reign of Terror, Instigators of trouble, in the hands of mischief makers, subversive activities' in his book. He could have commented these as tea plantations might have been completely termed as 'Colonial Enclaves' which in their norm should be free from trade union activity. However, he said that there was lack of uniformity in respect of wages and other forms of remuneration from one garden to another. Further, he hinted that the Darjeeling planter had the tradition of exploitation of the workers on the ground that gardens were considered as private property of British planters. These were the reasons why CPI could easily penetrated deep into the gardens and became successful in its venture. This role of CPI is recognised by every other trade union organisations later on in Darjeeling.

Discussing the origin of trade union movement in tea industry, the 15th September, 1945 is to be always remembered as on that date the first union known as Darjeeling Tea Garden Workers's Union was established under the leadership of Sushil Chatterjee, Ratanlal Brahmin, Ganeshlal Subba, B.B. Hamal and B.B. Chherti for the tea plantation workers. The trade union movement in the hill areas was further intensified on a solid footing due to emergence of various veteran political leaders of the region. This made the common workers more vocal to their grievance. Both strikes and lockouts became positive features of the industrial scene in the hill region.

In the early 1950's under the able leadership of Deo Prakash Rai another union known as Darjeeling District Chia Kaman Shramik Sangh was formed. The union was affiliated to the local party known as Gorkha League. Regardless of their differences, these unions cooperated each other for the common cause of the plantation workers. For example, in 1955 both the unions cooperated for the restoration of 14 points demands of the workers and jointly called a strike. This strike became successful as workers got some favour from the management, for the first time.

In the early 1960's, under the leadership of Dr. Maitree Bose, another union known as National Union of Plantation Workers was formed with Dr. Bose as President and L.M. Pradhan as General Secretary.

The trade unions of Darjeeling hills raised the issue of non-payment of wages of workers in Fagu T.E. in 1962-63. After a long struggle and intervention of Labour Commissioner, Government of West Bengal, their payment was made. Again, in 1964, unions had to intervene in the dispute between management and labour in regard to *Khatland* (kitchen land). After a long persuassion with the management the land was returned back to the workers. Similarly, the issue of closure of Rungeet T.E. arose and here in this case unions even threatened the management to open the garden by union themselves if management did not open it in this case Government had been compelled to intervene the situation and at the initiative of Labour Minister, the garden was opened. Again, the Avongrove Tea Estate was opened after following many formalities.

During the decade, unions rose the issue of frequent changes of management and problems associated with such changes, quality of management, emergence of directors with merchant background, without having any experience of tea industry, quick profit making of the garden owners and low profile of Government authorities in finding faults of the owners were the basic issues of the workers. In such situation, the unions had no alternative except to demand for the nationlisation of tea industry in the region. In this respect, Government also reacted positively and nationlised some tea gardens like Pandem, Rangeroong T.E., Rungmook and Cedar T.E., Via-Tukvar T.E., Pashok T.E., Rungneet T.E., Luksom T.E., etc. Such trade union movement was further strengthen by the reports of Rege Committee on Tea Plantation Workers (1944) and National Labour Conference (1969) which observed that tea plantation workers were helpless and unorganised till 1947.

The spectacular feature of all the three trade unions had respective political affiliations. For instance, NUPW (INTUC), Darjeeling District Chia Kaman Mazdoor Union (CITU) and Darjeeling District Chia kaman Shramik Sangh (Gorkha League) had their respective philosophy. Each union played the role of pressure creator on the living conditions of the plantation workers. During the period, interestingly after the separation of CPI with CPI(M) formar lost hold of the plantation workers. The division of trade unions along the ideological lines got momentum. Such ideological struggle between the unions cropped up so many problems and prospectives in the hill gardens. Negatively, the fragmentation of unions helped the fragmentation of workers into different groups which blurred the development of worker-leadership in the gardens. Women workers, though in majority, played a passive role in trade union movement. Union leaders felt that union works as part time jobs. This caused the inter-union rivalries which caused the lives of many workers in the gardens. This helped the management to follow the "divide and rule policy" in the industry. Under the circumstances, collective bargainings for the workers became weak. Thus, most of the agreements were unrealistic. This caused again the inter-union rivalries at garden like Chungtong T.E. where on May 13, 1985, a CPI(M) worker was murdered. The issue was raised in Legislative assembly, Calcutta. Such events in the garden started loosing the confindence of leaders and workers started devaiting from the trade union activities. So, in this juncture, workers started looking for different alternative of the survival. Till this time, i.e. 1985, The Gurkhaland agitation under the leadership of Subash Ghising reached far and wide corner of tea estates of Darjeeling Himalaya. During the agitation, no union could work for the plantation workers. After the formation of Darjeeling Gurkha Hill Council, 1988, another trade union known as Himalayan Plantation Workers Union emerged in 1989 for the plantation workers.

Trade Union Movement in Nineties

After the GNLF agitation, the trade union movement has turned its direction to different dimension. Interestingly, after 1989 all the previous national trade unions had been replaced by the HPWU. All those national unions have no locus standi among the workers today in the industry. Recently, in 1998, another union known as Darjeeling, Terai and Dooars Chia Kaman Mazdoor Union had been emerged under the political patronage of Communist Party of Revolutionary Marxist - the splinter from state Communist Party of India (Marxist). However. HPWU with 88% of plantation workers as members, DTDCKMU with 6% members from the gardens and DDCKSS with 3% members are functioning in the hill tea plantation today. Interestingly, all the three political parties are regional parties which have defined their union as the organisations of isolated tea garden working population in the isolated Himalayan region of the country.

Before we delve into the trade union movement in detail in the Himalayan tea industry, let us see the sociology of working class in order to arrive at a conclusive generalisation.

The plantation workers of Darjeeling Himalaya have 41588 households with 52,913 workers. They are all Nepali castes and tribes. The traditional Nepali society can be conceptually classified into two groups, viz, Tagadhari and Matwali on the basis of certain social and ritual criteria. Tea plantation workers of Darjeeling have still preserved this traditional system to some extent today inspite of considerable changes in their culture. Some of the Tagadharis have been adapting the way of life of Matwalis in the plantations. Among the Tagadharis, Chhetris are on the front in this respect. Even among the Chhetris, as Matwalis do, are carrying their rituals with the sacrifice of animals and using locally made wine known as *Jnar* or *Nigar* (made of fermented millet). It is observed from this study another 30,000 casual workers are engaged in high plucking season (between March to November) every year. It means that altogether, 82,913 people are directly involved as workers in the tea plantations of Darjeeling Himalaya. Besides, another three and half lakhs population are indirectly dependent on the tea plantation industry which earns about 140 crores rupees foreign money every year (Pramanik Probir: Statesman: 30: December: 1999). Interestingly, it is transparent from the Table 15.1 that employment of female workers is higher than the male counterpart.

Table 15.1.
Tea Plantation Workers in Darjeeling Himalaya (1999)

Sl. No.	*Caste Status*	*Male*	*%*	*Female*	*%*	*Total Worker*	*%*
	Tagadhari						
	(Jharra)						
1.	Bahun	100	0.4	150	0.5	250	0.5
	(Thimaha)						
2.	Chhetri	216	0.9	400	1.4	616	1.5
3.	Thakuri	50	0.2	200	0.7	250	0.5
	Matwali						
	(Setho)						
4.	Newar	507	2.0	551	2.0	1058	2.0
5.	Mangar	1270	5.1	1376	5.0	2646	5.0
6.	Gurung	762	3.1	826	3.0	1588	3.0
7.	Rai	13180	32.2	14277	51.6	27457	51.9
8.	Limbu	1778	7.1	1926	7.0	3704	7.0
9.	Tamang	5080	20.1	5503	19.9	10583	20.0
10.	Sunuwar	254	1.0	275	1.0	529	1.0
11.	Bhujel	254	1.0	275	1.0	529	1.0
12.	Thami	254	1.0	275	1.0	529	1.0
13.	Sherpa	254	1.0	275	1.0	529	1.0
14.	Lepcha	254	1.0	275	1.0	529	1.0
	(Kalo)						
15.	Kami	507	2.0	551	2.0	1058	2.0
16.	Damai	254	1.0	275	1.0	529	1.0
17.	Sarki	254	1.0	275	1.0	529	1.0
	Total	**25228**	**47.7**	**27685**	**52.3**	**52913**	**100.0**

It is observed that female outnumbered (52.3%) the male (47.7%) due to the fact that Nepali male population are interested for non-plantation works. It means that male mobility from the plantations are encouraged by the plantation system. This has double benefits for the industry. One is to get good jobs from females and secondly to curtail certain benefits for the families of the workers. Still another reason for the employment of more number of women workers is due to the logic that females are more obedient, than the males and more simple minded than male counterpart. Moreover, it is believed by all the planters that finger tips of the females are very sensitive to pluck the qualitative tea leaves only. Generally, it is also believed that females can render the similar tender care to tea bushes as they do in case of their children.

The Table 15.1 indicates that 97.9% tea plantation workers are Matwalis while the percentage of Tagandaris is only 2.1%. On the whole, the Matwali castes constitute the main working force of the plantations. Among the Tagadharis, Bahun is dominant caste though its percentage is slightly lower than Chhetris and Thakuris (Thimaha Tagadharis) with 0.5% and 1.5% respectively. Tagadharis (both Jharra and Thimaha) are purely Hindus hailing from Nepal. They are called Tagadharis which means that they wear sacred threads and are not supposed to drink or use wine in the rituals. Next to the Chhetris, Thakuris are there. But these two castes seem to have been almost insignificant in so far as their separate caste identities are concerned (Sharma: 1997) in the plantations of Darjeeling Himalaya.

Traditionally, Thakuris were treated to be the ruling caste in Nepal (Bista: 1991). They had royal patronage in Nepal. But after coming to the plantations, they have been gradually assimilating among the Chhetris. Thus, Thakuris and Chhetris form an integral part of the Thimaha category of Tagadhari group. They cannot do priestly jobs. Socially, they seem to have been assimilating themselves into the Matwali way of life and found to have claimed themselves as the descendents of Khas Matwalis of Nepal Himalayas.

Similarly, it is also observed from the Table 1 that among the Setho Matwalis, Sherpas (1.0%), and Lepcha (1.0%) are Scheduled Tribes and Kami (2.0%), Damai (1.0%) and Sarki (1.0%) are Scheduled Castes. The Lepcha and Sherpa along with Thami (1.0%) and Tamang (20.0%) are predominantly Buddhists. The other groups of Matwalis, i.e. Kalo Matwali (Kami, Damai and Sarki) along with Rai (51.9%) Limbu (7.0%), Mangar (5.0%), Gurung (3.0%), Sunuwar (1.0%), Bhujel (1.0%) of Setho Matwali group have form a dominant group though Rai, Limbu, Gurung, Mangar, Bhujel, Newar etc. are mainly Hindus but they practice animistic rituals. Historically, Kami, Damai and Sarki were treated as untouchables by Bahuns, Chhetris, and Thakuris in Nepal but the Matwali castes had no such conception of so-called untouchability. In other words, the Setho Matwalis had no difference with the Kalo Matwalis in Nepal and Sikkim.

Among the Matwalis, the most dominant caste is Rai (51.9%) and Tamang (20.0%). They were early migrants to tea plantations in Darjeeling hills from Nepal and Sikkim. Following Rai and Tamang, Limbu (7.0%) emmigrated to the plantations. The main reason for migration of these castes were due to the fact that they were ousted by the house of Gorkhas in Nepal during the latter half of the eighteenth century. These castes strictly practised animistic religion in Nepal and vehemently disagreed to follow the Brahmanical rites practised by Bahuns and Chhetris in Nepal during the latter half of 17th century. It is therefore observed that these three castes along with other Setho Matwalis (including the scheduled castes such as Kami, Damai and Sarki) and Scheduled Tribes like Lepchas and Sherpas have formed the most dominant group in tea plantation industry of Darjeeling hills or Eastern Himalaya.

It is also observed that Sherpas were migrated from eastern Nepal to the tea plantations following Rai, Limbu, Mangar, Gurung, Tamang in the beginning of 19th century. It is also observed that among the Lepchas, indegeneous Lepchas did not prefer to work in tea plantations as they were shifting cultivators. Only the Lepchas who were ousted from Sikkim to Nepal during early Chowgel dynasty had migrated to the plantations as Kamanee Coolies. The migrant Lepchas were mainly landless agricultural labourers in Nepal. The poor economic conditions forced them to migrate to the plantation industry for employment. Thus, Lepchas, Sherpas, Rais, Limbus, Tamangs and Thamis had migrated to the plantations mainly during the formative period of tea industry in the Eastern Himalaya. They were beef-eaters which was then prohibited strictly in Nepal. This may be the strongest reason for their migration to Munglan or India (Pradhan, 1991) or Indian Himalayas. They were followed by castes like Gurungs, Mangars, and Newars who were also not in favour of following Hindu rites and rituals in Nepal and Sikkim and gradually migrated to tea plantations of the Darjeeling Himalaya.

The Tagadharis as it is revealed from the present study in tea plantations of Darjeeling are the latest migrants. They migrated here from the urban areas of Darjeeling, Kurseong and Kalimpong after the forties of the 19th century. Another reason for their late migration to Munglan in general and tea plantations in particular was due to the establishment of Panchayati Raj adminitration in Nepal and opening of terai belt of Nepal due to Indo-Nepal Anti Malarial Project. This helped the landless Tagadharis to make an easy pretext to migrate to the plantations for permanent employment as wage labourers and white color jobs. Still another reason for their latter migration to tea industry was that they were ruling class in Nepal both at grassroot and national levels. This may be the reason why here in tea plantations also Ratanlal (a Brahmin) led the workers to mobilise and formed trade union for the first time in tea plantations of Darjeeling Himalaya, in early forties of 19th century (Dahal: 1995).

Recent Trends in Trade Union Movement

The manifestoes of the Himalayan Plantation workers Union (GNLF), Darjeeling, Terai and Dooars Chia Kaman Mazdoor Union (CPRM) and Darjeeling District Chia Shramik Sangh (Gorkha League) reveal the fact that tea garden workers in the Himalayan region feel deprieved of the welfare measures enshrined in the government acts on the ground that they belong to separate ethnic community. Ethnically, they are Gurkhas (Nepalis) and culturally they are as good as any other tribal population of the Himalayas. So, the formation of trade unions is in the line of regional political ideology and this might be the apparent reason why the central union leaders and leaders of political parties are same. However, the nomenclature of the unions are different from the regional political parties perhaps due to the question of acquiring registration certificates from the government of West Bengal.

The history of trade union movement in the Himalayan tea industry appears to be externally related to poor working conditions of the workers but internally it is related to the sense of deprivation of a ethnic community by the outside management personnel. To the garden workers, if the past management personnel were British colonialists then the present management are outsider or as good as the British colonialists. They are outsiders as they do not have much concern about the socio-economic upliftment of the plantation workers. Talking with garden managers, it is understood that ninety percent of managers feel that their present job as managers in the region are stepping stones for their higher professional career.

The plantation workers also feel that government and government Acts are mainly meant for management to manage the workers with minimum facilities including wages. The government and management always keep each other satiated with the various tactics. Hardly, workers come across the government officials in the plantations or know government officials to ventilate their grievances directly. It is also observed from the study that management and government feel that tea industry including the workers are their custodials. Under the changed situation especially after 1991 the management and government are in one side and plantation workers on the other as they can be easily retrenched or downsized.

Unlike Dooars (Jalpaiguri District) and Terai (Siliguri Sub-division of Darjeeling District) tea plantations of West Bengal, hill tea plantations have its own background, as we discussed in earlier chapters, in so far as the formation of trade unions is concerned today. Ethnic dimension or base is the basis of the plantation workers in terms of local ethnic meaning and definitions. This is another reason why other popular unions of national significance have not been able to get hold of tea plantation workers today in Darjeeling hills. Another reason to the union leaders for having such ethnic base of unions is due to the government policy which has whimsically consider all the hill population particularly tea garden workers as the migrants or the descendents of migrants from Nepal. Still another reason to have such an ethnic base of the unions is due to the fact that government has incorporated all Bhutias including the Refugees from Tibet into the category of Scheduled Tribe of the region.

After discussing this characteristic features of present trade union movement in the Himalayan tea industry today, let us see the involvement of tea plantation workers in the trade union movement today. Discussing the involvement of workers in the unionisation process, special thrust has been given to the socio-economic background of the workers.

It is apparent from the Table 15.2 that Bahuns is in the G.N.L.F. led Himalayan Plantation Workers Union with only 0.4% while their percentage in Darjeeling, Terai and Dooars Chia Bagan Mazdoor Union (CPRM) is 1.5% and in other unions like NUPW, DDCKSS, DDCBMU etc. are 2.0%. While 3.1% of Chhetris are in DTDCKMU (CPRM), Again, only 1.0% of Chhetris are in HPWU (GNLF). The percentage of Chhetris in DDCBMU (CITU) is 1.8% and 1.9% of them are in other unions. Similar picture is found in case of Thakuris in so far as their involvement in the trade unions is concerned. On the whole, it is seen from the table that only 4.0% of plantation workers are from the Tagadharis and 96.0% of them are Matwalis.

Among the Matwalis, 53% of members of Himalayan Plantation Workers Union comes from Rai caste followed by 19.3% of members from the Tamangs, 6.7% of Limbus and 4.8% of Mangars are members in the HPWU. Similarly, 2.9% of Gurung and 2.1% of members from Kamis are the members of the HPWU. The percentages of other castes in the union is not so significant.

On the whole, it appeared from the above table that 71.6% of Tagadharis support the Himalayan Plantation Workers Union on the ground that they believed themselves as the real Gurkhas. The rational behind this is that traditionally the Tagadharis used to contend themselves as real Gurkhas (protectors or worshippers of cows) people (Northey and Morris: 1976, Pradhan: 1991). Such a legacy had helped them to be the staunch supporters of the G.N.L.F. led union though the top leadership of the union is in the hand of Matwalis. Secondly, Tagadharis, though recent settlers in tea plantations as Sukumbasis, have along with Matwalis been declared as an integral part of Gurkha Community of the region by the Gurkha National Liberation Front. So, their safety and security is assured as they cannot be retrenched as in the past (Deo Prakash Rai: 1963) from the plantations in the light of the provisions of the Industrial Disputes Act, 1947 which stresses

Table 15.2
Involvement of Workers in Trade Unions

Sl. No.	*Caste Status*	*HPWU*	*%*	*DTDCKMU*	*%*	*DDCKMU*	*%*	*Others**	*%*
	Tagadharis (Jharra)								
1.	Bahun = 250	171	0.4	52	1.5	16	0.9	11	1.1
2.	(Thimaha)								
	Chettri = 616	457	1.0	106	3.1	32	1.8	21	1.9
3.	Thakuri = 250	171	0.4	52	1.5	16	0.9	11	1.1
	Matwalis								
	(Setho)								
4.	Newar = 1058	899	1.9	106	3.1	32	1.8	21	1.9
5.	Mangar = 2646	2249	4.8	265	7.8	79	4.5	53	4.9
6.	Gurung = 1158	1350	2.9	158	4.6	48	2.7	32	3.0
7.	Rai = 27457	25138	53.9	846	24.8	944	53.5	529	48.9
8.	Limbu = 3704	3148	6.7	371	10.9	111	6.3	74	6.8
9.	Tamang = 10583	8996	19.3	1058	31.0	317	18.0	212	19.6
10.	Sunuwar = 529	450	1.0	52	1.5	16	0.9	11	1.1
11.	Bhujel = 529	450	1.0	52	1.5	16	0.9	11	1.1
12.	Thami = 529	430	1.0	54	1.9	16	0.9	10	1.1
13.	Sherpa = 529	428	0.9	74	2.2	15	0.8	12	1.1
14.	Lepcha = 529	425	0.9	4	01	60	3.4	40	3.7
	(Kalo)								
15.	Kami = 1058	979	2.1	52	1.5	16	0.9	11	1.1
16.	Damai = 529	450	1.0	52	1.5	16	0.9	11	1.1
17.	Sarki = 529	450	1.0	52	1.5	16	0.9	11	1.1
	Total = 52913	**46650**	**88.2**	**3416**	**6.5**	**1766**	**3.3**	**1081**	**2.0**

*NUPW/DDCKMU/DDCWU etc.

for "Last Come First Go." However, the 28.4% of Tagadharis support other union like Darjeeling Terai and Dooars Chia Kaman Mazdoor Union (CPRM), Darjeeling District Chia Bagan Mazdoor Union (CITU), NUPW, Darjeeling District Chia Kaman Shramik Sangh (Gurkah League), DDCKMU etc. on the ground that these 28.4% of workers have some sort of social affinity with the leaders of these unions. It is because of the fact that concept and implication of *Afno* (relatives) *Mancee* and *Arka Manche* (non-relative) has played a significant role in the Nepali society (Bistä : 1991) and in the plantation also (Sharma : 1999). They considered the trade union leaders as *Thulo Manche* (Big sort) and themselves as *Sano Manche* (Common Coolies) of the society.

Interestingly, on the whole, 86.1% of Matwalis support HPWU on the ground that almost all the leaders including leaders of GNLF are Matwalis in the tea plantations of Darjeeling hills. They believe that *Jat Bhai* (own castes-Matwalis) can only understand the problems of fellow brothers nicely. Rest of Matwalis (13.9%) support the other unions as mentioned above due to their affinity with the leaders of the unions who can walk together from cradle to crematorium of the people. But they do not expect from such unions anything extra than the HPWU which is the only most powerful union that can extract benefits from the management judicially.

Finally, it is also seen from the table that 88.2% of tea plantation workers are the supporters of HPWU, 6.5% of them are the members of DDCKMU (CPRM), 3.3% of them support DDCKMU (CITU) and others (2.0%) support other unions like DDCKSS (Gorkha League), NUPW and DDCKMU, etc. This shows that HPWU is the only single most powerful trade union in the Himalayan Tea Plantation industry.

To conclude the section, it can be said that trade union movement in the Himalayan region is in the ethnic line rather than cosmopolitan dimension (Bhowmik: 1995). This may be the effect of West Bengal leftist rule in the state which stress for national question rather than international brotherhood as the way of life. This observation can be supplemented by the fact that all the top leaders of all unions of Terai and Dooars tea plantation workers belong to Bengali community while all the workers there are either Adivasis or Nepalis. To be more broader in explanation, the same is found in South Indian tea plantations and Assam where concept of nationalism has played significant role in the formation and evolution of trade union movement, and this has led to the leadership in the hands of dominant communities of the areas. Thus, the trade union movement in tea plantation industry of Darjeeling Himalaya is a movement of community participation rather than the participation of purely toiling mass as in case of other areas of the nation. Occupationally, all the Nepali castes are considered as toiling class in India and therefore the already toiling class need not to be reoriented for working class status separately. This may be the reason why only trade unions having regional philosophy and having same organisational goal, i.e., achieving distinct ethnic identity in the plantation enclaves is the central objective of trade union like their respective political parties have keep in their manifestoes. The question of job security, better working condition etc. are of peripheral interests to the trade unions. So, the trade union movement in the tea plantation industry of Darjeeling is the history of ethnic movement of workers being suffered and suffocated agonised in tea plantations which are located in far and wide area of the hill terrains of Darjeeling Himalaya which is ironically called as "Plantocracy" within the Indian Democracy (Sharma: 1999).

Ideology of the Himalayan Trade Union Movement

The veteran trade union leader of the Himalayan Plantation Workers Union observed "In the modern world every trade is looked up with trade-union which has the main responsibility of protecting workers right. In fact, trade and trade unions are the two poles of the same earth. They are quite separate but principally the same. One cannot survive without the other. When the welfare of the workers is properly looked then the industry survives. It is a known fact that the sickness of tea industry in some cases of Darjeeling tea industry is due to the absence of welfare of the workers". Further, he states 'Industry must survive so the industrial workers survives'.

The manifesto of the Himalayan Plantation Workers Union runs like:

1. The land including the households given to the workers must be registered in their name ;
2. The educated youths of the gardens must be given opportunity to become assistant managers or opportunity is to be given to the children of workers for training so as to become the assistant managers of the gardens ;
3. Harmonious industrial relations among the workers, management, owners and union is badly needed to save the industry in the changing context ;
4. Socio-economic life upliftment of the workers ;
5. Promotion of the people engaged in the industry.

Let us examine the manifesto of the trade union in detail in order to arrive at a generalised conclusion. The concept of identity brought about by the ethnic movement under Hillmen Association, Pranta Parised and Gurkha National Liberation Front in Darjeeling Himalaya had has made clear that any time workers have to leave the gardens if the *Badli* system (substitute basis of labour recruitment) is stopped on the application of pro-rata system by the management. So, the union feel that the land given to the workers i.e., local inhabitants must be registered in their name. By now, workers have understood that tea garden lands belong to the government and management including the owners of the tea companies are simply extracting profit. This became very apparent by the example of tea gardens like Pashok and Vi-Tukvar where the workers have owned the land in their control and government is silent. It is also observed that in these two gardens, the workers have completely managed the pluckings of tea leaves and sell to the neighbouring gardens. It proves that workers can survive if they became determined (Bhowmik : 1981). One may be really confused with the situation there. As it is already mentioned that only 22.0% of the male folk depends on the garden jobs in Darjeeling tea industry while 78.0% of them work outside the gardens or are engaged in non-plantation jobs. So, the closure does not caused any starvation in the workers' households. Only the female workers of the past have become housewives today. It is also observed that the female housewives have been engaged in cattle farming, agriculture or other jobs to help their male folks in family earnings. To the union leaders 'the closure enables the workers at least to bring their land back to them'. Hence instead of purchasing land for their graveyard from the management since the inception of tea industry, workers have now their own land for graveyards. This is the most impressive objective of the HPWU for having practical orientation of trade union movement in the industry. This might be the apparent reason why 88.0% of tea plantation workers are the members of the HPWU.

The union (HPWU) also has exerted consciousness among the workers that educated youths of the workers and children are to be given opportunity for becoming assistant managers in the gardens, so that the quality of the workers can be improved in the long run. The General Secretary of the HPWU feel that everything has been changed in the industry along with the change of the character of the government except the structure of the management caders who are brought from outside on the colonial believe that they can easily control or manage the workers as strangers. This concept has proved wrong today as the commitment towards it is to be emerged from within the hearts of the people and not by the repressive measures of management cadres from outside the region or community. This idea might have some relevance to the tea garden owners as recently they have started to recruit local youths as assistant managers in the gardens. Even the personality like J.P. Gurung, the senior manager of Darjeeling Plantation Industries Limited, has been given opportunity to become General Manager of the Company today. Of course, this appears to be more important to the planters to have local people in the mouthpiece organisation, i.e., Darjeeling Planters Association. This might be the background to appoint a local lady as Assistant Secretary in the association. Further, Darjeeling Planters Association has not allowed other national management associations in Darjeeling.

Considering the present plight of the Darjeeling tea industry at the global market, it is observed that workers, unions, management and owners have started believing the fact that confrontation no more can work for maintaining harmonious industrial relations in the industry. This is the ample reason why the occurrence of strike and lockouts as weapons to workers and management respectively provided by the Industrial Disputes Act, 1947 is decreasing day by day in Darjeeling. These weapons might have been used as defensive weapons instead of offensive ones by the concerned parties in the recent years. The glaring instances to suppliment the fact is Lingia T.E. and Moondakote T.E. which were opened within very short time of its closure. Similarly, HPWU refused to go on strike as Terai and Dooars workers did in 1999 though the HPWU was also one of the partners of Coordination Committee of Plantation Workers Union call for the strike.

In regard to the socio-economic upliftment of the workers, electrification of tea gardens, drinking water, schools, sanitation in respect of urinals and toilets, creches and other welfare facilities as enshrined in the Plantation Labour Act, 1951 are the other emergent issues of the union. Housing facility are inadequate though in every tripartite meeting, they assure of 8.0% new construction of houses (Puckka type) every year in the gardens. The Land-labour ratios to 1:4 has not done in most of the gardens considering the difficult terrains of the hill plantations.

Ever since the inception of tea industry at Darjeeling, workers were recruited as captives in the industry and they were to relinquish the gardens as soon as they would leave on superanuations under the *Hatta Bahira* system of the management. This forced the retired workers to settle in nearby areas and this gave birth of the present township of Darjeeling. Kurseong and Mirrik. This happened because no worker was given opportunity to come up in the management hierarchy. So, the workers used to live and die as workers only. This might be the reason why now the workers do not believe on the trade unions hailing from Calcutta and New Delhi which according to workers have betrayed them a lot ever since 1947.

It is clear from the above discussion that HPWU is trying to interpret the socio-economic problems of the workers as the ethnic problems of the community as a whole. To a union leader, every outsider feel that every Nepali is *Doke* (Coolie to carry basket of bamboo) which today is completely wrong. To appease the workers by providing minimum amenities for the time being appears to be the management policy and to lockout if they resented further or to change management cadres continuously have proved the hypothesis is true that tea industry is still lingering with colonial forces of production (Bhowmik: 1981). Occurences of T.B. diseases, poor quality of rations, poor medical facilities etc. made the workers weak though the tea made by them are best in the world. Everybody speaks about the best quality about tea of Darjeeling but nobody speaks the poor hands that make the best tea - an union leader said. Similar opinions are noted from the leaders of Darjeeling, Terai and Dooars Chia Mazdoor Union (CPRM) and Darjeeling District Chia

Kaman Shramik Sangh (Gurkha League). It can not be believed on the opinion of management that work culture of workers been deteriorating day by day on the ground that the workers are same as they were there since five generations. To the workers, it is the negligence of the management that has created poor work culture in the Hamalayan tea industry. Management always feel to manage workers with meagre investment. In fact, they are least bothered about the socio-economic upliftment of the workers as most managers feel that they are temporarily posted in the plantations and said to the workers that tea industry is their property as workers have to stay there for ever. The lack of commitment of managers is responsible for the sickness of Darjeeling tea industry. All these made the workers in the State of Slaves (Lozovsky: 1935). Interestingly, even in 1984 the boon year of Darjeeling Tea Industry, management never said of their sound position in the tea market as they would viewed that workers would ask for more and more facilities if they would said this to the workers.

Concept of Ideology

The Soviet Sociologist, I.N. Moskvichow (1974) states that "Ideology as a whole indicates the goals, means and forms of practical and above all, political activities of social groups and individuals. Accordingly, it supplies the justification for various social, political, moral and aesthetic ideals". In reality, most of the workers may be unaware of the role of ideology in their trade unions. It is the trade union leaders who lead and influence the activities of the workers in the framework of ideology by guiding and leading the workers in their movement (Bhowmik: 1981). In the present case it is the ideology of Gurkha National Liberation Front, Gurkha League and Communist Party of Revolutionary Marxist which have shaped the activities of trade unions in tea industry. As it is already mentioned that these three dominant ideologies have same ideological goal-formation of separate state for Gurkhas living in India. This issue was cropped up in the hills since 1917 under the Hillman Association (1917), and later on Pranta Parisad (1980) and Gurkha National Liberation Front (1984) till the formation of Darjeeling Gurkha Hill Council (1988). Thus, the ideology of the unions, unlike in other gardens of Terai and Dooars, is to protect Gurkhas or Gurkha workers working in tea industry. In the views of the management, had there been other unions of Terai and Dooars gardens then all the hill plantations would have been already closed by 1995. It is the local unions having specific ideology that have protected the tea industry. Thus, the trade unions here have twin objectives, one is to protect the workers by fighting for better working conditions and secondly, to aware workers for the restoration of separate ethnic identity in the region. In the idea of Shri Kumai "Gurkhas by nature are working class in Bengal and Bengali Community is the ruling class."

Limitations of Trade Union Movement

Bhowmik (1995) observed "Trade unions in tea have made positive contributions towards improvement of workers' lives. They played an important role in changing labour relations by breaking down the wall of fear. They have made the workers aware of their rights and taught them to fight for them. The ordinary worker realises the need for trade union and that is why one raerely finds a worker who does not belong to a union. However, there are several limitations in the trade union movement here."

In spite of widespread unionisation, plantatrion workers remain the lowest paid in the organised sector. Trade unions have been ineffective in improving the wage structure inspite of the increased profitability of the industry during the last decade and half. Wages have increased only marginally. The wage rate has rather decreased in the industry.

Further, Bhowmik (Ibid) observes that "trade unions have also failed to force the employers to implement the provisions of the Plantation Labour Act, 1951. As already mentioned that the Act stipulates for 8% of labour houses should be made puckka or permanent structure. If it was sticked properly than the 1969 would be the year when all the workers, houses would have been converted into puckka type. The implementation of the other provisions relating to labour welfare is even worse. The supply of drinking water is nil in hill gardens. The medical facilities would have to be improved rather it is observed from the study that it has decreased considerably on the pretext of incurring loss by the management. It is said that no union has been able to launch movement for the total implementation of Plantation Labour Act, 1951 in toto till today in the gardens. It is found that no union and worker report to labour Department about the non-fulfilment of the Act in toto. This has certainly proves the fact that trade unions lack enthusiasm to deal with non-wage issues of the workers. Moreover, the management prefer better to pay light fine for not fulfilling the provisions of the Act rather than giving the total facilities to the workers. Not a single garden has appointed Labour Welfare Officer in Darjeeling hills till today though the Government of West Bengal has instructed to do so. Unions do not show any interest or create pressure on the management. In fact, they are busy to carry on the political activities of their parties. The issue like Provident Fund, Gratuity. Family Pension etc. appears to be far cry or the imagination of the trade unions in the industry. On the other hand, management are happy not to pay Provident Fund, Gratuity, Family Pension accordingly which in fact is beneficial to the plantation owners. It is observed that it would be more beneficial to the management if more and more workers remain in absent especially in pruning seasons. Trade unions have also not been able to educate the workers about the losses of one day absent in the industry. All these limitations along with the multiplicity of unions have weaken the bargaining power of the unions in Darjeeling tea industry. The glaring instance is the North Tukvar T.E. where unions had to negotiate with management against the interest of the workers in 1999 when management were beaten by the workers.

There is therefore an acute need to impart trade union education and build an awareness of the statutory rights of the workers. The average tea plantation workers needs access to information on matters relating to his work and welfare facilities. The role of trade unions in this direction is very important so as to have enlighten work the force to face the challenges of liberalisation.

Commitments of Workers to Trade Unions

In this section, an attempt has been made to study the commitment and attitudes of the workers to trade union movement in tea industry of the region. The concept of Commitment not only involves the performances of the workers in trade unions but also the acceptance of the relevant norms of the reorganisation by orienting their behaviour accordingly. The commitment to the unions involves discipline, rules of the organisation. The Commitment also implies the acceptance of the ways of the unions for workers. The various scholars have various ideas of the concepts of commitment. Sharma (1974) views that commitment of the workers cannot be obstructed by the social differences. Here, in the present study, the commitment is operationalised from the point of view of the support structure of the workers to their trade unions in various activities. The degree of support has been studied here in the study.

The commitment and attitudes of the young Tagadhari and Matwali workers (37.3%) having little better educational standard is a such that they do not pay the union subscription regularly. So, the commitment and attitude of these young workers are not positive rather these workers may be characterised as the *passive* supporters of the unions. Similarly, 27.8% of Matwali workers especially young workers having less than 10 years of service and having little education standard appeared to have poor commitment to the unions. This is because of the fact that they expect something mirracle within a night, from the unions.

The workers commitment towards the unions in the area of attending the union meeting is also not so encouraging. It is observed that 17.9% of young Tagadhari workers donot attend the union meetings regularly at the unit level. Similarly, 58.4% of Matwali workers especially young one having little exposure to outside world and education donot attend the union meetings regularly. This may be the simplest reason why tea workers are devoid of adequate knowledge about unions, problems of the workers and industry as a whole.

The workers commitment and attitude to strike is rather activated over the years in the hill gardens. But, in the present study it is observed that 25.6% of young Tagadhari workers having higher educational standard donot participate in the strike while they have not interest in it. Similarly, 6.1% of young Matwali workers donot attend the strike. It shows that the strike to the workers is to be done by the union executives and they have nothing to do with it in the plantations.

Another aspect of the unionisation is the enrolling of new members in the unions. Interestingly, it is observed that 41.4% of Tagadhari workers have poor commitment and vague idea about the significance of this aspect. These workers are comparatively young and literate and overambitious. Similarly, 13.7% of young workers from Matwali group do not help unions to enroll new members.

The workers commitment to read notice board of the unions is also very poor, as 90.4% of Tagadhari workers of which 50% young workers donot go through the notice board of the union. Similarly, 89.1% of Matwalis of which 60.0% young one donot go through the union notice board. This keeps them in darkness about the relevent informations about unions, labours and industry.

Any trade union movement can sustain its existence through its activities of various types. Besides the implementation of various labour legislations regarding rights and responsibilities of the workers, trade unions have other social responsibilities. To test the success of the unions, the responses of the workers about it can be done. It is explored from the present study that 98.5% of plantation workers have poor commitment about the diversified activities of the unions. It is seen from the study that of 98.5% of the workers 70.0% of young workers have very poor commitment to unions about this aspect. It shows that the workers are very aware of economic activity of the workers organisations. But the other aspects of union activities is still unknown to the workers.

The attitude or commitment of the workers in union-management relation is apparent as 77.1 % of them said that union may be successful in negotiation if they have political unionists in the truest sense of the term. But in the area of failure in the negotiation, the commitment of workers is very weak as 80.0% of them said that incapable union leader is responsible for the failure in negotiation.

Talking to the workers, it is noted that 79.7% of workers showed commitment that they are union members and they have joined unions for better welfare facilities. Only 16.6% of workers have joined unions for the unity of working class identity in the industry.

However, it is a question that emerges from the discussion why workers lacks commitment to unions. In this respect it is noted that 75.7% of them said that unions do nothing for the betterment of the workers. Another 21.1% of workers said that workers commitment towards the unions is marginal due to the emergence of multiplicity of unions in the gardens. Since the plantation society is a closed society, it is very difficult to declare their distinct membership to any particular union operating in the garden.

The workers' commitment of the unions is quite fragile as they have not been able to distinguish between the union and political fund as written in the Indian Trade Union Act, 1926. Only 13.5% of Tagadhari and 6.0% of Matwali workers especially young one having little bit educational standard have been able to distinguish the two types of funds. On the whole, 6.2% of the plantation workers are committed to the unions in this aspect of trade union movement.

The affiliations of the unions to various political parties is a general phenomenon of unionisation today. But it is found that 89.1% of Tagadhari and 97.4% of Matwali workers have very poor commitment to unions in this aspect, as they donot know the nature and type of affiliations to political parties. Only 2.8% of the workers having little educational standard and being the members and officials of the unions are committed to the unions.

As per the responses of the workers which portrays their commitment to unions regarding their acquintance with the union leaders, it is noted that 31.6% of Tagadhari and 6.0% of Matwali workers donot have any acquintance with the union leaders. It shows that their commitment to the unions is half-hearted yet they have been fully unionised in the last fifty years of independence. Comparatively, Tagadharis donot have much concern with the union leaders who are mainly Matwalis. Again, these 31.6% of Tagadharis especially young educated workers and 6.0% of young Matwali workers having little educational background are not at all committed to the unions in this respect of activities.

The commitment of workers towards unions is expected to be apparent if we see their payment of union subscription, especially after getting their Bonus. In other times they say that they would pay the union subscription after getting the Bonus. It is observed that 29.6% of Tagadhari and 38.7% of Matwali workers donot pay the union subscription even after getting the Bonus. The study also highlights that unless repeated persuasion is done, workers donot want to pay union subscription even after getting Bonus or any other payment.

The workers commitment towards unions in the area of knowledge about the involvement of central leaders in unit level elections was studied. It is found that 61.1% of Tagadhari and 94 5% of Matwali workers donot know about it. On the average, 6.2% of the workers are appears to be committed to this aspect of the unions as they replied in positive. Again, they are found to be either little educated or the members of executive committees of unions.

The commitment of workers in regard to conflict management is mix in nature in the sense that conflict among the workers is solved (98.9%) by the unions. Interestingly, it is observed from the study that almost all the conflicts in regard to terms and conditions of work are solved by the management. The workers attitude to the conflict management is limited to economic aspect only. The conflict between the unions are to be solved by the police intervention only.

The commitment of workers regarding the understanding of union ideology is also not much encouraging. It is observed from the study that inspite of complete unionisation of tea plantation workers, 94.2% of workers donot know exactly the ideology of unions. Of course, they know the ideology about the Gurkhaland issue or the restoration of Gurkha identity well as activated by G.N.L.F. party and its frontal organisation (HPWU).

In the changing industrial scenario involvement of all in all the aspects of industry or developmental process is highly indispensible. In industrial arena, participation of people in elections is very important, so in the case of union elections. But unlike in other industries, tea industry management is indifferent to it. Even 99.7% of Tagadhari and 99.7% of Matwali workers donot know whether the management declares holidays in election days or not. It shows that the workers commitment to union elections is hardly to be complete or total. They are still in this case, marginal in attitude or involvement.

The workers commitment and attitude on the unions regarding value of internal leaders or leadership is another area of unionisation, it is observed from the study that 69.5% of Tagadhari and 15.1% of Matwali workers stated that only the central leaders are given value by the workers and management as they call central leaders in times of emergency. But interestingly, slowly, significance of internal leadership is realised by the management as 83.7% of workers said that these days they have started to involve the local leaders in solving the garden problems. This shows that the significance of rank and file leaders is a bare reality for the tea industry also.

The commitment of workers to unions can also be judged from the point of view of nature of acquiring receipt of union subscriptions. It is found that 76.8% of Tagadhari and 86.2% of Matwali workers stated that they donot receive any receipt from the unions of their subscription payment. Only 13.9% of the workers are getting the receipt of subscription payment. They are found to be either hailing from literate group of workers or executives of the unions.

The significance of receipt of union subscription is still beyond the actual commitment of the workers in the plantations.

The commitment of workers regarding the submission of annual returns by the unions to Labour Commissioner is another area of unionisation. It is observed that 98.3% of Tagadhari and 98.1% of Matwali workers donot know whether actually the unions do it accordingly or not. It shows that workers are apathetic to this activity.

The Bonus is another area of union activity and Bonus is considered as an integral part of wages of the workers. Over the year since 1965, the unions have to fight for this also at Calcutta every year just before the Durga Puja. But interestingly, 79.4% of Tagadhari and 96.1% of Matwali workers donot know how the Bonus is brought by the unions. Further, they do not know to acquire Bonus, the union leaders have to go to Calcutta. They know the Bonus but donot know the process of getting it. So, the commitment of workers to unions in this aspect is very poor. Only 20.6% of Tagadhari and 3.9% of Matwali workers know this or have commitment to unions in this aspect. They are found to have been either the literate workers or the executives of the unions.

The workers commitment to unions can also be understood from their awareness regarding the knowledge of recognition of unions. Here again, 96.4% of Tagadhari and 99.3% of Matwali workers have no idea about it. Only 3.6% of Tagadhari and 0.7% of Matwali workers have commitment to this aspect of the unions as they know that their unions are recognised by the management, government and society as a whole.

Though the unionisation claims that workers are confirmed of the fact that unions protect the interests of the workers, it is noted from the study that 14.2% of Tagadhari and 3.9% of Matwali workers said that the unions donot protect the interests of the workers. It shows that still the sizeable sections of workers donot believe that Trade Unions can protect the interests of the workers. So, they are not so much committed to unions about this also.

Counting the commitment of workers to unions regarding the wage revision, it is observed still 98.7% of Tagadhari and 99.8% of Matwali workers donot know how the wages of the workers are revised. Only 1.3% of Tagadhari and 0.2% of Matwali workers are aware of it. Like in other aspects of the commitment to unions, they are either literate or union officials or exposed to outside society.

The workers commitment towards their unions was further tested on the activities regarding productivity raising, population control, quality of life, creation of additional employment channels aspects. It is noted that HPWU have thrust on employment of youth, while the other unions stressed on productivity raising, population control etc. But workers could not ascertain which aspect of union activity is prime importance for them.

The workers commitment in regard to their choice for external and internal leaders, it is noted that 90.7% of them opted for external leaders. It shows that still their commitment to union leaders is for outsiders.

The number of unions in one industry and the choice for one or many was asked to the workers. It is noted that 81.1 % of workers have choice for multiple unions in the plantation industry. Only 18.9% of the workers showed commitment for one union in one industry of the region.

The commitment of workers regarding their idea about the utilisation of union fund was noted, and found that 81.1% of workers said that the unions are utilising the fund properly. While 18.9% of them said that the union funds are not properly utilised by the unions. These 18.9% of workers were little conscious due to their better educational standard.

Again, 98.0% of workers have no commitment to know about the conciliation or agreements done by the unions about their work related issues. In fact, it is also noted that workers do not have haunch to involve themselves in the negotiations etc. with the management. Everything is to be got done for them by the unions.

In framing the Charter of Demands, the commitment of rank and file workers is very poor as it is found that 95.8% of workers still do not know as what is a Charter of Demands. This may be the reason why sometimes it is called that Charter of Demands is of the unions rather than of the workers.

The plantation workers is so much so committed to state that unions are to be politicised that 91.0% of them said that unions must be affiliated with political parties in order to make feel the management that even a minority union is something important as it has political backing.

The commitment of workers regarding the significance of Panchayati system in the plantation has negative reaction as 94.4% of them feel that only union is most powerful than Panchayat. It shows that the importance of Panchayati system is very vague among the plantation workers. Further, 97.5% of workers said that only trade unions are recognised by the management and Panchayat leaders have no role to play in the plantation industry.

Inspite of so much love for the trade unions, 96.2% of plantation workers are not satisfied with the registration process of the union which means they have no commitment on the legal registration of unions and unions as legal entity.

The commitment of workers to unions in regard to causes of strike is also not very positive as 83.6% of them said the main cause of strike is to acquire more and more welfare facilities for the workers. In fact, for the last decade, the unions are fighting for better social status of the workers by raising the overall quality of life. Interestingly, the workers participate in unions having commitment to show majority of working class solidarity of Gurkha community in the Himalayan tea plantation industry. This appears to be the stronger point for their commitment in unions But, when strike fails, workers said it is due to the strike called by rival (95.4%) unions. It shows that the commitment of workers to strike has decreased due to the multiplicity of unions.

The workers responses regarding the satisfaction on the grievance redressal procedure is somewhat discouraging as 90.3% of them are not committed to the procedure of grievance redressal procedure in the plantation. Similarly, their commitment in regard to the dispute settlement machineries is also discouraging as 94.4% of them are not satisfied with the machineries. But 82.3% of the workers feel that they have commitment on strike which can prove that workers are a big power to the management. Again, their commitment in making sense (75.6%) that strike can help raise in wages is wrong.

The workers commitment regarding the work style is different today than in the past as 68.7% of them said that work to rule the day should be the principle today. It shows that the commitment of workers in regard to work is positive in the sense that involvement in intentional strike should be avoided (0.1%) in the plantations of the hills considering challenges coming to the industry.

The above discussion shows that the commitment of the workers to their unions is more or less positive and it can be improved if they are provided with sufficient trainings on trade union education to prove that workers can be the best friends of the industry if they are informed with sufficient informations of present day economy of the industry.

16

TRADE UNIONS AND WORKERS PARTICIPATION

An attempt has been made in this section to study the workers participation in the various activities of trade unions in the Himalayan tea industry. By 'Participation', here we mean the support of workers to the unions.

Union Subscription

Collection of funds is an important function of trade unions. However, the funds are collected whenever the unions require the same. One of the sources of fund collection is the subscription made by the workers. Every year, a sum of Rs. 20 is collected from each worker as annual subscription. Interestingly, the payment of subscription is not regular by the workers. This is the aspect which was taken for the study to know the support structure of the workers towards their unions.

Table 16.1.
Payment of Union Subscription

Sl. No.	*Caste Status*	*Total Workers*	*Paying Subs.*	*%*	*Donot pay Subs.*	*%*
1.	Tagadhari = 1,116	1,116	700	62.7	416	37.3
2.	Matwalis = 51,797	51,797	40,000	77.2	11,797	27.8
	Total	**52,913**	**47,000**	**88.8**	**5,913**	**11.2**

It is observed from the Table 16.1 that 62.7% of Tagadharis pay union subscription while 37.3% of them do not pay the subscription regularly every year, while 77.2% of Matwalis pay union subscription and only 27.8% of them do not pay the subscription. On the whole, it is observed that 88.8% of the plantation workers pay the union subscription to their respective unions and only 11.2% do not pay the subscriptions. From the table it is observed that payment of subscription as an important source of union fund or income structure has been understood by the workers. However, the 11.2% of them have not been either convinced about it or asked for the subscription by the unions. So, their participation at the level of paying subscription at 88.8% shows the fact that unionisation of tea plantation workers in Darjeeling Himalaya is a bare reality in the truest sense of the term.

Trade Union Meeting

Another indicator of workers participation in trade union movement is attending the union meetings at the garden level, whenever called for. Interestingly, it is observed from the Table 2 that only 17.9% of Tagadharis attend the meetings while 82.1% of them do not attend the meetings held at the gardens. On the other hand, 58.4% of Matwalis attend the meetings and 41.6% of them donot attend the meetings. On the whole, 57.5% of the workers attend the meeting while 42.5% of them do not attend the meeting of the unions. It shows that the significance of attending the meeting to equip

Table 16.2.
Caste and Trade Union Meetings at the Gardens

Sl. No.	*Caste Status*	*Yes*	*%*	*No*	*%*
1.	Tagadharis = 1,116	200	17.9	916	82.1
2.	Matwalis = 51,797	30,225	58.4	21,572	41.6
	Total = 52,913	30,425	57.5	22,488	42.5

with informations are not much found with the plantation workers. Groupwise, Tagadharis are found with least interest to attend the meetings, because they are of the opinion that merely attending meetings of the unions do not suffice the very purpose unless the unions allow to go through the policy matter of the unions which lie with the Matwalis who have occupied the dominant positions in the trade unions of the region.

Participation in Strike

To call strike and sustain it is one of the important functions of trade unions. It is transparent from the Table 16.3 that 74.4% of Tagadharis participate in strike while 25.6% of them do not participate in the strikes. Those who (25.6%) do not participate in strikes expressed that their unions sometimes exert violence when lot of problems including deaths take place. But surprisingly, it is also observed from the table that 93.9% of Matwalis participate in strike and only 6.1% of them do not participate in strikes. It is explored from their ideas that Matwalis do not scared of violence even if any takes place while doing the strikes as they are considered themselves as martial race. However, on the whole, it is observed that 93.5% of the workers participate in strikes while 6.1% do not so as they do not have faith on strike or their leaders of the unions.

Table 16.3.
Caste and Participation in Strike

Sl. No.	*Caste Status*	*Yes*	*%*	*No*	*%*
1.	Tagadharis = 1,116	830	74.4	286	25.6
2.	Matwális = 51,797	48,625	93.9	3172	6.1
	Total = 52,913	**49,455**	**93.5**	**3,458**	**6.5**

Enrolment of New Members in Unions

To convince friends and fellows for becoming members of a union is another area of workers participation in trade union movement. It is transparent from the Table 16.4 that among the Tagadharis, only 58.6% try to help the unions for enrolment of new members in the union, while 41.4% of them do not do it on the ground that it is very hard to convert people from the political party or political ideology of a union to another union ideology.

Table 16.4.
Caste and Union Enrolment

Sl. No.	*Caste Status*	*Yes*	*%*	*No*	*%*
1.	Tagadharis = 1,116	654	58.6	462	41.4
2.	Matwalis = 51,797	44,696	86.3	7,101	13.7
	Total = 52,913	**45,350**	**85.7**	**7,563**	**14.3**

On the other hand, 86.3% of Matwalis try to convince people in this direction while 13.7% of them do not so on the ground that as union leaders of other unions are happend to be their *Afno Manche* (relatives). This indicates the fact that concepts of *Afno Manche* and *Arkka Manche* (Non-relatives) have played an important role in the enrolment process of the trade unions in the Nepali society of the plantation industry of the Himalayan region.

Union Notice Board

To participate in information sharing is another important function as a part of trade union activity by the members and officials of unions. Surprisingly, it is noted from the Table 16.5 that 9.6% of Tagadharis and 10.9% of Matwalis participate in reading the notice board of the unions while 90.4% of Tagadharis and 89.1% of Matwalis do not go through the notice boards of the unions or do not visit the union offices. On the whole, it is observed from the table that only 10.8% of the plantation workers read union notice boards and 89.2% of them do not go through it, or hardly they visit union offices. Interestingly, these 10.8% of the plantation workers are either the members of executive committees of the unions or are connected with some social (Samaj) activities of the plantations. It is therefore observed that the general rank and file workers do neither read the notice boards nor do they know to read it nor unions do have any notice boards in the plantations. So, the workers do not know the latest know-how of the unions in which they are the members.

Table 16.5.
Reading Notice Board of Unions

Sl. No.	Caste Status	Yes	%	No	%
1.	Tagadharis = 1,116	107	9.6	1,009	90.4
2.	Matwalis = 51,797	5,625	10.9	46,172	89.1
	Total = 52,913	**5,732**	**10.8**	**47,181**	**89.2**

Workers Awareness on Union Activities

The awareness of plantation workers regarding the nature of activities of the unions is an important indicator to assess the level of trade union movement in tea industry. It is found from the table 16.6 that 96.2% of the Tagadhari workers are aware of economic activities of the unions while 9.0% of them are confirmed of social activities of the unions.

Table 16.6.
Workers Awareness on Union Activities

Sl. No.	Caste Status	Eco	%	Ideological	%	Social	%	Others	%
1.	Tagadharis = 1,116	1,074	96.2	30	2.7	10	0.9	2	0.2
2.	Matwalis = 51,797	51,031	98.5	630	1.2	100	0.2	36	0.1
	Total = 52,913	**52,105**	**98.5**	**660**	**1.2**	**110**	**0.2**	**38**	**0.1**

But 98.5% of Matwali workers are aware of the economic activities of the unions. On the whole, 98.5% of tea plantation workers understand union as an instrument of economism of the workers. Thus, the importance of changing role of unions after the liberalisation of Indian economy has not reached to the gardens in so far as the workers awareness to multiple roles of trade unions is concerned. It is thus quite natural to generalise that trade unions as management is still in the traditional stage of development in tea industry of the Himalayan region.

Trade Union Role in Negotiations

The traditional concept of trade unions has been sharpen by their role as one of the important instrument for negotiations for the workers. It is observed from the table mentioned below that the most important reason

(57.2%) for successful negotiation is due to the capable union leaders for Tagadhari workers followed by the strong political base (17.9%). But 78.4% of Matwali workers believe that strong political base of the unions can help to do negotiations successfully. Only 16.7% of Matwali workers do believe for

Table 16.7.
Reasons for Successful Negotiations by Unions

Sl. No.	Caste Status	Solidarity	%	Rational Demand	%	Capable Leader	%	Pol. Base	%
1.	Tagadharis = 1,116	150	13.4	128	11.5	638	57.2	200	17.9
2.	Matwalis = 51,797	2,068	4.0	431	0.8	8,685	16.7	40,613	78.4
	Total = 52,913	**2,218**	**4.2**	**559**	**1.1**	**9,323**	**17.6**	**40,813**	**77.1**

capable union leaders as a criteria for successful negotiations. On the whole, it is observed that 77.1% of workers believe for strong political base of the unions as the criteria for successful negotiations, while 17.6% of them believe for capable union leaders as the criteria for successful negotiations. The table protrays the fact that strong political base of unions can have dominant role for doing successful negotiations with the management and government even after the liberalisation of Indian economy in general and tea industry in particular.

Workers and Political Party

In order to assess the political influences of parties, workers were asked to state their support to various political parties. It is therefore observed from the Table 8 that 64.5% of Tagadhari workers support the Gurkha National Liberion Front while 12.5% of them support Communist Party of Revolutionary Marxist and 17.9% of them support Communist Party (Marxist) while 4.5% of them support either Congress (1) or Gurkha League. But 77.2% of Matwalis are the supporters of G.N.L.F. party and 16.8% of them are the supporters of C.P.R.M. party and 3.9% of them are the supporters of either Congress(I) or Gurkha League parties of the region. On the whole, 77.0% of the tea plantation workers of the Darjeeling Hamalaya are the supporters of G.N.L.F. and

Table 16.8.
Members of Political Parties

Sl. No.	Caste Status	G.N.L.F.	%	CPRM	%	C.P.I. (M)	%	Others	%
1.	Tagadharis = 1,116	720	64.5	140	12.5	200	17.9	50	4.5
2.	Matwalis = 51,797	40,000	77.2	8,686	16.8	1,111	2.1	2,000	3.9
	Total = 52,913	**40,720**	**77.0**	**8,826**	**16.7**	**1,311**	**2.5**	**2050**	**3.9**

16.7% of them are the supporters of C.P.R.M. party. It is observed from the table that both G.N.L.F. and C.P.R.M. as well as Gurkha League have regional philosophy as already mentioned in the previous chapter of their own. The national parties like Congress(I) and C.P.I. (M) have hardly 3.0% members from among the tea plantation workers today in the region. According to the views of 85.0% of tea plantation workers, the national political parties do not bother about the ethnic problems of smaller ethnic communities of the country. This is the reason why to them, it is wise to support the local political parties which look after the problems of the plantation workers.

Workers and Their Length of Service

Studying the plantation workers in the region, we observed the workers who in fact do not know their ages. Many workers have been working even after seventy years of their age. They are allowed to work on the ground their health is good but nobody knows accurately their ages. This is most spectacular in case of workers who are old while this is not found in case of young workers. Their length of service have well been maintained especially after 1970. This is evident from the following table.

It is observed from the Table 9 that 38.2% of Tagadhari workers are working in the plantations for the period of 05-10 years followed by 35.8% of them working during the last 10-15 years. The Tagadhari workers working between 15-20 years are 9.0% and 9.3% of them are working for the last 20-25 years. Still 6.3% and 1.2% of Tagadharis are working during the last 25-30 years and 30-35 years respectively. But interestingly, 58.3% of Matwalis are working for the last 5-10 years. Again, 38 2% and 3.2% of Matwalis are working for 10-15 to 15-20 years respectively. On the whole, it is transparent from the table that 57.8% of plantation workers belong to the range of 5-10 years of service, 38.2% of them in the range of 10-15 years of service and 3.3% of them in the range of 15-20 years of service. It is transparent from the table

Table 16.9.
Workers and Length of Service

Sl. No.	*Caste Status*	*Years*						
		5-10 (%)	*10-15 (%)*	*15-20 (%)*	*20-25 (%)*	*25-30 (%)*	*30-35 (%)*	*35+ (%)*
1.	Tagadharis = 1,116	400 (35.8)	426 (38.2)	100 (9.0)	104 (9.3)	70 (6.3)	12 (1.2)	4 (0.9)
2.	Matwalis = 51,797	30,186 (58.3)	19,777 (38.2)	1,620 (3.2)	118 (0.2)	50 (0.1)	26 (0.1)	20 (0.1)
	Total = 52,913	**30,586 (57.8)**	**20,203 (38.2)**	**1,720 (3.3)**	**222 (0.4)**	**120 (0.2)**	**120 (0.2)**	**24 (0.1)**

that tea industry does hardly employ people who are above 25 years of service in the plantations rather they perfer to give young workers in *Badli* (substitute) basis (Sharma: 1997). It is because of the fact that plantation jobs are purely manual in character and hence physical stress is much in carrying out the duties in the high terrains. So, the 30 and plus years of service at the plantations is hardly found in case of 0.2% workers who are old workers having not known their actual date of birth. It means that most of the workers cannot work beyond 30 years in the plantations.

The Unsuccessful Negotiations

Quite often, in the recent years, trade unions have not been able to be successful in negotiating the management relating to terms and conditions of work of the plantation workers in the light of the various government legislations, or previous terms of agreements both Biprtrite or Tripartite. The plantation workers view that there are number of reasons for failure in negotiations by the unions. It is transparent from the following Table 16.10 that 64.5% of Tagadharis feel that weak political base of the union caused for such failure in negotiations by a particular union. Again, 27.8% of Tagadharis believe that incapable union leaders is responsible for failure in negotiations. Further, 5.4% of Tagadharis stated that the disunity of the workers is responsible of failure in negotiations.

Table 16.10.
Reasons for Failure in Negotiations

Sl. No.	*Caste Status*	*Disunity of workers (%)*	*Non Rational Demand (%)*	*Incapable Leader (%)*	*Non-pol Base (%)*	*Non-Mngt (%)*
1.	Tagadharis = 1,116	60 (5.4)	6 (0.5)	310 (27.8)	720 (64.5)	20 (1.8)
2.	Matwalis = 51,797	780 (1.5)	94 (0.2)	42,007 (81.1)	8,857 (17.1)	59 (0.1)
	Total = 52,913	**840 (1.6)**	**100 (0.2)**	**42,317 (80.0)**	**9,577 (18.1)**	**79 (0.1)**

But on the other hand, 81.1% of Matwali workers believe that incapable union leaders are responsible for failure in negotiations. Only 17.1% of them believe that non-political base of the unions are responsible for the failure in this respect. Further, 1.5% of Matwalis believe that disunity of the workers as an important reason for failure in negotiations. On the whole, it is observed that 80.0% of the plantation workers feel that incapable union leaders are responsible for failure in negotiations. Only 18.1% of the workers feel that non-political base as the reason for failure in negotiations. It shows that leadership qualities is very important determining variable for the success in doing successful negotiations by the unions in the Himalayan region. It is also understood that role of management is of little significance in so far as the failure of negotiations by the unions of the plantation industry is concerned.

Joining Unions

Studying the West Bengal tea plantation workers. Sarath Davala (1995) in Employment and Unionisation in Indian Industry observed that all the plantation workers of the West Bengal are unionised. To test his study, an attempt has been made here to assess the reason for joining the unions by the workers. Further, Bhowmik (1995) observed that it is wise to have unions no matter whether it is weak or strong while working in tea industry.

It is transparent from the above Table 16.11 that 37.2% of Tagadharis join the unions to stand against the exploitation by the management. Another 28.4% of them have joined the unions for better welfare facilities. Again, 9.4% of them feel that there will be the prospect left for them if they join unions for their promotion. This has been followed by another 10.5% of them who join unions for restoring unity among the working class in the plantations. On the other hand, 80.7% of Matwali workers join unions for better welfare facilities while 16.7% of them join unions for unity of workers. Still 2.2% of them join unions to get rise in wages. On the whole, 79.7% of plantation workers have joined unions for better welfare facilities and 16.6% of them have joined unions for unity of the plantation workers. Interestingly, 2.3% of them have joined unions to get rise the wages of the workers. It shows that these 2.3% of the workers have still no idea about the way how their wages are fixed or revised at after every three years interval. It is also observed that hardly any worker could tell us the meaning of minium wages that they get and it is regulated to them through Minimum Wages Act. 1948 by the tripatrite agreements at Calcutta.

Table 16.11.
Reasons for Joining Unions

Sl. No.	*Caste Status*	*Wage* (%)	*Welfare Facility* (%)	*Rise in* (%)	*Better Exploitation* (%)	*Unity* (%)	*Stand Against Unemp-loyed youth* (%)
1.	Tagadharis = 1,116	42 (3.8)	317 (28.4)	117 (10.5)	415 (37.2)	105 (9.4)	120 (10.6)
2.	Matwalis = 51,797	1,160 (2.2)	41,842 (80.7)	8,660 (16.7)	56 (0.1)	65 (0.1)	14 (0.1)
	Total = 52,913	**1,202 (2.3)**	**42,159 (79.7)**	**8,777 (16.6)**	**471 (0.9)**	**170 (0.3)**	**134 (0.3)**

Indifference to Unions

Tea plantation industry is an isolated entity and its workers are therefore kept at enclaves (Bhowmik : 1981) having still little exposure to the outside world (Sharma : 1999). Being isolated entity or location, it is observed that the workers very often loose their hearts from becoming the members or working steadily for the trade union movement. There are still gardens where leaders of the Central Committees from Darjeeling have not ever visited. This helps management to discourage the unit leaders, to left unions and join the hands of the management. This has caused the rank and file workers to left the unions alone. Besides, the reasons mentioned above, there are other reasons too for not joining the unions. This is clear from the following Table 16.12.

It is observed from the table 16.12 that 33.3% of Tagadhari workers feel that multiplicity of unions in the plantations is responsible for not joining the unions by the workers in the truest sense of the term. Further, 25.7% of them state that these days unions do nothing for the workers or betterment of working class. Again, 24.5% of Tagadharis believe that infiltration of outside non-worker leaders having vested interests is responsible for the workers to abstain from involving union activities of the plantation. On the other hand,

Table 16.12.
Reasons for Not Joining Unions

Sl. No.	Caste Status	*Fear of Victimisation (%)*	*Outside Leader (%)*	*Multiplicity of Unions (%)*	*Political Interference (%)*	*Union do Nothing (%)*
1.	Tagadharis = 1,116	77 (6.9)	273 (24.5)	372 (33.3)	107 (9.6)	287 (25.7)
2.	Matwalis = 51,797	97 (0.1)	114 (0.2)	10,803 (20.9)	1,037 (2.0)	39,746 (76.7)
	Total = 52,913	**174 (0.3)**	**387 (0.7)**	**11,175 (21.1)**	**1,144 (2.2)**	**40,033 (75.7)**

76.7% of Matwali workers feel that workers hesitate to join unions because unions do nothing for them. Again, 20.9% of Matwalis state that multiplicity of union is responsible for the workers' hesitation to join unions. On the whole, it is observed that 75.7% of the workers feel that workers hesitate to join unions as unions do nothing for them. Further, 21.1% of the plantation workers feel that multiplicity of unions in the plantations are responsible for the workers' hesitation to join unions. It shows that workers want to be the members of the unions provided the unions can do something for the real welfare or benefits of the workers.

Fund Collection

It is observed from the study that due to lack of wholetimers of the unions (Bhowmik: 1981) trade unions are not able to collect the fund regularly in the plantations. This aspect has also mentioned by the National Commission on Labour (N.L.C.: 1969) as a handicap on the part of trade unions. Secondly, since the gardens are located in far flunged terrains of the Hamalaya, it is not possible for the union executives to visit each and every workers households and collect the union fund. Of course, to collect the fund is a right given by the Indian Trade Union Act, 1926. However, in this Act, a distinction is made between union fund and political fund. Former is compulsory while latter is optional to the workers. Any trade union movement is considered successful provided this distinction is made clear to the rank and file workers while collecting the union funds. To make the workers clear about this making distinction is the primordial duty of unions.

Table 16.13.
Workers Awareness about the Distinction Between Union and Political Funds

Sl. No.	*Caste Status*	*Yes*	*%*	*No.*	*%*
1.	Tagadharis = 1,116	151	13.5	965	86.5
2.	Matwalis = 51,797	3,105	6.0	48,692	94.0
	Total = 52,913	**3,256**	**6.2**	**49,657**	**93.8**

It is apparent from the above Table 16.13 that 86.5% of Tagadhari workers and 94.0% of Matwali workers do not know the difference between the political and union funds. The ample reason for such confusion is due to the fact that no union endeavours to clear this distinction to the workers while collecting the funds. Only 13.5% of Tagadhari and 6.0% of Matwali workers know the difference. On the whole, 93.8% of the workers donot know the difference between the two types of funds and only 6.2% of them know the distinction. They are found either the officials or executive members of the unions. This may be the reason why workers while giving the subscription say 'Party Fund' rather than the union fund. Even if they do know the difference between the two types of the fund, they pay it as they want to make feel the unions that they are ready to participate in union activities. It is explored from the study that Nepali workers believe on *Sath Dino* (to cooperate) in the local affairs of the workers.

Union Affiliation

Every Union keeps liaison with the national federation having a distinct political philosophy which defines the functioning of the union at the national, regional and unit level. Such affiliation to be known to the unions is also to be made known to the workers to widen the trade union movement. The Himalayan trade unions have also specific affiliations to various federations and political parties. The following table makes it clear about their affiliations.

Table 16.13(A)
Trade Unions in Darjeeling

Sl. No.	*Name of Trade Union*	*Name of the Affiliated Federation/ Political party*
1.	Himalayan Plantation workers union	Tea defence Committee for Plantation Workers' Rights (Hind Mazdoor Sabha) and G.N.L.F. Party.
2.	Darjeeling, Terai and Dooars Chia Kaman Mazdoor Union	Co-ordination Committee of Tea Plantation Workers' Union and C.P.R.M. Party.
3.	National Union of Plantation Workers'	Indian National Trade Union Congress, (I.N.T.U.C.)/ Co-ordination Committee of Tea Plantation Workers' Union./ Congress (I) Party.
4.	Darjeeling District Chia Kaman Mazdoor Union	Centre of Indian Trade Union/Committee of Coordination Plantation Workers Union/ C.P.I. (M).
5.	Darjeeling District Chia Kaman Shramik Sangha	Gurkha League/Coordination Committee of Tea Plantation Workers' Union
6.	Darjeeling Pahari Chiabari Karmachari Sangha.	Tea Defence Committee for Plantation Workers' Rights. HMS.

It is revealed from the above Table 13(A) that the most strongest HPWU is with HMS federation which is mainly anti-leftist federation while smaller unions are with Coordination Committee of Tea Plantation Workers' Union which is a leftist federation. To assess the significance of such affiliation of unions to the federations and parties, workers awareness were studied so as to know the level of trade union movement in hill plantations.

Table 16.14.
Workers Awareness Regarding Affiliation of Their Unions

Sl. No.	*Caste Status*	*Aware*	*%*	*Donot Aware*	*%*
1.	Tagadharis = 1,116	122	10.9	994	89.1
2.	Matwalis = 51,797	1,371	2.6	50,426	97.4
	Total = 52,913	**1,493**	**2.8**	**51,420**	**97.2**

It is observed from Table 16.14 that 89.1% of Tagadhari and 97.4% of Matwali plantation workers donot know or aware about the affiliation of their unions with the national federations or political parties. Only 10.9% of Tagadhari and 2.6% of Matwali workers are aware or know the affiliation of their unions with the national federations and political parties. They are found to be either the executive members of the unions or comparatively literate workers. The 97.2% of the tea plantation workers do not even know the names of their unions. They simply called parties for their unions. It is therefore generally concluded that trade union activities of the plantations are fully meshed with political activities of the political parties. So, like other unions of the country, Himalayan trade unions are fully concerned with political unionism to characterise trade union movement as economic unionism through political parties.

Workers and Union Leaders

Ramaswamy (1977) observed that indifference of workers with the union leaders make help to grow tyrany in the unions. Such apathy of the workers to the leaders and unions make unions corrupted and anti-workers in their approach and actions. The Himalayan tea plantation workers are expected to be more distant in so far as their day-to-day interactions with the union leaders are concerned as they reside in distant difficult terrains of the Himalaya. So, their personal acquintance with the leaders and vice-versa may be thin.

Table 16.15.

Acquintance of Workers, Leaders and Union Executives

Sl. No.	*Caste Status*	*Know Leader*	*%*	*Donot Know*	*%*
1.	Tagadharis = 1,116	763	65.4	353	31.6
2.	Matwalis = 51,797	48,697	94.0	3,100	06.0
	Total = 52,913	**49,460**	**93.5**	**3,453**	**06.0**

It is observed from the Table 16.15 that 65.4% of Tagadhari and 94.0% of Matwali workers know the union leaders not exactly as a union leaders but leaders of political parties. Interestingly 31.6% of Tagadhari and 6.0% of the Matwali workers do not even know the leaders of the unions as parties' leaders or even some of them have never heard the names of the union leaders. On the whole, 93.5% of the plantation workers know leaders by persons or they know the names of the leaders while 6.5% of them donot at all know the leaders of the unions. From this, we can say that trade unions are still in childish stage of development in the tea industry. Even 93.5% of the workers have very little personal interactions in their day to day life. Such indifference to union leaders is due to tyranical nature of union leaders and illiteracy of the plantation workers. Further, some workers said that union leaders are *Thulo*

Manche (Big sorts) and they considered themselves as *Sano Manche* (Common Coolies) and hence hardly, they dare to come nearer to the leaders. So, what is needed to bring them to the proximity of leaders and unions is to motivate, educate and participate them in modern way so that trade union movement can get fresh breath to face the challenges brought about by the changing economic scenario.

Bonus and Union Subscription

It is known from the study that most of the workers desire to pay their union subscription at the time of Bonus payment. Unfortunately, most of the workers feel that to get bonus means to get extra wages in the form of prize. They do not have any idea that it is the money that they are getting for their labour as per the payment of Bonus Act, of the Government. It is apparent from the Table 16.16 that 70.4% of Tagadhari and 61.3% of Matwali workers pay union subscription after getting the bonus. But it is also observed from the Table that 31.6% of Tagadhari and 6.0% of Matwali workers do not pay subscriptions even after getting their Bonus payment.

Table 16.16.
Bonus Payment and Union Subscription

Sl. No.	*Caste Status*	*Pay*	*%*	*Donot Pay*	*%*
1.	Tagadharis = 1,116	786	70.4	330	29.6
2.	Matwalis = 51,797	31,760	61.3	20,037	38.7
	Total = 52,913	**32,546**	**61.5**	**20,367**	**38.5**

It is observed from the above table that on the whole, 61.5% of tea plantation workers pay union subscription after getting the Bonus while 38.5% of the workers donot pay union subscription even after getting their Bonus. It shows that the subscription as the main source of union fund is still not completely known to the plantation workers of the plantation industry. This is the reason why unions are financially weak and this has led the unions to be submissive or defensive rather offensive and assertive in acquiring the rational demands of the workers.

Political Leaders and Union Elections

In holding the union election, the role of central leaders is very important. Such role of central union or political leaders must have been clear to the rank and file of workers in order to have successful trade union movement in the industry. The involvement of central leaders make a lot of difference when the management of the plantations have to hear the suggestions of the leaders who are mainly politically supported by political parties.

Table 16.17.
Awareness of Workers Regarding the Involvement of Central Leaders in Union Elections

Sl No.	*Caste Status*	*Know*	*%*	*Donot Know*	*%*
1.	Tagadharis = 1,116	429	38.4	687	61.6
2.	Matwalis = 51,797	2,834	5.5	48,963	94.5
	Total = 52,913	**3,264**	**6.2**	**49,650**	**93.8**

It is noted from the above Table 16.17 that 61.6% of Tagadhari and 94.5% of Matwali workers do not know the role or involvement of the central trade union leaders in the plantation level union elections or in the election days. Only 38.4% of Tagadhari and 5.5% of Matwali workers know the involvement of central union leaders in the elections or elections days. On the whole, it is observed from the table that 93.8% of plantation workers donot know the involvement of central leaders in the unit level elections. Only 6.2% of them know such involvement of the central leaders in holding elections. These 6.2% of workers happened to be the officials of unions at the plantation level. It is also observed from the table that comparatively Tagadharis are more aware about the importance of involvement of central leaders in the elections though they are numerically less than Matwalis. This may be due to their leadership concept of organisational legacy of the past both in Nepal and Sikkim (Pradhan: 1991).

Workers and Conflict Management

Conflicts are basic facts of life in group and organisations. Thus, the conflicts are inevitable features of organisational life and hence conflicts are inescapable aspect of life. In organisations, conflicts take place in many forms and types. Robbins (1967) defines conflict as a process in which an effort is purposively made by 'A' to offset the efforts of 'B' by some form of blocking that will result in frustrating 'B' in attaining his or her goals or furthering his or her interests. In an organisational life, conflicts occur when two or more parties pursue mutually exclusive goals, values and events. It is based on the assumption that there are two or more parties whose interests or goals appears to be incompatible. Tea industry being an organisation must have the mechanisms for managing the conflicts which may be of different types. At the industrial level, tea industry has its own system of management of conflicts. Bhowmik (1995) observed that any industrial level conflicts of plantation industry are managed by the involvement of tripartite committee at the state level. The committee is consisting of Consultative Committee of

Plantation Associations (management organisation), Coordination Committee of Tea Plantation Workers' Union which have fifteen constituent unions and Tea Defence Committee For Plantation Workers' Rights consisting of eight constituent unions operating in the tea industry of North Bengal of West Bengal. It is clear from the above discussion that tea plantation level conflicts are solved by the tripartite body. But interestingly, it is observed from the study that garden level problems or conflicts are left to them only.

It is observed from the above table that 95.2% of conflicts between the two families regarding elopement of girls by boys, deaths, land disputes and other disputes are solved by the local Samajs (social organisations) which in many plantations are caste and community associations, 2.1% of the conflicts

Table 16.18.
Workers' Responses on Conflict Management in Tea Industry

Sl. No.	*Areas of Conflict*	*Union*	*%*	*Management*	*%*	*Samaj*	*%*	*Police*	*%*
1.	Two Families	1,007	1.9	1,115	2.1	50,373	95.2	420	0.8
2.	T/U & Management	288	0.5	51,620	99.4	—	—	5	0.1
3.	T/U & T/U	119	0.2	1,022	1.9	80	0.25	1,6929	7.7
	Worker/worker	52,307	98.9	386	0.7	209	0.4	11	0.1

are solved by the intervention of management and 1.9% of conflicts are solved by the trade unions. It shows that issues related to social interactions like marriages, death, land disputes, *jari* (fine to male who elope the wife of another person), rituals etc. are the areas of local Samajs. These issues are normally considered as cultural issues where the management or unions have very little roles to play. But if there are conflicts between management and unions relating to the terms and conditions of services of the workers in the light of various Government Acts then such conflicts are solved (99.4%) by the interventions of management associations and central committees of the unions. However, in such conflicts, management has to take initiative as unions and police have little power except in exceptional cases like murders, theft and other criminal activities in the premises of the plantations. While, it is observed from the Table 16.18 that 97.7% of conflicts between or among trade unions are solved by police and only 1.9% of conflicts are solved by the management as it disturbs the smooth functioning of the industry. Again, 98.9% of conflicts between the two workers are solved by unions themselves.

The Union Ideology

In a broad sense, ideology can be regarded as the consciousness of a society, class or social group. This consciousness is determined by the material conditions of existence of the group concerned and it provides the main directions, principles and goals of their practical activity. In other words, ideology is a systematic totality of views, ideas and theories which expresses the interests and aspirations of a given social group (Bhowmik: 1981). Thus every ideology have generalised interpretations of character and course of human actions as motive forces. These principles may or may not be scientific or legal. It is understood from the earlier discussion on trade union movement of tea industry in hill Darjeeling that most of the present dominant trade unions have similar ideology relating to ethnic identity to be attained first by attaining the terms and conditions of service which are their peripheral interests. Thus, I.N. Moskvichov (1974) might be correct when he said that "ideology as a whole indicates the goals, means, and forms of practical and above all political activities of social groups and individuals". It is practical on the ground that most of the workers may not aware of the role of ideology in their trade union organisations. They are the leaders who lead the workers through their activities in the framework of ideology in the form of trade union movement. A mass movement across the history of Darjeeling Tea Industry has been taken place which are mainly known as ethnic movement guided by distinct "identity ideology". Whatever, the movement that taken place in Darjeeling Tea Industry like Pranta Parisad movement, Gurkhaland Movement or Nepali Bhasa Movement etc. are purely guided by the separate political ideology for the formation of separate state within the union of India.

Table 16.19.

Workers' Awareness Regarding Union Ideology

Sl. No.	*Caste Status*	*Know*	*%*	*Don't Know*	*%*
1.	Tagadharis = 1,116	49	4.4	1,067	95.6
2.	Matwalis = 51,797	3,031	5.9	48,766	94.1
	Total = 52,913	**3,080**	**5.8**	**49,833**	**94.2**

It is observed from the above table that 95.6% of Tadadhari and 94.1% of Matwali workers donot know about the ideology of the unions, they are rather found clear about the separate slate of Gurkhaland for which they shade their blood and sweat. For instance, they are aware about the party ideology of G.N.L.F. that harps on separate state. Hardly 4.4% of Tagadhari and 59% of Matwali workers have fair idea about the ideology of the unions. Again, they are found to be either the officials of trade unions or are comparatively literates than others of the plantations. On the whole, it is observed from the table that 94.2% of plantation workers do not know the ideology of unions. The 5.8% of the workers have little idea about the ideology of unions and its place in trade union movement in the Himalayan tea industry. It shows that ideology may be an intergral part of trade unions, it does not affect the workers. Radhakamal Mukherjee (1945) might be correct as he said that "Workers are too illiterate to understand the implications of Communist Ideology and on whole flock to those who promise fulfilment of the largest economic and social hopes". This statement is correct in case of the Himalayan tea plantation workers who are totally functionally illiterates. Secondly, minority unions have no locus standi in the plantations. It is simply observed that such unions have only leaders not the followers in the plantations. Further, the term 'ideology' is often considered as Communist ideology and it has presently little impact among the tea plantation workers in the Himalayan tea industry. Rather workers are fed up with the ideology they have been heard since the last thirty years without any practical relevance.

Tea Industry and Union Elections

In an industrial society like tea plantation industry, union is not only important for workers to protect their interests but to the management also to establish the fact that industry without union is a myth. In order to have a representative union, management in the light of Indian Trade Union Act, 1926 should have to see that the union elections are properly held as in case of other elections. This can in whole lot be justified the question of 'Recognition' by the management in the light of the provision of Indian Trade Union Act, 1926. Thus, the election of unions are not myth. The workers' awareness regarding the union elections are important in order to make the trade union movement a success.

Table 16.20.
Workers Awareness Regarding the Declaration of Holidays in Election Days of Unions

Sl. No.	*Caste Status*	*Know*	*%*	*Don't Know*	*%*
1.	Tagadharis = 1,116	17	15	1,099	98.5
2.	Matwalis = 51,797	175	3.4	51,622	99.7
	Total = 52,913	**192**	**0.4**	**52,721**	**99.6**

It is transparent from the Table 16.20 that 98.5% of Tagadhari workers do not know whether the management declare holidays in the election days of the unions or not. Similarly 99.7% of Matwali workers also do not know the issue. On the whole, 99.6% of the plantation workers donot know the issue. In fact, hardly management declare holidays for union elections. This might be the reason why the most of election of unions are held on Sunday or any other closed holidays. Because of the closed holidays most of the workers do not get information about the election of unions or remained busy in other business. Secondly, it is also observed in many gardens that workers do not know the place of elections as well as they donot know the timings of the elections. Thus, most of the workers fail to cast votes. It is understood from the union offices that hardly 10 to 15% of the plantation workers attend the union elections. This has created a lot of confusions in claiming the exact membership strength of the unions on the one hand and the very concept of industrial democracy has been spoiled on the other in tea industry of the Himalayan region.

Management Priority for Central Leaders

Rank and file leaders are far cry of Indian democracy. The rank and file leaders can come from the industry which can solve the problems in the industry itself. Interestingly, it is observed from the following table 16.21 that 69.5% of Tagadhari workers feel that rank and file or unit leaders are hardly invited by the management at troubled times. But on the other hand, 84.9% of Matwali workers believe that external non-worker leaders is to be invited by the management in times of emergency in the gardens.

Table 16.21.

Leaders to be called by Management in Emergency Times

Sl. No.	*Caste Status*	*Central Leaders*	*%*	*Unit Leaders*	*%*
1.	Tagadharis = 1,116	776	69.5	340	30.5
2.	Matwalis = 51,797	7,834	15.1	43,963	84.7
	Total = 52,913	**8,610**	**16.3**	**44,303**	**83.7**

Only 35.5% of Tagadhari workers feel that external non-worker leaders are to be given due privilege by the management. On the whole, 83 7% of the Himalayan tea plantation workers advocated for involvement of external union leaders in times of emergency in the plantations. This shows that the independence of plantation workers is secured through is secured through both non-worker and external leaders for all issues of the plantations. This has hinder the growth of rank and file leadership in tea industry. Such dependence on non-plantation worker-leaders is the creation of plantation system (Bhowmik: 1981), which has employed 52.0% of women workers who are less assertive for holding the union protfolios due to their double roles (Bhadra: 1997) as plantation worker and housewives. By nature, they are rather docile, humble and submissive (Sharma : 1997).

Union Subscription Receipts

The success of trade union movement can also be assessed from the proper receipts received by the members from the unions after paying the union subscriptions from the union offices. It is transparent from the Table 16.22 that 76.8% of Tagadhari workers donot get any receipt of the subscriptions paid to their unions. The 86.3% of Matwali workers donot

Table 16.22.
Workers' Response on Receipt of Union Subscription

Sl. No.	Caste Status	Yes	%	No	%
1.	Tagadharis = 1,116	29	23.2	857	76.8
2.	Matwalis = 51,797	7,118	13.7	44,679	86.3
	Total = 52,913	**7,377**	**13.9**	**45,536**	**86.1**

get any receipt from the union office whatsoever. Only 13.9% of them said that they get the receipt because of them being the officials of the unions or they are comparatively little conscious about the significance of the receipts to them in being the members of the unions. This is the issue which has weaken the image of trade unions as whosoever collecting the subscriptions is not found to be sincere enough to deposit all the collected money to the union offices.

Annual Returns of Unions

As per the Indian Trade Union Act, 1926, every trade union has to submit their return of the income and expenditure to the office of Labour Commissioner. Such record of income and expenditure of the unions are to be informed to the members of the unions. This will help to escalate the doubts of the workers about the proper utilisation of union fund. But it is evident from the following Table 16.23 that 98.3% of Tagadhari and 98.1% of Matwali workers donot know whether their unions submit their annual

Table 16.23.
Submission of Union Annual Returns

Sl. No.	Caste Status	Know	%	Donot Know	%
1.	Tagadharis = 1,116	19	1.7	1,087	98.3
2.	Matwalis = 51,797	564	1.1	51,233	98.1
	Total = 52,913	**583**	**11.1**	**52,330**	**98.9**

returns or not to the offices of Labour Commissioners. Further, it is also observed that they have never come across the names of labour commissioners or Assistant Labour Commissioners both at Darjeeling and Siliguri. On the whole, 98.9% of tea plantation workers do have no idea about this aspect of trade union movement. Only 11.1% of them know about this. They are found to be directly or indirectly involved in the affairs of the executive committees of the trade unions.

Workers Awareness about Bonus Meeting at Calcutta

The workers' perception in regard to the participation of their unions in Bonus meeting or tripartite agreements at Calcutta has been studied in this section. It is observed from the Table 16.24 that 79.4% of Tagadhari

Table 16.24.
Workers Perception of Participation of Unions in Bonus/ Agreements Meetings at Calcutta

Sl. No.	*Caste Status*	*Know*	*%*	*Donot Know*	*%*
1.	Tagadharis = 1,116	230	20.6	886	79.4
2.	Matwalis = 51,797	2,013	3.9	49,784	96.1
	Total = 52,913	**2,243**	**4.2**	**50,670**	**95.8**

and 96.1 % of Matwali workers do not know this. Only 20.6% of Tagadhari and 3.9% of Matwali workers know that just before Puja festival their union leaders rush down to Calcutta for doing agreements on Bonus. Similarly other industrial level agreements are done at Calcutta. These workers are either officials of unions or little more conscious of the way how Bonus is acquired. Interestingly, Tagadharis (20.6%) is more conscious about it than the Matwalis (3.9%). On the whole, it is transparent from the table that 95.8% of the plantation workers donot know about their participation through unions in Bonus or other meetings at Calcutta. This may be the reason why some union leaders said that unions means to arrange everything for workers from cradle to crematorium. Again, this may be perhaps the ample reason to characterise unions as "Economic Unionism" even at the advent of 21st century.

Union Recognition

Recognition of trade unions by the management and the plantation society is another dimension of trade union movement. The recognition as a social process has to be percolated down to the workers. Some of the managers viewed that every union has to be given recognition by the management to avoid unnecessary problems created by even a small union in the plantations.

It is observed from the above Table 16.25 that 96.4% of Tagadhari and 99.3% of Matwali workers do have no ideas about the union recognition. Only 3.6% of Tagadhari and 0.7% of Matwalis know about the recognition of their trade unions. They are found to be either the officials of unions or conscious citizens of the plantations or plantation system. On the whole, 99.2% of them do not know the recognition of trade unions. However, it is known that changes in the political power structure, the question of recognition of trade union also undergo changes. Till 1984, CITU led Darjeeling District Chia Bagan Mazdoor Union was a recognised union but after the formation of Darjeeling Gurkha Hill Council, its Himalayan Plantation Workers Union is the only most recognised union in the Himalayan Plantation industry. It is a recognised union both for the management and society as a whole. Thus, question of union recognition is directly interlinked with the power structure in the region or state.

Table 16.25.
Workers' Awareness Regarding Union Recognition

Sl. No.	*Caste Status*	*Know*	*%*	*Don't Know*	*%*
1.	Tagadharis = 1,116	40	3.6	1,076	96.4
2.	Matwalis = 51,797	364	0.7	51.433	99.3
	Total = 52,913	**404**	**0.8**	**52,509**	**99.2**

Protection of Workers' Interests and Unions

Unions are meant for the protection of workers rights or to protect the multiferous interests of the workers. This is what everybody knows that trade unions should see the interests of workers first.

It is transparent from the Table 16.26 that 85.8% of Tagadhari and 96.1% of Matwali plantation workers believe that having unions means the protection of the interests of workers. However, 14.2% of Tagadhari and 3.9% of Matwali workers do not know the main functions of trade unions. On the whole, 95.9% of the workers have deep conviction about the fact that the main function of trade unions is to protect the interests of the workers.

Table 16.26.
Unions and Protection of Workers' Interests

Sl. No.	*Caste Status*	*Yes*	*%*	*No*	*%*
1.	Tagadharis = 1,116	957	85.8	159	14.2
2.	Matwalis = 51,797	49,768	96.1	2,029	3.9
	Total = 52,913	**50,725**	**95.9**	**2,188**	**4.1**

Only 4.1% of the plantation workers do have no idea about the role of trade unions in the changing industrial scenario.

Unions and Wage Revision Board

As already mentioned that the wages of the workers are revised at every three years interval and to revise we have Wage Board which is a tripartite body consisting of representatives of Unions, Management and Government. Yet this aspect is found to be more or less not known to the rank and file workers. This is apparent from the responses of the workers in the following table.

Table 16.27.
Union and Wage Revision Board-workers' Responses

Sl. No.	*Caste Status*	*Know*	*%*	*Donot Know*	*%*
1.	Tagadharis = 1,116	14	1.3	1,102	98.7
2.	Matwalis = 51,797	95	0.2	51,702	99.8
	Total = 52,913	**109**	**0.2**	**52,804**	**99.8**

Interestingly, it is observed from the Table 16.27 that 98.7% of Tagadharis and 99.8% of Matwalis donot know the fact that union representation is there at wage revision board at Calcutta at every three years. Only 1.3% of Tagadharis and 0.2% of Matwalis have fair idea about this fact. However, they are found to be the officials of unions. It shows that common rank and file are still indifferent to this aspect of unions. On the whole it can be said that the participation of plantation workers in this aspect of trade union is still in the primitive stage.

Workers' Awareness about Union Areas of Operations

Under the changed situation, the role of trade unions must have also been diversified into various functional dimensions to get ready the tea workers to face the challenges brought about by the liberalisation of our economy. Such can be clear if we study the knowledge of workers about such diversified activities of the unions.

Table 16.28.
Workers' Responses About the Work Preferences of Unions

Sl. No.	*Name of Union*	*Productivity*	*%*	*Population Control*	*%*	*Quality of Life*	*%*	*Creation of Additional Emp.*	*%*
1.	H.P.W.U. (G.N.L.F.)	2008	3.0	2.2	0.1	740	1.4	50143	94.8
2.	D.T.D.C.K.M.U. (C.P.R.M.)	960	1.8	13	0.1	230	0.4	51710	97.7
3.	D.D.C.K.M.U. (C.I.T.U.)	51480	97.3	213	0.4	5.5	0.1	1165	2.2
4.	Others*	2114	4.0	50630	95.7	100	0.3	69	0.1

**N.U.P.W., A.I.T.U.C., G League*

The Table 16.28 portrays the fact that H.P.W.U. give more and more stress on their manifestoes for the creation of additional employment (98.8%) in the industry with the management. Similarly, it is found that 97.7% of workers said that this D.T.D.C.K.M.U. under C.P.R.M. party give importance for raising the productivity in the industry. Further, union like N.U.P.W., D.C.K.S.S., A.I.T.U.C. stress for the control of population in the industry. But 97.3% of workers said that D.D.C.K.M.U. (C.I.T.U.) wants the productivity raising. It is apparent from the table that issue like productivity, population control and creation of additional employment potentialities in and around the plantations appear to be tne agendas for trade union movement in the industry today. In fact, three issues are the centre of attention of not only unions but also of management and government policy to sustain the industry in the new century to come.

Rank and File Leaders Vis-a-vis External Leadership

It is an established fact that trade union movement to a large extent depend on the nature of leadership. It is the believes of the people concerned to the industry that unless and until the rank and file leadership emerge in the industry, trade union movement remains standstill. The workers desire for type of leadership was studied in this project.

Table 16.29.

Workers' Preference for Type of Leaders

Sl. No.	*Caste Status*	*Rank and File*	*%*	*External*	*%*
1.	Tagadharis = 1,116	779	69.8	337	30.2
2.	Matwalis = 51,797	4,118	7.9	47,679	92.1
	Total = 52,913	**4,897**	**9.3**	**48,016**	**90.7**

It is seen from the Table 16.29 that 69.8% of Tagadharis prefer for rank and file leaders. To them, rank and file leaders can understand the genuine problems of the workers as part of the system, while 92.1 % of Matwalis prefer for outside leaders. To them, management gives little importance to the rank and file leaders who are mostly illiterates. On the whole, hardly 10.0% of plantation workers prefer for rank and file leaders. It shows that tea plantation workers are still have no idea about the importance of rank and file leaders. To have more and more non-worker leaders will be much beneficial to management too so as to exploit workers at the isolated enclaves. So, the management encourages for external leadership of the unions. This is the reason why unions have bad names for corruption and tyrany in the unions. This has been further enhanced by the multiplicity of unions at the plantations since the last three decades.

One Union in one Plantation

"One Union in One Plantation" appears to be a far cry in the plantation industry. The workers were asked to respond to this aspect also to assess the significance of the one union in one industry as we found in other industries of the country.

Table 16.30.

Workers' Options for One Union in One Industry

Sl. No.	*Caste Status*	*One Union*	*%*	*Multiple Union*	*%*
1.	Tagadharis = 1,116	960	86.0	156	14.0
2.	Matwalis = 51,797	9,024	17.4	42,773	82.6
	Total = 52,913	**9,984**	**18.9**	**42,929**	**81.1**

It is observed from the Table 16.30 that 86.0% of Tagadhari workers prefer for one union in one industry while 82.6% of Matwali workers prefer for multiple unions in one industry. On the whole, it is observed from the table that 81.1% of plantation workers prefer for multiple unions and only 18.9% of them prefer for one union in one plantation. Such choice for multiple unions is responsible factor for deteriorating trade union movement in tea industry of Darjeeling Hemalaya following which each and every agreement goes mostly in favour of management in the recent years and many gardens have even closed down for ever.

Fund Utilisation in Unions

Utilisation of union fund is another area of union activity in the plantations. The particulars of utilisation of union fund must be made clear to the workers in order to make trade union movement a successful ones.

Table 16.31.
Workers' Response on Utilisation of Union Fund

Sl. No.	*Caste Status*	*Proper*	*%*	*Improper*	*%*
1.	Tagadharis = 1,116	163	14.6	953	85.4
2.	Matwalis = 51,797	42,763	82.6	9,034	17.4
	Total = 52,913	**42,926**	**81.1**	**9,987**	**18.9**

It is transparent from the Table 16.31 that 85.4% of Tagadhari workers responded that unions donot utilise their union funds properly while 82.6% of Matwali workers responded that unions utilise their funds properly. On the whole, 81.1% of plantation workers feel that funds are properly used by the unions. But 20.0% of workers believe that unions are corrupted in so far as the proper utilisation of fund is concerned. It is therefore apparent that all workers are not sure about the utilisation of fund by the trade unions of the plantations of the region.

Conciliation and Agreements

Trade union is the medium to educate the workers regarding the various aspect of collective bargainings, conciliations and agreements done for the workers. So, it is expected that plantation workers are aware of details of conciliations and agreements.

It is observed from the Table 16.32 that 96.8% of Tagadhari and 98.5% of Matwali workers donot know about the details of conciliation and agreements. They are found to be the officials of unions who (1.6%) know details about conciliations and agreements. Therefore, can be said that ordinary tea plantation workers donot know about the conciliations and agreements done by the unions. This means still the workers are not aware about what is Collective Bargainings in the clear sense of the term.

Workers' and Charter of Demands

To do collective bargaining, preparing the Charter of Demands is important to be submitted to the management.

Interestingly, it is observed from the above Table 16.33 that 97.7% of Tagadhari and 95.8% of Matwali workers donot know their role in framing the Charter of Demands. Similar opinion is done in case of Matwali workers. On the whole, it is observed that 95.8% of tea plantation worker

Table 16.32.
Workers' Awareness about Details of Conciliation/Agreement

Sl. No.	*Caste Status*	*Know*	*%*	*Donot Know*	*%*
1.	Tagadharis = 1,116	36	3.2	1,080	96.8
2.	Matwalis = 51,797	791	1.5	51,006	98.5
	Total = 52,913	**827**	**1.6**	**52,086**	**98.4**

Table 16.33.
Role of Workers' in Framing of Charter of Demands

Sl. No.	*Caste Status*	*Yes*	*%*	*No.*	*%*
1.	Tagadharis = 1,116	26	2.3	1,090	97.7
2.	Matwalis = 51,797	2,197	4.2	49,600	95.8
	Total = 52,913	**2,223**	**4.2**	**50,690**	**95.8**

feel that they donot have any role in framing charter of demands as they are not informed before preparing the same by the unions. It shows that preparing Charter of Demands and submitting it to the management is purely the exclusive function reserved for unions and workers have nothing to do with it. So, it reveals the fact that trade union movement in tea industry is still in the traditional form and interestingly it is also accepted by management and government.

General Functioning of Unions

Another area of enquiry of study was in respect of workers' participation in trade union movement by studying their satisfaction structure in the functioning of unions in general.

It is found from the Table 16.34 that 83.3% of Tagadhari workers are not satisfied with the functioning of the unions while 53.1% of Matwali workers are satisfied with the functioning of the unions. Again, 46.2% of Matwali workers are not satisfied with the union functioning. Those who are satisfied are of the opinion that it is better to have unions rather than to have singular dominance of management. Interestingly, 46.9% of the plantation workers are not satisfied with the general functioning of the unions. These workers, according to the union officials, have found to have tendency to change their membership from one union to another. Plantation being a closed society,

Table 16.34.
Functioning of Unions and Workers' Satisfaction

Sl. No.	*Caste Status*	*Satisfactory*	*%*	*Not Satisfactory*	*%*
1.	Tagadharis = 1,116	186	16.7	930	83.3
2.	Matwalis = 51,797	27,886	53.8	23,911	46.2
	Total = 52,913	**28,072**	**53.1**	**24,841**	**46.9**

the change of their membership from one union to another becomes more transparent to all the workers. This sometimes create inter-union rivalries in the plantations.

Workers Reference for Non-worker Leaders in Unit

The trade union movement has been further weakened by the presence for non-worker leaders by the workers and management in the plantations.

Table 16.35.
Workers' Preference for Non-worker Leaders in Unit Level Union

Sl. No.	*Caste Status*	*Yes*	*%*	*No*	*%*
1.	Tagadharis = 1,116	736	65.9	380	34.1
2.	Matwalis = 51,797	40,213	77.6	11,584	22.4
	Total = 52,913	**40,949**	**77.4**	**11,964**	**22.6**

It is observed from the Table 16.35 that 65.9% of Tagadhari and 77.6% of Matwali workers prefer for non-worker leaders at the unit level union. Only 34.1% of Tagadhari and 22.4% of Matwali workers prefer for non-worker leaders at the unit level union. The execessive preference for non-worker leaders (77.4%) at the unit level union by the workers is due to the fact that such non-worker leaders belong to middle class educated people who can balance the management bureaucracy and exploitation. It is found from the study that management cannot make fool the educated leaders regarding the terms and conditions of services of the workers. Further, they can easily understand the implications of agreements and problems and prospect of tea industry.

Political Affiliation of Unions and Workers

Surprisingly it is observed that workers have deep faith on the political affiliation with the political parties. But it is also observed from the study that they do not know the fact that unions can have affiliation not with political parties rather they can have affiliation with national federations having

Table 16.36.
Workers' Options for Affiliation to Unions

Sl. No.	*Caste Status*	*In favour*	*%*	*Against*	*%*
1.	Tagadharis = 1,116	268	24.0	848	76.0
2.	Matwalis = 51,797	4,135	8.0	47,662	92.0
	Total = 52,913	**4,403**	**8.3**	**48,510**	**91.4**

similar political ideologies of political parties. Till date non-worker has been taught about this reality that unions may have affiliation with national federations directly and not with the political parties. Unions can borrow the political ideologies of political parties in order to get support from the parties at the government platform.

It is transparent from the Table 16.37 that 76.0% of Tagadhari and 92.0% of Matwali workers prefer against the affiliation of unions with the political parties. On the whole, 91.4% of tea plantation workers have opted against the political affiliation of unions. Only 8.3% of them have opted in favour of affiliation. It is therefore clear from the table that unions can keep existence even without having their political affiliation with national federations or political parties. But majority of workers feel it as obligatory on the part of unions to affiliate themselves with one or another political parties to reach voices to the government, Legislative Assembly or Parliament.

Introduction of Panchayati System in Tea Industry

With the introduction of Panchayati system in the tea plantation industry, the role of unions vis-a-vis panchayat has become quite controversial. The plantation workers were asked their reactions about power structure of union and panchayat in the study.

Table 16.37.
Workers' Reactions on The Role of Unions and Panchayat and their Power

Sl. No.	*Caste Status*	*Union is Powerful*	*%*	*Panchayat is More Powerful*	*%*
1.	Tagadharis = 1,116	969	86.8	147	13.2
2.	Matwalis = 51,797	48,995	94.6	2,802	5.4
	Total = 52,913	**49,964**	**94.4**	**2,949**	**6.6**

With the increasing importance of Panchayati Raj in the country, the Himalayan Tea Plantation workers were also brought under the purview of Panchayati Raj System. Recently in 1998, this had become very important issue in the state though completely Darjeeling District could not be brought under it. However, the workers were asked to react about it and to express their feeling about the priority that management gives in the plantations to these two types of systems. From the above Table 16.37, it is observed that 86.8% of Tagadhari and 94.6% of Matwali workers feel that trade unions are more powerful than the panchayat as dealt by the management. On the whole, it is noted that 94.4% of tea plantation workers feel that unions are more powerful than panchayats. They said this in the light of their experiences that management always gives preference to unions than panchayats. Only 5.6% of them stated that Panchayat are more powerful than unions. It shows that panchayati system as the revival of old type of organisation though it made parallel to unions is not much prefered by the plantation system as it has created a confusion and contrast between the two organisations which have again equal legal sanctity. This might be apparant reason why the plantation have still further deteriorated to a damaging extent in so far as the developmental works are concerned. Both the organisations try to get the projects at their disposal. This is more precarious in the plantations where union and panchayat have different political background and support. Secondly, Panchayat as a traditional organisation is found to be more important for Tagadharis who were in the past the custodians of panchayat as rulers of villages both in Nepal and Sikkim and Matwalis had no upper hands in the panchayats as they were mainly toiling mass (Pradhan : 1991). Having Matwali majority in the plantations as plantation workers, the spirit of Panchayati Raj has not been really successful both in organisation and functioning. Thirdly, the dominant Himalayan Plantation Workers Union (G.N.L.F.) is against the introduction and functioning of panchayati system in the Himalayan tea plantation industry especially in hill plantations excepting Terai gardens of Darjeeling District. Even in the Terai areas, the panchayat members hail from outside the plantations. The panchayat members of the plantations of Terai have been working at behest of union leaders of various unions. Moreover, whatever the conciliations and meetings take place in the plantations being convened by the management, only union leaders take part actively and panchayat leaders or members have been obtained from participation.

Recognition of Union Vis-a-vis Panchayat Leaders

The question of union recognition is assured by the Trade Union Act, 1926 in the industry. The recognition of panchayat is not apparent in tea industry as we find in villages. The developmental works of panchayat in tea industry appears to be thin since inception. (1998) as so far no significant progress is noted by the workers. So, its recognition has been bleak for the plantation workers.

Table 16.38.

Trade Union, Panchayat and Management Recognition

Sl. No.	*Caste Status*	*Trade Union*	*%*	*Panchayat*	*%*
1.	Tagadharis = 1,116	965	86.5	151	13.5
2.	Matwalis = 51,797	50,602	97.7	1,195	2.3
	Total = 52,913	**51,567**	**97.5**	**1,346**	**2.5**

It is observed from the above Table 16.38 that 86.5% of Tagadhari and 97.7% of Matwali workers feel that trade unions are better recognised by plantation management than the panchayats. But interestingly, it is also observed that 13.5% of Tagadharis feel that panchayat are also to be recognised by the management sooner or latter as it is also a legal organisation of the government for tea plantation workers, while 2.3% of Matwali workers feel that Panchyat is better recognised than unions by the management on the ground that it is less politicised than unions. On the whole, it is observed that 97.5% of plantation workers feel that unions are more recognised by management than the panchayat. Such observation was further supplimented by the opinions of management that unions are related to tea industry while panchayat is not directly concerned with the industry. So, unions are more important than Panchayat in tea industry. Again, the unions have good hold with workers. Hence management feel that they donot have much concern with the panchayat leaders while carrying on the activities of the industry.

Union Registration

The registration of union is another important area of trade union movement. With the passage of fifty years of independence it is expected that the unions must have taught the workers about the process of union registration so as to make succes0s the trade union movement—a success in the real sense of the term.

Table 16.39.

Workers' Satisfaction Structure on Union Registration Process

Sl. No.	*Caste Status*	*Satisfied*	*%*	*Not Satisfied*	*%*
1.	Tagadharis = 1,116	186	16.7	930	83.3
2.	Matwalis = 51,797	1,829	3.5	49,968	96.5
	Total = 52,913	**2,015**	**3.8**	**50,898**	**96.2**

It is observed from the above Table 16.39 that 83.3% of Tagadhari and 96.5% of Matwali workers are not satisfied with the process of union registration. To the workers, it is not known them how the union is registered. They donot know who is the appropriate authority to be approached for the union registration. Only 16.7% of Tagadhari and 3.5% of Matwali workers know about the process of registration. They are found to be the leaders or officials of unions. It shows that rank and file tea plantation workers are not aware of the registration process of the unions. On the whole, 96.2% of the plantation workers donot know the process and only 3.8% of them know it being directly involved in the unions as officials of the unions or organisations. So, it can be said that on the basis of observations made during our field work that union registration as part and parcel of trade union activity is still outside the purview of workers participation. It is also found that political leaders are more interested to get registered an union than the rank and file workers. It means that political leaders by and large do union registration. Further, workers said that they donot understand the wide formalities of union registration which involves knowledge and skill and such abilities are not lies with the rank and file workers. This lack of skill and knowledge being illiterate or semi-literate has hindered the workers to shoulder the responsibility of getting the union registration in the plantations.

Workers' Satisfaction on Panchayat

The recent efforts to introduce panchayat system in hill tea plantations by the government has invited lot of confrontation from the Darjeeling Gurkha Hill Council especially after 1998 on the ground that hill tea gardens are already under the control of DGHC which is separate developmental organisation than other existing in the plain areas of Darjeeling and Jalpaiguri districts. This might be the reason why Government of West Bengal has dropped down the idea of introduction of panchayati system in the hill tea gardens. However, to know the people about the acceptance of panchayati system, an enquiry had done in this study, to assess their satisfaction structure about the introduction of panchayat system in the plantations of Darjeeling Himalaya.

Table 16.40.

Workers' Preference for Introduction of Panchayat

Sl. No.	*Caste Status*	*Prefer of Panchayat*	*%*	*Not Prefer for Panchayat*	*%*
1.	Tagadharis = 1,116	33	3.0	1,083	97.0
2.	Matwalis = 51,797	1,029	2.0	50,768	98.0
	Total = 52,913	**1,062**	**2.0**	**51,851**	**98.0**

It is observed from the Table 16.40 that 97.0% of Tagadhari and 98.0% of Matwali workers are not in favour of introduction of Panchayati system in the plantations of the Himalayan region. On the whole, 98.0% of plantation workers are not in favour of introduction of panchayati system. Only 2.0% of them are in favour of introduction of panchayati system on the ground that it might create further confusion with trade unions. Management are of the view that the industry has to unnecessarily listen the grievances of unions and panchayats simultaneously. This has further overburdened the industry as both the organisations quite often exert political pressures and commotions in the plantations. Such a picture is more damaging in plantations where unions and panchayats members hail from two different political parties. Thus, the very objective of introducing Panchayati system as a national commitment has so far not yet been reaped good harvest in the tea industry of the region.

Workers and Strikes in Tea Industry

Strike as an ultimate weapon for workers in the light of Industrial Disputes Act, 1947 has also common in tea industry. However, with the passage of time specially after 1991, the strike as a constitutional right appears to become an defensive mechanism as unlike in the past when it was considered as an offensive mechanism as no union wants to linger strike for even couple of days today in the Himalayan tea plantation industry. It is being supplimented by the view of Shri N.K. Kumai, President of Himalayan Plantation Workers who refused to call strike in 1999 as he told the authors that to call strike for one days involves a loss of nine lakhs rupees for the workers and in a week they loss fifty four lakhs rupees. This is the direct loss. He added that in one day strike, industry loss round about ninteen lakhs rupees which sometimes becomes irrepairable throughout the year.

Table 16.41.
Workers' Awareness about The Causes of Strikes

Sl. No.	*Caste Status*	*Wages* (%)	*Retrench-ment* (%)	*Poot working Condition* (%)	*Welfare* (%)	*Bad Behaviour of Management* (%)
1.	Tagadharis = 1,116	4 (0.4)	6 (0.5)	608 (54.5)	465 (41.7)	33 (2.6)
2.	Matwalis = 51,797	4 (0.1)	10 (0.1)	7,842 (15.1)	43,790 (84.5)	151 (1.0)
	Total = 52,913	**8 (0.1)**	**16 (0.1)**	**8,450 (16.0)**	**44,255 (83.6)**	**184 (0.3)**

It is observed from the above Table 16.41 that 83.6% of causes of strike is due to poor welfare facilities of the workers in the light of Plantation Labour Act, 1951 and 16.0% of the causes of strike is due to the poor working conditions. However, it is also observed from the table that 54.5% of causes of strike is due to poor working conditions to Tagadharis while 4 1.7% of causes of strike is related to welfare to them. Interestingly 2.6% of strike is due to bad behaviour of management to the view of Tagadharis, while 84.5%

of causes of strike is due to poor welfare facilities to Matwalis and 15.1% of causes of strike is due to poor working conditions to Matwalis and 1.0% of causes of strike is due to the bad behaviour of management. On the whole, it is observed that 83.6% of causes of strike is due to poor welfare facilities of the workers and 16.0% of causes of strike is due to poor working conditions to the plantation workers. It shows that still strike is mostly centered around the various provisions of Plantation Labour Act, 1951 and other labour legislations like Employees Provident Fund Act, Gratuity Act, Bonus Act, etc. This might be the apparent reason why trade union movement in tea industry is still not able to shift its emphasis from "Economism" to "Dynamism" for overall development of society as a whole.

Workers' Participation in Strike

Regarding the participation of workers in strike, a mixed responses have been observed in the study. During these years the issue is gaining low ebb in so far as the trade union movement in tea industry of the Himalayan region is concerned. However, workers take part in it simply because they do not invite any confrontations.

Table 16.42.
Reasons for Workers' Participation in Strike

Sl. No.	*Caste Status*	*Fulfill Demand (%)*	*Show Majority (%)*	*Fear of Assault (%)*	*Picketings (%)*	*Other Social Reasons (%)*
1.	Tagadharis = 1,116	686 (61.5)	265 (23.7)	107 (9.6)	8 (0.7)	50 (4.5)
2.	Matwalis = 51,797	4,135 (8.0)	45,833 (88.5)	341 (0.7)	468 (0.9)	1,020 (2.0)
	Total = 52,913	**4,821 (9.1)**	**46,098 (87.1)**	**448 (0.8)**	**476 (0.9)**	**1,070 (2.1)**

It is observed from the above Table 16.42 that 61.5% of Tagadhari workers participate in strike to fulfil demands of the unions while 23.7% of them participate to show majority in front of management. Again, 9.6% of Tagadharis stated that they participate in strike due to the fear of assaults and 4.5% of them stated that they participate in strike to avoid social boycott by other workers. Interestingly, 88.5% of Matwalis stated that they participate in strike to show majority in front of management. Again, 8.0% of them stated that they participate in strike to fulfil demands of the unions. On the whole, it is observed that 87.1% of plantation workers participate in strike to show majority and 9.1% of them participate to fulfil the demands of the unions. Only, 2.1% of them stated that they participate in strike to avoid social boycott by the society. Such social boycott involves isolation of such workers' families from involving in social activities like marriages, death ceremonies; festivals and other important social occasions, refuse to transact exchanges of goods and services in the household affairs of the society.

Workers' Indifference to Strike

With the excessive indifference of Government towards the industry after 1991 in general and workers in particular, the faith of workers towards the strike called by the unions is diminishing steadily. This may be the reason why we see in this study that during the last ten years there is hardly any strike taking place for long period in the Himalayan plantation industry.

Reasons for Avoiding Strike by the Workers

Another important emerging problem of present trade union movement is non-participation of workers in the strikes. It is observed in the present study that workers hesitate to participate in strikes because they donot invite problems in their family life as normally strike called for violence which cause for fatal consequences.

Table 16.43.

Causes of Non-participation of Workers in Strike

Sl. No.	*Caste Status*	*Fear of Victimisation Management (%)*	*Illegal Strike (%)*	*Unjust Demand (%)*	*Strike by Rival Union (%)*	*Not good to Strike (%)*
1.	Tagadharis = 1,116	8 (0.7)	61 (5.5)	207 (18.5)	731 (65.5)	109 (9.8)
2.	Matwalis = 51,797	11 (0.1)	35 (0.1)	118 (0.2)	49.743 (96.1)	1,890 (3.6)
	Total = 52,913	**19 (0.1)**	**96 (0.2)**	**325 (0.6)**	**50,474 (95.4)**	**1,999 (3.8)**

It is observed from the Table 16.43 that 65.5% of Tagadhari and 96.1 % of Matwali workers donot want to participate in strike due to the fact of strike by rival unions, while 18.5% of Tagadhari believe that such strike is called for unjustified demands. Again, 9.8% of Tagadhari and 3.6% of Matwali workers feel that it is not good to strike in the changing situations when tea industry of the region is passing through the tough time in the international markets. On the whole, it is seen that 95.4% of plantation workers believe for non-participation in strike due to the strike is not total rather partial normally called by rival unions having political vested interests. But 3.8% of the plantation workers believe that it is not good to strike. Thus, it can be said that strike as an ultimate weapon of workers is going to be defensive rather offensive as in the past. Similar is the case of lockout as the ultimate weapon of the management when it is observed today in Darjeeling Himalayan plantation industry that management and unions donot use their weapons normally and even if they use them, they use them for a very short period. In fact, they do not want to linger the strike and lockout for longer duration. Rather they believe on negotiation, education and trainings for avoiding the use of such weapons. Such observations can be supplimented by the lockouts called in gardens like Glenburn, Lingia, Moondakotee, Nagrifarm etc. in 1999 for shorter durations. Interestingly, the problem cropped due to the assault of manager by the workers in North Tukvar T.E. in 1998 was negotiated shortly even if the workers did not get any additional benefits after the incident. In this case the Himalayan Plantation Workers Union had to take defensive side to solve the problem by agreeing the terms of the management. According to the General Secretary of the Union, workers had committed mistakes by physically assaulting the manager. Superintendent of Jaishree Tea Company and Assistant Managers of North Tukvar T.E.

Workers' Grievance and Redressal Procedure

It is an accepted fact that redressal procedure of workers grievances is still vague to the workers because the workers donot understand the wide formalities of the procedure involved.

Table 16.44.
Workers' Satisfaction on Grievance Redressal Procedure

Sl. No.	*Caste Status*	*Satisfied*	*%*	*Not Satisfied*	*%*
1.	Tagadharis = 1,116	248	22.2	868	77.8
2.	Matwalis = 51,797	4,864	9.4	46,933	90.6
	Total = 52,913	**5,112**	**9.7**	**47,801**	**90.3**

It is transparent from the above Table 16.44 that 77.8% of Tagadhari and 90.6% of Matwali workers are not satisfied with the grievance redressal procedure followed in tea industry of the region. But 22.2% of Tagadhari and 90.3% of Matwali workers are satisfied that the grievance redressal procedure is with the years glyding by becoming simple as local union leaders and management try to solve the problems at Darjeeling itself without referring to the Joint Labour Commissioner's office at Siliguri or Labour Commissioner, Calcutta. On the whole, 90.3% of the workers are not satisfied with the procedure and only 97% of them are satisfied with it. It is known from the study that majority of workers are not satisfied with the procedure on the ground that unusual tactics are followed by unions and management and such tactice are not comprehensibly to the rank and file workers. Secondly, hardly any worker can understand well about the concept and meaning of conciliation, negotiation and agreements. So, it appears from this that handling of grievences of the workers are the exclusive areas of the central trade union leaders only.

The Industrial Disputes in Tea Industry

The dispute settlement machineries for plantation workers of the government have not been much successful considering the non-implementation of Plantation Labour Act, 1951 in toto.

Table 16.45.
Workers' Satisfaction Structure on Dispute Settlement Machinery

Sl. No.	*Caste Status*	*Satisfied*	*%*	*Not Satisfied*	*%*
1.	Tagadharis = 1,116	147	13.2	969	86.8
2.	Matwalis = 51,797	2,804	5.4	48,993	94.6
	Total = 52,913	**2,951**	**5.6**	**49,962**	**94.4**

It is observed from the above Table 16.45 that 86.8% of Tagadhari and 94.6% of Matwali workers of Darjeeling Himalaya are not satisfied with the dispute settlement machineries of the government. Only 13.2% of Tagadharis and 5.4% of Matwalis are satisfied with machineries. On the whole, 94.4% of the plantation workers are not satisfied with the machineries of industrial disputes and only 5.6% of them are satisfied with it. To the plantation workers, such machineries donot decide any issue promptly. Further, lot of money is required to get the disputes settled from the machineries. So, it is proved the handling of such delicate industrial disputes require mutual trust, and respect, participative practices, collective communication and information sharing (Karan: 1999: 4-5), between the management and labour in tea industry.

Workers' View on Strike as Means to Prove Them A Great Power

Quite often during the last fifty years, workers were considered a cheap labour force commonly known as Coolies by the management in plantation industry (Bhowmik: 1981). Considering recent changes at the global village, labour is becoming as an important factor of production or resource of the industry. To assess the view with workers, some observation had been done in this study.

Table 16.46.
Workers Viewed as a Big Power

Sl. No.	*Caste Status*	*Yes*	*%*	*No*	*%*
1.	Tagadharis = 1,116	796	71.3	320	28.7
2.	Matwalis = 51,797	42,763	82.6	9,034	17.4
	Total = 52, 913	**43,559**	**82.3**	**9,354**	**17.7**

It is transparent from the above table 16.46 that 71.3% of Tagadhari and 82.6% of Matwali workers feel that workers are a big power in tea industry as it is basically a labour intensive industry. On the whole, 82.3% of plantation workers feel that workers is a big power without them no work can be completed in tea industry. But on the other hand 17.7% of workers feel that they are not a big power in industry as they are very cheap having the value of Rs. 34.80 only per day as wage they get. However the workers feel that they feel a big power under the banner of unions. So, if there is no union there will be no agency to say that workers a big power of the industry and management may revert to their earlier style of exploitation of workers. This is so as it is apparent from our experiences that still management is functioning notionally in the line of past legacy which was left to them by the British planters. To prove them a big power, strike is to be called for as and when require to erase out the legacy that present management still lingering in the plantations of Darjeeling hills.

Strike and Wage Raise

It is a general believe that strike can help raise wages of the workers. To organise strike is another important area of trade union movement in industry. The occurences of strike is going to be very limited in tea industry during the last one decade in Darjeeling hills. Even the nine days strike called by other unions in Terai and Dooars areas could not take place in tea industry of Darjeeling Himalaya in 1998. Even they refuse to have a token strike for one single day.

Table 16.47.
Strike and Wage Raise

Sl. No.	*Caste Status*	*Yes*	*%*	*No*	*%*
1.	Tagadharis = 1,116	229	20.5	887	79.5
2.	Matwalis = 51,797	39,765	76.8	12,032	23.2
	Total = 52,913	**39,994**	**75.6**	**12,919**	**24.4**

It is observed from the Table 16.47 that 79.5% of Tagadhari workers reacted in negative while 23.2% of them (Matwalis) reacted in positive. This shows that Tagadharis are far conscious about the fact that wage can be increased not by doing strike but by tripartite agreement on the basis of Minimum Wages Act, 1948 of India through Minimum Wages Board consisting of members of management, unions and government at every three years. Interestingly, 76.8% of Matwali and 20.5% of Tagadhari workers still believe that wages can be raised by resorting to strike. On the whole, 75.6% of plantation workers believed strike as a way to raise wages. This happens because 96.0% of plantation workers are Matwalis who are still appeared to be tribals (Dash: 1947) having very limited knowledge about the organisational aspect of trade unions and their functionings. However, 24.4% of the workers among mainly Tagadharis donot believe on the fact that strike can help the wage raise for the plantation workers.

Workers' Response on Quality of Work Life

Tea industry being the outcome of colonial system of agro-based type had followed covert type of exploitation after the independence of the country. To react with such type of system, workers with the mobilisation of trade unions followed gherao, go-slow, tool-down strike, gate meetings, etc. etc. in tea industry as the style of work life. But after 1991 it is expected that such types of work styles must have been transformed into "work to rule" the day-the new philosophy brought about by the liberalisation of Indian economy.

Table 16.48.
Workers' Responses for Work Styles

Sl. No.	*Caste Status*	*Gherao*	*%*	*Go-slow*	*%*	*Tool-Down Strike*	*%*	*Work to Rule*	*%*
1.	Tagadharis = 1,116	13	1.2	300	26.9	107	9.6	696	62.4
2.	Matwalis = 51,797	9	0.1	16100	31.1	15	0.1	35673	68.9
	Total = 52,913	**22**	**0.1**	**16400**	**31.0**	**122**	**0.2**	**36369**	**68.7**

It is observed from the above Table 16.48 that 62.4% of Tagadhari and 68.9% of Matwali workers stated that everybody of the garden has to work for eight hours per day as per the provision of Plantation Labour Act, 1951 in changing industrial scenario. Interestingly, 26.9% of Tagadhari and 31.1% of Matwali workers believed that sometimes they have to adopt "go-slow", type of work in order to inform the management that they are not satisfied with the existing working conditions of gardens. In regard to traditional style of gherao and tool down strike, only 10.8% of Tagadhari workers stated that in positive as they said these days, the ways of ventilating their grievances are sometime important to improve the working conditions of the plantations. On the whole, it is observed that 31.0% of workers believe on go-slow, as a process to inform the management faults. But 68.7% of the workers stated that under the changing situation, philosophy of 'Work to Rule' as a norm is to be strictly followed as the quality of work life in the plantation industry of the region. It shows that the traditional style or quality of work life through gherao, go-slow and tool-down strike have slowly becoming redundent as majority of them (68.7%) believe on "work to rule the day" in the plantations.

From the above discussions, it is important to note that the workers can rightly participate in the trade union activities and activities of industry if they are properly motivated, trained and given opportunities to exploit their calibre. To do so, the basic tendency of unions to keep everything secret to be made transparent to the rank and file workers of the industry. Secondly, management also has to realise the fact that no more workers are the mess of the system as today the workers are very much exposed to outside world. Thirdly, political interferences in the matters of industry should be avoided to make it really liberalised from the age old concept of enclave economy.

17

ETHNICITY AND TRADE UNION MOVEMENT

It is observed in the earlier chapters that trade union movement in tea gardens of the Himalayan region is mainly an ethnic movement. We understand that the basic objective of trade union movement is to protect the interests of working class. This concept of class interest was championed by Communists in the hill tea gardens since 1946. But whenever the unity of working class in tea gardens was diffused to ethnic cause, it became absolute and sessionist for the government of West Bengal. There are certain reasons why such ethnic movement lead under the banner of trade unions was made absolute by the West Bengal government. To make this clear, let us discuss comparatively the following historical-cum-socio-cultural background of trade unions in Dooars and hill tea gardens of West Bengal.

First, the trade union movement in Dooars gardens was initiated and organised by outsiders hailing from Bengal-Assam Rail Road workers Union. Bhowmik (1981) observed that 'the workers of the Dooars showed signs of collective action only after the trade union organisers of the Bengal-Assam Rail Road Workers' Union under an attempt to organise them in early 1946', while in Darjeeling Tea gardens, local leaders like Ratanlal Brahmin, J.L. Subba, B.B. Hamal, and others initiated and organised the tea garden workers before 1946 and formed tea workers union. The garden workers accepted the trade union movement not because of the influence of communist class ideology but because of having "affective tie" of the leaders of the union with the workers. We will explain the concept of "Affective Tie" a bit latter in this chapter.

Secondly, it is wrong to brand the 'Class' factor as a determining variable for the origin and growth of trade union movement in Darjeeling hills. It is the ethnic traits like *Daju-Bhai* (brothers), *Bichara* (pitty feeling), *Afnoo Manche* (relatives) that help local leaders to sustain the trade union movement. Therefore, it is wrong to dilute the class framework into the ethnic scenario.

Doing this would only harm the framework of communist ideology itself while it certainly does not help improving the scenario at tea plantations.

Thirdly, had it been purely the trade union movement, if it brought about by the Communists and national political parties there would have been no ethnic movement like Gurkha National Liberation Front or Praanta Parisad for the separate identity in Darjeeling hills, as it is already mentioned that the movement had deep roots at the gardens of the Darjeeling hills.

Fourthly, the trade union movement as it is called by the Communists sense in the gardens have had peripheral class interests. It is peripheral, as issues relating to terms and conditions of services of the workers as a class are mainly dealt at par with other workers of tea industry of North Bengal in the light of Plantation Labour Act, 1951. Had it been purely trade union movement in the generic sense, than there would have been no movement in the closed gardens like Pashok T.E., Via-Tukvar T.E., Puttong T.E. etc. during 1984-1988.

Fifthly, it can be accepted that there was a trade union movement in Dooars gardens having both the workers and management from similar socio-economic and cultural background of the country, while in Darjeeling gardens, both under the grip of British colonialism and now neo-colonialism or neo-colonialist-system, owners and management, are outsiders having different socio-cultural background. It is inter-class conflict in Dooars tea gardens while it is inter-ethnic conflict in hill tea gardens of Darjeeling.

Finally, the top leadership of the Dooars gardens is in the hands of Bengali community (Bengali Babus in gardens) and Bengali leaders at the central committees of the unions while all the union leaders of the central committees are the local people from the same ethnic community in Darjeeling gardens.

It is apparent from the above discussion that ethnicity has played a significant role in Himalayan trade union movement. Daniel Bell, a prominent Sociologist, has defined ethnicity as 'Affective Tie'. His contention of ethnicity has been taken here as the analytical tool for studying the trade union movement in tea industry.

Another important reason for having this analytical tool is that, from the organisational point of view, day by day, having no affective tie of the owners and management, the tea gardens are getting sick and state government has shown little inclination to rejuvinate the gardens. It is also interesting to note that until now there is not a single Lepcha, Bhutia and Nepali tea estate owner. All the gardens are owned by plainsmen while hillmen are kept satisfied with a few managerial posts (Subba : 1992). Thus, the ownership of hill tea gardens provides a clear picture of ethnic stratification.

The ethnic ideology is driving force behind the trade union movement in the hill tea industry. Let us discuss ethnic ideology which is concerned with the ideology of identity.

Ideology of Identity

The ideology of identity is primarily the ideology of insecurity of tea garden workers being exploited at turn in the hands of the British colonialists and Indian neo-colonialist-planters and owners of tea industry.

The planters and owners of the gardens since its inception have treated the garden workers as an ethnic community of mercinary character. Whatever the development the tea garden owners did was primarily for alleviating their poverty rather than providing them prospects for advancement as of other leading communities in the region. The industrial relationship between the owners and workers (two separate ethnic groups) is the relationship of holding power and authority by owners and workers without such powers and authority. Such relationship is always in strain form sometimes covert and some other time in overt forms. Both groups feel threatened of each other's positions-privileged (owners) and underprivileged (workers). Owners always try to ensure its privileges and workers try to overcome its hardships. Of course, being the Himalayan region, the owners/management sense of insecurity is deeper than the workers who have the privileges to acquire extra-territorial helps across the borders. Another reason for having such ideology is that the workers often have experienced the inherent indifference to national trade unionism. To the workers nationalism may be important for other ethnic communities but they have nothing to do with it as they feel of losing their place or identity in the gardens. Here identity is mainly meant for them the culturo-linguistic-cum-social preservation and development.

To explain such issue like identity, let us discuss some pertinent sociological hypothesis to prove that why the sense of insecurity pervades in the minds of the workers. The first hypothesis is the increasing population and restricted employment potentialities in the gardens. Mainly the unemployed youths are engaged for 5 to 6 months in a year in Bigha (allotted) works leaving them utter unemployed in rest of the year. Another hypothesis is that 'transfered anger' of the workers looking the lavish way of life of management and their families. The genesis of this feeling is the history of one and half century of colonial hegemony of enclave economy. Another hypothesis is that all communities in India got separate state identity based on separate ethnicity except the Gurkhas or Nepalis. Instead of recognising their status, planters and owners consider them simply barbaric, Coolies to be tamed brutally in the enclaves.

Still another hypothesis is that the tea gardens as the source of people's livelihood (cheap slogan of the management) has been stagnated as the owners of the gardens have no feeling of socio-economic development of the workers who belong to other ethnic groups. This might be the strongest reason why now there are only 70 tea gardens and hence the number of gardens decreased from 96 in 1981 to 70 in 1999.

Another important hypothesis behind this identity issue is the economic deprivation and negligence in providing the various incentives in the light of labour legislations of the government.

It is an established fact that the Himalayan tea industry is very famous for its quality which has attracted the world markets with handsome revenues. But the hypothesis it provides "ample means of livelihood to workers" appears to be wrong as the lion's share of the profit goes to the trader-owners from Calcutta, Delhi, Mumbai and South India. This has affected the inter-ethnic relations between the garden workers and management who belong to the plain communities.

Thus, in the eyes of academicians and political leaders, the working class movement in the gardens is trade union movement to suit their own timid interests but to the workers it is ethnic movement of course under the banner of some organisations.

To suppliment the above contention, let us cite the ground reality with ample evidences that lead to characterise the recent ethnic movement in tea gardens. Had it been the trade union movement then there would have been clashes not only between the G.N.L.F and C.P.I.(M) the ruling party of the state but between G.N.L.F and other national political parties also. It should be pointed out here as earlier in Pranta Parisad movement also, tea belt was the bastion of clashes and even death fury of the people, ever since 1977 when the Left Front government was formed in the state. But the Marxist influence in tea gardens was not complete as Deo Prakash Rai, the charismatic leader was assured of Rai votes and it is already mentioned that Rai is the most dominant caste among other castes in tea plantations. So, only a few tea gardens were the stronghold of Marxists where the numerical strength of Rai caste was much lesser compared to Tamangs, Sunuwars, Gurungs, Mangars as well as Limbus. After the death of Deo Prakash Rai (the Gurkhali leader) of All India Gurkha League, the C.P.I. (M) got the opportunity to break the All India Gurkha League control and spread fast in the tea gardens especially after 1980. He was succeed over by a Marxist Tamang Dawa Lama. Sociologically having no second rank Rai leader and coming of Tamang leader. C.P.I. (M) penetrated far and wide corners of the industry in the Himalayan region. It was so happened because the Tamang comes next to Rai in strength in tea industry of the region as workers. Instead of following National Union of Plantation Workers having a Bhutia leader (Dawa Norbula) Rais rather preferred to support the Tamang C.P.I. (M) leader. Prior to that, the C.P.I. (M) cadres were looked down upon by other unions as illiterates and idiots and now C.P.I. (M) also started treating the AIGI and NUPW in the same fashion after 1980. This caused the death of 6 AIGI workers at Samabeong T.E. such C.P.I. (M) brutality forced the garden workers to join it forcefully. Such brutality could be easily sustained with careful patronage of the state government. The important point to note is that the politics of brutality was the process of unionisation under C.P.I. (M) which became an instrument for reckoning with the ideology of identity latter on in late eighty under the G.N.L.F. movement as ethnic movement in tea gardens. Because of this politics of brutality under C.P.I. (M) there appeared to have been a clash at Arya Tea Estate and Bloomfield T.E. of Darjeeling.

Identity vis-a-vis Trade Union Movement

After 1984, in every tea garden, trade unions of the past became dysfunctional, though there were leaders but without members. One Indrajit Pradhan, the leader of C.P.I. (M) of Ambootia T.E. was killed for the first time. By 1987, in each and every garden, local committee was formed by G.N.L.F. under the charge of a convener.

Now, there were only central leaders at Darjeeling and all the unit leaders of C.P.I. (M). N.U.P.W. and A.I.G.I., either left tea gardens or surrendered to G.N.I.F. committees. The central leaders of the unions were mum and hidden in cosy rooms at Darjeeling. In the mean time, another local C.P.I. (M) leader was killed at Som T.E. in August 1986. Another severe clash taken place with C.P.I. (M) workers at Teesta Valley T.E. where many workers were injured and finally they surrendered to G.N.L.F. local committee.

In September, 1980, two CPI (M) supporters were killed at Samsing T.E. and ten houses of the workers were ransaked. In October, 1986, 3 houses of CPI (M) leaders were looted at Tukvar T.E. and 3 houses were put on fire at Arya T.E. in the same month. In CPI (M) stronghold Singtam garden, a large number of GNLF houses were put on fire and 13 rounds firing was done by police. In November, 1986, 50 CPI (M) houses were burnt down in the same areas at Tukvar, Badamtam and Phoobsering Tea Estates. The thirty houses of CPI (M) were put on fire at Tukvar T.E. In November, again, 30 houses of CPI (M) were burnt down at Rungmook T.E. In June, 1988, 4 persons were kidnapped and others injured at Sepaidhura T.E. In May, 1988, 4 persons were killed at Oaks T.E. Again, in February, 1989, 2 persons were killed in Rungmook T.E.

Feedback of Ethnic Movement in Tea Gardens

After the ethnic movement was over, almost all the tea gardens came under the grip of the Himalayan Plantation Workers Union under the patronage of G.N.L.F. The identity proved that trade union in the Himalayan tea industry is not merely concerned with terms and conditions of services of the workers rather it had social objectives and implications. For Sociologists, the Social Impact Studies of the ethnic movement is important to assess the degree of ethnic base of trade union movement. Professor Frendenburg (1986) agreed the following propositions for such movement of ethnic type :

1. Socio-cultural variables need to be examined as well as economic or demographic ones;
2. Social Impact Assessment Study should not be limited to whatever data may appear to be available;
3. Social Impact Assessment Study should not he limited variables that are easily quantified and/or politically silent;
4. "Quality of life" is a key dependent variable to be looked into and;
5. Social Impact Assessment Study focus more on the tendency of projects to redistribute resources at all levels.

At the industrial level, the ethnic movement for restoring ideology of identity was a complete success. The tea industry was already degrading badly with the indifference of owners and management to local ethnic community. In the month of August, 1986, D.P. Sharma reported that tea industry was in 'Doldrums' with growing indiscipline among the workers and tea gardens had to close down one after another. Among the tea estates, Badamtam was the first garden to close down having 1300 workers under the prestigious Goodricke company. The garden had total man-day lost of 10,408 every day. Similarly, in July, 1987 Shymal Sarkar reported that 7 day strike just concluded incurred a loss of Rs. 4 crores. Plucking of tea leaves of second flush was done in 5 out of 72 gardens. Excepting Ranli-Rungliot, Makaibari, Longview, Sepaidhara. Lingia, Marrybong, Choogtong and Singtam Tea Estates all other gardens were closed down in the period as they had stronghold of GNLF. The worst affected gardens were Happy Valley, Tindharia, Soureni and Arya. Almost 75,000 permanent and temporary workers lost Rs. 65 lakhs of rupees in 7 days But according to Bharat Bhajoria, the then Chairman of Darjeeling Planters Association, estimated lost of wages was 8 crores. Similarly, in March, 1988, Shekar Gupta reported that loss of wages was 8 crores of rupees in a single year. They reported that almost all tea gardens were cut off from the rest of the world without fuel, transport and other raw materials due to destruction of roads and bridges. Another report of Vinayak in August. 1988 shows that the estimated production loss in 1986 and 1987 was one million kilograms or Rs. 5 crores and 1.1 million kilograms or loss of 8 crores respectively. The man-day lost were also reported to be 3,30,000 in 1986 and 6,00,000 in 1987. In Tukvar T.E. (Puttabong) which is owned by Jayshree Company of Birls Group, production had fallen from 3.39 lakhs Kg. in 1986 to 2.32 lakhs kgs. in 1987.

Interestingly, it is noted here that not a single worker died of hunger, during the four years of movement. So, it proves the fact that if the Himalayan tea gardens are closed down for ever no Gurkha or Nepali dies of hunger or starvation. Such thing is absolutely proved by Pashok and Via-Tukvar T.E. which were closed down for ever in 1990 when both the gardens were with more than four thousand workers and even now they are still surviving. Thus, the socio-cultural variables were found to be the determining variable for identity movement rather than purely the economic deprivation of working class in the Marxian phraseology. Another point is to mention is that if the trade union movement under CPI(M) had deep dent in tea estates for the last 25 years, then how yesterday's CPI(M) leaders left CITU and joined Himalayan Plantation Workers Union (GNLF) today.

In fact, it was the common understanding grown among the workers that CPI(M) is a Bengali party and such suspicion could not be wipe out from the simple minds of the workers. "Marxist or Non-Marxist, they are first of all Bengalis" comments an intellectual at Darjeeling. Interestingly, no hill CPI (M) leaders like Bengali CPI (M) cardres at Siliguri or at Calcutta referred that it would be another partition of Bengal if separate Gurkhaland state is made or carved out from North Bengal which was in the past outside the state of West Bengal. This might be the reasons why CPRM was formed in Darjeeling hills and its trade union wing is known as Darjeeling, Terai and Dooars Chia Bagan Mazdoor Union was formed in late nineties.

Another reason why Nepali Marxists shifted their loyalty to Himalayan Plantation Workers Union was due to the policy of CPI(M) leader Mr. Jyoti Basu who ordered Nepali Marxists to go for a fratricidal clash with Nationalist Nepalis in the gardens. It was his contradictory step for being the exponent of Anti-Terrorist Act imposed at Punjab in 1985, in the region.

It was found that in Chogtong and Singtam tea estates CPI(M) supplied money and arms to CPI(M) caders there to fight against GNLF activists and CPI(M) gave one lakh rupees as compensation to the members of CPI(M) whose houses were set on fire by GNLF supporters. Further, in those two gardens, the numerical strength of GNLF was very marginal and CPI(M) and state police therefore combinedly attacked the GNLF houses. Even the salary and wages of CPI(M) workers were paid by the managers but GNLF supporters did not get the same. The local criminal known as Man Singh Rai of CPI(M) of Tukvar tea estate asked by the CPI(M) party high command to kill the GNLF both at Darjeeling gardens and Siliguri. At that time, police had withdrawn his criminal charges and allowed to roam freely. In fact all these instances proved the fact that Marxist government in West Bengal behaved in no different way from the rightists of the past in so far as the identity issue of the people in general and plantation workers in particular is concerned in the Himalayan region. After the formation of Darjeeling Gurkha Hill Council in 1988, though lot of workers were discontent, almost all the workers shifted their membership to Himalayan Plantation Workers Union which is a frontal organisation of plantation workers in tea and cinchona plantations of the region because they said that they had already tested the salt of both rightist and leftist trade unions in a better way since 1947.

Future of Trade Union Movement

On the basis of above observations some propositions may be made regarding the future of trade union movement in the region. The trade union as the organisation for workers rather than of the workers are going to become an instrument to support party in power at Darjeeling hills. As N.K. Kumai, the veteran trade unionist of HPWU once stated that the union officials should not criticise DGHC efforts in tea gardens, the unionisation of tea plantation workers in the Himalayan region is not purely based on 'Class Interest' rather than the interests of G.N.L.F. which has so far pretended to stick to ethnic identity of the plantation workers including all the people of the region.

Secondly, the trade union movement is one sided game of HPWU today when it claims that to raise issues of the workers of the gardens means to raise question of an ethnic group relating to their socio-economic conditions in the region. Raising the ethnic question to HPWU is only their legitimate right and no other union has this power as they have in the past betrayed the people and workers.

Thirdly, HPWU feels that other unions are anti-establishment in nature and actions.

Finally, still the majority of workers feel that DGHC is as good as Gurkhaland and this might be the reason why more than 85% of plantation workers support HPWU.

On the basis of this present state of development of trade union movement, workers do whatever HPWU asks for both union and general elections.

Since HPWU has started to convince the workers that tea garden land is also not theirs and every effort is therefore to be made to convert the land theirs, there is every possibility of total closure of tea gardens by 2020 in Darjeeling hills so will be the end of trade union movement. This is one future proposition.

Another possible proposition drawn from the present trade union movement is to shift union emphasis from being complacent to workers and management to tea industry in the truest sense of the term.

It is observed from the opinions of the workers that tea industry has helped to solve only thirty percent of their problems and remaining seventy percent of their problems are to be solved by themselves. Still they are supporting the union on the ground that it is their own people (Afno Machees) who have formed it and functioning whatsover way though in many cases not upto the mark of their satisfaction.

The trade union movement in tea industry of the region is found to have been taken place on the patronage of political parties. Of course, in most of the period and cases, same ethnic background of the local leaders hailing from the same ethnic community could gather adequate momentum. It is trade union movement to the political parties only while to the workers all the party leaders are consisting of the people of their own ethnic community so they support the unions which to them are the frontal organisations of political parties in the region. One final point to note is that the workers support unions having their own people because what they believe is 'Blood is thicker than water' principle.

Hence, the participation of workers in most of the cases is passive in early stage of movement and intense in middle stage and even violent in the climax and latter on dwindles down slowly to non-existence. Thus, the trade union movement often repeats, develops and decays but in every moment of the movement, the motivational process of unionisation is found to be completely on ethnic line both in pre-British period, after the independence, today and even in future to come.

Setbacks of Present Trade Union Movement

It is observed by our visits to the Himalayan tea industry that managers always feel to somehow satiate the central leaders of the unions. They said that if the CPI(M) would have been in power in Darjeeling hills for another one decade or so then by 2000 all the tea gardens would have been closed. The managers were of the view that nationalisation policy of tea gardens of government was responsible for deteriorating conditions of tea estates because of poor work culture of the workers which were brought about by the nationalisation of tea industry in Darjeeling hills. Doing this, go-slow, strike etc. were increased by leaps and bounds till 1988. But the present leaders of dominated HPWU discouraged to do so to the workers on the one hand and curtailing certain legitimate rights of the workers by undertaking hasty agreements with the management on the other. Take for instance of North Tukvar T.E., Happy Valley T.E., Glenburn T.E., Lingia T.E., Moondakote T.E. etc., where HPWU even agreed that no additional housings would be made for the workers during the next two years from 1998 to 2000. It shows that the existing tyrany of HPWU is mounting like anything in the region. Here in these cases, the local leaders of gardens were not allowed to say anything in the matter (Ramaswamy : 1977) because the item 'housing' comes under the industrial level negotiation of central committee of HPWU.

Another setback of present Himalayan trade union movement is in respect of excessive politicisation of the workers instead of unionisation under the HPWU as even there is no independent union flag of HPWU in gardens.

The question of drinking water, electricity, roads, and bridges appears to have been not taken care of by HPWU or other unions and drinking water problem is very acute in the gardens almost throughout the year. When we discussed this problem with the central leaders, they said that our workers are accustomed to carry drinking water from distant *Dharas* (springs) and *Jhoras*. Thus, the negligence of health aspect relating to drinking water of workers is another drawback of unions.

The Himalayan Plantation Workers Union leaders are seen busy with materialistic aspects of the workers like Wage negotiation, Bonus negotiation, Khetland negotiations but regarding Gratuity, Provident Fund and Family Pension of the workers they do not want to play any concrete role because most probably they do not have any idea about these aspects of trade unions or trade union movement. It was learnt from the rank and file leaders and workers from the gardens that thousands of retired plantation workers in every garden have not received their provident fund since the last twenty years. This is another severe drawback of trade union movement today in the region.

We asked them about the reasons for not getting these claims acquired by leaders. They said that as leaders are *Thulo Manchees* (big sorts), they cannot dare to complain them about these aspects now and then.

Coming to the question of creche, not a single garden has so far any creche and no union leader till today has pressurised the management for the same. There is no Labour Welfare Officer in the hill tea gardens. The efficiency of Labour Welfare Officer of course is known to all the top leaders of Himalayan Plantation Workers Union, Darjeeling District Chia Kaman Mazdoor Union, Darjeeling District Chia Bagan Workers Union, Darjeeling, Terai and Dooars Chia Kaman Mazdoor Union and Darjeeling District Chia Kaman Shramik Sangh but they perhaps feel that if Labour Welfare Officer is appointed then their status and role in the gardens will be minimised. This is the logical contention of Darjeeling Planters' Association also in regard to the appointment of Labour Welfare Officers in tea gardens of Darjeeling Hills.

Another setback of present trade union movement is in the education of children of the workers. After implementing the children education cess of 8 paise per kilogram of made tea, the management feel that they donot have any other role to play and unions too do not bother about the issue and never ask the District Primary School Board about the proper utility of education cess paid by the management of every garden of the region. This may be the apparent reason why educating Nepali youths is purely the duty of guardians. It is because of this, especially the young boys and girls are going out of the gardens from the families who can afford them to send out for education and jobs and they hardly come back to join tea gardens isolated life. Perhaps this is the reason why majority of workers are women. Only 23 per cent of male workers from 48 per cent are purely the plantation workers in the gardens. Women have on the other hand, because of their double roles at family and work place, little inclination to trade union activities in the gardens.

The garden workers also show little botheration about their health aspect. Most of the hospitals do not have medical doctors and trade unions too do not have care of this aspect of the workers resulting which thousands of workers are suffering from Tuberculosis and even an Aids patient was found in Marybong T.E. in 1998.

In so far as the question of recreational facilities of the workers is concerned, most of the gardens do not have play ground, libraries and other indoor and outdoor game facilities. Cultural programmes are hardly organised. Instead, every union and management has allowed video shows at night when many young boys and girls are gathered and undergo illicit relationship. Many workers see night shows and in the next day they remain absent. It does harms to the workers not only in respect of wage cut but also reduction in Gratuity, Provident Fund and Family Pension. Not a single trade union has opposed this resulting which the socio-economic conditions of the workers is deteriorating day by day. Drinking alcohols is increasing by leaps and bounds in the garden Bhattis (liquor hearths) and here in this respect also no trade union shows any interest to advise the management or workers to avoid indulging in drinking habit. It is further observed that almost 50 per cent of income of male workers are spent on liquors.

Inspite of normalcy brought about by Darjeeling Gurkha Hill Council, the inter-union violence and murders is still encouraged by trade unions in the gardens among the fellow workers. This has helped the management to continue with the colonial policy of Divide and Rule in the gardens. The traditional style of criticising and counter-criticising is still prevalent among the workers and trade unions.

Another drawback of trade union movement is that each and every so-called trade union leaders belonging to different caste groups are busy with the formation of caste samajs (Caste Panchayats) with respective caste members (workers) resulting which the trade union movement is losing its grounds. Still another factor for weak framework of trade union movement today is that the working class has been cut across by various religious subsects like Pranami Dharma, Sai Dharma, Satsang Dharma, Christainity, etc., in the gardens. Such things are gathering momentum because the educated members of the workers do not want to comeback to the tea gardens after their education outside.

All these instances indicate the fact that trade union movement in the Himalayan tea industry is in premature stage of its development. Previously, the trade union movement was a movement of Mutual Compliant type calling strike, go-slow, etc., excessively, even now and then and present one is of Mutual Compliance type (Walton: 1992) having excessive compliance to management by curtailing down almost all the legitimate welfare facilities of the workers in the industry. Almost all the leaders of unions appear to have been at the easy reach of the management. Hardly the central leaders of the unions visit the gardens except in big social occasions or elections of unions as Thulo Manchess (big sorts) or chief guests and special guests.

18

CONCLUSION

Nothing short of organisation is the actualisation of Industrial Democracy. Restoring the industrial democracy through an organisation having 'Affective Tie' of workers and leaders, the trade union movement emerged in the Himalayan Tea Plantation Industry. Launching trade union movement, the leaders since early forties of 19th century as well as workers had to align with the Bengal Government so as to restore ethnic identity. Despite of having dissimilar racial, cultural, linguistic and historical backgrounds with the Bengal Government, the Himalayan plantation workers had to make artificial liaison with central trade union leaders of national trade unions like CITU and NUPW. This is observed in the present study as in most of the times the trade unions of ethnic political parties like All India Gurkha League, Pranta Parisad and Gorkha National Liberation Front have ruled the Himalayan region in general and tea plantation industry in particular.

The influence of Bengal Communists in tea plantations was excellent only in the formative period of trade union movement in early forties of the 19th century in Darjeeling plantations due to the affinity of union leaders with the workers. But later on after 1950, Communists lost their locus standi in the gardens, due to the ethnic leadership of Deo Prakash Rai of AIGL. He could mobilise the tea garden workers to the fullest extent with the tactical patronage of Congress party till 1980. In fact, shared cultural values of the party ideology of AIGI were accommodative for tea garden workers. The AIGI gave an ethnic mobilisation in the form of an organisation which was latter on synchronised with trade union organisation known as Darjeeling District Chia Kaman Shramik Sangh.

The Marxist concept of class is the later ascendancy in the history of trade union movement in the Himalayan tea industry. While mobilising the work force, it was the ethnic political forces which had already grown in the plantation industry of a separate community being smashed down by bigger imported philosophy of outsiders hailing from other central or majority ethnic groups of the country.

It is observed in the study that both the management of the gardens as owners/management and government big sorts belong to the central ethnic groups of the country. The ethnicity as the analytical tool for studying the bases of trade union movement in the region has been operationalised as 'a separate ethnic group of having a common language, tribal background of the Himalayas and ever neglected peripheral community of borderland coolies to be tamed to whatever extent as possible'. The broader ethnic people of the gardens as management cadres and higher government officials taunt, insult and even despised the local coolies stating or calling "Kanchas" which is understood in derogatory sense by the ethnic people in Darjeeling Himalaya.

Those were the background reasons why trade unions supported every ethnic movement in the region. Though Marxists feel that ethnicity as a "false consciousness", it is the ethnic base of majority ethnic group's rule in the region since last fifty years of independence which legitimised the ethnicity as the guiding principle of mainland Bengal and other states of the country. For example, 'while only one Indian state is ruled by sixteen ethnic groups in sixteen states out of twenty six states today (Subramanian : 1 999). The Bengal Marxists are protagonists of self-rule by the concerned ethnic group but since its ruling in the state, problem started in the Himalayan region as they rejected the demand of the region in Darjeeling hills.

The foregoing chapters show that how the trade union movement of the Himalayan tea plantation industry as 'isolated enclaves' had ethnic rather than class consciousness that shaped the structure of the movement itself in the truest sense of the term though Marxists have baised remarks on this ethnic base of unions as sessionist ones. It is because of the fact that democracy is just not of the people, for the people and by the people, it is always of the majority community, for the majority community and by the majority community (Subba : 1990).

Unlike in other areas of the country, tea industry was established at Darjeeling Himalaya with the assistance of Mr. Gossain, who was by ethnicity a Nepali and it was he who procured tea seeds and plants from Kumaon hills and Tibet to the British colonial planters in the region. Similarly, it was Dakman Rai who was also a Nepali by ethnicity who encouraged his fellow Nepalis for joining tea gardens and work with all deligence and devotion giving perseverance to work. The plantation workers served both colonial British planters and neo-colonial planters of Indian origins as 'Sahibs' characterising or degrading themselves as 'Coolies' for ever. They gave blood, sweats and even their beautiful females to satiate the planters, management cadres and owners at work places and outside.

In the present study, it is also observed that trade unions are understood by the workers as the frontal ethnic organisations of political parties and not vice-versa. Being a marginal ethnic community in tea plantation industry, the question of identity is much prominent and this has resulted into the formation of union ideology as the ideology of separate identity.

Trade union here is not meant in the sense as understood by Communists in terms of the agent of the workers to fight against the owners of production for the protection of workers rights. The owners of production is not conceptualised in terms of merely the owners as a class but a separate ethnic group hailing from the mainland of the country and they have separate ethnic background. It is they who own the means of production and it is the local ethnic community who do not own the means of production. Former always try to dominate the latter group. Had it been accepted as the trade union movement in tea industry by the government then there would have been no violence in recent agitation under the G.N.L.F. This sense of superiority of management and inferiority of workers will be there in the industry for ever to come as it is only when ethnodevelopment takes place and if it really takes place then there will be the chances of the emergence of class consciousness among the workers. Here the class consciousness is overshadowed by ethnic consciousness. Such ethnic consciousness is observed among the workers in their participation in trade union activities. They participate in trade unions or trade union activities in areas like strike, processions and meetings of the unions as they are asked to do so by the central leaders of the unions belonging to regional political parties.

Conclusion

To the workers, previous trade unions mainly CITU and NUPW were the mouthpieces of other ethnic groups of the country. They understood the fact that previous unions used to manage workers for the fulfilment of the satisfaction of majority ethnic group of Bengal. The workers have no hope of the noble assurance of national trade unions as workers feel that these unions are liars of the people in the plantations of the region. They cheated people there like anything in the past. This was more spectacular when CPI(M) was totally rooted out from hills after the formation of Communist Party of Revolutionary Marxists in 1995, by the old CPI(M) leaders like Dawa Lama and R.B. Rai (ex-M.L.A. and ex-M.P. respectively) from Darjeeling hills.

The ethnic movement in tea industry is a class or trade union movement of an ethnic group against another ruling ethnic group (owners/management). This might be purely a trade union movement for outside ethnic group in normal time while it is an ethnic movement to the same ethnic group when it erupts out at gigantic height that reflects cultural, social, economic and emotional reality of the group. Such instances are plenty here in the plantations. The ethnic movement was there ever since 1917 when the Hillmen Association was formed at Darjeeling. It was subsided with whimsical assurances of the then British government. It again emerged in 1920 under Nebula, still later on under Gurkha League, Communist Party of India during fifties of 20th century. Language movement in sixties and separate state demand after 1980, under Pranta Parisad and Gurkha National Liberation Front. Though today G.N.L.F. has been subsided with Darjeeling Gurkha Hill Council, there is every possibility of similar movement in near future as it is found that the workers are not satisfied with the functioning of D.G.H.C. though they mainly support Himalayan Plantation Workers Union which is the frontal organisation of G.N.L.F.

The socio-cultural relations or 'Affective Tie' between the leaders and workers is only the string that has helped to lead the trade union movement in tea industry of the Himalayan region. The common cultural traits like *Daju-Bhai* (brothers), *Afno Manches* (relatives and neighbours). *Bichara* (feeling sorry to people or leaders) etc. etc. have helped to form, sustain and even foster the distinct type of trade union movement of an ethnic community in inaccessible Himalayan tea industry. Otherwise, the sense in which other trade unions work in tea industry of the country as the organisation of workers of all sects, castes, community, religious sects etc. has no bearing in the Himalayan tea industry as the unionisation process of the far and wide corners of the tea industry of the country has not yet reached (Sharma : 1997) to tea industry of the region under study.

Bibliography

Bhowmik, Sharit : Class Formation in the Plantation System, People's Publishing House, New Delhi, 1981.

.... : Tea Plantations in West Bengal, in Sarath Davala (Ed.) Employment and Unionisation in Indian Industry, Friedrich Ebert Stiftung, New Delhi, 1995.

Bista, Dor Bahadur : Fatalism and Development. Nepal's Struggle for Modernisation, Orient Longman, Calcutta, 1993.

Caplan, L. : Land and Social Change in East Nepal : A Study of Hindu-Tribal Relations, Routledge and Kegan Paul Publication, London, 1970.

Chhetri, Shanti : Women Workers in the Informal Sector, Gyan Sagar Publication, Delhi, 1999.

Dahal, Mohan P. : Ghuk Dai Na Guk Ne Pehar Ko choro (in Nepali) Pratima Prakashan, Pradhan Nagar, Siliguri, 1997.

Dasgupta, Manas : Tea Plantation Workers in the Eastern Himalaya, of Sarkar, R.L. and Lama. M.P. (Ed.), Atmaram and Sons, Delhi, 1986.

Government of India : Plantation Labour Act, 1951. Trade Union Act, 1926.

Industrial Standing Employment Orders Act, 1946.

Industrial Disputes Act, 1947.

Maternity Benefit Act, 1961.

Payment of Bonus Act, 1972.

Payment of Gratuity Act, 1965.

Employees Provident Fund Act, 1952.

Minimum Wages Act, 1948.

Government of West Bengal : West Bengal Plantation Labour Rules, 1956, Plantation Labour in West Bengal, 1994.

Griffith, S.P. : The History of Indian Tea Industry, Routledge, London, 1967.

Haimendorf, C.Von, Furer : Caste and Kin in Nepal. India and Ceylon, Asia Publishing House, Bombay, 1966.

.... : Anthropology of Nepal, Vikas Publishing House, New Delhi, 1978.

Hunter, W.W. : Statistical Account of Bengal, Government Printing Press, Calcutta, 1874.

Karan, A.K. : Role of Labour Admistrators. A New Orientation, in Spotlight (a Journal of West Bengal Labour Services Association), Annulipi Press, Calcutta, 1999.

Lozovsky, A. : Marx and the Trade Unions, London, 1935.

Moskvichov, L.N. : "End of Ideology": Theory: Illusions and Reality. Moscow, 1974.

Mukherjee, Radhakamal, : The Indian Working Class, Macmillan and Company, London, 1945.

O'Malley, I.S.S. : Bengal District Gazetteer 'Darjeeling' Alipore Government Printing Press, Calcutta, 1905.

Pradhan, Kumar : Gurkha Conquests, Oxford University Press, Calcutta, 1991.

Ramaswamy, E.A. : The Worker and His Union, Allied Publishers, Private Limited, Bombay, 1977.

Robbins, N. : Organisational Behaviour, Prentice Hall Inc, London 1992.

Sarkar, R.L. and Lama, M.P. : Tea Plantation Workers in the Eastern Himalayas. Atmaram and Sons Publication, New Delhi, 1986.

Sharma, Khemraj : Tea plantation Industry in India. N.L. Publishers, Dibrugargh, Assam, 1999.

Sen, Sukumol : Working Class in India : History of Emergence and Movement (1830-1970). K.P. Bagchi and Company, Calcutta. 1977.

Subba, Tanka, B. : Ethnicity, State and Development, Har-Anand Publication, New Delhi, 1990.

Subramanian, Narendra : Ethnicity and Populist Mobilisation, Oxford University Press, Calcutta, 1999.

Tea Board of India. 1990, Govt. of India, New Delhi.

Xaxa, V. : Economic Avalism and Structure of Class, Como Publications, New Delhi, 1997

INDEX

S

T